# Politics and Racism Beyond Nations

"Based in the author's detailed research on memories of genocide and other traumas, *Politics and Racism Beyond Nations* is a passionate plea for confronting many of the most urgent problems we face in our current world, while showing the wider relevance of anthropology to these concerns. Will make for a useful and popular book for students."
—David Sutton, *Professor of Anthropology, Southern Illinois University, USA*

"In *Politics and Racism Beyond Nations*, Linstroth analyses the multiple impacts of racism and "othering projects" in the United States and beyond. One of the strengths of this book is how Linstroth draws on a wealth of interdisciplinary and multidisciplinary theoretical frameworks while bringing them to life through thick narratives of diverse individual experiences, such as members of the LGTBQIA+ community and Buddhist monastics. Through theory, people's experiences, and his extensive anthropological research, Linstroth weaves topics that range from racism and othering, immigration, nationalism, terrorism, and racial trauma. Although theoretically focused, this book addresses issues of extreme relevance in our current world.

This book is unique in how Linstroth connects diverse issues and its holistic approach. He discusses the role of the state and society in sustaining structural violence in tandem with the toll it takes on the minds and bodies of citizens. Additionally, Linstroth provides hope and a way to move our humanity forward through education and respect toward all living beings taking a Buddhist perspective. This book explains how othering and racism operate. It also illustrates how to use our interdependency and love for each other to restore our humanity. This book is insightful and contributes to the ongoing dialogue on how to create a world in which all living beings can thrive."
—Jacqueline N. Font-Guzmán, *Professor at the Center for Justice and Peacebuilding, Eastern Mennonite University, USA*

"Politics and racism as basis of crises and conflict remain topics of perennial interest in today's world, not least because they are experienced the world over with associations on the big questions and major subjects of the century, including nationalism, genocide, terrorism, immigration, trauma, and love and peace. J. P. Linstroth's magnificent book brilliantly interweaves poignantly the big questions on these major subjects from a multidisciplinary perspective. Spiced by a diverse collection of ethnographic narratives from Europe, Asia, and the

Americas, this volume presents theoretical analyses of politics and racism across nations and brings a valuable service to the comparative study of the subjects. The volume is the latest work in what I can describe as Linstroth's gift in sharing with the readers an extraordinary array of the major human concerns of the early twenty-first century. This author's fascinating ideas and lucid writing provide rewarding knowledge to scholars across the social sciences."
—Fonkem Achankeng, *Professor at College of Education and Human Services, University of Wisconsin, USA*

"Dr. Linstroth's eclectic approach to some of the most poignant challenges of our time provides a fresh look at transnational issues such as racism and politics. An anthropological perspective allows Linstroth to transcend the narrow confines of the nation-state in order to focus on lived experiences. Rather than providing specific solutions, the book forces the reader to challenge conventional wisdom and to accept the intrinsic complexity of the human condition. Linstroth blends a healthy concern for social justice with academic expertise."
—Otto Federico von Feigenblatt, *Program Director and Professor of Educational Leadership—Latin Division, Keiser University*

J. P. Linstroth

# Politics and Racism Beyond Nations

A Multidisciplinary Approach to Crises

J. P. Linstroth
College of Arts and Sciences
Barry University
Miami Shores, FL, USA

ISBN 978-3-030-91719-7     ISBN 978-3-030-91720-3  (eBook)
https://doi.org/10.1007/978-3-030-91720-3

© The Editor(s) (if applicable) and The Author(s), under exclusive licence to Springer Nature Switzerland AG 2022

This work is subject to copyright. All rights are solely and exclusively licensed by the Publisher, whether the whole or part of the material is concerned, specifically the rights of translation, reprinting, reuse of illustrations, recitation, broadcasting, reproduction on microfilms or in any other physical way, and transmission or information storage and retrieval, electronic adaptation, computer software, or by similar or dissimilar methodology now known or hereafter developed.

The use of general descriptive names, registered names, trademarks, service marks, etc. in this publication does not imply, even in the absence of a specific statement, that such names are exempt from the relevant protective laws and regulations and therefore free for general use.

The publisher, the authors and the editors are safe to assume that the advice and information in this book are believed to be true and accurate at the date of publication. Neither the publisher nor the authors or the editors give a warranty, expressed or implied, with respect to the material contained herein or for any errors or omissions that may have been made. The publisher remains neutral with regard to jurisdictional claims in published maps and institutional affiliations.

Cover illustration: © Marina Lohrbach_shutterstock.com

This Palgrave Macmillan imprint is published by the registered company Springer Nature Switzerland AG.
The registered company address is: Gewerbestrasse 11, 6330 Cham, Switzerland

*This book is dedicated to my father John P. Linstroth, Sr. and to my mother Dr. Carol Dorgan, and to all the indigenous peoples in Brazil who struggle for recognition, especially to all the urban Amerindians I knew so well. Additionally, it is dedicated to all those who have ever experienced discrimination and/or racism—may we all overcome.*

# Foreword

J.P. Linstroth provides readers with a tour-de-force exploration of the nature and interconnections of racism, nationalism, terrorism, hatred, and violence as he calls for humanity to nurture tolerance, compassion, and mindfulness instead. His is an urgent plea to change our destructive ways: "we are all interrelated and need each other for the survival of the planet." Linstroth's crucial message is to put aside divisiveness and act in concert to right the wrongs we are inflicting on each other and the Earth. "Humanity is in existential crises," writes Linstroth, "on the verge of its own destruction." The various "-isms" that contribute not only to immense human suffering around the world but also to humanity's death march to oblivion must be forsaken and replaced by humane values and life-affirming practices if any of our grandchildren will be survived by their grandchildren. These are "heavy" topics, but of the utmost importance for a world on the brink. Linstroth rightly puts the shared responsibility on every one of us alive today, noting through a Buddhist lens that "we are all inter-beings on the planet Earth and have the responsibilities of taking care of it and saving the environment as we are interrelated to it."

A unique and valuable aspect of *Politics and Racism Beyond Nations* is its anthropological holism. Rather than focusing on a particular case of racism, nationalism, or genocide, Linstroth pulls from numerous examples that circumscribe the world to show how the harmful and ugly patterns recur in different places and times. As an anthropologist, Linstroth has conducted ethnographic interviews and fieldwork in various cultural settings, for example, in Amazonia, the Basque region of Spain, among

Central American refugees living in the United States, with self-identifying homosexuals, and among Buddhist monastics. Most chapters in Linstroth's book begin with excerpts from the numerous interviews that he has collected, thus allowing the people to speak for themselves about the traumas they have faced.

One of Linstroth's recurring points is that trauma can have both immediate and enduring—even intergenerational—consequences, to individuals and social groups. Linstroth explains, "These are memories about social exclusion and negative memories formed from negative experiences that may have become routine. These are memories of 'discrimination, prejudice, racism, stereotyping, and labeling, which demean individuals and collectives to such an extent as having permanent consequences.'"

Institutionalized racism in the United States is an example. Linstroth recounts how nearly 30 years ago he interviewed one of the legendary Tuskegee Airmen, a member of the African American squadron that inflicted heavy damage on the Axis powers during World War II, accruing over 1700 missions flown and nearly one hundred Distinguished Flying Crosses in the process (as well as various other awards for valor and eight Purple Hearts). Eighty-four Tuskegee Airmen lost their lives in service to their country, which was operating under Jim Crow segregation practices at the time. Linstroth learned from the Tuskegee Airman, then in his 80s, that his grandfather had been a slave, his father a sharecropper, and even after he had earned his university degree and served his country in times of war, the only job he could get was as a janitor.

Institutionalized racism and the weight of its legacy continue in America today as reflected in gross disparities and inequities in employment, education, health care, delivery of "justice," and more. Lawyer Bryan Stevenson (2015: 254–255), in *Just Mercy*, recounts how his African American client Walter McMillian was sentenced to die for a crime he did not commit. Readers can glimpse the trauma Mr. McMillian endured through Stevenson's heart-wrenching description that includes McMillian's own words:

> Then I watched [on television] his expression change, and he began talking with more animation and excitement than I'd ever heard from him. … "They put me on death row for six years! They threatened me for six years. They tortured me for with the promise of execution for six years. I lost my job. I lost my wife. I lost my reputation. I lost my—I lost my dignity." He was speaking loudly and passionately and looked to be on the verge of tears.

"I lost everything," he continued. He calmed himself and tried to smile, but it didn't work. He looked soberly at the camera. "It's rough, it's rough, man. It's rough. I watched worriedly while Walter crouched down close to the ground and began to sob violently."

Stevenson (2015: 313) reflects:

I felt the need to explain to people what Walter had taught me. Walter made me understand why we have to reform a system of criminal justice that continues to treat people better if they are rich and guilty than if they are poor and innocent. ...Walter's case taught me that fear and anger are a threat to justice; they can infect a community, a state, or a nation and make us blind, irrational, and dangerous.

As an Anthropology student decades ago, I learned in my classes that there is no biological validity to racial classifications—that "race" is a social construct. Should there be three races, or five, 205, or 2005? It arbitrarily depends on whether one lumps or splits in playing this classificatory pseudo-scientific game. What is biologically real is the human micro-variation that has nothing to do with "race," within and among different populations, typically with greater genetic variability existing *within* the same human population than between different populations. And features of human variation (e.g., whether a person's fingers are long or short or their blood type AA or AB) really has no bearing on issues of social equality, rights, or opportunities. Renowned anthropologist Ashley Montagu (1905–1999), who himself early in life had felt the painful sting of prejudice against Jews, was instrumental in the creation of the UNESCO Statements on Race (https://en.unesco.org/courier/july-august-1950). The title of his book captures the main message: *Man's Most Dangerous Myth: The Fallacy of Race*, first published in 1942.

It is a sad commentary indeed that 80 years later, as Linstroth aptly demonstrates, the fallacy of race still cries out for further myth-busting (Brace 2005; Fuentes 2012; Kendi 2019). In 2005, in a book sardonically titled *"Race" Is a Four-Letter Word*, biological anthropologist C. Loring Brace (1930–2019) wrote: "When it is finally realized that there is no coherent biological entity that corresponds with what people generally assume is meant by 'race,' all those claims extolling or denigrating various aspects of racial worth will be deprived of any validity. Race, then, is a social construct that should be dealt with solely on the basis of the conventions that govern social behavior." Race as a social construct, lacking any biological reality, is a theme picked up by Linstroth. He quotes from Ibram X. Kendi's best-selling *How to Be an Antiracist* on the history behind the concepts of race and racism. Kendi calls out race and racism as mechanisms of domination and exploitation employed by those in power:

> Racist ideas are not natural to the human mind. Race and racism are power constructs of the modern world. For roughly two hundred thousand years, before race and racism were constructed in the fifteenth century, humans saw color but did not group the colors into continental races, did not commonly attach negative and positive characteristics to those colors and rank the races to justify racial inequality, to reinforce racist power and policy.

Today, concepts of race and racism permeate some societies, such as the United States, so thoroughly across historic, social, political, and economic realms that Kendi's (2019) assertion that racism is not natural to human thinking or Brace's conclusion that biology lends absolutely no support to the concept of race is "apt to be greeted with frank incredulity" by the public (Brace 2005: 4).

Linstroth reflects upon racism not only in the United States against immigrants, minorities, and Native Americans, but also as contributing to tragedies and trauma inflicted on indigenous peoples from Australia, Brazil, Canada, and other parts of the world. For example, Linstroth recounts how President Jair Bolsonaro of Brazil considers indigenous peoples "animals in zoos." As expressed in a quotation presented by Linstroth in his book from the renowned anthropologist David Maybury-Lewis, one of the co-founders of Cultural Survival, "Indigenous peoples are those who are subordinated and marginalized by alien powers that rule over them. It follows that they are relatively powerless, and so they become prime targets for genocide." An outrageous and egregious example of the abuse of indigenous people followed closely on Bolsonaro's election in 2019. A new wave of 20,000 illegal gold miners invaded Brazil's indigenous Yanomami reserve, spreading Covid-19, polluting streams with deadly mercury, shooting at people, and otherwise wreaking ethnocidal and ecocidal hell upon the Yanomami and their land (Sponsel 2021: 109; Survival International, https://www.survivalinternational.org/tribes/yanomami).

What can be done to rid humanity of racism in its various manifestations? Riane Eisler and I recently collaborated on a book titled *Nurturing*

*Our Humanity*, elaborating upon Eisler's seminal work on domination, partnership, and cultural transformation. The word "humanity" of course has two meanings. To quote *Merriam-Webster*, one meaning is: "compassionate, sympathetic, or generous behavior or disposition," (being *humane*), and the second meaning is: "the quality or state of being human" (being *human*). Meanwhile, "to nurture" means "to promote the development of someone or something." Thus, "nurturing humanity" is a double-entendre for promoting compassionate, *humane* actions and for nourishing *humankind* overall, as members of the same species.

Eisler first presented the partnership-domination continuum in her now classic 1987 book *The Chalice and the Blade*. That book title presents two metaphors for power: the chalice reflecting partnership and the blade for domination. *Nurturing Our Humanity* utilizes the partnership-domination construct and explores the implications for enhancing partnership for human betterment and survival on a troubled planet.

The domination-partnership model is really a continuum. At one end, domination-oriented societies have rigid top-down hierarchies maintained through physical, psychological, and economic control across various types of social institutions. Specifically, males rank higher than females in domination systems. The acceptance of abuse and violence, from child- and wife-beating to racism, exploitation, torture, slavery, and warfare, constitutes another component of domination systems. The abuse may be direct and physical, as in torture, unjust incarceration, and genocide, as well as institutionalized, for instance, in a social acceptance of police brutality, or more generally, in the repression, injustice, and social inequities that become embedded in a society's norms, values, practices, and institutions. A final component of domination systems is that violence is viewed as inevitable, even moral. For example, domination practices such as extermination, enslavement, and torture are considered necessary and morally justifiable.

By contrast, core features of partnership systems support equity, caring, and the promotion of well-being for all members of a society. A democratic and egalitarian focus is manifested in values, norms, social institutions, and practices. An equal partnership between women and men is manifested in partnership systems; women and men are equally valued and respected. Partnership systems reject abuse and violence. Partnership societies may not be totally free of aggression, but violence is not built into partnership values, traditions, and institutions.

Finally, while cruelty and violence are recognized as human possibilities, they are not considered moral or inevitable. In partnership-oriented societies, human relations are based on principles of equality, mutual respect, compassion, caring, and cooperation for the social good.

The point in reviewing tenets of a domination-partnership model is that the various examples of racism, terrorism, extreme nationalism, sexism, genocide, ecocide, and other forms of trauma-inducing abuse that Linstroth considers in this book all fit within domination systems. A second reason for presenting this lens is that it clearly shows there are more prosocial, life-enhancing, humane alternatives to domination. Egalitarian societies exist. Non-warring societies are found in every corner of the planet. Racism is not everywhere present; the "race" concept is a recent historical phenomenon, and shifting orientation toward partnership values and practices provides a guiding beacon for moving humankind beyond racism. Humans have again and again created partnership systems in prehistory and history around the world (Eisler and Fry; Fry and Souillac 2017). In short, partnership-oriented social systems exist, so therefore they are possible. As Eisler and I emphasize in *Nurturing Our Humanity*, the peoples of the world would benefit substantially by shifting to partnership orientations and social systems.

Partnership societies extended way back over human prehistory as part and parcel of the nomadic forager lifeways that spanned most of the human existence on Earth. At the national level, examples of partnership-oriented societies can be found today in the Nordic countries of Denmark, Finland, Iceland, Norway, and Sweden. In *Nurturing Our Humanity*, we review numerous studies on human health, happiness, and well-being to substantiate that partnership systems are better for individuals, families, communities, and nations than domination systems with their dehumanizing and destructive features such as direct and institutionalized violence and racism.

Given the serious challenges facing humanity in the twenty-first century, working together as partners for human survival is urgent and mandatory. As Linstroth writes, "Our very humanity depends upon how we as human beings from varying societies across our world treat fellow human beings with dignity and respect." On an interdependent planet facing major challenges, understanding the origins, natures, and impacts of partnership and domination systems on human lives and societies is crucial to human well-being and survival. Linstroth likely would agree, for he writes, "If human beings are to avoid nuclear destruction, environmental nihilism and an impending 6th extinction of millions of animals on our planet (including ourselves), and elude climatic catastrophe, we must think in terms of "inter-being" before it is truly too late."

Beliefs that humans are naturally competitive, aggressive, racist, or xenophobic can promote fear, distrust, even hatred, and a reluctance to work together. These negative assumptions about human nature can lead also to pessimism, about creating more caring social institutions, assuring genuine justice under the law, and promoting human well-being; about eliminating racism, discrimination, prejudice, and other gross inequities within nations and around the world; about moving politics and international relations beyond arsenals and armaments; and about pushing back against exclusive nationalisms that are totally out of step with implementing the imperative pan-human cooperative agenda necessary for survival on an interdependent planet. Understanding the strong partnership underpinnings and potentials of human behavior offers a prescription for human survival and well-being. When the prosocial and peaceable tendencies of humans are recognized along with the long-standing legacy of partnership-based societies, then the possibilities of creating, in the twenty-first century, social institutions and practices that support genuine social justice, racial equality, human rights, and well-being become possible.

Greensboro, North Carolina
20 September 2021

Douglas P. Fry

## References

Brace, C. Loring. 2005. *"Race" Is a Four-Letter Word: The Genesis of the Concept.* New York: Oxford University Press.

Eisler, Riane. 1987. *The Chalice and the Blade: Our History, Our Future.* San Francisco: Harper and Row.

Eisler, Riane, and Fry, Douglas P. 2019. *Nurturing Our Humanity: How Domination and Partnership Shape Our Brains, Lives, and Future.* Oxford University Press.

Fry, Douglas P., and Souillac, Geneviève. 2017. The Original Partnership Societies: Evolved Propensities for Equality, Prosociality, and Peace. *Interdisciplinary Journal of Partnership Studies,* 4 (1), article 4.

Fuentes, Agustín. 2012. *Race, Monogamy, and Other Lies They Told You.* Berkeley: University of California Press.

Kendi, Ibram X. 2019. *How to Be an Antiracist.* London: Oneworld.

Montagu, Ashley. 1942. *Man's Most Dangerous Myth: The Fallacy of Race.* New York: Columbia University Press.

Sponsel, Leslie E. 2021. *Nonkilling Anthropology: A New Approach to Studying Human Nature, War, and Peace.* Honolulu: Center for Global Nonkilling.

Stevenson, Bryan. 2015. *Just Mercy: A Story of Justice and Redemption.* New York: Spiegel and Grau.

# Prologue

### A Note on My Mentor

Let me begin by stating how honored I feel that J.P. Linstroth asked me to write the prologue for his latest book. After all, this section is usually reserved for the authors to tell their book's story, their journey, their inspiration. Linstroth entrusted me to shed some light into how this book came into being, using a voice that is not his own. J.P. Linstroth has been my mentor who helped me grow from student to scholar. With that in mind, please forgive me if this is not your everyday prologue, but a note on how J.P. Linstroth's humanity and quest to work for a better world for all drives his scholarship and vice versa.

To understand Linstroth's motivation behind this book, one cannot separate the Oxford-educated cultural anthropologist from the person whose life choices were often driven by supporting those who are less privileged and whose voices he helped elevate. At first glance, one will see an academic who is broadly concerned with advancing peace research. One will also see him as a scholar serving on the Board of Directors of the International Peace Research Association Foundation, whose mission is "to advance the field of peace research through rigorous investigation into the causes of conflict and examination of alternatives to violence."[1] In his fieldwork, which is saturated with ethnographic "thick description," Linstroth has heard many stories from many people around the world and written about them. In this book, Linstroth's own journey as an academic, a cultural anthropologist, a peace and conflict researcher, a non-profit worker, a student, and a teacher becomes part of the story. This book has components of his own journey as an academic, but more importantly as an anthropologist who is concerned about the well-being of all humans, especially those who have been traditionally marginalized.

The following paragraphs are my humble attempt to share my interpretation of J.P. Linstroth's experience and authority to take on a vast landscape of issues such as nationalism, racism, terrorism, genocide, trauma, tolerance, and love with vastly different groups of participants, including Basques, Brazilians, Amerindians, Buddhist monastics, Guatemalan-Mayas, and self-identified homosexuals. I also attempt to show how in my work with J.P. Linstroth, I have been able to see behind the researcher and learned what has inspired him. Covering tremendous ground of social theories, Linstroth weaves the notions of "othering" and "structural violence" throughout his entire book. But first, I attempt to answer the simple question: Why now? Without doubt, this book comes at a time when our world needs no less than a complete paradigm shift. J.P. Linstroth recognized this context and clearly situated this book within.

One does not have to look beyond headlines to recognize the importance of a book that covers the spectrum from racism and genocide to tolerance and love. The challenges, I admit, seem overwhelming. We must acknowledge that the state of the world is not right and that we are deeply entrenched in destructive social systems built and upheld by domination and inequality. There is a planetary crisis; there is a full-on assault on issues of peace, justice, and the environment; there is a rise in authoritarianism; the U.S. foreign policy which has major impacts on the entire world operates within a racism-militarism paradigm, where food, money, and other resources around the world are distributed extremely unequally; and the 85 richest people of the world possess as much wealth as the 3.5 billion poorest. Most people who will read this book probably are quite familiar with this story, the old story. Those are challenges that might lead us to become sarcastic and bury our heads in the sand—the problems are too big, too overwhelming, too uncomfortable. The bad news is that the problems will not go away if we ignore them. And if such global inequality is not taken on at its core, I am afraid our "work for good" will always fall short. This book scrutinizes the old story, but also attempts to build a new one.

As the reader will see in this book, J.P. Linstroth's inspiration has always been to name the problems, historicize them, intellectually explore them, and offer pragmatic as well as aspirational pathways forward. Linstroth includes and analyzes large social reflections and theories by Ibrahim Kendi or Pierre Bourdieu, as well as critical research on nationalism by his former students Jacqueline Font-Guzman and Michael Fonkem Achankeng. At the same time, he can passionately—dare I say angrily—write about the impact of the populist bigotry by world leaders like former U.S. President Donald Trump and his obsession with "white homogeneity" and Brazilian President Jair Bolsonaro with his blatant disdain for Brazil's indigenous population and other minorities, and everyone else who does not fit the homogenized "us" of the power-holders.

This leads me to point out the two most dominant theoretical threads in the book, which I also consider to be the ones that must be urgently addressed should we seek meaningful change in the world. First, the examination of "the othering project" is one of the continuous threads throughout this book. By asking "how humans 'other others,'" we can start unpacking what is claimed in the title "Politics and Racism Beyond Nations." Paloma Ayala Vela, another former student of J.P. Linstroth, and I (2013) attempted to address the notion of "otherness" by suggesting undoing previously reified understandings of "the other" and instead embrace differences not as threats but as opportunities to appreciate the broader human family. Second, a key theoretical distinction made throughout the book is that of direct and indirect violence. As a peace and conflict scholar, I am convinced that this distinction sets our discipline apart through its systematic examination of different forms of violence. Most commonly associated with Johan Galtung, structural violence is understood as the ongoing and institutionalized harm done to individuals by preventing them from meeting their basic needs for survival, well-being, identity, and freedom. Linstroth's inclusion of racist rhetoric, for example, into the understanding of violence then becomes even more nuanced of so-called soft or symbolic violence from Pierre Bourdieu as modes of socio-cultural domination hidden in everyday life and dominant discourses.

What Linstroth has been able to do is to create a coherent narrative about such subjects because he approached his research endeavors with his full self. His approach to research has always had a clear connection to how he views his role in the world. And this role, like my own, is that of an educated white male who is grappling with his privileges and wants to make the world a better place. While being a rigorous academic, Linstroth never ceased to center the participants he worked with in his inquiries. In other words, Linstroth never entered the field as a neutral observer in a social science laboratory, but as a trained anthropologist who cared about research participants and their contexts. I have personally been privileged to learn from and participate with J.P. in such studies where we examined the sense of self and sense of belonging of Guatemalan, Haitian, and Cuban immigrants in Florida. In fact, a while after the research study was concluded, J.P. Linstroth left the halls of academia to dedicate himself full time to lead the Guatemala Maya Center in Palm Beach, Florida, whose mission is "to assist, advocate, and provide services to Maya refugees and others as appropriate in the areas including, but not limited to, education, health, immigration, cultural continuity, and family preservation and empowerment consistent with the Maya culture as we embrace our new environment."[2]

As the title implies, this is a book about racism. It does not go unnoticed by me that J.P. Linstroth, who self-identifies as a white male, has asked me, another white male, to write a prologue. Both of us must recognize our identities as white male scholars in a space where patriarchy and white supremacy are key contributing factors to the many societal ills drawn out by Linstroth. We then must ask ourselves how can we use our training and privileges while at the same time re-thinking Western perspectives of being in the world? How can we make sure that as academics whose voices are heard we do not reinforce the exact structures we aim to transform? How can we as white scholars center the views of marginalized people for whom we claim to be champions? Linstroth, as we learn in his book, did not use his doctorate degree from Oxford University, one of the world's foremost prestigious universities, to seek high academic status and recognition. Nor did he use his Fulbright research scholarship to advance his career on the backs of the Amerindians in Brazil he studied. His scholarly inquiries were never isolated from the realities he was examining. He discovered prejudice, hate, and trauma, but also indigenous paradigms for cooperation and being in the world. He shows in this book how and why empathy and cooperation are part of humanity. He does that wonderfully by drawing from principles of Buddhism as well as by making the case for re-indigenization of society "if humanity is to survive into this century and beyond." Throughout the writing, J.P. Linstroth notably addresses his identity and privileges, recognizes his anti-racist aspiration, and in doing so attempts to unpack what Peggy McIntosh calls the "invisible knapsack" of white privilege.

I cannot help but see this book as a notable peace research contribution. It is interdisciplinary in its nature and rigorous in its analysis, but as

Elise Boulding, Johan Galtung and the many other founding mothers and fathers of our field have demanded, it has the normative aim of non-violent conflict transformation. After all, Galtung envisioned theories guiding peace workers to contribute to positive peace—peace with justice. Where does this leave us? Linstroth's motivation to write this book was to provide an educational opportunity for the betterment of the world. Not only does he want us to use his work to better understand genocide in that it goes beyond mass atrocities, but he also issues a call to action to halt the ongoing genocides against indigenous peoples worldwide. We are in a transformative time, and we cannot shy away from the big picture of transformative thinking that he offers. Tremendous challenges cannot be seen in isolation which might lead to the false belief that there are "fixes." The paradigm shift in a process of human development will always be aspirational, but perhaps never complete. I look at this book as bringing together years of research and original voices of people Linstroth talked to on his journey to create a more tolerant world.

Portland, Oregon                                                             Patrick Hiller
October 2021

## Notes

1. https://iprafoundation.org/
2. https://www.guatemalanmaya.org/mission-and-purpose

## References

Bourdieu, Pierre. 1984. *Distinction: A Social Critique of the Judgement of Taste*. Cambridge: Harvard University Press.
Galtung, Johan. 1969. Violence, Peace, and Peace Research. *Journal of Peace Research* 6 (3): 167–91.
Hiller, Patrick T., and Paloma Ayala Vela. 2013. The Journey to Conflict Resolver: Peace-Scapes. In *Conflict Transformation: Essays on Methods of Nonviolence*, ed. Rhea A. DuMont, Tom H. Hastings, and Emiko Noma, 152–166. Jefferson, NC: McFarland.
McIntosh, Peggy. 2019. White Privilege: Unpacking the Invisible Knapsack (1989). In *On Privilege, Fraudulence, and Teaching as Learning*. Routledge.

# Acknowledgments

A book is really a celebration. So much is collected in a book, not only knowledge, but the personal debts one accrues in writing it. I have accumulated many personal debts over the years, especially among family and friends. Without the support network of such people in my life this book would have been impossible to write. Some more than others have greater importance, mostly because they have had the most profound impact on becoming who I am as a human being, scholar, and writer. These are: my mother, Carol Dorgan; my father, John P. Linstroth, Sr.; my sister, Molly Del Re; and my brother, Michael Linstroth. So too, there are my brother-in-law, Joe Del Re, and my sister-in-law, Robyn Linstroth, and my nieces, Ali and Peyton from my sister and brother-in-law, and my niece, Ruby, and nephew, Bo, from my brother and sister-in-law. There are also the extended families of my brother-in-law and sister-in-law.

To all of them, cheers! Thus, I celebrate this book with my family and friends. Thank you all!

I would like to recognize a few of my friends below. Please also know, while I try to recognize everyone, I may have forgotten some, and if so, please forgive me in my forgetfulness.

First and foremost, I am grateful to my mother, Carol Dorgan, and my friend Conor Nixon for suggesting I should collect my opinion editorials and make them into a book. I am truly appreciative of their suggestions.

Moreover, I am truly grateful to Douglas Fry for agreeing to write the Foreword to this book and to Patrick Hiller for agreeing to write the prologue to this book as well.

Then there are my college friends: Bob Nix, Joseph Rondinelli, David Butler, John Stankard, John Forsythe, and Jim Seeley. There are also Oxford friends: Conor Nixon, David Waters, Lorcan Kennan, Frank Humphreys, Shond Laha, and Jon Stark; some Basque friends: Oier San Martin and Abraham Albisu; academic colleagues and friends: Hamdesa Tuso, Marie Olson-Lounsbery, David Sutton, Julia Chaitin, Otto Von Feigenblatt, Douglas Fry, Dru Gladney, José Exequiel Basini Rodrigues, Raimundo Nonato da Silva, Sandra Ott, Roger Goodman, (the late) Marcus Banks, Jeremy MacClancy, Stephen Sussman, Robin Wright, Glenn Shepard, Gillian Bickley, and Verner Bickley; former PhD students, Patrick Hiller, Paloma Ayala, Jackie Font-Guzman, Michael Fonkem, and Yanira Aleman-Torres; and some new friends, Cassia Araujo, Brian Knowles, and Tony Spaniol.

What is more, I am grateful to the following monastics Geshe Lama Phuntsho, Geshe Lobsang Tsultrim, Ajahn Amaro Bikkhu, and Sister Peace (An Nghiem) for answering my many questions about Buddhism and being patient with me in learning from them. It was an honor, for you to take the time with me.

Furthermore, I am grateful to Bob Nix for introducing me to Serene Washburn. Without Serene, I would never have been introduced to the Tibetan and Bhutanese Buddhist monks she knows so well.

Likewise, I am grateful to anonymous participants Sean, Chad, and Robert for being brave and sharing their life stories about growing up gay and what it means to be homosexual. Thank you.

Moreover, I am grateful to psychologist Maria Basualdo, LMHC, for her insights into the trauma of immigrant children—thank you, also.

In addition, I am grateful to all the Basques I encountered during my fieldwork in the Spanish Basque Country and afterward, and to the anonymous Guatemalan-Mayan immigrant participants and also to those Guatemalan-Mayas who lent their voices to share their stories of genocide—thank you.

What is more, I am so grateful to all the urban Amerindians I came to know in Manaus, Brazil, and the following peoples from eight indigenous groups: Apurinã, Kambeba, Kokama, Munduruku, Mura, Sateré-Mawé, Tikuna, and Tukano—thank you all.

Also, I am appreciative of Ian Trottier for including me monthly on his radio show *Discussions of Truth* as the "Linstroth Report." Further, I am indebted to Tom Hastings, Editor, for publishing my opinions in *PeaceVoice*, and to Joshua Frank, Managing Editor, and Jeffrey St. Clair,

Editor, for publishing my opinions in *CounterPunch*. Importantly too, I would like to recognize Aimée Valdes, manager of Restaurant Casa Santiago, for her friendship.

As a teacher at Royal Palm Beach High School, I would like to recognize the administration, faculty, and students there, and extend the same recognition to Barry University, where I am an adjunct professor.

Additionally, I am immensely grateful to the Palgrave Macmillan editorial team for their careful editing and formatting of this book. I am especially grateful to my editor at Palgrave Macmillan, Elizabeth Graber.

Furthermore, I would like to recognize the library staff at Palm Beach State College (PBSC) Library. I am particularly grateful to David Pena for his support as Director of the Library at the Palm Beach Gardens Campus and for inviting me to give a talk to the college. Additionally, I am also grateful to the Palm Beach State College Library staff, particularly: Amanda, Heather, and Vincent.

And of course, to you too, the reader, for picking up and hopefully reading my work. Thank you all with profound gratitude.

Additionally, I am immensely grateful to the Palgrave Macmillan editorial team for their careful editing and formatting of this book, particularly Vipinkumar Mani, Vinoth Kuppan, Brian Halm, and Sylvia Anand. I am especially grateful to my editor at Palgrave Macmillan, Elizabeth Graber.

# Permissions

I would like to thank the following people and organizations for permission to reprint in modified forms in parts or whole some of my past articles and a book chapter. First, I am thankful to *CounterPunch* and the Editor Jeffrey St. Clair and Managing Editor Joshua Frank for allowing me to reprint modified versions of my opinion editorials with *CounterPunch*. Also, I am thankful to Tom Hastings, Editor, for allowing me to reprint modified versions of opinion editorials in *PeaceVoice*.

Furthermore, my thanks are extended to Taylor & Francis for allowing me to reproduce some of the narratives from my article, "Mayan, Cognition, Memory, and Trauma," originally published in *History and Anthropology* (2009, Vol. 20, No. 2, pp. 139–182), especially the following pages: pp. 147–149 and pp. 167–168 [license number: 5087611085129]. Likewise, I am also grateful to Taylor & Francis for allowing me to reproduce narratives (pp. 131–132) from my book chapter titled: "Urban Amerindians and Advocacy: Toward a Politically Engaged Anthropology Representing Urban Amerindigeneities in Manaus, Brazil" (originally published in *Indigenous Studies and Engaged Anthropology: The Collaborative Moment*, editor Paul Sillitoe, 2015, Chap. 6, pp. 115–145, Surrey, UK: Ashgate Publishing Ltd., now a subsidiary of Taylor & Francis) [query ID: 600045385]. Also a thank you to *EuroScientist Journal* for allowing me to republish my opinion editorials from them.

I would also like to thank the *Houston Chronicle*, the *Des Moines Register*, *Naiz*, and the *Londondery Sentinel* for allowing me to reprint versions of articles which appeared in those newspapers. Furthermore, I am grateful to Proverse Publishers for allowing me to reprint the poem "Eco por Un Grito Moderno."

## Contents

1 **Introduction**   1
   *Outline of the Book*   12
   *Bibliography*   15

2 **Immigration and Racism**   17
   *Introduction*   26
   *Myths on Race and Invasion of the "Caravan Horde"*   28
   *Border Policies from Hell*   32
   *Borders on Insanity?*   36
   *Arundhati Roy on Indian Migrant Worker Oppression and India's Fateful Coronavirus Crisis*   41
   *Conclusion*   45
   *Bibliography*   51

3 **Nationalism and Terrorism**   53
   *Introduction*   62
   *Celebrating Terrorism?*   63
   *End of an Era for ETA? May Basque Peace Continue*   66
   *Fear and Loathing for the So-Called New IRA*   69
   *Footnoting History for the Sake of History and for the Sake of Peace*   72
   *The Problems with an Imagined Community*   75
   *Nations, Nationalism, and Non-nation Political Movements*   77
   *Conclusion*   81
   *Bibliography*   86

| | | |
|---|---|---|
| **4** | **Cultural Genocide, Genocide, and Amerindian Genocide** | 87 |
| | *Deposition: Carlos* | 87 |
| | *Deposition: Victor* | 88 |
| | *Deposition: Ines* | 89 |
| | *Deposition: Felipe* | 90 |
| | *Deposition: Miriam* | 91 |
| | *Introduction* | 95 |
| | *Protecting the Most Vulnerable from Genocide* | 96 |
| | *Will Ethnocide in Western China Become Genocide?* | 99 |
| | *Why Indigenous Lives Should Matter* | 102 |
| | *Preventing Brazilian Indigenous Genocide and Protecting the Amazon* | 106 |
| | *The Politics of Denial, the Brazilian President, and the Fate of Amazonia* | 109 |
| | *Genocidal Disease (COVID-19) as It Is Happening in Amazonia* | 112 |
| | *Bolsonaro's Continuous Follies and the Extermination of Brazilian Indians* | 117 |
| | *The Genocide We Are Allowing in Amazonia* | 124 |
| | *Conclusion* | 127 |
| | *Bibliography* | 138 |
| **5** | **Racial Trauma and Racism** | 139 |
| | *Introduction* | 149 |
| | *A Racist President and Racist Trauma* | 153 |
| | *What About the Amerindians During the Coronavirus Pandemic?* | 157 |
| | *Coronavirus, Poverty, and Structural Violence* | 161 |
| | *Malcolm or MLK?* | 165 |
| | *Why Race Is Everything in America!* | 170 |
| | *Why Natives in the United States Support #BlackLivesMatter* | 175 |
| | *Conclusion* | 179 |
| | *Bibliography* | 193 |
| **6** | **Environment, Humanism, Science, and Tolerance** | 195 |
| | *Introduction* | 208 |
| | *Teaching Tolerance* | 212 |
| | *Primates Are Us: Being Self, Being Others* | 215 |
| | *Mother of Us All* | 218 |

| | | |
|---|---|---|
| | *The Science and Politics Behind the Brazilian Amazon Mass Fires* | 222 |
| | *Bolsonaro Fiddles While the Amazon Burns* | 225 |
| | *Why the Developing World Cannot Flatten the Curve with Coronavirus (COVID-19) and Beyond* | 229 |
| | *Why a Race Is Not a Virus and a Virus Is Not a Race* | 232 |
| | *History and Science as Candles in the Dark* | 235 |
| | *Conclusion* | 242 |
| | *Bibliography* | 252 |
| 7 | **Empathy, Love, and Peace** | 255 |
| | *Introduction* | 293 |
| | *It's Not Batman, or Superman, or Wonder Woman, But Peaceworkers* | 301 |
| | *In the Name of "Love"* | 304 |
| | *What Is Love?* | 308 |
| | *Why a "Re-indigenization" of Society Makes Sense* | 311 |
| | *Conclusion* | 315 |
| | *Bibliography* | 320 |
| 8 | **Concluding Remarks** | 323 |
| | *Bibliography* | 338 |
| **Bibliography** | | 339 |
| **Index** | | 357 |

# CHAPTER 1

# Introduction

At the beginning of the twenty-first century, it is somewhat dismaying that "critical race theory" (CRT) has been so roundly critiqued by many present-day conservatives in the United States. Then again, following the presidency of Donald Trump, it may not be very surprising at all. Some, such as the current governor of Florida, have gone so far as to bar teachers from teaching CRT in public schools (K-12), or at least voicing their opinions on the subject.[1]

Nevertheless, "critical race theory" purports to help reduce the inequalities in society by pointing out structural inequities in regard to race, racism, and power (see Delgado and Stefancic 2017). In other words, critical race theory is an academic subfield, originating in the legal field, which proposes to aid society and societies in overcoming discrimination and racism and in educating about structural violence evident against minorities within society and societies.

This book is aligned with "critical race theory" (CRT) but aims to reach beyond it in the broad subjects it covers such as: immigration, nationalism, terrorism, genocide, trauma, and love and peace. The title, *Politics and Racism Beyond Nations*, evokes an understanding of the politics of racism from a global perspective in that hatred of immigrants is broadly shared by populist regimes the world over; in that racism may lead to genocide; in that the oppression of ethno-nationalist minorities may lead to terrorism; and as a consequence of racism, trauma ensues—all of these subjects are covered in this book. The book is also unique by bringing together knowledge derived from anthropology, biology, indigenous studies, neurology, peace studies, political science, psychology, and sociology, and other academic disciplines. As such, this book takes on "big questions" and "big subjects," and because of this, it is interdisciplinary and multidisciplinary in scope and thereby relevant to many scholars and students alike from an array of academic disciplines.

Additionally, the book introduces each chapter by providing rich ethnographic narratives from informants based upon the author's past and present research on nationalism, racism, genocide, terrorism, trauma, scientific tolerance, and love and peace, as well as some auto-ethnographic narratives from the author's perspective about researching such themes. Interviewed peoples include Basques, Brazilian Amerindians, Buddhist monastics, Guatemalan-Mayas, and self-identified homosexuals.

Specifically, *Politics and Racism Beyond Nations* addresses the following issues: "immigration and racism"; "nationalism and terrorism"; "cultural genocide, genocide, and Amerindian genocide"; "racism and racial trauma"; "environment, humanism, science, and tolerance"; and "empathy, love, and peace." In essence, the "othering" project is discussed and how it became particularly human. Hate and racism are not only tied to a historical post-colonial perspective but likewise how biology acts upon selves to create others through new findings from cognition, endocrinology, neurology, and psychology. For example, racism against immigrants is a particular problem in our world today, whether in the United States, Europe, or Australia. Likewise, "white nationalism" has become reformulated by juxtaposing so-called Others with nativist beliefs, and in the extreme, how such persistent negative ideals in turn have inspired genocide.

Moreover, we find populist movements continue to be dangerous. Populism, whether in Austria, Australia, Germany, Great Britain, Hungary, or the United States, demonstrates how reactive political perspectives, especially those espoused by political leaders, targeted immigrant groups and likewise supported a conservative philosophy of keeping intact national ideals and racist white ideals (see Gingrich and Banks 2006 on neo-nationalism).

To this, we may add perspectives from less developed nation-states such as those of Brazil and India, whereby an overwhelming fear of communism prevailed as if Brazil might become like Venezuela; or whereby Hindu nationalism may remain the major political religion of the Indian nation at the expense of other major religions like Buddhism, Islam, and Jainism. Hence, in the former instances we have Jair Bolsonaro becoming president in a political wave against labor and socialism in Brazil, whereas in the latter, Narendra Modi rode the wave of Hindu nationalism to become Prime Minister of India.

Nationalism and nationalist extremism tie into nationalist terrorism. European nationalist causes of terrorism, as in the case of Northern Ireland and the Basques, are now largely relics of the past. Yet, occasionally, the remnants of such terrorist nationalisms rear their ugly heads in the form of celebrations in favor of Basque terrorism or even in worse cases, the cause of deaths of journalists such as by the so-called New IRA (Irish Republican Army). While such nationalisms may be somewhat passé, other types of nationalist formations do persist in places elsewhere in the world like British Southern Cameroon, Catalonia, Falkland Islands, Kenya, Kurdistan, nationalist insurgents in Myanmar, Puerto Rico, Quebec, Scotland, Somalia, South Sudan, Wales, and Western Sahara. In some cases, violence persists because of a sense of nationalist "imagination," to paraphrase Benedict Anderson, whereas in most other cases throughout the world, peoples persist in the belief that new national formations are still possible.

With racism against immigrants there is an "othering" based upon hate, that is a hatred toward new immigrants and those peoples who are not yet incorporated into national wholes. Neo-nationalists, populists, and so-called nativists assert immigrant peoples can never be part of the nation because of their supposed foreignness and because such alien people allegedly threaten local jobs. On the other hand, with nationalist movements and nationalist insurgencies there is an "othering" of difference, as in the belief of belonging to separate ethno-nationalist groups and therefore a worthiness of creating new nation-states. Even so, present-day nationalist movements around the world are certainly not the same as those on the eve of World War I and certainly not poised to transform the current world order. Rather, such nationalisms and nationalist movements establish why such conflagrations are difficult to do away with. This is especially so since many such nationalisms prove why the ghosts of colonialism still haunt us today and many colonial conflicts have not been entirely resolved, inclusive of racism, and the remnants of colonial thinking.

Indeed, nationalism not only rears its ugly head in terms of aspiring ethno-nationalists wishing to have their own nation-states but among established nation-states and their attempts at eradicating their own minorities. State systems have proven to be especially deadly as evident in the twentieth-century and its many conspicuous genocides (e.g., Cambodia, Guatemala, Rwanda), but most notoriously, the Holocaust

(*Shoah*) and the German Nazi extermination of 6 million European-Jews. Fascism of the kind in Germany, Italy, and Spain, demonstrated how extreme nationalism, along with expansive militarism, and racism, projected notions of eradicating difference whether in terms of political ideologies (e.g., communism), or against minorities (e.g., Jews, Basques, Catalans, Roma, and so on). Present-day examples of this sort include the Chinese against the Uighurs, the Burmese against the Rohingya, the Brazilians against Amerindian peoples, and the northern Sudanese Muslims against peoples in Darfur. Genocidal violence may be mostly understood as directed by states. Such genocidal projects are for the most part state-directed violence.

Theoretically speaking, I ask, what is a state? Beyond the likes of James Scott and his classic work *Seeing Like a State* (1998), I pondered how states may create systems of social conformity and social exclusion and how such systematization may be entwined with a racialization of ideals within a perceived social order for society. States, in general, are systematized entities directed by projects of social control and the expansiveness of power. The argument here is initially somewhat similar to Dru Gladney's (1998) thesis in *Making Majorities*. Yet, by contrast, I attempt to examine why the "state project" may be a bit more encompassing to include non-nation-state nationalists, genocide, some aspects of human biology, and trauma. By examining not only causes of statehood and causes for statehood but to include also the effects from statehood, such as resulting atrocities may perhaps get us further along in understanding how humans "other others." Not only how majorities and minorities are made but what some minorities aspire to be and how majority projects may be interrelated to our own biological and neurological selves. Ultimately, perhaps, such an examination may lead us away from extremism and toward more peaceful resolutions.

Moreover, historically speaking we must not forget that state societies are relatively recent phenomena, and the modern nation-state, even more recent. As Douglas Fry (2013: 547) points out: "First, despite the fact that in the twenty-first century a global system of nation-states is taken as a fact of life, the first states, appearing in the form of ancient civilizations, are only several millennia old, whereas the modern version of the state, the nation-state, is only a few hundred years old. Second, politically-speaking, it has not always been this way and it does not always have to be this way. In other words, there is nothing inherently natural or normal about a global system based on nation-states." Yet, if we are to move toward more harmonious resolutions to our conflicts, we must recognize organizations like the United Nations are essential frameworks for creating more universal models of peace, and envision how better to cooperate globally may be even beyond the parameters of the current UN model.

In this book, *Politics and Racism Beyond Nations: A Multidisciplinary Approach to Crises*, I demonstrate how differences are created on many levels to reveal how the "othering project" is evident through national policies of immigration, through aspiring nationalisms, through genocidal inhumanity, and the subsequent effects of such othering evident in racial trauma. Likewise, I expound how science may illuminate intolerance by proving why homosexuality, for example, is at least substantially a biological phenomenon and how after all the discussion on hatred from racism, difference, and persecution we may examine notions of empathy, love, and peace through Amerindian and Buddhist perspectives. Particularly, when considering Amerindian philosophies about nature and Buddhist philosophical perspectives on "inter-being" we may reach toward more loving views of self, humanity, and the environment.

Even so, there is much to overcome in terms of "violence," whether at the individual, societal, or state levels. Nevertheless, it is beyond the scope of the book to suppose all types of violence may be overcome in directing our thoughts toward Amerindian and Buddhist perspectives. Still, such ontological views are worth thinking about and worth postulating about in terms of rethinking our Western standpoints beyond national security concerns and more toward environmental views of being in the world. Some might even say, it is incredibly naïve to try to be gentler and kinder. Yet, if we do not upend our current thinking of the sort of bellicose and environmental nihilism in their present forms, we may find ourselves in a nuclear war, or a planet in a Sixth Extinction beyond repair, or amidst global climate change past restoration.

As the book will establish, violence may be recognized as belonging to categories of "indirect violence" and "direct violence." In the former category, I explore how rhetoric, such as racist rhetoric, contributes to a milieu of indirect violence. Likewise, such indirect violence may be embedded within society through structures of violence, in other words, through those institutions which limit an individual's capacity and potential of being a whole person because of poverty, lack of housing opportunities, lack of educational opportunities, lack of employment opportunities, and so forth. Indirect violence of these sorts, racist rhetoric, and structures of oppression may in fact lead to more directed violent behavior against those individuals being oppressed. Moreover, from lack of opportunities, some oppressed individuals may resort to violence themselves as a means of being heard in a system which stifles their voices (e.g., African-American riots in the Watts neighborhood of Los Angeles during the 1960s in the United States).

Aside from rhetoric and the institutionalization of violence, which I am here claiming to be "indirect" influences, there of course are the direct aspects of violence and directed actions against individuals who are being oppressed. In the most extreme forms, such violence culminates in genocide against specific groups and peoples because of their ethnicity, race, and/or religion and how majorities wish to maintain a hegemonic hold on power within societies. After Antonio Gramsci, I am here thinking of hegemony as an all-encompassing force of control and in specific terms how such socio-cultural hegemonic forces, for example, negatively purport to cleanse society of undesirable ethnicities (e.g., through white supremacist movements, nativist movements, and/or majority ethno-nationalist forces). This is what I characterize as "negative hegemony," or hegemonic majority projects and hegemonic-directed forces leading in some cases to genocide (e.g., Nazi Germany against European Jews, Guatemala against Mayan Indians, Brazil against Amerindian Natives, China against Uighurs, and Myanmar against Rohingya).

For immigration policies of the United States, especially when millions of immigrants arrived in the late nineteenth and early twentieth centuries, a certain nativist xenophobia was directed at Asians—especially Chinese and Japanese. In this regard, social marginalization in official circles included the Chinese Exclusion Act of 1882 and the Gentleman's Agreement of 1907 against the Japanese. Xenophobic policies continued with Japanese internment during World War II under Franklin Roosevelt. Recently, the rhetoric against migrants was epitomized by the Trump administration's policies against Guatemalans, Salvadorans, Hondurans, and Mexicans crossing the U.S. southern border and the policy of separating children from families. Furthermore, racist rhetoric and violence against Asian-Americans in the United States has been exacerbated by the COVID-19 pandemic.

Social conformity and social exclusion in association with those aspiring for statehood among non-state nationalists are likewise quite evident. This is true for example among Basques and Catalans and many other groups elsewhere in the world. What one finds is that the "imagined community" of Benedict Anderson is really quite beyond his original conceptualization.

Among nationalists, and their competing ideologies regarding who will become the better patriot, or rather, what part of the movement is more patriotic, the moderate or the radical, there is a sense of "re-imagining and re-imagining and re-imagining" as a continual process along with the evolution of socio-cultural practices. Nationalism is a re-imagination which not only holds onto so-called rituals and traditions but is likewise transformative through its re-inventions and not just from adhering to "inventions of traditions" as described by Hobsbawm and Ranger (1983) but new inventions and new devices to keep alive the nationalist zeal and to make the nationalist project conform to a currency of the moment through the Internet, social media, music, television, and communicative possibilities through cell phone technologies. Among non-state nationalists, the nationalist project is a continuum of socio-cultural identities whereby the idea of a nation is always a mesmerizing possibility, the possibility of becoming, and the possibility of legitimacy. Such is the power of possible statehood as a talisman to non-state nationalists like Basques, Catalans, Scots, and Welsh, for example, whereby the state continues to have numinous qualities as a kind of secular religion along with all the secular religio-ritual practices toward nationhood.

Therefore, it is not difficult to imagine how nation-state policies may operate on a type of continuum or pendulum from initial "racist" projects against immigrants and then swinging toward extremes of genocide when "othering" oppression supported the very view of the state itself as a juxtaposition of racial purity against the impurity of minorities like Jews and Roma as it did in Nazi Germany. In this book, I am not arguing how states have evolved from beginning auspices of one type of prejudicial and racist view to the next but rather explain their features and their consequences. Indeed, a central feature of this book is understanding the consequences of hate and violence through racial trauma.

In *Politics and Racism Beyond Nations*, I argue how prejudices and racism have caused particular kinds of trauma. Today, we know also that trauma may be genetically passed on from mothers to their offspring and so there are certainly biological elements of trauma beyond the social. Yet, in my view, psychological trauma, whether in relation to genocidal survival or in association with racism, may be analyzed in terms of "time." In a previous article, "Mayan Cognition, Memory, and Trauma" (2009), I maintained how trauma may be conceptualized "diachronically" and "synchronically." "Diachronic trauma" I asserted happens over time and may occur on a regular basis, which I characterized as resulting from "racism" and its often everyday qualities. On the other hand, "synchronic trauma" I characterized as those traumatic experiences remembered as happening in particular episodes. Both diachronic trauma and synchronic trauma may be part of the memories of individuals or particular groups within different societies. Individuals and groups may have both diachronic and synchronic traumas because such traumas are often associated with specific memories and form overall qualities of memories over time. Specifically, synchronic trauma is associated with episodic memories and diachronic trauma is associated with semantic memories—the first being memories of episodes in time and the second being continuous memories over time. Such memory forms are not necessarily separate, nor are these necessarily separate forms of time memories. Episodic and semantic memories may be part of the same memories while diachronic and synchronic traumas may be part of the same repertoire of memories about traumas.

Additionally, the types of memories associated with genocide may be explained, I will argue, from rethinking Whitehouse's (2004) "imagistic mode of religiosity" through a secular reconfiguration by demonstrating how genocidal traumatic memories are also episodic and imagistic with flash-bulb-like qualities and imprint on the individual in very negative ways, not just through dramatic religio-rituals. As such, I will expound how: "traumatic recollections of escaping genocide are similar, in cognitive patterning but not in kind, to recollection processes for engaging in traumatic ritual activities like circumcision, scarification, and other bodily-mutilating rites" (Linstroth 2009: 160). Furthermore, I will assert that some traumatic memories, particularly those from childhood, may be part of storytelling for a group. Such autobiographical memories are different though. They give a sense of being there, a "we" sense, but in actuality are those memories of adults passed on to children similar to what Maurice Bloch (1998) described among Zafiminary children about a noteworthy massacre of a village in Madagascar. Thus, I will summarize these memories in the following fashion. "It proves I think that one does not have to have actual memories but memories which are shared between families and villagers as becoming 'we' memories of social trauma. In this manner the cognition of trauma is also a social process more than simply a form of individual recollection, especially indigenous discourses of storytelling, which are just as indelible and enduring" (Linstroth 2009: 165).

Moreover, aside from traumatic memories associated with genocide, there are those traumatic memories associated with "racism" and "structural or symbolic violence." I will contend such memories categorized with racism have different qualities than episodic and flashbulb memories of remembering particular episodes of egregious violence (e.g., assassinations, executions, massacres, and murders). Memories of "structural violence" tend to be those of the everyday sort. As I will argue in relation to immigrants, such memories "are traumatic to a different degree than those of flashbulb-traumatic memories. What these memories allude to are more semantic in character because they point to a way of knowing discrimination and oppression, which not only may be carried from such experiential episodes or 'schema' from their home countries but may be reinforced in host countries" (Linstroth 2009: 166). These are memories about social exclusion and negative memories formed from negative experiences that may have become routine. These are memories of "discrimination, prejudice, racism, stereotyping, and labelling which demean individuals and collectives to such an extent as having permanent consequences" (Linstroth 2009: 166). Memories of "structural or symbolic violence" are repetitive and routinized and may as a consequence become social norms and thus such memories have "semantic" qualities (Linstroth 2009). These are schemas of recurrent experiences embedded in, for example, the institutionalization of racism whereby the individual may be prevented from proper education, employment, and/or housing. Such memories are associated with those structures of society which oppress and prevent certain peoples, minorities, from having normal lives. This is everyday violence but a violence which is most often subtler and perhaps less overt but nonetheless for many just as devastating and powerful.

As such, trauma in the book has been envisioned in regard to how minorities are treated by states and institutionalized systems. My research among Guatemalan-Mayas and Brazilian Amerindians has demonstrated how memories are interwoven with experiences of trauma and how analyses of time may likewise reveal why particular sorts of memories are cognitively related to aspects of time, in other words, episodic-synchronic and semantic-diachronic. In the first instance, I examine how genocidal memories may be linked to synchronic and imagistic experiences of trauma, while in the latter, I consider how structural or symbolic violence of racism may be related to everyday qualities of semantic trauma. By considering these varying threads about trauma, I will show how intense violence may be for the negative influences on human cognition in its worst renditions through genocidal actions and in its subtler forms through structures of oppression.

Beyond trauma of the former types, *Politics and Racism Beyond Nations* was also written in order to create a more respectful and tolerant world in which to live in. Tolerance, not only extends to peoples of different ethnicities and peoples from different religions, but those with so-called different sexualities as among the LBGT (Lesbian, Bisexual, Gay, and Transsexual) community as well. In this case, science is viewed as possibly elevating the discourse of intolerance to bring about an understanding through LBGT awareness whereby such sexualities often have underlying biological bases. Even so, among humans, as in most activities humans do, even sexualities may be socially manipulated for cultural ends as evident among the former homosexual rituals practiced by some Papua New Guinean peoples such as the Sambia (Herdt 1981), or for example, when some rural Albanian women swear themselves as lifelong virgins to become men in order to run male-dominated farmsteads (Young 2000).

I felt compelled to write about tolerance because I know people who are intolerant. Unfortunately, their belief systems are often encompassed by religious points of view which stipulate those from the LGBTQ community identify with their sexualities solely as a matter of choice rather than partially from biological causations. As a socio-cultural anthropologist, I believe that one's sexuality may be variable according to cultural attributes, cultural traditions, and cultural norms as much as it is socially constructed. Nonetheless, one cannot discount the biological factors of sexual identity either. And while I certainly believe religious beliefs and their variations should be protected, however, such views should be filtered if they become intolerant. In many ways, religion may try to depict the world as it ought to be rather than what it is, which may include, for example, supplanting evolutionary biology. Religion cannot replace biology. Even so, religion may attempt to present alternative ideas about the world based on ancient texts but not necessarily able to displace, for example, biological, medical, and neurological facts. If religions are part of belief systems based in faith about interpreting the world, science accounts for interpreting the world through experimentations and empirical observations about the natures of realities and for the latter proving if observed realities are or may be more or less true from such careful observations and not simply in the former from faithful religio-convictions. In other words, magical thinking cannot replace realities we know to be true from careful scientific observations (e.g., the Earth is "not" 6000 years old according to the Bible but 4.5 billion years old according to geology).

Indeed, as Frans de Waal (2013: xiv), from a primatologist's perspective, has rightly pointed out: "empathy may be our only hope." On the other hand, anthropologist Douglas Fry (2013: 5) elaborated that "in the ever-more interdependent world community, global cooperation to successfully address climate change and other shared challenges to human survival is critically needed, and holding an erroneous warlike image of human nature only hinders the process of working together on the scale that is necessary."

Additionally, Fry (2013: 346) states it is important to approach "peace and security within a new global cooperative paradigm" and explains: "first, to have *vision* that conflicts can be solved without war, second, to recognize the role of global *interdependence* as a key to promoting *global cooperation*, and third, to focus on creating multiple *identities* ranging from the local community to the global community. I like to play with the 'Us versus Them' concept and say in this interdependent world of the twenty-first century that we need to 'Expand the Us to include the 'Them.'"

This is why the book also explores a new paradigm for cooperation and peace based upon indigenous Amerindian worldviews and Buddhist philosophy. The concept of "inter-being" is well known among Brazilian Amerindian peoples and Native peoples in general. The notion that "all" so-called beings, non-human animals and humans, have spirits along with sacred spaces and sacred objects, is an essential component to indigenous religio-thought. In other words, all beings have a purpose and deserve to be treated with respect. Likewise, we find this interrelatedness philosophy in Buddhism, especially from proponents like Vietnamese Buddhist and living saint Thich Nhat Hanh. This book examines these ideas of inter-being in detail both in Amerindian and in Buddhist traditions based upon my fieldwork in Manaus, Brazil (2009), studying Apurinã, Kambeba, Kokama, Munduruku, Mura, Sateré-Mawé, Tikuna, and Tukano Amerindians, and from ethno-biographic interviews with Buddhist monastics (2020).

Humanity is in existential crises on the verge of its own destruction in terms of environmental annihilation and in the midst of the Sixth Extinction as well on the verge of self-destruction from the very real possibility of all-encompassing nuclear warfare. If we realize how interrelated we are, not only as human beings across the globe, but how interrelated we are to all non-human beings as well and how dependent we are on our environment may prove to be a significant way forward in creating the peacebuilding blocks necessary in order to prevent further environmental disaster or ultimately nuclear extinction. Through education, we may be able to create the necessary means whereby a truer understanding of human beings in relation to their environment, each other, and non-human beings, may be the difference between survival or extermination.

Moreover, *Politics and Racism Beyond Nations* asks where can we go from here as humans? Part of the answer, at least, is examining how humans are not solely incited to be violent but why we are also predisposed as peaceful beings. This is framed with a discussion with Buddhist monks and a Buddhist nun who have been asked how they envision a more peaceful world. Thus, the book likewise demonstrates how and why empathy and peaceful resolution are part of the human social complex. Why "love" in human terms stems from empathic capacities of mammals, and is akin to emotive capabilities of our closest relatives, other primates, and among humans, why love is an elevated and ideal emotion beyond evolution representing the best part of our communality and abstract ideals.

## OUTLINE OF THE BOOK

### *Chapter 2*

Chapter 2 provides a critical view of the former Trump administration and its populist stance against Latin American immigrants. It also critiques the Indian Hindu nationalist administration of the Modi government for its lack of concern for rural migrant laborers. The populism of the Trump administration and the Modi government demonstrate how xenophobic the former was and how the latter excluded lower socio-economic classes from aid.

### *Chapter 3*

Chapter 3 examines how ethno-nationalist sentiments remain active and prominent well after the establishment of peace processes in the case of ETA (Basque Homeland and Freedom, *Euskadi Ta Askatasuna*) following 2011 and in the case of the IRA (Irish Republican Army) following the Good Friday Agreement of 1998. Additionally, I will demonstrate how ethno-nationalist minorities like Basques, Catalans, and (some) Northern Irish Catholics have sustained perspectives of ethno-subordination. This has lead them to imagine respectively an independent Basque Country,

Catalonia, and a united Ireland (Northern Ireland with the rest of Ireland). Moreover, I critique how Basque celebrations of the return of political prisoners jeopardize their peace process, while the murder of a journalist by the New IRA also jeopardized the peace process in Northern Ireland.

## Chapter 4

Chapter 4 is about creating connections between violence of the past and violence of the present as perpetrated against indigenous peoples and by interweaving narratives and understanding current genocidal practices. Depicted in this chapter are the genocides against Guatemalan-Mayas, Sentinelese Jarawa Islanders, Western Chinese Uighurs, Brazilian Amerindians, and to a lesser extent about the genocides against indigenous peoples in Canada, United States, and Australia. In general, I try to make sense of these genocides. For example, why do some human beings try to eliminate other groups of human beings in their entirety? What are the geneses of such mass murder? What are the consequences of such mass murder? And, how can such mass murder be prevented?

## Chapter 5

Chapter 5 analyzes the biographical narratives of racism against Guatemalan-Mayan immigrants and Brazilian urban Amerindians. It will be demonstrated how racism causes trauma in Guatemalan-Mayan immigrants and Brazilian urban Amerindians by understanding how memory forms of trauma may be divided between particular episodes of experiential trauma or "synchronic trauma" or experiential trauma over long periods of time or "diachronic trauma." Thus, this chapter also broadens the discussion of racism by addressing current affairs in the United States and beyond, for example, Trump's racist rhetoric; the consequences of the murder of George Floyd and African-American deaths at the hands of the police; racism against Native Americans in the United States; the racialized issues surrounding COVID-19 and Native peoples in Brazil. What is more, the chapter examines the "politics of racism," not only how race is a social construct but how racism plays a fundamental role in the political landscape for political leaders like former President Donald Trump and current Brazilian President Jair Bolsonaro.

## Chapter 6

Chapter 6 depicts the narratives of three gay men and what to them it meant growing up homosexual. The chapter is meant to inspire greater comprehension through science and how science may lead to more tolerance. For example, by better understanding the biological bases for LBGT constructions may aid in some manner toward social acceptance of same-sex and/or alternative sexual identities beyond hegemonic hetero-constructions. In this chapter, I am also promoting a kind of tolerance through neurobiology and primatology. Explored in this chapter are how different neurochemicals and different brain regions affect human behavior. Likewise, I investigate what non-human primate behaviors tell us about being human. Furthermore, the chapter explores the destruction of the Amazon and the negligence of Brazilian President Jair Bolsonaro in preventing mass fires and why race must not be associated with diseases.

## Chapter 7

Chapter 7 examines the narratives of four Buddhist monastics, three Buddhist monks and one Buddhist nun. Some of the questions asked of them were: What is love? What is peace? How can we make a better world? One of the major themes in the chapter is the notion of "inter-being." In other words, how can we become more respectful of each other, toward all human beings, but likewise toward all living beings from the Buddhist perspective, especially from the likes of Buddhist Zen Master Thich Nhat Hanh. Also, how such forms may be carried forward in the West through a "re-indigenization" of society, respecting the environment and an appreciation for all living beings will make the world a better place according to an Amerindian ethos. Another aspect of the chapter is celebrating the work of average peaceworkers, whereas other analyses in the chapter address what is love from the inspirations of Dr. Martin Luther King, Jr. and from biological perspectives.

### NOTE

1. Florida is the fifth state to ban "critical race theory" after Arkansas, Tennessee, Oklahoma, and Idaho so far as of June 2021. https://www.forbes.com/sites/carlieporterfield/2021/06/10/florida-becomes-fifth-state-to-bar-schools-from-teaching-critical-race-theory/?sh=7bea16c85044

## Bibliography

Bloch, M. 1998. *How We Think They Think: Anthropological Approaches to Cognition, Memory, and Literacy.* Oxford: Westview Press.
Delgado, R., and J. Stefancic. 2017. *Critical Race Theory: An Introduction.* 3rd ed. New York: New York University Press.
Fry, D.P., ed. 2013. *War, Peace, and Human Nature: The Convergence of Evolutionary and Cultural Views.* Oxford: Oxford University Press.
Gingerich, A., and M. Banks. 2006. *Neo-Nationalism in Europe and Beyond: Perspectives from Social Anthropology.* Oxford: Berghahn Books.
Gladney, D., ed. 1998. *Making Majorities: Constituting the Nation in Japan, Korea, China, Malaysia, Fiji, Turkey, and the United States.* Stanford, CA: Stanford University Press.
Herdt, G. 1981, new edn. 1994. *Guardians of the Flute: Idioms of Masculinity.* New York: McGraw-Hill.
Hobsbawm, E., and T. Ranger, eds. 1983. *The Invention of Tradition.* Cambridge: Cambridge University Press.
Linstroth, J.P. 2009. Mayan Cognition, Memory, and Trauma. *History and Anthropology* 20 (2): 139–182.
Scott, J.C. 1998. *Seeing Like a State: How Certain Schemes to Improve the Human Condition Have Failed.* New Haven, CT: Yale University Press.
de Waal, F. 2013. *The Bonobo and the Atheist: In Search of Humanism among the Primates.* New York: W. W. Norton & Company.
Whitehouse, H. 2004. *Modes of Religiosity: A Cognitive Theory of Religious Transmission.* Walnut Creek, CA: AltaMira Press.
Young, A. 2000. *Women Who Become Men: Albanian Sworn Virgins.* Oxford: Berg.

CHAPTER 2

# Immigration and Racism

*In the summer of 1991, I began working with an advocacy group, which later became known as "The Guatemalan-Maya Center." At that time, I was translating from Spanish to English stories of civil war atrocities and genocide in Guatemala from recent Guatemalan-Indian arrivals. The stories were, to say the least, horrific. They told of villages being set fire by Guatemalan soldiers; women who were raped by soldiers; they told of children murdered; people fleeing villages to the mountains. Story after story had similar themes—death, torture, villages destroyed. Some stories also told of the atrocities perpetrated by the guerrillas against villagers. These were the guerrillas who were fighting the Guatemalan military. And because the Guatemalan Army often could not locate the guerrillas in the mountains and the remote villages, where many of these Mayan Indians lived, the Mayas were caught in the middle of the conflict, and used by both sides. The stories of these Guatemalan-Mayan refugees were moving stories and were part of the political depositions I translated in order for these Guatemalan-Maya refugees to obtain green cards. These were refugees who somehow had made it to South Florida, in many cases on foot, to escape the Guatemala Civil War (1960–1996).*

*They fled the war at the time in Guatemala and I was amazed how all of them reiterated the same kind of story with the same basic plot—their father was killed; they saw people being burned to death; they had been raped; they watched their father or mother or brother and/or sister die before their own eyes, but they had survived, somehow; they watched the village priest being murdered; they had no time to bury their dead; they had fled to the mountains*

© The Author(s), under exclusive license to Springer Nature Switzerland AG 2022
J. P. Linstroth, *Politics and Racism Beyond Nations*,
https://doi.org/10.1007/978-3-030-91720-3_2

and then escaped Guatemala altogether; they left everything behind; their uncle's body was found with his head chopped off; the helicopters came and shot at everyone in the village with machinegun fire but they escaped, somehow; the military came and rounded up the men; the guerrillas came and rounded up the men; my father disappeared, and on and on and on. I wondered, "how had all of these people survived?" You could see the desperation in their eyes. Many women were with young children, some children suckling at their mothers' breasts. There was a general sadness among them, a kind of unutterable shock. What psychology circles (DSM-V, Diagnostic and Statistical Manual of Mental Disorders, 5th ed.) now call "post-traumatic stress disorder" (PTSD). At the time, I was just considering graduate school in Anthropology. But I knew this work with these refugees, even then, was really important. These were Mayan Indians: Chuj, Ixil, Kanjobal, K'ixe', Mam, and other ethnic groups. I spent the summer as a volunteer translating story after story, tragedy after tragedy, not knowing whether any of my translations of their broken Spanish to English, and their seeking asylum in the United States would be successful. (Later, I was told many of them had indeed received green cards due to my translations. The translations were sent off to immigration lawyers in Miami, Florida, who worked on their asylum cases, mostly pro bono.)

Then, one day, as I took a break from translating and transcribing the distressing and dreadful stories, one of the center leaders, herself a Kanjobal-Mayan woman, who spoke good English, and who had herself arrived with her family years before at the height of the killings and genocide there (1981–1983), said to me: "You know a lot of their stories are just exaggerations. Many of them are just repeating what they heard." I was flabbergasted by her comment. "Exaggeration?" I asked her, astonished, "You mean you are telling me what they are saying to me isn't true?" She said: "I don't know but a lot of them just repeat what they have heard. They want asylum here and are desperate to stay here."

Years later, in 2005, when I interviewed this same population, Guatemalan-Mayas, again for a joint grant project, after having completed a PhD at the University of Oxford in Social and Cultural Anthropology, I was much more aware how to conduct such interviews and more cognizant of their biographical and social meaning. I realized that even if these Guatemalan-Maya refugee stories of atrocities, horror, and genocide, were, even partially true, and even if many of them were hearsay, did not detract from their veracity. The fact such stories were partly true did not reduce or weaken the genocide these people had experienced, or their relatives had experienced. Such stories were how these Mayan Indians told stories of genocide; how they had collectively experienced such violence; how they had survived as a people from a concerted *effort to wipe them out.* I realized the value of their telling, even if they were repeated over and over, different versions of the same story, variations of genocide, but the repetitive pattern allowed them to mnemonically memorize what they had told me. Repeated patterns allow for memory and are patterns of oral history, particular not only to these Indians, but similar to the way oral histories are told by indigenous peoples everywhere. I realized these were "oral histories," oral histories of genocide the Guatemalan-Mayas had experienced. And regardless, if it was a cousin, or an uncle, or a father or a mother, or a grandparent, or other relative who had told them, or if they had in fact witnessed such atrocities themselves, or not, but heard them from neighbors, they were true stories. They were "true" stories to these people because they were survival narratives. They were oral histories that would be remembered their whole lives. Stories they would tell to their children and their children to their children, and so on. And therefore, they were really important eye-witness accounts, living memories, and survivor accounts from Indians who had been surviving genocide from Europeans for more than 500 years, with the Guatemalan genocide being the latest. While I just translated from Spanish to English their words, it was not until later, I realized as a researcher their value as historical testimonies of genocidal survival, especially the more horrific years between 1981 and 1983 when the so-called Silent Holocaust in Guatemala took place, and afterward as the civil war continued on until 1996.

Of course, later waves of Guatemalan immigrants in later years arrived for different reasons, mostly economic, to find work in the United States. As relatives safely adapted to life in the United States, other relatives sought asylum also and to meet up with their relatives who had made it here and found jobs here. Those migrants who manage to stay and work illegally, send thousands of dollars home to their families in Guatemala, known as "remittances." In turn, this money sent home converts into millions and has helped many poor families throughout rural Guatemala to survive. Later generations also left Guatemala because of the threat of gangs, but most of them knew they were certain to find better jobs in the United States with migrant work such as picking fruit and vegetables, or landscaping, or meatpacking, or in restaurants. The trek was worth it for many, the money was so much better. So, for most new Guatemalan-Mayan immigrant arrivals even with the looming threat of Immigration and Customs Enforcement (ICE), making it to "El Norte" was worth the risks. They could find a new life here, a life where they could earn a decent living, a life much better than in their native Guatemala.

\* \* \*

Twenty-two years after I first worked with the Guatemalan-Mayas on their political asylum cases, I took a job as the Executive Director of "The Guatemalan-Maya Center." It provided me with a unique opportunity to continue my advocacy work with immigrant populations and to fight for their rights in South Florida. Most often, it was thankless work. Some of the notable issues I worked on were "wage theft," when Mayan immigrants worked overtime, and were not paid for the extra hours. Other issues, were mostly associated with education, trying to get Mayan-immigrant families to teach their children with books and to read to their children, while their Indian culture did not normally promote such formal learning. These are people with Limited English Proficiency (LEP) learners and most migrants who come to the United States never finished grade school. Many among them, their first language was their Indian language, and their Spanish was sometimes broken and grammatically incorrect. At best, many of them, the adults who crossed the border, if not most of them, made it to the fourth grade. In rural areas, children were called upon to take care of their subsistent farmlands in the highlands and to take care of brothers and sisters if they were older.

So, a majority of my work involved "immigrant advocacy," whether speaking to the local city council, school officials, local law enforcement, the Florida Department of Children and Families (DCF), the Children Services Council, local lawyers, local media outlets, other immigrant advocacy groups, the Guatemalan Embassy, or public healthcare officials, and so on. Often my time would be spent meeting such disparate organizations in order to promote the rights of people who are, more often than not, voiceless. Immigrants mostly exist in the shadows of our society for fear of deportation. They work in the margins and they are more likely to do jobs most Americans find undesirable, such as picking fruit and vegetables in the fields; housecleaning; cooking, dishwashing, and bussing at restaurants; gardening and landscaping; meatpacking; car-cleaning; poultry industry work; ranch-hand work; and construction. For many reasons, their illegal work and their illegal status are the underbelly of the American economy, and which for most Americans are least understood. Most Americans are wholly ignorant how reliant they are on illegal migrant work. They are not cognizant that most of these migrant workers receive paychecks and pay federal taxes through their paychecks. Thus, while their voices are largely silent, they are nonetheless important in upholding many industries we rely upon and take for granted.

In recent years, following my tenure at The Guatemalan-Maya Center, and under the former Trump administration, migrant children, those mostly from El Salvador, Guatemala, and Honduras, have been separated from their parents. This separation of children from their parents has caused

2 IMMIGRATION AND RACISM   21

*enormous amounts of stress to these families. Children are psychologically scarred for life from such parental disconnection according to many leading mental health experts. In present circumstances, the economic situation and the violence migrants have experienced in their home countries are terrible. Many families have been threatened with violence for various reasons, and believe it is worth making the approximate 1300-mile journey to the U.S./ Mexico border through the perils of Mexico, where often migrants find numerous abuses against them, inclusive of murder, rape, and robbery. Most of these migrants would rather face such abuses in transit countries like Mexico than stay in their homelands. Furthermore, some scientists have argued that "climate change" has instigated forced displacement of many in Guatemala as well as elsewhere.[1] Such refugees have been called "climate refugees" and evident in Guatemala, for example, by a dry region in the central part of the country, where drought is apparent and ongoing, in Spanish known as "El Corredor Seco" (The Dry Corridor). This has created a situation of rampant famine, where small-plot farmers are unable to subsist because of crop failure from the growing dry conditions.*

\* \* \*

*From the short documentary report from Univision (2019): "The Legacy of the 'Zero Tolerance Policy': Traumatized Children with No Access to Treatment".[2] ["Adayanci Pérez, aged 6, is one of 4256 children who were separated from their parents at the U.S./Mexico border as part of the former Trump administration's 'Zero Tolerance' policy according to the ACLU.[3] A more recent, Inspector General Department of Health and Human Services Report (HHS), puts the number at 2737 and another 1556 non-accounted-for children for a total of 4293.[4] Adayanci's father made the journey to the United States for a better life and better education for his daughter. Yet, both father and daughter were detained at the U.S./Mexican border. Adayanci was separated from her father for three and a half months. Her father was deported back to Guatemala while Adayanci stayed in the United States and was placed with an American family without the consent of her Guatemalan family. Her father was given phone numbers in Michigan but the numbers did not work. Finally, after Adayanci, was found, she was finally reunited with her Guatemalan family in Guatemala. Soon following the reunification with her family, her mother asked Adayanci: 'Why are you crying? Why are you like this?' She just says, 'I don't want anything, I just want to stay here.'" Adayanci was diagnosed with post-traumatic stress disorder before returning to Guatemala. Her family did not know because the clinical report she brought home with her was in English.* "*The symptoms of post-traumatic stress in children can go from fear, disassociations, loss of memory or choosing not to talk, as if the child has lost contact with reality. If one does not resolve traumatic childhood events, a sure disposition factor for future traumas is created ... I can't express, I can't find words to describe the systematic abuse of children,*" *remarked María Basualdo, psychologist, expert in trauma and migration. Migrants make the long trek through Mexico to the United States, often with the help of a "coyote" (a smuggler), with whom they go into debt. Migrants are sometimes given a year to repay the coyote, or else the coyote threatens the family with death of one of its members. Such arrangements in Guatemala are illegal but they happen all the time. Adayanci and her family live in a very poor and rural area of Guatemala and do not have the financial means of paying for the psychological care of Adyanci from her trauma. According to recent studies, as many as 400 children who were separated at the U.S./Mexico border have not been reunited with their parents and families. (In 2019, the number of children not yet united with their parents changed to about 150 children.) For these children alone, the psychological toll will be enormous, if not irreversible.)*[5]

* * *

*As a follow-up to this short media report, I caught up with the psychotherapist Maria Basualdo, LMHC, to ask her more about the psychological effects on children from the family separation policies at the US/Mexican border. As she explains the issue:* "*A young child would perceive separation as abandonment. They cannot discern and understand what is going on, and therefore, perceive the absences of his or her parents as abandonment, thus lack of love. Of course, age and time of separation are crucial variables that would affect how traumatizing the experience is. Trauma is a subjective experience and there are multiple factors that influence how events affect children. Most of these children who suffer separation at the border, already come from highly traumatic lives. The odyssey they suffer when they came to the United States, days of waiting in the dessert, and the suffering from hunger and fear.*" *She further elaborates by stating:* "*Trauma also diminishes the ego, and as such, trauma becomes a point of deficiency. So, the child perceives himself as insufficient, not worthy of love. Children are rapidly symptomatized because they cannot verbally articulate or understand the complex emotions they are confronted with.*" *Additionally, she goes on to say:* "*Abandonment produces a feeling of helplessness, and this is the most traumatic experience for a child (nothing can replace the home or the affection of the parents, no institution or care) ... And, childhood events are crucial and constitutive of the psychic structure. Primary relationships form at* an early age and then function as role models for future relationships." I then asked Ms. Basauldo a subsequent question: "What will potentially happen psychologically to these children who have been separated at the US/Mexican border if they are 'not' properly treated by a mental health expert to deal with their past traumas of parental separation?" And her answer was as follows: "This is hard to predict. It does not 'only' depend on the exposure to treatment but also to make certain they get the right type of treatment. PTSD is a very complex diagnosis and requires taking into consideration multiple factors. It is crucial to focus on the subjective experience of the patient and reframe it. Children need to be reassured; they need to have the certainty that they are loved by their parents. There are preexistent factors, vulnerability, and history that need to be considered for a treatment plan. At the same time, the intrapsychic history or preexisting or predisposing biological or psychological factors, are necessary but are not necessarily sufficient to develop trauma. Some argue, however, that the prevalence and severity of trauma depends more on subjective factors than the actual stressor. What really matters, and this is crucial for treatment, is a very careful understanding of the meaning that the patient attributes to the traumatic event(s); the value assigned to it; and, what it means to him or her." I then asked her: "Will these children who have experienced parental separation at the U.S./Mexican border carry their psychological traumas into adulthood? And what will be the psychological effects in adulthood of such trauma?" Her response: "Absolutely, childhood traumas are constitutive and determine future behaviors and attachment styles. They set a worldview and they mold future relationships. Trauma is the antecedent of how a person conceptualizes the world and relates to it. They may in future ask such questions to themselves such as: 'Do I trust others?' 'Is the world hostile?' 'Should I defend myself at all times?' And as such, trauma shapes the personality of the individual." To understand further, I went on to ask: "In your clinical opinion what is the difference between child parental separation 'post-traumatic stress disorder' (PTSD) and other forms of PTSD?" And in answering, she remarked: "PTSD presents with a constellation of symptoms according to DSM [Diagnostic and Statistical Manual of Mental Disorders, 5th ed.]. But, again, trauma is a subjective and biased experience. The stressor is needed but irrelevant as what really matters is how the event is perceived and interpreted by the subject, what it means to her. There are no different forms of PTSD, there are different subjective experiences of trauma and how people develop symptoms. It is complex and responds more to the history of the patient than the stressor which may have caused or triggered the symptoms. The mere presence of a stressor is necessary, but not sufficient. At the same time, the intrapsychic history or preexisting or predisposing biological or psychological factors, are necessary but not sufficient to *develop trauma. Some argue, however, that the prevalence and severity of trauma depends more on subjective factors than the actual stressor. What really matters, and this is crucial for treatment, is a very careful understanding of the meaning that the patient attributes to the event, the value assigned to it, what it means to him or her."* And finally, I asked Ms. Basauldo: "How do children view their parents when they are returned to their parents? How do children psychologically cope with the reunification? How may psychologists, such as yourself, help children who have been traumatized from child-parent separation?" And Basualdo answered: *"Depending on how the children experienced and internalized the traumatic experiences, would result in how they dealt with their parental reunification. Hence, children may become reactive and upset and blame their parents for abandoning them. Or, they can become clingy and develop separation anxiety. Depending on the age of the child, they may develop different forms of attachment which might carry on in future relationships throughout their lives. Because trauma is a subjective experience, it is very difficult to predict or generalize what could happen during reunification. As I mentioned, I do not work (and I haven't) worked with children who have been separated from their parents. Hypothesizing about this really depends on the age and symptomatology of the child. My perspective is treatment with children is more psychodynamic than it is behavioral. At its core, I would try to work 'projectively' (i.e., projective), using playing therapy and drawings to first understand how this trauma was perceived and experienced, redefining and reassuring safety. Children often develop regressive symptoms which behavioral approaches tend to extinguish. In my opinion, the core of therapy with children is helping them express what is going on internally. A symptom is a way of expressing, so when the child wets his or her bed, he or she 'is saying something'. I often say that we need to let the symptom talk, so extinguishing it could be counterproductive. Of course, if the child presents with self-injury behaviors, a more straightforward and behavior approach needs to be used. The core of reunification is to give the child back a sense of reassurance and safety, eradicating any sense of blame or guilt, or, lack of self-worth that she or he might have developed as a result of the trauma. Family therapy is also needed as the child acts in direct response to their given environment. Children do not react to trauma in identical ways (neither do adults) because trauma always implies an interaction between the external and the internal worlds, and the internal world is by definition, unique. Thus, we cannot conceive trauma as a direct response to an objectively traumatizing event or trigger, even though such an event(s) might be extremely violent. Assuming that the trauma is caused by the external event, is to strip away any possible subjectivity, any history, any psychological structure. Precisely, a subjective traumatic experience(s) is (are) always the consequence of a very specific and unique interaction between an event(s) or trigger(s) and the way that event is experienced and symbolized (or conceptualized to use more cognitive jargon). As such, the internal world of the child responds to multiple variables, and therefore, needs to be analyzed to develop a treatment plan. The child's history, personality, previous traumas, belief system, family history, etc., all need to be encompassed and taken into consideration to understand the unique way that the child experienced the traumatizing event(s). According to psychoanalysis, any trauma is always a childhood experience, an internal conflict that arises when the child is confronted with the external world. Children have (in the early stages), structurally, essential features of helplessness and defenselessness, which in turn makes them more vulnerable to traumatizing events. Consequently, children are extremely dependent on their parents to form their own psychological structures. Early childhood is the stage of most psychological vulnerability. Also, their personal histories really matter. Sometimes, children have been traumatized before. And, trauma in such instances becomes accumulative."*

\* \* \*

Julia Le Duc, Associated Press photograph—Father and daughter drowned migrants faced down along the banks of the Rio Grande River

Press photograph of former President Donald J. Trump, 45th President of the United States

## Introduction

In order to understand the complexities of racism against new immigrants in the United States and the political movements against such people, one must, I believe, analyze the concepts of ethnicity and populism and their epistemological possibilities. As Dru Gladney (1998: 1) posits: "Majorities are made, not born … Numerically, ethnically, politically, and culturally, societies make and mark majorities and minorities under specific, historical, political, and social circumstances." While I am in agreement with Gladney, in my view, we need to expand social arguments to include the cognitive, and even, may I dare say the biological today (see Chap. 6). By this I mean how we create differences in our minds, and which is also a different consideration of Anderson's (1983) *Imagined Communities*, how nations are constituted and defined. Furthermore, in reminiscing about what Marcus Banks discussed in his seminal book *Ethnicity: Anthropological Constructions* (1996: 186–187), that ethnicity is probably as much in the researcher's mind as much as it is in the subject's mind, we now have answers for what this means for the latter. What I am asserting here is something akin to Maurice Bloch's distinction between the transcendental social and the transactional social. He states (2013: vii): "I argue that the transcendental social consists of social-order phenomena created and maintained by rituals. The transactional social is governed by norms and ways of doing things that are largely subconscious" (see Chap. 6).

In terms of ethnicity, what I mean by it are those actions, categories, identities, and norms, which are often carried out at the subconscious level and whereby differences are maintained through cognitive underpinnings, social networks, and boundaries. In the case of immigrants, the implication according to Andreas Wimmer (2013: 27) is "that ethnicity does not emerge because 'minorities' maintain a separate identity, culture, and community from national 'majorities,' … Rather, both minorities *and* majorities are made by defining the boundaries between them." Even so, I argue these boundaries are exacerbated in populist movements, especially those which emphasize xenophobic claims (see also, Barth 1969). Hereby, the politics of populism whether in Brazil, the United States, or India, evident by some examples in this book, exaggerate Nativist accusations, allegations, and declarations as to warp meanings of ethnicity and wherein serve a homogenizing project.

In recent years, especially with the last Trump administration, notions of populism came to the fore in regard to issues about immigration. By populism I am advocating the ideational definition proposed by Cas Mudde and Cristóbal Rovira Kaltwasser (2017: 6): "As a thin-centered ideology that considers society to be ultimately separated into two homogenous and antagonistic camps, 'the pure people' versus 'the corrupt elite,' and which argues that politics should be an expression of the *volonté générale* (general will) of the people."[6] The populism of Donald J. Trump railed against the so-called mainstream media, the deep state, and new immigrants. The "sociocultural grievances have remained remarkably constant: 'our way of life' is attacked by the 'liberal elite' who use an oppressive (federal) state and a far too expensive and expensive welfare state to stifle the initiative and values of the people while providing 'special privileges' to non-deserving minorities" (Mudde and Kaltwasser 2017: 25). As

Joseph Lowndes (2017: 240) purports: "Donald Trump, adored by supporters as a disruptive teller of unvarnished truths, watched his poll numbers rise with each outrageous statement—be it about Latin American immigrants, Muslims, women, or his political opponents. Yet again, this performance of the low was also loaded with its own visceral sense of abjection."

In this chapter, I also discuss the problems associated with Prime Minister of India, Narendra Modi, and his Bharatiya Janata Party (BJP) (Indian People's Party) and their association with rural migrant workers who were left stranded by the Modi administration because of a nationwide lockdown for Coronavirus (COVID-19). It is important to realize as Jaffrelot and Tillin (2017: 188) maintain that: "The Hindu nationalist variant of populism poses a threat to India's democracy because of its exclusivist overtone. Majoritarianism, here, means that the largest ethnic group is bound to govern the country and that minorities may end up as second-class citizens." Modi gave no consideration to these internal migrants caught by the lockdown and eventually forced to migrate home for lack of food and money.

In general though, populist ideology assaults those that threaten the homogeneousness of the people. As Mudde and Kaltwasser (2017: 18) avow populism: "Can legitimize authoritarianism and illiberal attacks on anyone who (allegedly) threatens the homogeneity of the people." Populists argue that the so-called liberal elite "favors *the interests* of the immigrants over those of the native people" (Mudde and Kaltwasser 2017: 14). As such this chapter provides a critical view of the populist stance, especially as espoused by the last Trump administration against Latin American immigrants, and lastly, against the Modi administration for its lack of concern for rural migrant laborers.

## Myths on Race and Invasion of the "Caravan Horde"

The last presidential administration of Donald J. Trump seemingly promoted racist discourse against hapless immigrants and the so-called threat they posed.[7] Indeed, Trump and his administration focused on immigrants as the major threat to the security of the nation. Such hyped-up racist rhetoric was not only dangerous and hyperbolic but completely false. The so-called compassionate conservatism years of the George W. Bush presidency were long gone.[8]

This vitriol against the caravan of Central Americans and Mexicans on their way to the border of the United States in 2018 was all out of proportion to any real threat. These people are poor and are fleeing situations of untenable violence in their home countries. Some of this violence has been caused by U.S. policies in the region.

Furthermore, Trump staged the national guard at the border in 2018 for photo opportunities of soldiers building coil wire fencing. Moreover, Trump's words of racist hatred had also inspired and summoned numerous posse of armed militias to the U.S./Mexican borderlands.

Fear-mongering and racism against immigrants however is nothing new in the history of the United States. Toward the end of the nineteenth century and at the turn of the twentieth century, many in the United States promoted "Nativism"—an all-white America where good jobs belonged to whites, not foreigners.[9] This was the historical period known as the "Second Industrial Revolution," the "Gilded Age" and the "Progressive Era"—a time of enormous economic transformation for the country through industrialization and urbanization.[10]

Those on the West Coast in states like California blamed the loss of jobs and low wages on Chinese immigrants. This followed with the passage of the Chinese Exclusion Act by the U.S. Congress in 1882. In 1907 there was also a "Gentleman's Agreement" with Japan to restrict Japanese emigration.[11]

By 1924 the U.S. Congress passed the "Immigration Act," thereby limiting immigration from Eastern and Southern Europeans such as those with Greek, Italian, Polish, and Jewish origins and almost banning all Asians altogether.[12]

During the mid-nineteenth century, a huge wave of Irish immigrants came to the United States because of the "Great Famine" (1845–1849) in Ireland.[13] These Irish worked in the worst jobs possible. They built the railroads connecting the country to the West Coast, constructed canals, and provided cheap labor for much of northern industry. In this period, the Irish were viewed as dogs, drunkards, and non-human apes. (Ironic because they were white.)

Conditions in manufacturing were generally deplorable for all new immigrants in the Gilded Age. Workers were not protected and required to work 14-to-16-hour hour days, six days a week (sometimes seven) and almost 365 days a year with little or no time off. Children (as young as ten or younger) worked too and were not required to attend school. A typical unskilled laborer at the time earned no more than $8–$10 per week.[14]

Upton Sinclair's historical novel, *The Jungle* (1904), illustrates these hazardous conditions for immigrants in Chicago's meatpacking industry—lost limbs and digits, no workman's compensation, unsanitary conditions, and dangerous work.[15]

In the Chicago Haymarket Riot of 1886, several German immigrants were unfairly accused of instigating a protest where policemen were killed.[16] The injustice of the following trial was so evident that the governor of Illinois commuted some of the sentences of those accused. (Again, these were white immigrants.)

Fears of immigrants, even those born as Americans, were also evident during World War II with the internment of Japanese-Americans into concentration camps. Some 100,000 Japanese-Americans were imprisoned between 1942 and 1945.[17] Yet, there was no evidence such Americans posed any real threat to other Americans because of their Japanese heritage. But mythologies persist. Immigrants are easy scapegoats and targets because they often do not have a voice to protest such falsehoods against them.

Indeed, immigrants are often the hardest working populations, wanting a better life for themselves and their families. We find this in new immigrant populations coming from Mexico and Central America to the United States today. These are people who work in the fields picking our fruits and vegetables; doing domestic work and caring for our children; laboring in meatpacking plants; working in landscaping and mowing our lawns; and preparing our food in the restaurant industry.

I have been advocating on behalf of the Guatemalan-Maya population in South Florida since 1990. Many of these immigrants arrived here from the genocide and civil war in Guatemala in the early 1980s where the United States was indirectly involved, having trained the country's military leaders in the School of the Americas.[18]

During the 1980s the United States intervened more directly in the civil wars in Central American countries like El Salvador and Nicaragua.[19] Such U.S. military interventionism was against the spread of communism yet caused greater instability in the region.

Moreover, U.S. economic trade policies of the 1990s such as NAFTA (North American Free Trade Agreement) have consistently undermined the economic opportunities of those living in countries like El Salvador, Honduras, and Guatemala.[20] Employers in Central America have consistently violated minimum wage agreements and fair labor conditions.

If we are to be honest, these 5000-people coming from El Salvador, Guatemala, Honduras, and Mexico in 2018 posed no real threat to the security of the United States. Moreover, it was not difficult preventing them from crossing our border.[21] But the mythologies created by the former Trump administration will most likely persist in the American imagination.

Let me dispel some these myths about this so-called caravan threat of 2018. There was no threat of Middle Eastern terrorists amongst this caravan of mostly poor Central Americans. Nor was there credible evidence to back up such claims. Nor was the Democrat Party responsible for organizing the caravan. Migrant caravans have been coming to the U.S./Mexican borders for years under both Republican and Democrat administrations. Traveling in numbers makes the journey safer for these migrants. Often migrants are victims of real threats of violence along the way—murder, rape, and robbery. Nor was the Honduran government financially supporting the caravan. What was more, U.S. economic aid to the region has worsened the situation for those countries rather than bettered it. The former Obama administration's support for "Alliance for Prosperity" has in fact exasperated inequalities and caused more violence.[22] And finally, these people cannot just return to their home countries and apply for political asylum there. They must be in the United States to apply for asylum and citizenship.

The situation in Central America is a humanitarian crisis on a large scale. It is a crisis to much an extent caused by U.S. policies in the region. We have often treated those South of the border as inferior and lesser peoples since the beginning of our imperialist aims in the Western Hemisphere with the Monroe Doctrine, then the Roosevelt Corollary, and U.S. military interventionism over the last one hundred years throughout the Americas and the Caribbean.[23]

Do not be fooled by Trump's racist rhetoric. These immigrants are desperate human beings wanting a better life for their families. They are not security threats. They should be protected and sheltered and given the same opportunities as our ancestors arriving at Ellis Island. Rather, Emma Lazarus' words (1883), should echo with everyone: "Give me your tired, your poor, your huddled masses yearning to breathe free, the wretched refuse of your teeming shore."[24] This is the true America and the ideals we all hold dear.

## Border Policies from Hell

Who was not rightly moved by the photograph of a Salvadoran father and his daughter drowned and laying on the Mexican side of the Rio Grande River in 2019?[25] The father, Óscar Martínez Ramírez, was only twenty-five years old and his daughter, Valeria, was almost two, with her dainty and diminutive white arm draped over her father's nape, both faced down in the muddy river bank—and were both yet more unnecessary U.S./Mexican borderland deaths as both Democrats and Republicans continue debating how to deal with our so-called southern border crisis.

The photo was taken by Mexican photo-journalist, Julia Le Duc for the Mexican newspaper, *La Jornada*, but making the Associated Press (AP) circuit.[26] It is a shocking and unsettling photo—reflecting a something, which should not be. The young man's wet black t-shirt pulled up nearly over his head and above his daughter's head, his shorts more like swim trunks. And comparable to all photos of the newly dead, the father-daughter appeared to be just resting along the river bank—as if exhausted from an arduous swim, a momentary repose perhaps—but nonetheless, reflecting the eternal in their deaths, a disquieting stillness, never to awaken in their final embrace.

How much more can the American people accept about our border policies from hell? And this past Trump administration separating children from their parents and holding them in unconscionable conditions in less than adequate border facilities—how much more? So, is the current Biden administration doing any better than the Trump administration with its border policies? Evidence suggests not much better but there is some improvement.[27]

In 2018, there were almost 300 borderland deaths.[28] And instead of ameliorating the situation, the Trump administration made it worse because of borderland policies by cutting off a significant portion of U.S. development aid to El Salvador, Guatemala, and Honduras.[29] This had have the opposite effect on these countries than as an intended foreign policy punitive measure. From a recent Congressional Research Service report in March 2019, it was clear the Trump administration was trending to limit the amount of U.S. aid to Latin America and the Caribbean compared with previous administrations.[30] Contrary to Trump, development aid to Central America may have staunched flows of migration through funding for ceasing gang violence, alleviating food insecurity, providing viable labor opportunities, and reducing poverty.

For one, immigration problems were not limited to the U.S./Mexican border. More people from foreign countries are overstaying their visas through airport arrivals in general than coming to the U.S. southern borderlands.[31] This has been true for the last several years. In a 2017 study in *the Journal on Migration and Human Security*, the authors state: "In 2014, about 4.5 million US residents, or 32 percent of the total undocumented population, were overstays" and that "Overstays accounted for about two-thirds (66 percent) of those who arrived (i.e. joined the undocumented population) in 2014."[32] According to a Department of Homeland Security report, there were a total of 701,900 overstay events in 2017.[33] Moreover, in general, undocumented migrants in the United States have steadily declined over the last few years. And beyond Trump's pomposity, Mexico has actually done quite a lot in detaining Central Americans and also by providing them with humanitarian visas to stay in Mexico.[34]

While certainly there is a southern borderland crisis, because according to U.S. Customs and Border Protection statistics, the number of apprehended families along the Southwest U.S./Mexico border had increased by 463 percent from 2018.[35] Even so, the U.S. detention facilities at the border are wholly inadequate for processing new immigrants, and especially neglectful for young child care. Columbia University Law Professor and Director of Columbia's Immigrants' Rights Clinic, Elora Mukherjee, reported on the deplorable conditions of children held in U.S. custody at the Clint Facility in Texas. As Professor Mukherjee explained: "In twelve years representing immigrant children in detention, I have never seen such degradation and inhumanity. Children were dirty, they were scared, and they were hungry."[36]

As a result of the outcry from such reports about inhumane conditions for migrant children and families at U.S. detention facilities along the U.S./Mexico border, the Acting Head of U.S. Customs and Border Protection (CPB), John Sanders, resigned on June 25, 2019.[37]

In my view, our modern problems of U.S./Mexico border policies began with former President Donald J. Trump himself and his racist rhetoric. (Notably, the Biden administration has tried taking a different U.S. border policy stance.) Even so, some people, such as U.S Border Patrol officers, were forced to carry out the executive orders of their bosses, however, wrongly conceived. And some realized such directives were morally wrong.

The anthropologist Marilyn Strathern (1988), in her well-regarded book *The Gender of the Gift*, described "social agency" this way: "Persons or things may be transferred as 'standing for' (in our terms) parts of persons. This construction thus produces objects (the person as a 'part' of a person—him or herself or another) which can circulate between persons and mediate their relationship."[38] In other words, our infernal U.S. border policies were an extension of former President Trump's xenophobic bombast against migrants and immigrants, and no less inflammatory than his remarks following the unfortunate incidents in Charlottesville, Virginia in 2017.[39]

Thus, in my opinion, Trump's hateful speech about Central American migrants, about undocumented immigrants, about foreigners, those from "sh**hole" countries—all had negative cascading effects in general. Children and others were dying at the U.S./Mexican border because the former Trump administration wanted such tragedies to resonate as deterrents for those who wishing to cross and/or seek asylum in the United States.[40] According to a 2018 Human Rights Watch report, titled "In the Freezer: Abusive Conditions for Women and Children in U.S. Immigration Holding Cells," facilities at the border were needlessly dangerous. According to the report: "We found that conditions in holding cells at the southern border are often poor and in several critical respects identical to those previously found by US courts to be in violation of CBP's [U.S. Customs and Border Protection] obligations and prior commitments."[41]

The holding cells are made of concrete and those detained are given Mylar blankets (a foil often used for marathon runners following their runs), in rare cases a mat. The temperatures are set incredibly low and this is why they are known as "freezers" (*hieleras*). Of those interviewed, none were given soap, toothpaste, or toothbrushes, and none were allowed to shower for days. The conditions were indisputably unsanitary and extremely stressful to children. More so, Trump officials saw nothing wrong with such reprehensible detention conditions as one Trump lawyer justified to Judges on the U.S. Court of Appeals for the 9th Circuit.[42]

In many cases, immigrant detainees are held for many days, in traumatic settings, allowing for immunity weakness and children falling ill, particularly from parental separations. As Human Rights Watch (2018) described: "In some cases, we heard that immigration agents attempted to separate mothers and young children. For instance, Miriam F. told us that after she went to the border post in El Paso, Texas, to request asylum in early September 2017: 'They first told me they were going to separate me and my daughter. They also said this to the other mothers. We all began to cry.

We said that our children were still very small. My daughter is six years old.'"[43]

The claims of Human Rights Watch have been supported by an ACLU 2018 report documenting abuse and maltreatment of child immigrants in U.S. custody.[44] In psychological terms, according to Harvard University's Shorenstein Center, separating children from mothers, and/or families, causes conditions of "child neglect," exacerbating possibilities of mental health problems into adulthood as bipolar disorder and schizophrenia, and increasing risks for violent behavior.[45]

As a summary of the former Trump administration's child detention at U.S. southern border, I leave you with a poem from my award-winning poetry book *Epochal Reckonings*. In it, I wrote about what conditions might be like for a child in U.S. detention along the southwestern border:

**Eco por Un Grito Moderno**[46]
A room lit by blazing glaring fluorescent lights...
    Cold and nondescript...
        A detention facility in El Norte...
            The wee hours of a bleak morning...
"Mamaaaaaa!!!..."
The wailing voice of a small child...
    "Mamaaaaaa!!!..."
Only 3 or 4...
Wailing inconsolably...
Her tiny fists pounding the small table...
    A uniformed woman murmuring....
Indistinctive...
Sliding over colouring books and a rainbow of crayons...
To the little pounding hands...
And the little hands shoving them away...
Carelessly...
Without care...
    "Mamaaaaaa!!!..."
On a shelf nearby...
Children's books...
Colourful books...
Lettered child blocks...
Wooden, bright letters...
Some stuffed dolls...
A Winnie the Pooh...
A Mickey Mouse...

A Donald Duck...
  "The Donald" Duck's eyes chewed out...
Cartoon arched blue eyes...
With irises gone...
Face chewed up...
With a perfect blue suit...
And a perfect blue hat...
Its yellow bill with white stuffing coming out...
  "Mamaaaaaa!!!..."
A child's face in agony...
Red from crying...
Brown from the sun...
Sweaty strands of black hair...
Criss-crossing the small forehead...
  An "Eco por un Grito" moderno...
A child's face from David Alfaro Siqueiros...
Crying and wailing...
And inflating, larger and larger...
A child's mouth...
Becoming a great chasm of wailing...
  "Mamaaaaaa!!!..."
Filling the room...
In eternal absence...

## BORDERS ON INSANITY?

Anyone who has seriously studied the so-called immigration issue in the United States knows the problems extend well beyond the U.S. southern border with Mexico. In fact, the U.S./Mexico border itself is a varied geographical region, stretching from Texas through New Mexico through Arizona to California—a terrain of unforgiving deserts and a daunting river and in some places formidable rocky escarpments and ravines. And building a wall across such a great expanse of nearly 2000 miles is all but impractical. Even so, the former Trump administration won a huge victory from the U.S. Supreme Court (*Donald J. Trump, President, et al. v. Sierra Club, et al. 2019*) for the approval of using billions in military funds to construct Trump's grand wall.[47]

In order to protest such wall construction, various artists, both Mexican and American, staged numerous artworks along the borderlands and on the already extensive wall system. One of my favorites, is a black-and-white giant baby overlooking the wall from the Mexican side—a quizzically huge baby face—underlining how children are being treated at the border in U.S. detention facilities.[48] Another of the more creative and recent projects, were "pink seesaws" extending through the wall, whereby Mexican and American children may seesaw up and down in play. Thus, demonstrating a barrier does little in preventing borderland human interactions nor deny borderland mutual interests on either side of such fencing.[49]

When examining the so-called immigration issue, we soon realize there is an enormous class difference in how it is being addressed. For example, there is considerable evidence to suggest more visitors to the United States overstay their "tourist visas" than cross the U.S./Mexican border.[50] So, those with the means to buy an airplane ticket and apply for student visas, or tourist visas, or work visas, are more likely to overstay and the immigration numbers bear this out, far exceeding southern border crossers. Yet, practically nobody in the media or politicians discuss the "overstayers" as a problem.[51] Many indigenous poor and overall the indigent from the Central American "Northern Triangle"—El Salvador, Guatemala, and Honduras—would rather risk their lives trekking through Mexico to make it to the United States than remain in their home countries.

Why are so many Central Americans willing to gamble with their lives to come to the United States? What are conditions like in their home countries? Why is the United States cutting off developmental aid to these Central American countries?

Before answering these important questions, let me address certain political memes, those partisan ideas becoming copied and popularized among Republicans about immigrants. One is that Democrats want "open borders" is a complete nonsense. Another is that immigrants are coming to the United States to take away your healthcare and will be given a "free ride" on everything—another complete nonsense.[52] At least, Democrats will more likely be more guarded about immigrant healthcare in coming months. If the United States were to provide such coverage to undocumented immigrants it would be an outlier among first world countries according to the *New York Times*. And currently, like European countries, it does not.

No serious person believes in "open borders." The United States of America will protect its borders, regardless if a Republican or a Democrat is in the White House. We are a nation-state and all nation-states protect their borders in some fashion. And yet, our immigration policies cannot be based upon racism or xenophobia either but upon practical considerations.[53]

After all, we are a nation of immigrants and built by immigrants, as well as a post-genocidal society from our maltreatment of our Native American population, and a post-slavery society from our maltreatment of African-Americans. Moreover, new migrants, undocumented aliens, do the jobs most other Americans do not want to do.[54]

They work in restaurant-kitchens cooking your food; they bus your tables at restaurants; they do the landscaping for your yards; they pick your fruit and vegetables; they work in the poultry and the meatpacking industries; they work as domestics and clean your houses; they clean your hotel rooms; they take care of your children; and they work many hours and for lower wages; and above all else, they pay federal income taxes.

One of the tactics used in the 2020 presidential election was "fear politics."[55] Immigrants were being scapegoated because it is easy to pick on a population without a voice. Blaming immigrants for the ills of society is easy and it detracts from focusing on real issues and on real societal problems. Scapegoating immigrants has a long Nativist history in the United States with the "Gilded Age" (1865–1890), and populist targeting of unskilled workers from Eastern and Southern Europe; with the Chinese Exclusion Act, limiting Chinese emigration to the United States (1882); and with the Gentleman's Agreement, limiting Japanese emigration to the United States (1907).[56]

Unfortunately, the same racist fears against immigrants were expressed then as are expressed now: white jobs will be lost; immigrants are ruining society; immigrants do not do their fair share; and why should we care about those people; they don't belong here; they should go back to where they came from; they are not us because they are not white and so on—the worst kind of white nationalist discourse.

So, returning to the previous questions: why would anyone risk their lives to cross the U.S./Mexico border? And what are conditions like in immigrant home countries: El Salvador, Guatemala, and Honduras? And why did the previous Trump administration cut off aid to these Central American countries?

In the so-called Northern Triangle of Central America, gang violence is rife; climate change has created drought conditions for small-scale and subsistence farmers[57]; mining companies have polluted water sources[58]; NAFTA (North American Free Trade Agreement) have made small-scale farming untenable; cash-crops such as coffee in Guatemala have been affected by blight[59]; police violence and paramilitary violence are rampant. In sum, conditions for most are unbearable and unlivable, especially for those living in poor and rural areas which are least developed.[60]

So, families are willing to hazard homicide, rape, robbery, and harsh environmental conditions on a journey to cross the U.S./Mexican border because survival conditions in their home countries appear much worse than such a perilous trek. Moreover, by cutting off development aid to El Salvador, Guatemala, and Honduras, undoubtedly make supportable circumstances much, much severer, and as such, foment a "self-fulfilling prophecy" for a "border crisis."[61] In fact, this is what the Trump administration probably wanted. In creating a border crisis by limiting development aid to Central America was a distraction from real issues within the United States than by concentrating on our southern borders as the sole problem of our country.

What have been the specific policies of the prior Trump administration in preventing migrants from seeking "asylum"—a request for protection and safety in another country for fear of one's life in one's home country? According to Heyman and Slack and The Center for Migration Studies (CMS 2019), and others, migrants have been refused requests of asylum if they are subjected to expedited removal, even if migrant fears were justified that returning to their home country may result in their deaths.[62] Further, migrants have been criminally prosecuted in order to deter other migrants from coming to the United States. Perhaps the most inhumane of all, children have been separated from their parents at the border and have been held in deplorable conditions without access to soap, toothpaste, or showers for as long as three months or more.[63] Additionally, Mexico along with Guatemala have been declared "safe third countries" in order to prevent asylum claims in the United States in 2019.[64]

Whatever the reason for turning away migrants at the U.S./Mexican borderlands, and preventing asylum seekers from entering at U.S. ports of entry (POEs), endangers the lives of asylum seekers stranded in northern Mexico, leaving them homeless, and exacerbating the tenuous situations of an already vulnerable group. In these Mexican cities along the border, there is "a high level of death, violence, and criminal exploitation" in the words of Slack and Heyman (2019).[65]

By blockading asylum seekers at the U.S./Mexican border, and specifically non-Mexicans, such people are particularly defenseless and besieged, and thereby subject to all sorts of violence, as victims of assault, fraud, and robbery, and as victims of kidnapping for drug trafficking, for sexual exploitation, and for organ harvesting, among other horrors. Hence, under such circumstances, Mexico is not a "safe third country," nor is Guatemala for that matter because of the same and similar crimes as those in Mexico. Therefore, migrants cannot expect to be safe either in Mexico or Guatemala.

One important and undeniable effect of the so-called border crisis is the overt racism against Latin American immigrants in general as asserted by Heyman, Slack, and Guerra (2018) in their noteworthy article, "Bordering a 'Crisis': Central American Asylum Seekers and the Reproduction of Dominant Border Enforcement Practices."[66] As these authors explain: "The moral evaluation of that crisis differed, of course, in important ways. For some, a crisis of children and families needing assistance evoked powerful feelings of service and solidarity. For others, a crisis of disease-bearing, gang-ridden Latin American border migrants evoked anxiety over invasion. Crisis was, of course, overstated" (p. 774).[67]

Perhaps, the most unfortunate victims of the "border crisis" in 2019 were the children held in detention centers along the border and elsewhere such as the private detention facility in Homestead, Florida.[68] The psychological effects of young children being separated from parents were devastating and have been well-described by mental health practitioners.[69] Prolonged childhood trauma, for example, may adversely affect such children's mental health well into adulthood and affect how children as adults may negatively view authority figures.

As a final note, an interim report conducted by academic border experts and law professors, was released in April 2019 from the "Department of Homeland Security (DHS) Advisory Council Panel on Families and Children Care Emergency."[70] It proposed that "an enforcement-based approach to the current situation at the border that focuses on detention, limitations on access to asylum, restrictions on due process and a presumption that arriving Central American families present a threat. Such an enforcement focus is unwarranted and is doomed to be ineffective" (p. 2).[71]

As a nation, the United States must not succumb to racism, nor to dog whistles eliciting racist imagery. Nor should we listen to racist bombast about new immigrants. As the great South African leader of the anti-Apartheid movement, Nelson Mandela, once wrote in his autobiography, *Long Walk to Freedom* (1994): "No one is born hating another person because of the colour of his skin, or his background, or his religion. People must learn to hate, and if they can learn to hate, they can be taught to love, for love comes more naturally to the human heart than its opposite.[72]

## Arundhati Roy on Indian Migrant Worker Oppression and India's Fateful Coronavirus Crisis[73]

So far, we have discussed international migration and racism. Yet, it is important to consider how racism also relates to internal migrants like those in India and how internal migrant Indian workers were caught out by Coronavirus lockdown in India. Much of the data here is associated with the Indian activist and writer, Arundhati Roy and her reports about what happened to the plight of India's internal migrants ensuing India's severe COVID-19 restrictions in 2020.

In India there is never one story but thousands, even millions, and so the detrimental impact of Coronavirus (COVID-19) on this country of more than 1.3 billion, especially among the poor, has been profound, causing immense suffering. Nor did it help matters much when Prime Minister Narendra Modi shut India into immediate lockdown in 2020 without warning to mitigate Indians from contracting COVID-19.[74] Thousands of day laborers and migrant laborers were left stranded in large cities in 2020 without food or money in such places as New Delhi, Mumbai, Gandhinagar, Chandigarh, Chennai, Jaipur, and Lucknow, among others.[75] It was the largest lockdown in the world because of COVID-19.[76]

If such workers had prior warning, say at least a week's time, then it may have prevented such a massive humanitarian disaster. Yet, Modi and his BJP (Bharatiya Janata Party) government, did not seem to be concerned about these rural migrants when planning their lockdown. Thousands of migrants had to make the long trek home to their rural villages, while hundreds of them were dying along the way from exhaustion, heat fatigue, thirst, starvation, and road accidents.[77]

There was so much misinformation about COVID-19 in India, that a group of at least 400 university-affiliated Indian scientists, Indian Scientists' Response to COVID-19 (ISRC), were debunking myths about Coronavirus such as whether or not cow dung or cow urine would boost one's immunity against the disease.[78] What was worse, healthcare workers had been targeted with violence as carriers of Coronavirus as they had been in Mexico, and ethnic populations had been stigmatized and beaten because of false rumors about contagion.[79] For example, Muslims in India had been condemned as COVID-19 disease transmitters and as scapegoats, an ethnic population in India of about 200 million.[80] Moreover, Indian Muslims had been attacked, refused medical aid, and boycotted from such negative associations about them as so-called super-spreaders.[81]

As acclaimed Indian novelist and political activist Arundhati Roy explained in an interview (May 13, 2020) on *France24*: "Because in India a lockdown means something different than in Europe or America, because in India a lockdown means people compressed into physical spaces, not distanced, because people live in such small and squalid conditions, most people."[82] Indeed, as elsewhere in the developing world, where social distancing is near impossible, the same insalubrious conditions existed in India and still exist today. In India, the healthcare system is underfunded, and sanitary conditions are not good.

On March 24, 2020, Prime Minister Modi appeared on Indian television and announced a "total lockdown" of the Indian nation. All of India's markets were to be closed, as well as all public transportation and even private transportation would be disallowed.

In an opinion piece for the *Financial Times*, Arundhati Roy wrote about Prime Minister Modi's absolutist decision-making (April 3, 2020): "He [PM Narendra Modi] said he was taking this decision not just as a prime minister, but as our family elder. Who else can decide, without consulting the state governments that would have to deal with the fallout of this decision, that a nation of 1.38bn people should be locked down with zero preparation and with four hours' notice? His methods definitely give the impression that India's prime minister thinks of citizens as a hostile force that needs to be ambushed, taken by surprise, but never trusted."[83] Hence, it was ironic when epidemiologists and other scientists across the globe praised Modi for his firmness in locking down the country. Yet, such comments were mostly thoughtless without thinking about India's massive destitute population.

Roy went on to explain: "Many driven out by their employers and landlords, millions of impoverished, hungry, thirsty people, young and old, men, women, children, sick people, blind people, disabled people, with nowhere else to go, with no public transport in sight, began a long march home to their villages. They walked for days, towards Badaun, Agra, Azamgarh, Aligarh, Lucknow, Gorakhpur—hundreds of kilometers away. Some died on the way."[84]

The scenes in India of these day laborers, the so-called migrant workers, were beyond measure, a humanitarian crisis of untold thousands walking in desperation to their home villages. As Arundhati Roy expounded in the *Financial Times*: "They knew they were going home potentially to slow starvation. Perhaps they even knew they could be carrying the virus with them, and would infect their families, their parents and grandparents back home, but they desperately needed a shred of familiarity, shelter and dignity, as well as food, if not love. As they walked, some were beaten brutally and humiliated by the police, who were charged with strictly enforcing the curfew. Young men were made to crouch and frog jump down the highway. Outside the town of Bareilly, one group was herded together and hosed down with chemical spray."[85]

In her *France24* interview, Roy elaborated: "As for the workers, who are being called migrant workers, who by various schemes and economic policies, who were really swept out of the countryside into cities, and into very, very precarious, very low-paying jobs, and crammed into tenements on the edges of cities. And then, suddenly on the 24th of March [2020], they had no money, they had nowhere to live. They just had to leave. And there was no transport, as the whole world witnessed this. And until today, thousands of people are still walking. But the only good thing is, if we don't trust the figures entirely, the numbers of people getting infected is increasing. The numbers of deaths are nowhere near where they have been in Europe and America. So, why that is, everyone has theories."[86]

And yet for the mass exodus back to the countryside, Arundhati Roy proclaimed on *France24*: "There is going to be so much desperation, there is so much desperation. We are talking about a situation of mass hunger. A lot of people are walking. The reason people are walking to their villages is because they hope that you know that a little bit of land or some community support they will get ... there is millions of tons of food in government warehouses to be distributed ... Whether those people after going through this absolute trauma, will come back [to the cities], one doesn't know. Right now, there are still people being held in quarantine centers, detention centers. Some of them are being prevented from going home. There is talk of industries more or less forcing them to work in industries which are just opening up now."[87]

There were approximately 139 million who were considered to be migrant laborers and like most of the poor in India, were largely ignored and unnoticed by India's ruling elite class.[88] According to recent statistics, about 270 million Indians live at or below the poverty line (2011–2012) and more recently the numbers are estimated at 70.6 million.[89] Yet, Coronavirus has probably changed all of this, given the forced unemployment from the virus.

Prime Minister Narendra Modi has pledged about $266 billion in economic stimulus, or 10 percent of the gross domestic product (GDP) to address the COVID-19 issue and protect India's economy.[90] Yet, not much of anything is being done to help the migrant laborers making the arduous trek, mostly on foot, to their home villages. State governments have been quicker to act in aiding these hapless commuters in distributing food rations.

The 2020 lockdown has caused real desperation among the poor in India's rural areas such as among residents of a slum colony in Bengaluru (Bangalore) City.[91] Without work, they are struggling to feed their children and themselves, and worse, vegetable prices increased. Furthermore, ration cards are not being distributed as they were before the lockdown, and without men earning from migrant work, starvation is a real issue.

In 2020, one of these millions of migrant workers, Rampukar Pandit, whose anguished face was captured by a photographer on a New Delhi roadside, upon learning about his sickly child at home and with no public transportation to take him home.[92] He began walking to reach his eleven-month-old baby, a 745-mile journey to Bihar state, but was already exhausted without food on the excursion home. Pandit had only reached New Delhi's outskirts when his image was taken. When the journalist asked Pandit about how Modi's government has largely done nothing for migrant workers such as him, Rampukar asserted: "I am a nobody, I'm like an ant, my life doesn't matter. The government is only concerned with filling the stomachs of the rich."[93]

In a *Financial Times* article (May 23, 2020), political activist Arundhati Roy avowed: "The zero-planning [2020] lockdown has meant that in these last 59 days (make that 120 days of lockdown and a 10-month internet siege for Kashmir) India has witnessed a nightmare from which we [in India] may never fully recover. Unemployment was at a 45-year high before the lockdown. The lockdown is estimated to have cost 135m jobs."[94]

In all likelihood too, the migrant workers who were left stranded in India's major cities without food, shelter, or money, and who were forced to make their way to their home rural villages somehow, were spreading COVID-19 to the remotest areas of India. So, Prime Minister Modi's plan to save India with an extreme lockdown in fact may have done the opposite.

Coronavirus in all likelihood was spreading like wildfire among the faceless thousands to other nameless thousands—to everywhere in India.

In sum, Arundhati Roy in her celebrated novel *The God of Small Things* (1997) prophetically declared: "It was a time when the unthinkable became the thinkable and the impossible really happened."[95]

## Conclusion

While populism tends to exaggerate ethnic differences from political visions of xenophobia, this chapter really expressed the moral issues surrounding immigration and migration both in the United States and in India. The politics of difference and fear demonstrated how the previous Donald J. Trump administration exacerbated problems associated with new Latin American immigrants and directed negative populist rhetoric against voiceless people. Rather than protecting ethnic minorities, populist bombast and magniloquence expressed by former President Trump promoted white homogeneity. The prior Trump administration's immigration policies were meant to be punitive and separated families at the U.S./Mexican border, while being especially egregious for separating small children from their parents and holding them in detention in poor conditions for days, and in some cases much longer. Such borderland policies caused extreme trauma among children, who directly suffered from the former Trump administration's border restrictions and castigatory attitude toward immigrants. On the other hand, there was the policy of neglect by Indian Prime Minister Narendra Modi and his BJP party locking down the country for Coronavirus (COVID-19), which left thousands of rural migrant laborers stranded in major Indian cities. Both Trump and Modi hold to populist politics. For Trump, the realization that his popularity numbers increased with each outrageous statement against the handicapped, immigrants, women, minorities, or political rivals, and as such populist rhetoric became rewarded does little to detract from the fact that such political tactics are morally suspect. Moreover, the situation in India exposed Modi's standpoint against minorities and underlined class differences whereby thousands of rural migrant laborers became abandoned and forsaken for the COVID-19 lockdown. The irony is that PM Modi himself is from a lowly family background or "Other Backward Class" (OBC).[96] In sum, the immigration policies of the anterior Trump administration were tantamount to racism against minorities with little or no voice, whereas Modi's Coronavirus policies demonstrated his administration's policies of class discrimination.

## Notes

1. https://www.wlrn.org/post/guatemalan-climate-change-refugees-pouring-over-us-border-and-south-florida#stream/0.
2. Univision Short Documentary, Report: "The Legacy of 'Zero Tolerance' Policy: Traumatized Children with No Access to Treatment" Link: https://vimeo.com/294227617.
3. https://www.aclu.org/news/immigrants-rights/family-separation-two-years-after-ms-l/.
4. U.S. Department of Health and Human Services, Office of Inspector General (March 2020).
5. "The Legacy of 'Zero Tolerance' Policy: Traumatized Children with No Access to Treatment" Link: https://vimeo.com/294227617.
6. For an alternative approach to populism, see Gingerich and Banks (2006) on "neo-nationalism."
7. https://www.hrw.org/news/2018/05/22/trumps-racist-language-serves-abusive-immigration-policies#.
8. https://www.bushcenter.org/catalyst/opportunity-road/george-w-bush-on-compassionate-conservatism.html.
9. https://journals.sagepub.com/doi/pdf/10.1177/233150241700500111.
10. https://www.humanitiestexas.org/archives/digital-repository/brands-how-rich-got-rich-gilded-age-america-2011.
11. https://www.history.com/topics/immigration/chinese-exclusion-act-1882.
    https://www.history.com/topics/immigration/gentlemens-agreement.
12. https://en.wikipedia.org/wiki/Immigration_Act_of_1924.
13. https://www.history.com/topics/immigration/irish-potato-famine.
14. https://www.bls.gov/opub/mlr/cwc/american-labor-in-the-20th-century.pdf.
15. https://www.amazon.com/Jungle-Dover-Thrift-Editions/dp/0486419231/ref=sr_1_3?dchild=1&keywords=Upton+Sinclair+the+jungle&qid=1627591711&sr=8-3.
16. https://www.history.com/topics/19th-century/haymarket-riot.
17. https://www.archives.gov/education/lessons/japanese-relocation.
18. https://en.wikipedia.org/wiki/Western_Hemisphere_Institute_for_Security_Cooperation.
19. https://link.springer.com/chapter/10.1057/9780333983867_6.
    https://www.britannica.com/topic/20th-century-international-relations-2085155/The-world-political-economy.

20. https://www.citizen.org/wp-content/uploads/CAFTA-fact-sheet-Aug-2018.pdf.
21. https://www.bbc.com/news/world-latin-america-45951782.
22. https://www.coha.org/the-alliance-for-prosperity-plan-a-failed-effort-for-stemming-migration/.
23. https://en.wikipedia.org/wiki/Monroe_Doctrine.
    https://history.state.gov/milestones/1899-1913/roosevelt-and-monroe-doctrine.
24. https://www.nps.gov/stli/learn/historyculture/colossus.htm.
25. https://www.washingtonpost.com/world/2019/06/26/father-daughter-who-drowned-border-dove-into-river-desperation/.
26. https://apnews.com/article/caribbean-ap-top-news-el-salvador-international-news-immigration-2f8422c820104d6eaad9b73d939063a9.
    https://www.nytimes.com/2019/06/25/us/father-daughter-border-drowning-picture-mexico.html.
27. Under Biden, children likewise have been detained at the border. Although there has been a task force created to unify detained children with their families. The refugee cap under Biden has also risen compared with the former Trump administration. On the other hand, images of border patrol agents beating Haitian migrants with long horse reins on September 20, 2021 along the border have been disconcerting.
    https://www.npr.org/2021/09/20/1038918197/the-biden-administration-is-fighting-in-court-to-keep-a-trump-era-immigration-po.
    https://www.nbcnews.com/politics/white-house/white-house-says-images-border-patrol-whip-obviously-horrific-n1279663.
    https://www.bbc.com/news/world-us-canada-56255613.
    https://www.bbc.com/news/world-us-canada-58637116.
28. https://apnews.com/article/caribbean-ap-top-news-el-salvador-international-news-immigration-2f8422c820104d6eaad9b73d939063a9.
    https://www.theguardian.com/us-news/2019/may/23/migrant-child-us-custody-deaths-hhs-outcry.
29. https://www.cnn.com/2019/03/30/politics/state-department-aid-el-slavador-guatemala-honduras/index.html.
30. https://fas.org/sgp/crs/row/R45547.pdf.
31. https://www.npr.org/2019/01/16/686056668/for-seventh-consecutive-year-visa-overstays-exceeded-illegal-border-crossings.
32. https://journals.sagepub.com/doi/pdf/10.1177/233150241700500107.
33. https://www.dhs.gov/sites/default/files/publications/18_1009_S1_Entry-Exit-Overstay_Report.pdf.
34. https://qz.com/1602930/mexico-is-detaining-more-immigrants/.

35. https://www.cbp.gov/newsroom/stats/southwest-land-border-encounters/usbp-sw-border-apprehensions.
36. https://www.theatlantic.com/family/archive/2019/06/child-detention-centers-immigration-attorney-interview/592540/.
37. https://www.theguardian.com/us-news/2019/jun/25/john-sanders-customs-and-border-protection-resigns-cbp.
38. Strathern (1988: ???).
39. https://www.vox.com/2019/4/26/18517980/trump-unite-the-right-racism-defense-charlottesville.
40. https://www.cnn.com/2018/01/11/politics/immigrants-shithole-countries-trump/index.html.
41. https://www.hrw.org/report/2018/02/28/freezer/abusive-conditions-women-and-children-us-immigration-holding-cells.
42. https://www.youtube.com/watch?v=tRjUyr_36MY.
43. https://www.hrw.org/report/2018/02/28/freezer/abusive-conditions-women-and-children-us-immigration-holding-cells.
44. https://www.aclu.org/press-releases/aclu-obtains-documents-showing-widespread-abuse-child-immigrants-us-custody.
45. https://journalistsresource.org/politics-and-government/family-separation-child-health-research/.
46. This poem "Eco Por Un Grito Moderno" has been published in the book *Epochal Reckonings* (2020, Proverse Publishers), and previously published in the online magazine *CounterPunch*.
47. https://www.supremecourt.gov/opinions/18pdf/19a60_o75p.pdf.
    https://apnews.com/article/mexico-donald-trump-ap-top-news-courts-supreme-courts-5d893d388c254c7fa83a1570112ae90e.
48. https://mymodernmet.com/jr-street-artist-mexican-border-wall/.
49. https://www.theguardian.com/us-news/2019/jul/30/pink-seesaws-reach-across-divide-us-mexico-border.
50. https://www.theatlantic.com/international/archive/2019/04/real-immigration-crisis-people-overstaying-their-visas/587485/.
51. https://www.npr.org/2019/01/16/686056668/for-seventh-consecutive-year-visa-overstays-exceeded-illegal-border-crossings.
52. https://www.washingtonexaminer.com/opinion/democrats-double-down-on-open-borders.
    https://www.nytimes.com/2019/07/03/health/undocumented-immigrants-health-care.html.
53. https://www.theatlantic.com/magazine/archive/2019/04/david-frum-how-much-immigration-is-too-much/583252/.
54. https://www.newamericaneconomy.org/issues/undocumented-immigrants/.

55. https://www.latimes.com/opinion/op-ed/la-oe-abramsky-trump-politics-of-fear-midterms-20180923-story.html.
56. https://www.counterpunch.org/2018/11/09/myths-on-race-and-invasion-of-the-caravan-horde/.
57. https://www.theguardian.com/global-development/2019/jul/29/guatemala-climate-crisis-migration-drought-famine.
58. https://www.theguardian.com/environment/2019/jul/29/honduran-asylum-seeker-dam-protester.
59. https://foe.org/blog/nafta-renegotiation-threatens-family-farmers-environment/.
60. https://www.theguardian.com/global-development/2019/jul/30/el-salvador-water-crisis-privatization-gangs-corruption.
61. https://thehill.com/homenews/administration/443764-trump-officials-slow-walk-president-order-to-cut-off-central-american-aid-report.
62. https://cmsny.org/publications/heyman-slack-asylum-poe/.
63. https://www.washingtonpost.com/nation/2019/06/21/detained-migrant-children-no-toothbrush-soap-sleep/?noredirect=on.
64. https://foreignpolicy.com/2019/07/30/trumps-safe-third-country-agreement-with-guatemala-is-a-lie/.
65. https://cmsny.org/publications/heyman-slack-asylum-poe/.
66. https://www.researchgate.net/publication/332061146_Bordering_a_Crisis_Central_American_Asylum_Seekers_and_the_Reproduction_of_Dominant_Border_Enforcement_Practices.
67. https://www.researchgate.net/publication/332061146_Bordering_a_Crisis_Central_American_Asylum_Seekers_and_the_Reproduction_of_Dominant_Border_Enforcement_Practices.
68. https://www.amnestyusa.org/wp-content/uploads/2019/07/Homestead-Report_1072019_AB_compressed.pdf.
69. https://www.psychologytoday.com/us/blog/nurturing-self-compassion/201806/damage-separating-families.
70. https://law.utexas.edu/wp-content/uploads/sites/11/2019/05/expert-response-to-HSA-Advisory-Council-report-final-sign-on.pdf.
71. https://law.utexas.edu/wp-content/uploads/sites/11/2019/05/expert-response-to-HSA-Advisory-Council-report-final-sign-on.pdf.
72. https://www.amazon.com/Long-Walk-Freedom-Autobiography-Mandela/dp/0316548189/ref=sr_1_5?keywords=Mandela+long+walk+to+freedom&qid=1564650848&s=gateway&sr=8-5.
73. India has also grossly misrepresented and undercounted its COVID-19 death toll according to several news sources.
    https://www.npr.org/sections/goatsandsoda/2021/07/20/1018438334/indias-pandemic-death-toll-estimated-at-about-4-million-10-times-the-official-co.

https://thesciencesurvey.com/editorial/2021/06/10/the-problem-with-indias-underreporting-of-covid-19-cases/.

https://www.theguardian.com/world/2021/may/01/were-burning-pyres-all-day-india-accused-of-undercounting-deaths.

74. https://www.nytimes.com/2020/03/24/world/asia/india-coronavirus-lockdown.html.
75. https://www.theatlantic.com/ideas/archive/2020/04/the-pandemic-exposes-indias-two-worlds/609838/.
76. https://www.thelancet.com/journals/lancet/article/PIIS0140-6736(20)30938-7/fulltext.
77. https://www.bbc.com/news/world-asia-india-52672764.

https://www.aljazeera.com/news/2020/05/14/speeding-bus-kills-indian-migrant-workers-trying-to-walk-home/.

78. https://in.news.yahoo.com/cow-urine-kills-coronavirus-indian-060900135.html.
79. https://www.bbc.com/news/world-latin-america-52676939.
80. https://www.washingtonpost.com/world/asia_pacific/as-world-looks-for-coronavirus-scapegoats-india-pins-blame-on-muslims/2020/04/22/3cb43430-7f3f-11ea-84c2-0792d8591911_story.html.
81. https://www.washingtonpost.com/world/asia_pacific/as-world-looks-for-coronavirus-scapegoats-india-pins-blame-on-muslims/2020/04/22/3cb43430-7f3f-11ea-84c2-0792d8591911_story.html.
82. https://www.youtube.com/watch?v=CSZ-PtlY4HE.
83. https://www.ft.com/content/10d8f5e8-74eb-11ea-95fe-fcd274e920ca.
84. https://www.ft.com/content/10d8f5e8-74eb-11ea-95fe-fcd274e920ca.
85. https://www.ft.com/content/10d8f5e8-74eb-11ea-95fe-fcd274e920ca.
86. https://www.youtube.com/watch?v=CSZ-PtlY4HE.
87. https://www.youtube.com/watch?v=CSZ-PtlY4HE.
88. https://www.weforum.org/agenda/2017/10/india-has-139-million-internal-migrants-we-must-not-forget-them/.
89. https://en.wikipedia.org/wiki/Poverty_in_India.

https://www.washingtonpost.com/news/worldviews/wp/2018/07/10/india-is-no-longer-home-to-the-largest-number-of-poor-people-in-the-world-nigeria-is/.

90. https://www.cnn.com/2020/05/13/business/india-stimulus-covid-19-intl-hnk/index.html.
91. https://www.youtube.com/watch?v=9zpv0gZrQYs.
92. https://www.theguardian.com/global-development/2020/may/19/my-angel-man-who-became-face-of-indias-stranded-helped-home-by-stranger-coronavirus.

93. https://www.theguardian.com/global-development/2020/may/19/my-angel-man-who-became-face-of-indias-stranded-helped-home-by-stranger-coronavirus.
94. https://www.ft.com/content/442546c6-9c10-11ea-adb1-529f96d8a00b.
95. https://www.amazon.com/God-Small-Things-Novel-ebook/dp/B001NBEWN6/ref=sr_1_1?dchild=1&keywords=the+god+of+small+things&qid=1590390059&s=books&sr=1-1.
96. https://www.rediff.com/news/column/ls-election-sheela-says-is-narendra-modi-really-an-obc/20140510.htm.

## BIBLIOGRAPHY

Anderson, B. 1991, orig. 1983. *Imagined Communities: Reflections on the Origin and Spread of Nationalism.* London: Verso.

Banks, M. 1996. *Ethnicity: Anthropological Constructions.* London: Routledge.

Barth, F., ed. 1969. *Ethnic Groups and Boundaries: The Social Organisation of Culture Differences.* London: George Allen and Unwin.

Bloch, M. 2013. *In and Out of Each Other's Bodies: Theory of Mind, Evolution, Truth, and the Nature of the Social.* London: Paradigm Publishers.

Center for Migration Studies. 2018. *Blockading Asylum Seekers at Ports of Entry at the US-Mexican Border Puts Them at Increased Risk of Exploitation, Violence, and Death.* Josiah Heyman and Jeremy Slack https://cmsny.org/publications/heyman-slack-asylum-poe/

Gingerich, A., and M. Banks. 2006. *Neo-Nationalism in Europe and Beyond: Perspectives from Social Anthropology.* Oxford: Berghahn Books.

Gladney, D., ed. 1998. *Making Majorities: Constituting the Nation in Japan, Korea, China, Malaysia, Fiji, Turkey, and the United States.* Stanford, CA: Stanford University Press.

Jaffrelot, C., and L. Tillin. 2017. Populism in India. In *The Oxford Handbook of Populism*, ed. C. Rovira Kaltwasser et al., 179–194. Oxford: Oxford University Press.

Josiah, H., Jeremy, S., and Emily, G. 2019. "Bordering a 'Crisis': Central American Asylum Seekers and the Reproduction of Dominant Border Enforcement Practices" in *Journal of the Southwest*, 60 (4): 754–784. https://www.researchgate.net/publication/332061146_Bordering_a_Crisis_Central_American_Asylum_Seekers_and_the_Reproduction_of_Dominant_Border_Enforcement_Practices

Lowndes, J. 2017. Populism in the United States. In *The Oxford Handbook of Populism*, ed. C. Rovira Kaltwasser et al., 232–247. Oxford: Oxford University Press.

Mudde, C., and C. Rovira Kaltwasser. 2017. *Populism: A Very Short Introduction*. Oxford: Oxford University Press.

Rovira Kaltwasser, C., et al., eds. 2017. *The Oxford Handbook of Populism*. Oxford: Oxford University Press.

Slack, Jeremy and Josiah Heyman. 2019. Asylum and Mass Detention at the U.S.-Mexico Border during Covid-19. *Journal of Latin American Geography* 19 (3), 334–339.

Strathern, M. 1988. *The Gender of the Gift: Problems with Women and Problems with Society in Melanesia*. Berkeley: University of California Press.

Wimmer, A. 2013. *Ethnic Boundary Making: Institutions, Power, Networks*. Oxford: Oxford University Press.

CHAPTER 3

# Nationalism and Terrorism

It was 1996. I had been in the Spanish Basque Country for about two months in the little town of Hondarribia with a current population of about 17,000. It was fall weather and blue sky. The air was cool and crisp and welcoming. I was hanging around the fishing docks, trying to interview fishermen, learning about Basque fishermen culture. I was doing ethnographic fieldwork for my PhD (D.Phil.) in Social and Cultural Anthropology at the University of Oxford. Eventually, my focus would switch to studying the annual Alarde parade, a historical ritual, commemorating the town's victory over the French in 1638. Hondarribia, a beautiful and quaint coastal town, located along the Spanish-French border, where the frontier between the two countries are separated by the Bidasoa River. In the historic district, there is the castle and fort of Carlos V, now a luxury parador hotel. In the town's center and shopping area, there are charming two-story houses with balconies of bright green, blue, and red colors—the same colors of the fishing boats lining the fishermen's harbor (now mostly a defunct enterprise. On the other hand, Hondarribia now has a luxurious commercial harbor as well.)

On this fall day, I remember ducking into a small café bar for a pintxo (a type of Basque hors d'oeuvre) and a coffee around mid-morning. As I was enjoying my mid-morning snack, I was approached by a man in his fifties. He asked me in Spanish, "What are you doing here?" He repeated the question in English. I was startled a bit. "What do you mean? I don't understand?" I quizzically asked him in Spanish. The man persisted, "I mean, what are you doing here?" I told him I was doing anthropological research for my PhD at

© The Author(s), under exclusive license to Springer Nature Switzerland AG 2022
J. P. Linstroth, *Politics and Racism Beyond Nations*,
https://doi.org/10.1007/978-3-030-91720-3_3

the University of Oxford. Then, the man said: "Well, we don't want you here. You're 'not' welcome. Why don't you pack your things and leave? Otherwise, you might have a lot of problems." He explained to me that he was a representative of Herri Batasuna (the political wing of the Basque terrorist group, equivalent to Sinn Fein for the former Irish Republican Army, IRA) and he had heard all about me by other townspeople. So, I was trying to digest this undisguised threat. I wondered to myself, was doing a PhD worth it—a threat on my life? Had I indeed made a mistake by doing a PhD in an area with nationalist terrorism, a type of terrorism targeting businessmen, military personnel, policemen, and politicians. Therefore, I had to take this threat seriously.

After his initial query, I remember the man then went into some kind of rant about not liking researchers interfering there. People like me could not hide. And thoughts like: "I don't know who told you it was a good idea to be here but it is not. Your safety might be at stake if you stay. Do you understand what I mean?" I was a bit stunned. In reality, I had no idea what to say and stood at the restaurant counter in silence. It should be remembered this was 1996, when the Basque terrorist group, Euskadi Ta Askatasuna (ETA) [Basque Homeland and Freedom], was very active. They were especially active in this borderland area because many Etarras liked escaping from Spain across the French border and vice versa. Most of their hideouts at the time were in the French borderland areas of the Basque Country. "Indeed," I thought to myself, "What if I was over my head? Was I really doing something dangerous? After all, I was studying Basque fishermen. Ostensibly, I was not studying Basque terrorism at all, nor Basque terrorists. I was researching Basque fishermen." Yet, others might consider what I was doing as "dangerous fieldwork" because of the circumstances and because of the terrorist milieu in the region. Maybe it was perilous after all. Ultimately, the result of my fieldwork (1996–1997) would lead to my Oxford D.Phil. thesis, and eventually to a book, "Marching Against Practice: Political Imaginings in the Basqueland" (2015).

In the year before my fieldwork in Hondarribia began, in 1995, there was an attempt on the life of the Spanish Prime Minister José María Aznar, of the Popular Party (Partido Popular, PP), at the time a candidate for the Spanish PM-ship, when ETA tried blowing up his limousine. Fortunately, for Aznar, the limousine was armor-plated and protected him. The same year, there was also a thwarted plot to kill the King of Spain at the time, King Juan Carlos. In 1996, during my fieldwork year, the prison guard, José Antonio Ortega Lara, was kidnapped and almost starved to death by ETA. Ortega Lara was eventually rescued by the Spanish police in 1997, after 532 days of capture. The same year of '96, a politician was killed in the Guipuzcoan capital of San Sebastián and a judge murdered in Madrid as well as a high-ranking officer of the Basque police (Ertzaintza)—all victims of ETA. In the summer of 1996, ETA also set off bombs at the Catalan airport of Reus, near Barcelona, injuring many British tourists, at least thirty-three people, and that same summer, a sergeant in Spanish military as well as a Basque businessman were killed by ETA. A year later, in 1997, a lieutenant colonel of the Spanish military; a businessman; a hairdresser in Granada, Spain; a prison psychologist; a Supreme Court Justice; another Basque businessman; a national policeman; a Basque policeman; a high-ranking member of the Spanish national police; a member of the Guardia Civil; and a Basque Popular Party councilman—all were murdered and all were victims of Euskadi Ta Askatasuna, Basque Homeland and Freedom, the Basque Terrorist Group.

Yet, it was 1997 also when the Basque town councilor and Popular Party (Partido Popular, PP) member Miguel Ángel Blanco was kidnapped and then assassinated by the Basque terrorist group, ETA. Prior to the councilman's murder, ETA demanded the Spanish government move Basque political prisoners, who were scattered across Spain, to be closer to the Spanish Basque Autonomous Region. Nevertheless, the Spanish government ignored the terrorist group's demand. Blanco's death was a turning point in the Basque conflict. It caused millions of Spaniards to take to the streets and protest against ETA violence and an end to ETA. From then on, it was the beginning of an end for ETA. The Spanish government was to make a concerted military and police effort to strangle the organization with arrests of its members and halting its operations as well as police cooperation with the French government to do so. But ETA continued killing. In all, 829 people were murdered by the Basque terrorist organization, ETA, from the death of Spanish dictator Francisco Franco in 1975 until its permanent ceasefire in 2011.

Hence, when I received this death threat message from a member of Batasuna/ETA, I had to take it seriously. But in the end, I decided to carry on with my ethnographic fieldwork, and stay in Hondarribia, regardless of such unveiled intimidation. My fieldwork no doubt had its perils. The Spanish police thought Hondarribia might harbor terrorists too. Often, when taking the bus from Hondarribia to its sister town, Irún, the next Spanish town over, the Spanish police would often set up roadblocks. As I passed such roadblocks in the bus, the Spanish police conducting them wore masks to hide their identities and carried big guns like the H&K MP-5 or the SIG SAUER SWAT, along with their automatic pistols. Yet, perhaps the main reason for such roadblocks were to protect the main airport for the region, San Sebastián Airport (Donostiako Aierportua), which is located on the road from Hondarribia to Irún. Thus, while the police were protecting the airport, they were also signaling to ETA: "we are here." Additionally, the Basque police *force (Ertzaintza) would often park a couple of their vehicles in front of the fishermen's living quarters, a group of apartments near the port, as a reminder to Herri Batasuna supporters among the fishermen, they were watching them too. (This is the same apartment building where I lived with a family of fishermen for a couple of months while I was living in Hondarribia.)*

*Furthermore, when I did preliminary fieldwork in a small Basque fishing village, Getaria, in Gipuzkoa, I realized people did not want to be tape-recorded. Townspeople were paranoid what they might say and if ETA would find out. They did not want their words to be on record for fear of potential persecution. Such was the paranoia in the Basque Country at that time. The paranoia was palpable. So, even though I began recording conversations of women net-menders, wives of fishermen, it proved to be unwelcome. As a consequence, I stopped recording Basques. I had to learn to take good notes. I had to rely on my memory for conversations. Otherwise, I might run into some real trouble and I did not want that.*

*Even so, throughout that fieldwork year (1996–1997), I never knew if or when I might be threatened again? Nevertheless, I made lifelong friends with many Basques and gathered enough material for a doctoral thesis. But the threat of ETA, the terrorist group and their supporters, not wanting me in Hondarribia doing research, was always in the back of my mind. What would happen if they carried out their death threat? I suppose I was more worried about my family and my poor mother. But I persisted and stayed and managed living with several Basque families and recorded the significance of a Basque historical parade and commemorative event in which local women wanted equal access and equal participation in the event. Gender equality, or dismissing it, was on townspeople's minds. Most local women argued that the Alarde parade had nothing to do with gender equality but their town's traditions, all of which became central themes in my book "Marching Against Gender Practice."*

\* \* \*

*Years later, from 2009 to 2010, I found myself working as a senior researcher for the Peace Research Institute Oslo (PRIO) in Oslo, Norway. In the few years prior to this, I was an assistant professor for the "Peace Research and Anthropology' course at Nova Southeastern University (NSU). While at PRIO, I was contacted by Herri Batasuna/ETA for help and advice in their ceasefire and my thoughts on a permanent ceasefire with Spain. At the time, the Basques were looking for the same deal, Sinn Fein and the IRA had with the "Good Friday Agreement" (1998), more than a decade beforehand. HB/*

ETA believed a "peace process" was the best way forward to achieve their goal of political independence from Spain and France. (The goal of ETA and Herri Batasuna was always the political independence from Spain. Yet, as researchers like myself knew, such a dream was all but impossible. Spain was never interested in the Basque Autonomous Region becoming independent and seceding from the nation. And Province of Navarra, did not want to become part of a Basque Country according to many Navarrans.) Notable peace activist and human rights lawyer, Brian Currin from South Africa, became important and prominent to the Basque peace process. On the other hand, my role was mostly negligible.

Even so, I met in secret with two of the Herri Batasuna/ETA members at PRIO, myself and a Program Director. Then, following this, I met with the International Representative of Batasuna a couple of times for dinner. I remember him being a very affable fellow, a young man in his late twenties. He was just starting a family with his partner and he lived in the French Basque region (Iparraldia). His English was good, fluent. I remember he thought it a good idea, I write an article which explained the theoretical importance of nationalism as a viable vehicle for accepting the independence of non-nation territories. Of course, I had reservations. Nationalism was one of the main causes of World War I. Nationalism led to the Holocaust. Nationalism led to the Balkan Conflicts of the 1990s and so on. I was interested in coming to an understanding with Herri Batasuna/ETA how they were going to move forward with a peace process. Also, I knew the Spanish government was likely to be uncooperative. The Basques wanted a similar peace deal like the Irish Republican Army (IRA) and Sinn Fein had with Great Britain, Ireland, and Protestant Loyalists in 1998. It meant that Spain would treat the Basques, ETA and Herri Batasuna as equals—very, very unlikely. In subsequent years, as the ETA permanent ceasefire persisted, my misgivings proved to be true. By 2018, ETA had been completely dissolved. And to date, there has been no peace process, unfortunate for the Basque political prisoners, and in my view, unfortunate for the victims of ETA. Basques still want political independence, just as the Catalans do.

During this time, my Herri Batasuna/ETA friend put me in contact with the former director of a Basque newspaper, a newspaper which was forced close, and this same director had been allegedly tortured while in police custody. I took the opportunity to interview him over the phone and asked him about his torture experiences at the hands of Spanish authorities. It was an interesting interview. It seemed to prove Herri Batasuna propaganda about Spanish state torture to some extent, but not entirely. Torture, was one of the main arguments of Herri Batasuna and ETA for continuing the conflict against the Spanish state. Indeed, over the many years of the conflict, numerous Herri Batasuna supporters had claimed to have been tortured while in police custody. Yet, and as a researcher, I also knew some of the HB figures about torture were probably exaggerated. Regardless, HB members wanted to impress upon the world about the widespread aspect of the Basque torture for continued Basque political support. Nevertheless, I think it is true to claim, Spanish torture of Basque political prisoners did happen. It was well documented. So, again, here is another situation about "partial truths." If it was even partly true, those from the Basque "Patriotic Left" (Abertzaleak) had been tortured, then this was truly quite bad. It was certainly and unfortunately a major reason why the Basque conflict remained intractable for so many years. In addition, I was put in connection with another Herri Batasuna member who compiled a book about Basque torture. I doubted some of the compiled figures. Maybe some of it was true? Certainly, other Basque researchers demonstrated the veracity of some of the torture in the Basque region.[1]

Even so, nothing justified ETA terrorist violence, ever. Nothing justified the multitudes who died at the hands of ETA and nothing justified the necessity for creating more and more victims for independence over the thirty-six years since Franco's death up until 2011 with the permanent ceasefire. Basque terrorism produced a lot of "unforgivable damage." Basque terrorist violence psychologically affected numerous families in adverse ways and negatively affected Basque society as a whole. There was nothing good about Basque terrorism. There was nothing justifiable about Basque terrorism, no matter how much the Basque "Patriotic Left" (Abertzaleak) chose to justify it. Just as there is nothing good about any other type of terrorism, ever. It was destructive and harmful, and quite frankly stupid. In all, it was horrific. ETA's violence was altogether pointless. The more ETA terrorism lasted over the years, and the more lives were lost or those who continued to be injured from its nihilistic annihilation, the more senseless it became over time. Basque independence became a cause of mind-numbing folly and idiocy, rather than some glorious cause célèbre because of all the victims ETA left in its awful wake. Of course, ETA would argue, it was meant to attain its lofty goal of political independence and the victims were the "collateral damage" result of the ongoing war it had with the Spanish state. But one question, always, always remained—at what cost? And then other questions persisted as well, like: whose family would be destroyed next? And is Basque violence, really Basque culture? Surely, the ancient Basques had other worthy sociocultural attributes aside from political violence in Spain—such as their language (euskera), their traditions, their *sports, their symbols, their cuisine, their literature, their music, their mythology, and their social organization, and on and on, but not violence.*

*After I had met with Herri Batasuna/ETA on several occasions about achieving their peace process in Oslo, Norway, I was named as one of the "International Leaders" in Conflict Resolution and Peace Processes, a list of such peace mediators read out at the European Parliament, on March 29, 2010, in Brussels, Belgium by South African Human Rights Lawyer, Brian Currin. It became known as the "Brussels Declaration" in order to appeal to ETA to cease its terrorist violence with a permanent declaration of peace, and commending the Basque Patriotic (Abertzale) Left to support the peace process as well as petitioning to the Spanish government to recognize an ETA ceasefire. My co-signers of the "Brussels Declaration" were: Betty Williams, Nobel Peace Prize Laureate for her peace work in Northern Ireland; Denis Haughey, full-time assistant to John Hume, who had participated in the Northern Irish Good Friday Agreement; John Hume, Nobel Peace Prize Laureate for his peace work in Northern Ireland; Archbishop Desmond Tutu, Nobel Prize Laureate, who chaired the Truth and Reconciliation Commission in South Africa; Mary Robinson, first female President of the Republic of Ireland, and afterward, United Nations High Commissioner for Human Rights; Former President of South Africa, FW de Klerk, Nobel Prize Laureate, along with Nelson Mandela for his role in ending Apartheid; the Nelson Mandela Foundation; Aldo Civico, Director for International Conflict Resolution at Columbia University; Sheryl Brown, Virtual Diplomacy Director, United States Institute of Peace (USIP); Andrea Bartoli, Director of the Institute for Conflict Analysis & Resolution (ICAR) at George Mason University; Alan Smith, UNESCO Chair on Peace Education at University of Ulster; Christopher Mitchell, Emeritus Professor of Conflict Research, Institute for Conflict Analysis & Resolution (ICAR); Hurst Hannum, Professor of International Law, Fletcher School of Law and Diplomacy, Tufts University; Jon Etchemendy, Provost, Stanford University; William Kelly, Archive of Humanist Art; Albert Reynolds, Past Taoiseach, Prime Minister of the Republic of Ireland; Nuala O'Loan, Baroness, Member of the House of Lords, First Police Ombudsman of Northern Ireland, and Special Envoy to Timor-Leste for the Republic of Ireland; Raymond Kendall, former General Secretary INTERPOL; and Silvia Casale, former President of the European Committee for the Prevention of Torture and Inhuman and Degrading Treatment or Punishment.*

*Of all of the moments, when I met with the young man who was the International Representative of Herri Batasuna and ETA, one stands out to* me. *I remember walking in downtown Oslo, Norway with him and returning from a café. I said to him in passing, "You realize now it is all over, right?" I continued, "You realize that they [the United States, Spain, France] will not stop coming after you. After 9/11, everything changed, and the United States, Spain, and France are just going to try to get rid of all of you. You know that, right?" I think he understood me. I said my goodbyes and I left him in downtown Oslo.*

*And now, I think to myself, what a difference a few years make. Here I was meeting with a representative of Herri Batasuna/ETA, and telling him "it was all over." Their terrorism was over. How ironic this was. When in the first months of my fieldwork in 1996, I was being told by them to leave the Spanish Basque Country, or else. Ironic indeed, it truly was. And now I was telling Herri Batasuna/ETA there were not many alternatives left in their violent struggle. They had to give up their arms. Trying a peace process was their best option.*

*And in the following year, 2011, a permanent ceasefire was declared by ETA. It was over. Ironic, or not, it was over, and the Basques and Spain could enjoy peace. "At long last, there will be peace!" "Azkenean, bakea egongo da!"*

\* \* \*

Photograph of ETA (Euskadi Ta Askatasuna, Basque Homeland and Freedom) terrorist members

3 NATIONALISM AND TERRORISM 61

Photograph of New IRA (Irish Republican Army) parading in Northern Ireland

Photograph of Irish journalist Lyra McKee, who was murdered by the "New" IRA

## Introduction

This chapter examines how ethno-nationalist sentiments are practiced and how terrorist groups remain active well after the establishment of peace processes in the case of the permanent ceasefire of ETA (*Euskadi Ta Askatasuna*, Basque Homeland and Freedom) following 2011 and in the case of the IRA (Irish Republican Army) after the Good Friday Agreement in 1998. Moreover, I wish to demonstrate how ethnic minorities like Basques, Catalans, and Northern Irish Catholics have maintained their viewpoints of ethno-subordination and imagine respectively an independent Basque Country, Catalonia, and united Ireland (Northern Ireland with the rest of Ireland). As James C. Scott (1990: xii) has asserted: "Every subordinate group creates, out of its ordeal, a 'hidden transcript' that represents a critique of power spoken behind the back of the dominant. The powerful, for their part, also develop a hidden transcript representing the practices and claims of their rule that cannot be openly avowed." These political and social dynamics are still in play in Spain among the Basques and Catalans, and to some extent among the Catholic minority in Northern Ireland. The two former groups, both Basques and Catalans, earnestly seek recognition for independent states, while the "New" IRA has not let go of old grievances, long after the peace process between Northern Ireland, Great Britain, and Ireland. When peace processes take hold there is always the worry of a return to violence, whether in the Basque Country or Northern Ireland. As two commentators on the Northern Irish "Troubles" have declared: "Peace, if there is to be peace, will always be imperfect, and there will always be controversy: yet, for all that, it can be forecast with some confidence that the future will bring much improvement on the last three turbulent decades" (McKittrick and McVea 2002: 242). Indeed, in general, peace has brought much improvement to the Spanish Basque Country and to Northern Ireland. But, as this chapter establishes, there is still much political unrest in the Basque Country, Catalonia, and Northern Ireland.

Additionally, I consider how the notion of the "nation" is a debatable term, whereby competing nationalisms and visions for an "imagined community" are at stake. Such ideas are beyond the likes of Benedict Anderson (1983) because the nation itself may be divisible. Yael Tamir (2019: 147) contends: "Why must Spain be taken to be 'indissoluble' and 'indivisible'? Why cannot this unity be questioned? These questions are raised by the Catalans, the Basques, the Lombards, the Scots, leaving the old nation-states speechless as they witness their own national arguments being used against them." Nationalist politics are factionalized among nationalist secessionists. There is a broad spectrum of political parties, for example, and their adherents who contend are the true patriots of non-nation separatist movements. In the Basque Country, the difference used to be those who support violence as opposed to those who support independence through peaceful means. These political views imagine an independent nation in different ways and compete with one another to achieve secession.

In sum, this chapter, reveals how nationalist aspirations have been shaped in post-peace situations of the Basque Country and in the failures of other peace processes in Northern Ireland, for example. On the other hand, it also exposes how Catalans have expressed their desires for independence through a 2017 referendum for independence and what this tells us about non-nation political movements for secession.

## Celebrating Terrorism?

Our first president, George Washington, in today's political landscape might be viewed as a "terrorist," but more accurately, might be described as an "insurgent" or "rebel."[2] Indeed, our first thirteen colonies toward the end of the eighteenth century were fighting one of the great European superpowers at the time in Great Britain. After all, we fought the British in a type of guerrilla warfare and won with the help of another superpower at the time, France.

So, today, when hearing about terrorists celebrating we take a step back and ask—why? Or, what? Or, how? Indeed, the whole notion of "terrorism" conjures up "fear" as it once did when the notion was first popularized during the so-called Reign of Terror (*La Terreur*, 1793–1794) in the French Revolution.[3]

We do not often hear about terrorists openly celebrating in daylight with popular support. Yet, there are pockets of the world in which they still do so, whether in Northern Ireland, or Palestine, or in the case of this past weekend, in the Spanish Basque Country, *Euskal Herria*. And while celebrating terrorism may not be quite ubiquitous, it is not altogether uncommon either.

Some Spanish Basques were engaging in a war of terrorism against Spain, and partly, against France, from 1959 until 2011. By 2018, the Basque terrorist group, "Basque Homeland and Freedom" (*Euskadi Ta*

*Askatasuna*, ETA) was completely dissolved and their weapons verifiably decommissioned. Even so, ETA, after having become defunct, had not lost its popular support among a substantial portion of the population living in places like the Spanish province of Gipuzkoa.[4]

I spent almost two years in Gipuzkoa in the Spanish Basque Country in the late 1990s for my PhD research at the University of Oxford, initially to study Basque fishermen, and then to analyze a controversial and polemical commemorative parade known as the Alarde.

During the late 1990s, celebrating terrorism was everywhere in the Basque Country. There were the solemn and nationalist funerals for deaths of ETA terrorists. There were the protests against the arrests of ETA terrorists and the political protests for freeing all Basque terrorists and massive political rallies for an "independent Basque Country." Patriotic Basques (*abertzaleak*) hoped for a unified and independent Basque Country, uniting four Spanish provinces with three French provinces to form the irredentist state of *Euskadi*.

One of my first academic articles, "The Basque Conflict Globally Speaking: Material Culture, Mass Media, and Basque Identity in the Wider World" (2002), discussed how violent nationalists surround themselves in material symbols so as to enhance their power and to emphasize their cause for themselves and to others, whether at political funerals, or political protests, or in the form of political graffiti, or political jewelry, or political t-shirts, or other political material forms.[5] One of the most powerful and unifying symbols is the flag and in the Basque case, the Basque flag, known as the *Ikurriña*.

So, for me, it was no surprise to hear and read reports from Spain in recent days about Basque townspeople celebrating former Basque terrorists returning home after many years in prison. These former Basque terrorists (*etarrak*) were fêted as heroes. Basque townspeople were seen waving numerous Basque flags and applauding—the typical fanfare of Basque patriots.

Yet, such celebrations of terrorism were viewed elsewhere in Spain as outrageous and unwarranted.[6] In my view, they also put the Basque peace process back even further from becoming a reality. Some Spanish politicians even questioned whether or not such celebrations in fact constituted crimes.

However, as any scholar of nationalism knows, "independence movements" are emotionally bound, and hardcore nationalists like Basque patriots (*abertzaleak*), are exuberant to celebrate their Basqueness and even unify over those in the past willing to use violence in the name of an independent Basque Country. Similar exuberance has been seen among Spanish Catalans as well and Catalans voicing their support for the independence referendum in 2017 as well as protests against Catalan nationalist leaders arrested with similar political scenes of nationalism there.[7]

So, when former Basque terrorists returned home in 2019 to their Basque towns, José Javier Zabaleta to Hernani after twenty-nine years in prison and Xabier Ugarte to Oñati after twenty-two years in prison, the Basque patriotic supporters were out in full Basque pride, waving their red-white-green *Ikurriñak* and voicing their approval with ecstatic applause and political signs reading "*Presoak Etxera*" (Prisoners Return Home), along with fireworks.[8]

Following the uproar over the appropriateness of such celebrations, the Basque regional government (*Eusko Jaurlaritza, El Gobierno Vasco*) declared there will be no more future homages to Basque terrorists in the Basque region because of ethics and out of respect for the victims of terrorism.[9] Also, in 2019, the Secretary General of Coexistence and Human Rights of the Basque Regional Government, Jonan Fernández, asked the Basque patriotic left (*izquierda abertzaleak*) to desist in such celebrations "for the sensitivity and respect for the memories of the terrorist victims and the pain of their families" and because "it does not favor coexistence." The Basque Regional Government also iterated it sympathized with the suffering victim families and expressed its indignation about such festivities. Furthermore, the Basque Regional President (*Lehendakari*) Iñigo Urkullu issued a statement condemning the Basque patriotic left for their homages to former Basque terrorists.[10]

As someone who has lived in the Basque Country and has worked toward Basque peace, such celebrations supporting terrorism and lauding former terrorists do nothing to bring the Basque people toward peace, or Spain desiring more efforts toward reconciliation. Following more than fifty years of terrorism, more needs to be done toward recovery, truth commissions, and trust. The new "Memorial Center for the Victims of Terrorism" is an excellent beginning toward education, outreach, and understanding.[11] I can only hope for a sustained Basque peace as more and more former Basque terrorists return home and as reconciliation between ETA supporters and terrorist victims becomes essential for coexistence.

Certainly, the Basque people want peace and undoubtedly the Basque people deserve peace as well as the rest of Spain. More so, the victims of

ETA terrorism deserve respect and the knowledge that Basque terrorism is indeed over and done.
*Beti egon daiteke Euskal bakea*! (May there always be Basque peace!)

## END OF AN ERA FOR ETA? MAY BASQUE PEACE CONTINUE

On Thursday, May 16, 2019, we had news of the arrest of Josu Ternera, his full Basque name being Jose Antonio Urrutikoetxea Bengoetxea, the former leader of Basque terrorist group, *Euskadi Ta Askatasuna* (ETA, Basque Homeland and Freedom) near Saint Gervais-les-Bains in the French Alps.[12] The operation was conducted by the Spanish Guardia Civil and the French General Directorate of Interior Security (*Direction Générale de la Sécurité Intérieure*, DGSI). As Ternera represents some of the ETA old guard, the news was welcome. Yet, some serious questions remain in the present. Where are the Basques and Spain in their peace process? Will further arrests of ETA commandos and ETA leadership ease enough tensions for the Spanish government to resume talks with the radical Basque left (*Batasuna*)?

It has been ten years since ETA declared a permanent and verifiable ceasefire and in 2018, Ternera as spokesperson for the group, declared ETA's final dissolution.[13] Since 2011, many Basques have waited for a peace process and negotiations with the Spanish government along the lines of the "Good Friday Agreement" in Northern Ireland. Even so, successive Spanish governments during this time, both conservative and liberal, have not wanted to negotiate with Basque political parties who in the past supported violence against Spanish security forces, the military and police, as well as contra Spanish politicians.

Since ETA's inception in 1959 it was responsible for 829 deaths. In its final years, the terrorist group especially targeted conservative Spanish politicians from the Popular Party (*Partido Popular*, PP). Over its half-century history prior to conclusion, its paramilitary activities were responsible for numerous civilian deaths, military and police killings, criminal extortion, kidnappings, bombings, murders, and assassination attempts. All of this violence was presumably done in the name of independence for creation of a separate Basque Country or *Euskadi*—the irredentist idea of political secession of the so-called seven Basque provinces fissuring from Spain and France.[14]

As a political-military movement, ETA, did not arise in a vacuum. It came into being because of the Spanish Dictator Francisco Franco's

(1939–1975) policies of cultural oppression against Basques and Catalans.[15] Franco and his regime tried earnestly to eradicate the ancient Basque language (*euskera*) and Basque culture. Basque nationalism though began around the turn of the twentieth century through the writings of Basque politician, Sabino Arana Goiri.[16] But it was not until the 1960s, when Basques radicalized toward using violence, developing both a political platform and paramilitary strategies to counteract against the Francoist dictatorship, while also formulating separatist goals for the establishment of a Basque state.

When *El Caudillo*, Franco died, and Spain transitioned to democracy, it should have signaled an end to ETA. However, ETA continued and carried on its warfare with the Spanish police and Spanish military, and later Basque police as well. Its political ideology became Marxist and its politics leftist favoring environmentalism, feminism, and workers' rights. Its primary political rallies became those against the imprisonment and torture of its members and its political adherents.

When I conducted ethnographic fieldwork in the Spanish Basque Country (1996–1997), ETA had changed military tactics toward assassinating politicians and not just members of the security forces. By 1997, when a young PP Town Councilman, Miguel Ángel Blanco was kidnapped and eventually murdered by ETA, caused massive protests and unrest against "Basque Homeland and Freedom" throughout Spain with millions marching in favor of peace.[17] Indeed, many believed it was time for the Spanish government to publicly support terrorist victims' rights and to provide monetary support for victims' families and even pay for bodyguards for threatened politicians.

It was clear then, ETA's days were numbered. Most Spaniards saw ETA and the radical Basque left as criminals and not as revolutionaries as the Basque left saw themselves. Even, the Zapatista EZLN (Zapatista Army of National Liberation, *Ejército Zapatista de Liberación Nacional*) leader, Subcomandante Marcos, questioned ETA's Marxist aims and credentials comparative to the poor Indians in Chiapas, Mexico.[18]

In 2010 in Oslo, Norway, while I was working for the Peace Research Institute Oslo (PRIO), as a Senior Researcher, I had the opportunity for talks with some of the *Batasuna* leadership and for discussions toward suggesting ways forward in a possible peace process. My role was altogether minor compared to others such as the South African lawyer and peace activist, Brian Currin, also responsible for the creation of the South African Truth and Reconciliation Commission, and other notables as the

Irish Sinn Féin leadership, Gerry Adams and Martin McGuinness, as well as Nobel Laureates like Bishop Desmond Tutu and John Hume, among other peace dignitaries.

In March 2010, I was one of the signatories of what became known as the "Brussels Declaration," read out to the European Union (EU) Parliament: "We, the undersigned, welcome and commend the proposed steps and new public commitment of the Basque Pro-independence (*Abertzale* Left) to 'exclusively political and democratic' means and a 'total absence of violence' to attain its political goals.[19] Fully carried out, this commitment can be a major step in ending the last remaining conflict in Europe. We note the expectation that the coming months may present a situation where the commitment to peaceful, democratic, and non-violent means becomes an irreversible reality. To that end, we appeal to ETA to support this commitment by declaring a permanent, fully verified ceasefire. Such a declaration appropriately responded to by [Spanish] Government would permit new political and democratic efforts to advance, differences to be resolved and lasting peace attained." It was a welcome statement for a total commitment to peace—peace from years of Basque conflict and peace for all the Spanish people.

Now, a decade on from ETA's formal declaration of a permanent ceasefire in 2011, I reflect upon the meaning of Josu Ternera's arrest and what more can be done toward a Basque peace process. It is heartening that it was Ternera who made recorded statements of an official apology on behalf of ETA to the victims' families.

In their own words, ETA declared in 2018: "We know we caused a lot of pain during the long period of armed struggle, including damage that can never be put right … We wish to show our respect for those who were killed or wounded by ETA and those who were affected by the conflict. We are truly sorry."[20] These are truly remarkable words from those formerly hell-bent on achieving Basque independence at all costs—including willingness to die and kill for a political cause.

ETA further remarked: "We know, owing to our armed struggle, our actions have hurt people who bore no responsibility whatsoever. We have also caused damage that cannot be undone … We apologize to those people and their families. These words will not make up for what happened nor will they lessen the pain, but we speak them respectfully and without wanting to provoke further suffering."[21]

Unfortunately, the Association of Victims from Terrorism (*Asscociación de Víctimas del Terrorismo*, AVT), and the other victims' associations (*el*

*Colectivo de Víctimas del Terrorismo*, COVITE, *la Fundación Miguel Ángel Blanco* y *la Asscociación de Cuerpos y Fuerzas de Seguridad del Estado Víctimas del Terrorismo*), rejected the apology as a denial by ETA of its authentic responsibility for its use of violence from historical manipulation of the conflict by using the bombing of Guernica during the civil war as historical cover for its many atrocities.[22]

As Teresa Whitfield (2014) describes in her well-received book *Endgame for ETA*: "Spanish intransigence may uphold Spanish 'principles', but it also helps ensure that Basque society will remain deeply polarized and significantly hostile to Spain and Madrid. Over many years, ETA had inflicted great suffering on its victims and damage to the Basque Country and Spain. The ending of its armed activities had been unanimously welcomed, and its dissolution would be too. Peace is not worth any price, but nor does it come free."[23] Indeed, there are deep wounds to heal from the Basque conflict.

In 1960, around the time ETA began as a political organization, Dr. Martin Luther King, Jr. penned some of his own words about "personal suffering" in his short essay "Suffering and Faith."[24] He observed: "My personal trials have also taught me the value of unmerited suffering. As my sufferings mounted I soon realized that there were two ways that I could respond to my situation: either to react with bitterness or seek to transform the suffering into a creative force. I decided to follow the latter course. Recognizing the necessity for suffering I have tried to make of it a virtue. If only to save myself from bitterness, I have attempted to see my personal ordeals as an opportunity to transform myself and heal the people involved in the tragic situation which now obtains. I have lived these last few years with the conviction that unearned suffering is redemptive."

May there be healing and redemption from the Basque conflict.

## FEAR AND LOATHING FOR THE SO-CALLED NEW IRA

In 2019, I had a brief conversation with a friend of mine from Belfast, Northern Ireland, who now lives in the United States. We discussed, among other things, the so-called New Irish Republican Army (IRA) and its murder of Irish journalist, Lyra McKee, twenty-nine years old, on April 18, 2019.[25] Both of us expressed "fear and loathing," and just outright outrage about the New IRA and its renewed violence. After all, the "Good Friday Agreement" for peace in Northern Ireland was signed almost exactly twenty-three years prior, finally ending "The Troubles," which cost nearly 3500 lives.[26]

Most believed, perhaps naively, including myself, that such extrajudicial killings were relics of the past and behind us. The Northern Irish murders ended, or so we thought, with the "peace accords" at Stormont Palace and House of Commons in 1998. Even so, observers of the Northern Irish "Troubles" knew IRA "hardliners" remained after the peace deal had been signed. Those who could not accept peace in Northern Ireland and those who would not stop the violence until a utopic vision for a "unified Ireland" was achieved.

The tumultuous years of the "Troubles" lasted in Northern Ireland from the 1960s until 1998, but historically speaking, the violence between Irish Catholics and Irish Protestants has deep roots in the sectarian divide of Irish history dating back to the seventeenth-century "Plantation Era," which entailed the seizure of Irish owned land by the English Crown and overall colonization of Irish land by British settlers. The early years of the conflict between native Catholics against the settler Protestant British and Scottish "planter class" resulted in the Confederate Wars (1641–1653) and the Williamite War (1689–1691).

Fast forward to 1916 and the "Easter Rising" in Dublin, Ireland, where a concerted effort was undertaken to win Irish independence from Great Britain and establish the Irish Republic, again a time period 105 years from the present. It was led by the Irish Republican Brotherhood, the Irish Volunteers, and the Irish Citizen Army when the British were heavily engaged in fighting World War I. For many reasons, this historical period was instrumental in Irish history when Sinn Féin garnered a majority of Irish votes in 1918 and later would evolve into the political arm of the IRA.

From the 1960s to 1990s, the "Troubles" were a period of convoluted killings between Catholic Republican paramilitaries and Protestant Ulster-Loyalist paramilitaries, as well as the IRA against the British military and RUC (Royal Ulster Constabulary), a time of reprisals and counter-reprisals, resulting in assassinations, car bombings, civilian casualties, death threats, disappearances, hunger strikes, petrol bombs, political jockeying for power, political murals, prison sentences, sectarian community divisions, and continual terrorism.

Both Unionists and Republicans have united against dissident "New" IRA paramilitaries because of the murder of the journalist Lyra McKee in Derry during the Easter Week. After twenty-one years of relative peace, their willingness to dialogue is welcome, signifying we are undeniably in a new era of non-violent understanding where sectarian violence has no place in this "new" Northern Ireland. Talks about power-sharing between

Sinn Féin and the Democratic Unionist Party (DUP) have been revived since the breakdown of such discussions in 2017.

A statement by the "New" IRA's political party Saoradh (Liberation), "Tragically a young journalist, Lyra McKee, was killed accidentally"—was not good enough for the Northern Irish majority who supported the peace process and the Good Friday Agreement in 1998.[27] It was, in effect, beside the point.

After all, it was in the city of Derry where the infamous "Blood Sunday" incidents happened some forty-seven years beforehand on January 30, 1972.[28] It revolved around the British Army shooting at forty-eight unarmed Irish Catholic marchers who were protesting political internment. And then on that day, thirteen of them were killed straight away.

The present-day trials against ex-British soldiers and ex-Northern Irish police for the Bloody Sunday shootings and other security forces killings have tested the resolve and limitations of judicial courts in Northern Ireland. Questions are raised whether or not such ex-British soldiers and police should be charged at all with crimes of murder and attempted murder such as "Soldier F." Some 200 ex-soldiers and ex-policemen are said to be under investigation.[29]

Prior to the journalist's slaying, the Police Service of Northern Ireland/Royal Ulster Constabulary (PSNI/RUC) conducted a raid on the Creggan Estate in Derry searching for explosives and weapons as preventative measures against terrorism during the Easter weekend of 2019.

What ensued was a political riot. Its original intent evolving from a Saoradh demonstration commemorating the Easter Rising of 1916. To protest the police raid, dissident Republican militants set two cars ablaze with Molotov cocktails and began firing live rounds in the direction of police and gathered crowds. During the melee, Lyra McKee, was gunned down by some masked gunman among the New IRA paramilitary rioters. Under such circumstances, it is unclear how New IRA paramilitaries could defend Lyra McKee's homicide as accidental because of their murderous intent against the Northern Irish police.

This so-called New IRA was formed from those Republican paramilitaries who did not believe in the Northern Irish peace process along with young, impoverished, and unemployed youth who were born after the Good Friday Agreement and raised with sectarian beliefs.[30] The PSNI (Police Service of Northern Ireland) believe the New IRA may have several hundred members. On the other hand, the political situation in Northern Ireland has been exacerbated since 2016 from a potential

BREXIT failure and the threat of "borders" and "police checks" returning to Northern Ireland.[31]

Fortunately, the majority of former Provisional Republicans, and Sinn Féin politicians, do not support the New IRA nor the Saoradh, and their unrealistic goals for unification of Northern Ireland with the rest of the island.

On Wednesday, April 24, 2019, McKee's funeral was well attended by important British and Irish politicians, including at the time, the British Prime Minister Theresa May, Labour Leader Jeremy Corbyn, Irish President Michael Higgins, Irish Prime Minister Leo Varadkar, and Irish Minister of Foreign Affairs Simon Coveney. All the Northern Irish political parties were equally represented.

McKee was survived by her mother, two brothers, and three sisters. She was described as an LGBT activist and also survived by her partner Sara Canning. The service was at the Protestant St. Anne's Cathedral in Belfast, even though McKee was from a Catholic family. Her family wished her funeral to be well attended by the entire community. Her family described Lyra as a woman with a "warm and innocent heart" and who was a "great listener"; and who was also "smart" and "strong-minded"; and who believed in "inclusivity, justice, and truth."

We can only hope McKee's death will not be in vain. We can only hope the Good Friday Agreement remains in place and the political parties believe again in the peace process and not a return to violence.

As the Irish Nobel Laureate, novelist, playwright, and poet, Samuel Beckett, once declared: "Ever tried. Ever failed. No matter. Try again. Fail again. Fail better." On the other hand, the good people of Northern Ireland cannot afford to fail any longer and they know it.

## Footnoting History for the Sake of History and for the Sake of Peace

Recently, I was reminded of the short story by the Argentinian writer, Jorge Luis Borges, titled: "The Theme of the Traitor and the Hero" ("*El Tema del Traidor y el Héroe*") (1962) in which a fictional historian is compelled "not" to change the biographical history of an Irish hero because of nationalist interests.[32] It seems my own recent writing has inspired such liberal editing for the benefits of nationalism.

Such historical musings are curious but nothing new to me. In my past academic writing, I have examined how different historical interpretations of a Basque commemorative parade inspired quite differing viewpoints about the past and were dependent upon notions of feminism or traditionalism with very different political implications.[33]

In Borges' story, the hero is named Fergus Kilpatrick, an Irishman living around 1824. The story feels more like the murderous and traitorous times of the Republican independence movement, or the Easter Rising of 1916 in Dublin, Ireland against Great Britain. The narrator in the story, named Ryan, is the great-grandson of the Irish hero Kilpatrick. As the protagonist Ryan remarks: "That history should have copied history was already sufficiently astonishing; that history should copy literature was inconceivable."

Indeed, the whole idea of history meandering between irony and truth may be expected and likewise its similarities with history more ironic still. We find some histories paralleling literature, whether they be the literary plots of Shakespeare's *Julius Caesar* or Shakespeare's *Macbeth*, as Borges aptly points out. Yet, when so-called nationalists alter so-called small facts for their own political gains and purposes to change history, often they do so as a means of normalizing their political discourse. While such editorial renderings of opinions about conflicts may not be the intent of the original author, or historian, or no doubt, in some cases, peace activist and peace writer, altering facts and editing out content for political purposes may be somewhat dangerous. Because nationalism presupposes a particular perspective, a religiosity for the nation as an ideal above all else.

What Ryan discovered was that his great-grandfather, Fergus Kilpatrick, was perhaps a traitor. Rather than change his biographical history, Ryan thought better of it and kept his research knowledge secret. To Ryan, Kilpatrick would remain a hero for the good of the country, Ireland. As Borges writes about Ryan's thinking: "After a series of tenacious hesitations, he resolves to keep his discovery silent. He publishes a book dedicated to the hero's glory; this too, perhaps, was foreseen."

In 2019, I was grateful to have had my words for peace published in two nationalist publications. One was an article expressing my outrage over the "New" IRA killing of the young Irish journalist, Lyra McKee. The editorial piece was picked up by the Unionist newspaper *Londonderry Sentinel*, titled "Fear and Loathing for the So-Called 'New' IRA" (May 1, 2019).[34] In that piece, the editor decided to edit my writing by renaming the city of "Derry" as "Londonderry." To the outside observer such an edit may seem minor. However, place in Northern Ireland is everything with strong implications for "sectarian divides" between Republican Catholics against Protestant Unionists. Londonderry is the politicized and Unionized name of Derry. On the other hand, for Republican Catholics, Derry is still Derry.

Generally, such an edit may seem to be minor, but it makes my article about peace and staying the course with the Good Friday Agreement more politicized, whereas my original intent was to remain neutral and neither support Republican Catholics or Protestant Unionists in a conflict with resurfacing issues from time to time. After all, I am an outsider, a foreigner, and observing the ongoing post-Troubles Northern Ireland from a distance.

Likewise, my article favoring a Basque peace process and commenting on the recent arrest of the Basque terrorist, former member of Euskadi Ta Askatasuna, ETA, Josu Ternera, was picked up by the leftist-leaning, Abertzale left newspaper *NAIZ* (May 23, 2019).[35] The Basque editor decided in this newspaper to cut out a paragraph about the ETA killing of PP town councilor, Miguel Ángel Blanco. By editing out this paragraph, in effect, removed the blame of ETA for the killing of this young politician and thereby removing an important point in the article. That ETA murder in particular is a painful memory for the Basque Abertzale left because it exposes one of the worst episodes of their long tumultuous history of atrocities.

This history explains the next paragraph as to "why" millions marched across Spain in favor of peace back in 1997.

If the Basque peace process is to continue today, the Abertzale Left, Batasuna, must take unequivocal responsibility for such atrocities. It must confront these painful histories and apologize for them.

Having said this though, both the *Londonderry Sentinel* and *NAIZ*, published the majority of my words for peace and a call for renewal of peace processes in both places, Northern Ireland and the Basque Country. (Also, published under different titles in *PeaceVoice* and *Counterpunch*.)[36]

While to some, these are small footnotes; nevertheless, they are worth pointing out because there are varying "nationalisms" in competition with one another here and what becomes part of public discourse may become the dominant narrative of a given conflict. In the first instance, there are the competing ideals of Protestant Unionists versus Republican Catholics. In the latter case, there are competing visions between Basque nationalists and Spanish nationalists over hearts and minds in the Basque Country and Spain.

As Mahatma Gandhi once declared (1931): "What is true of individuals is true of nations. One cannot forgive too much. The weak can never forgive. Forgiveness is the attribute of the strong."[37] May the weak become strong in their forgiveness and may the strong become humble and forgive for the sake of peace.

## THE PROBLEMS WITH AN IMAGINED COMMUNITY[38]

Imagine the Texas Legislature authorizing a vote for Texan Independence—a referendum on the Lone Star State once again becoming an independent republic. Imagine that Texans vote overwhelmingly for independence, and that state lawmakers, contrary to the wishes of the U.S. president and the federal government, then vote to secede, something that has not happened in the United States since 1861, the eve of our horrible civil war. What would a current U.S. president do in similar circumstances? Most likely send in the military, have all members of the Texas Legislature arrested and put in federal prison, thereby putting an end to Texan secession.

This is basically what is happening in Catalonia, Spain. Except in this instance, following the Catalan vote for independence of Oct. 1, 2017, Spain's Prime Minister Mariano Rajoy, dissolved the Catalan legislature and called for new elections by December.[39] About 43 percent of Catalans voted, and of this number, 90 percent voted for independence, although a majority of Catalans abstained.[40]

In response, the Spanish prime minister invoked Article 155 of the country's constitution, which allowed him to suspend the autonomy of the region of Catalonia (Catalunya) and its powers of self-rule, including by adjourning its governing body and taking control of its regional police force, the Mossos d'Esquadra. In the current crisis, Rajoy has held his hand by arresting neither members of the Catalan Parliament nor Catalonian Parliamentary President Carles Puigdemont. Rajoy chose to fire them instead.[41]

Madrid then controlled the Catalan police force as well. But Rajoy did not deploy the military *en masse*, at least not yet, likely because he wanted to avoid exacerbating this internal constitutional crisis. Moreover, both the European Union and the United States support Spain on the matter of Catalonia.

In examining the Catalan independence vote, as well as the Scottish independence referendum of 2014, what is the takeaway here regarding independence movements in general? Consider those in Europe, for the Spanish Basques, the Flemish Belgians, the French Corsicans and so on. And take into account as well as such movements elsewhere in the world, for the British Cameroons, the Iraqi Kurds, the Burmese Karen, the Sri Lankan Tamils, the Palestinians, the Indian Sikhs and the Russian Chechens.

It may be argued that nationalism in its many guises, especially in its extremes, has caused plenty of damage. After all, much blood has been shed in the name of ethno-nationalist independence, or by means of the "hyper-state," or "pathological state," National Socialist fascism, genocide, and the purging actions of totalitarian regimes. Nationalism to preserve power, "patriotism" and "statism," therefore may be equally problematic.

Some ethnic minorities are so enamored of the promise of their own nation, they will do almost anything to achieve it, even to the extent of committing violence for their ideals. Theirs is a kind of religious fervor, a futuristic "imagined community," where any means necessary becomes legitimate to achieve nationhood.

Even so, it is difficult to enter into the global club and to be accepted among the already recognized 193 member countries of the United Nations.[42] The most powerful of states make such decisions. Those upsetting the balance, or pretending to do so, are inevitably excluded. In this latter category, we may also include indigenous peoples and their indigenous rights movements with their many similarities with ethno-nationalist minorities.

Neither Spain, nor the present world order will accept a Catalonian independent nation. So says the European Union, so says the United States and, by default, so says the United Nations. The only hope, therefore, is that this unrest not lead to bloodshed.

Some argue, especially subaltern intellectuals, whether self-determination should be granted wherever it arises and wherever there is a legitimacy to such claims among particular ethno-nationalist minorities. Yet, the worry among established countries and their governments, is if such claims are allowed and such peoples permitted their own nations and states, then it would be like pulling a string and allowing the whole garment to completely unravel. The nation itself might fall apart and can no longer be a sustainable whole or a prosperous union.

Governments today are simply not willing to allow for this. Secessionism means losing physical territory and losing economic gains. The most complex problems are those ethno-nationalist assertions in post-colonial situations where the major European powers such as Great Britain and France in the past divided up varying regions without heeding to varying ethnic territories. (The continent of Africa is a good example in this regard.)[43]

Simply put, problems of independence such as the one in Catalonia are not going away any time soon. The primary question to ask then is: will the nation-state still be a viable concept in the future?

## NATIONS, NATIONALISM, AND NON-NATION POLITICAL MOVEMENTS

Many may wonder what all the fuss in Catalonia, Spain is about—a previous 2017 referendum vote for independence, and in 2019, people rioting in the streets following the judicial conviction of Catalonian nationalist leaders for sedition, and violent altercations in Catalonian streets with the police. After all, Barcelona, the capital of Catalonia, is a travel hotspot but when it comes to Catalonian nationalism and Catalonian politics, such political movements may remain a mystery to many American observers.

On Monday, October 14, 2019, the Spanish Supreme Court sentenced nine Catalan leaders to prison terms for sedition and attempting to separate from Spain in 2017.[44] Of those convicted, were Oriol Junqueras, the former Catalan vice-president, who was sentenced to thirteen years, the most of any of the convicted, as well as others like Carme Forcadell, former speaker of the Catalan parliament, and political activists such as Jordi Cuixart, and Jordi Sànchez. Additionally, a new extradition order for the arrest of former Catalan president, Carles Puigdemont, was given. (He is currently self-exiled in Belgium.)[45]

In fact, many Americans are often unaware of their own nationalist sentiments. Take, for example, the kneeling controversy of the American football player, Colin Kaepernick in the National Football League (NFL) in 2016, and whether or not taking a knee during the national anthem is an appropriate form of political protest.[46] The act of kneeling during the national anthem provoked strong emotions in many Americans.

To those against, kneeling was viewed as sacrilegious by not respecting the sacral national anthem and the American flag. On the other hand, to those for, kneeling signified a form of protest against all of the police violence against African-Americans in recent years and for the "Black Lives Matter" movement. Moreover, former President Donald Trump weighed in on the issue and admonished NFL football players like Kaepernick who had the temerity of taking a knee during an American sacred symbolic ritual.[47] These actions are so controversial because our national symbols are so emotive and because they have great meaning to us all.

Whether or not we are aware of our own "Americanness," and what emotions such nationalism or patriotism evoke, is situation dependent. Indeed, the late anthropologist Benedict Anderson proposed the notion of an "imagined community" whereby strangers believe in the same symbols, who read the same national newspapers and news websites and so on and imagine themselves to be fictionally related and part of a community of the political imagination. Thus, the relatedness of patriotism is an important national fiction because of its emotional inspirations, and aspirations as well.

In terms of the United States, we might think of the Catalan separatist movement and the Catalan independence movement as equivalent to Texas seceding from the union, or Alaska, or even Hawaii. What would the federal government of the United States do in such cases? In fact, the issues were decided a long time ago in the American Civil War (1861–1865), and a few years afterward with the U.S. Supreme Court ruling in *Texas v. White* (1869) by making unilateral secession illegal.[48]

"Nationalisms" such as the Catalan case have been ongoing for some time. Catalonian nationalism has its historical antecedents reaching back to the Spanish Civil War (1936–1939) and beforehand and following the Francoist oppression of regional movements within Spain such as Basque and Catalan cultures, identities, and languages.

The Catalan case is not even unique in the world today. We see similar non-nation political movements in the British Isles among the Scottish and the Welsh, for example, and the failed Scottish referendum in 2014. In Canada, there is the Québec sovereignty movement with a failed 1995 referendum for independence. Such political movements lost their respective referendums for independence by very small margins, similar to Catalonia in 2017.

In fact, many ethno-nationalist peoples throughout the world may be categorized along the lines of failed nationalist movements. There are, for example, the British Cameroonians and their struggle for sovereignty within present day Cameroon as well described by Michael Fonkem.[49] The "Oromo Liberation Front (OLF)" for recognition of the Oromo people in Ethiopia and analyzed by scholars such as Hamdesa Tuso.[50] Elsewhere, we find the "Free Papua Movement" against Indonesia and for the independence and liberation of the people living in the western half of Papua New Guinea.

In some cases, such ethnic-based movements have suffered defeat as happened in Sri Lanka among the Liberation Tigers of Tamil Eelam (LTTE, or simply, Tamil Tigers) in 2009.[51] Or, in the case of Northern Ireland with the "Good Friday Agreement" (1998) there was a peace agreement between all interested political parties and combatants in the settlement of the Northern Irish conflict: namely, Great Britain, the Republic of Ireland, the Irish Republican Army (IRA) and their political supporters such as Sinn Féin, the Ulster Volunteer Force (UVF) and their political adherents, the Ulster Unionist Party, the Ulster Democratic Party, and related parties. Some thought because of the status of BREXIT, the "Good Friday Agreement" was in jeopardy with the possible return of "hard borders" between Northern Ireland and the Republic of Ireland.[52]

Of course, in the Middle East, there is the Palestinian movement in Israel, and among Palestinian refugee populations in Jordan and Lebanon, and the Kurdish movement in Syria, Turkey, and Iraq. And in Southeast Asia, there is the Kachin Independence Organization (KIO) in Myanmar.

Closer to home, there is the case of Puerto Rico, a territory of the United States with its own "Boricua" independence movement for territorial sovereignty. This has been excellently depicted in Jackie Font-Guzman's book *Experiencing Puerto Rican Citizenship and Cultural Nationalism* (2015).

Moreover, in the last thirty years, indigenous peoples have become increasingly political and demanding more rights within countries like Brazil as I have previously described in "Brazilian Nationalism and Urban Amerindians: twenty-first century dilemmas for indigenous peoples living in the urban Amazon and beyond" (2015).

In truth, there are so many non-nation-state political movements today seeking sovereign status, it is difficult to keep track of them all. In my own studies, I have examined how and why the Basques sought independence for so many years from Spain and why there is not one Basque nationalist movement but several competing factions. Most of these non-state political movements have splinter groups and varying opinions about how to achieve independence and national sovereignty. Nationalism in such cases are not one thing but many.

In returning to the NFL incident with Colin Kaepernick kneeling during the national anthem, both sides in the disagreement would still regard themselves as being American. This is so, even if one or other view might argue by allowing or by disallowing kneeling during the singing of the national anthem as equivalent to being un-American—exercising the right to protest or demeaning a national symbol. Who is more patriotic? Such conflicting views are similar among ethno-nationalist factions and struggles for independence.

In Spain, and since the Franco dictatorship (1939–1975) tried eradicating provincial identities as those in the Basque and Catalan regions, the country in transition to democracy and its federal constitution allowed for more autonomy among its regional peoples. Both the Basque Country (El País Vasco, or *Euskal Herria*) and Catalonia (*Catalunya*) have benefited enormously from considerable autonomy with their own powerful regional parliaments, regional judicial courts, regional police forces, regional taxation, and so on. On the other hand, the elimination of borders with the creation of the European Union (EU) has been mostly unsuccessful and, in many regards, has emboldened and exacerbated "nationalisms" within Europe as those among the Basques and Catalans.

Even so, Europe has long been aware of the dangers of nationalism. One only need to look historically back to World War I and World War II for reasons to be wary of nationalist ideals, when millions of lives were squandered because of nationalist claims, and the impositions of nationalist fanaticism.

The question of Catalonia is virtually the same one to be asked elsewhere and wherever such ethno-nationalist independence movements arise in the world. It is: what is a legitimate state?

There are those nation-states recognized by the United Nations and there are those political non-state ethno-nationalist movements which do "not" receive the same legitimacy. As Arnoldo Otegi, a prominent leader of *EH Bildu* (Euskal Herria Bildu, Basque Country Unite), the political separatist party once favoring "Basque Homeland and Freedom" (ETA) terrorist violence, remarked: "The line was that there was not a political problem in Spain, just a criminal one."[53] And Spain, among other so-called legitimate nation-states, may have good reason for rejecting such ethno-nationalist movements if they use violence for upholding their irredentist values. The Basque ETA was responsible for at least 829 deaths prior to their complete dissolution in 2018. Moreover, the numerous victims of Basque terrorism are still dealing with the trauma and horrors from the Basque conflict. And like the Catalan convicted nine, Otegi among other Basque separatist leaders, was arrested and convicted and served six years in prison (2010–2016) for dissidence and supporting terrorism.

If Texas, or Hawaii, or Alaska were to try to carve themselves off from the United States we might think like Spain. We might have the federal government take over the seceding state and impose military federal rule just as we had done so following the civil war during Reconstruction (1865–1876).

Yet, regardless, these non-state political movements are unlikely to go away any time soon. Nationalism or patriotism arouse strong emotions in people. And, for many reasons, nationalism is secular religion, it provides a great sense of "communal awareness" or an "imagined community" by which to uphold one's sense of identity and pride. The modern appeal of nationalism has been ongoing since at least the late nineteenth century. Again, the questions to be asked are: what is a legitimate state? And who decides? As legitimate nation-states determine the current world order, ethno-nationalist movements will remain non-nation political movements, always yearning for something more.

* * *

In an interesting twist of fate, as this book goes to press, the current Spanish Prime Minister Pedro Sánchez, on June 22, 2021, pardoned the nine Catalan leaders who were jailed for the attempted secession of Catalonia, stating that "the decision comes from the need to reestablish coexistence."[54] This is a good sign for relations between ethno-nationalists like those in the Basque Country and Catalonia and the Spanish government.

## CONCLUSION

In summary, we may ask again what is a legitimate nation-state? Do ethno-nationalist minorities like Basques and Catalans have valid claims to statehood? If not, why not? In ongoing peace processes how may violence be prevented when old grievances come to the fore such as happened with the death of the journalist Lyra McKee in Northern Ireland at the hands of the so-called New IRA?

In this chapter, I established how peace processes become jeopardized by those still willing to support acts of terrorism, whether in Basque Country with the celebration of the return of political prisoners or because of actual acts of violence as in the murder of a journalist by the "New" IRA in Northern Ireland. Likewise, I commented on how nationalists try to manipulate history or circumstances as in editing my own opinion editorial writing to suit nationalist purposes. In one instance, an Ulster Unionist newspaper, the *Londonderry Sentinel*, altered the name of Derry to Londonderry, and in another the Basque patriotic leftist newspaper *NAIZ* excised out a whole paragraph about the ETA killing of a Basque town councilman. Nationalists manipulate texts and histories to fit into their own narratives and visions of history and politics, and thereby transforming them into "their" nationalist histories and nationalist politics.

Basques and Catalans, and nowadays to some extent some Northern Irish Catholics, feel subordinated by dominant hegemonic forces. In the case of the Basques and Catalans, it is Spain and Spanish nationalism, and for the latter, it is the disagreement with the outcome of the 1998 Good Friday Agreement. As James Scott (1990: 136) contended: "Most of the political life of subordinate groups is to be found neither in overt collective defiance of powerholders nor in complete hegemonic compliance, but in the vast territory between these polar opposites." For Spain, "[p]olitical integration and national identification thus form the two sides of the nation-building coin" (Wimmer 2018: 1). Thus, the goal of nation-building is to reduce ethnic tensions and as such "undermine support for separatism … and eventually lead citizens to identify with the nation and perceive it as a community of lived solidarity and shared political identity" (Wimmer 2018: 1)—whereas Ireland would remain separate from the North.

Even so, secessionists remain viable forces in our world today as the cases of Basque and Catalan nationalists prove and, contra Andreas Wimmer (2018), nevertheless challenge nation-building in our world today. According to Yael Tamir (2019: 150): "The growing social and economic gaps, alongside the democratic crisis, provoke a discussion about fundamental political questions: How are we to define the boundaries of political units and who is to be included within them? Nationalism provides an acceptable justification: first to the question of the boundaries issue, then to the definition of 'the people,' and finally to distributive issues." The Basques and Catalans have irredentist ambitions of creating independent states, however unrealistic, and some Northern Irish Catholics even now hope for a "United Ireland," however improbable.

What I have shown here are how peace processes are vulnerable to long-term sentiments about intractable conflicts in the case of some

Basques celebrating the return of ETA prisoners and in the murder of a journalist in Northern Ireland. Moreover, I revealed how nationalists try to manipulate narratives for their own political purposes. In addition, I elaborated on how nationalist movements try to remain vital forces to be reckoned with as in the 2017 Catalan referendum for independence.

So, as Benedict Anderson (1983: 6) proposes: "Definition of the nation: it is an imagined political community—and imagined as both inherently limited and sovereign." We may further grasp how non-state nationalists "re-imagine" themselves and their nationalist aspirations again and again. We see this through the difficulties of maintaining peace processes as well as how states react to ethno-nationalist minorities like Basques and Catalans, and how nationalist views persist through revising narratives to achieve a uniformity to nationalist identity fitting certain nationalist ideals. These are unfinished identities and visions which are continually being re-imagined and always politically becoming with each political faction and each different political era (Biehl and Locke 2017).

## Notes

1. Since the Democratic Spanish Transition, after 1978 to the present, Zulaika and Douglass (1996, 204–205), stated: "over 14,000 Basques have been arrested for political reasons, and that about 85 percent of those arrested are subjected to torture and maltreatment of all kinds. If we take into account that this repression has taken place almost exclusively among the so-called patriotic-left, which votes for the pro-ETA Herri Batasuna Party and which accounts for about 250,000 Basques, approximately one out of twenty in their ranks has suffered the harrowing effects of arrest and potential torture during the democratic period."
2. https://www.newsweek.com/quora-george-washington-delaware-christmas-terrorism-406095.
   https://www.americanheritage.com/patriots-or-terrorists.
3. https://www.britannica.com/event/Reign-of-Terror.
4. https://www.theguardian.com/world/2018/may/02/basque-separatist-group-eta-announces-dissolution.
5. https://www.tandfonline.com/doi/abs/10.1080/13600810220138302.
6. https://elpais.com/politica/2019/07/29/actualidad/1564419016_676669.html.
7. https://www.houstonchronicle.com/opinion/outlook/article/Linstroth-The-problems-with-an-imagined-12327711.php.

8. https://www.diariovasco.com/politica/gobierno-vasco-exige-20190729102833-nt.html.
9. https://elpais.com/politica/2019/07/29/actualidad/1564404282_963105.html.
10. https://twitter.com/Gob_eus/status/1155782961272360960.
11. http://www.memorialvt.com.
12. https://www.theguardian.com/world/2019/may/16/fugitive-ex-leader-of-eta-josu-ternera-basque-detained-in-france.
13. https://www.theguardian.com/world/2018/apr/20/eta-apologises-basque-separatists-deadly-violence.
14. The seven Basque provinces are: Araba, Bizkaia, Gipuzkoa, and Nafarroa (Navarra) in Spain; and in France: Lapurdi, Nafarroa Beherea, and Zuberoa.
15. https://www.britannica.com/biography/Francisco-Franco/Francos-dictatorship.
16. https://en.wikipedia.org/wiki/Sabino_Arana.
17. https://english.elpais.com/elpais/2017/07/12/inenglish/1499853524_605938.html.
18. http://www.struggle.ws/mexico/ezln/2003/marcos/etaJAN.html.
19. https://icgbasquedotorg.wordpress.com/documents/brussels-declaration/.
20. https://www.theguardian.com/world/2018/apr/20/eta-apologises-basque-separatists-deadly-violence.
21. https://www.theguardian.com/world/2018/apr/20/eta-apologises-basque-separatists-deadly-violence.
22. https://www.rtve.es/noticias/20180420/victimas-rechazan-perdon-selectivo-eta-falta-autocritica/1718661.shtml.
23. https://global.oup.com/academic/product/endgame-for-eta-9780199387540?q=endgame%20for%20eta&lang=en&cc=us.
24. http://okra.stanford.edu/transcription/document_images/Vol05Scans/27Apr1960_SufferingandFaith.pdf.
25. https://www.theguardian.com/uk-news/2019/apr/22/lyra-mckee-friends-stage-protest-derry-offices-saoradh.
26. https://www.britannica.com/topic/Good-Friday-Agreement.
    https://en.wikipedia.org/wiki/The_Troubles.
27. https://en.wikipedia.org/wiki/Saoradh.
28. https://en.wikipedia.org/wiki/Bloody_Sunday_(1972).
29. https://www.theguardian.com/uk-news/2019/apr/25/up-to-200-ex-soldiers-being-investigated-over-troubles-allegations.
30. https://www.theguardian.com/news/2019/apr/20/poverrty-paramilitaries-derry-fertile-soil-revolt-killing-lyra-mckee.
31. https://www.theatlantic.com/international/archive/2019/02/brexit-threatens-peace-northern-ireland-remain-eu/582970/.

32. https://www.derechopenalenlared.com/libros/labyrinths-borges.pdf.
33. J. P. Linstroth (2015). *Marching Against Gender Practice: Political Imaginings in the Basqueland.* Lanham, MD: Lexington Books.
34. https://www.londonderrysentinel.co.uk/news/politics/fear-and-loathing-so-called-new-ira-2038115.
35. https://www.naiz.eus/en/iritzia/articulos/fin-de-una-era-para-eta-que-la-paz-vasca-puede-continuar.
36. http://www.peacevoice.info/2019/05/18/end-of-an-era-for-eta-may-basque-peace-continue/.
    http://www.peacevoice.info/2019/05/13/irish-return-to-political-violence/.
    https://www.counterpunch.org/2019/05/20/end-of-an-era-for-eta-may-basque-peace-continue/.
    https://www.counterpunch.org/2019/05/03/irish-return-to-political-violence/.
37. https://archive.org/details/HindSwaraj-CWMG-051/page/xxiv/mode/2up.
38. See Anderson (1991, orig. 1983) *Imagined Communities: reflections on the origin and spread of nationalism.*
39. https://www.bbc.com/news/world-europe-41783289.
40. https://www.cnn.com/2017/10/02/europe/catalonia-independence-referendum-explainer/index.html.
41. https://www.aljazeera.com/news/2017/10/27/mariano-rajoy-fires-catalan-regional-government.
42. https://www.un.org/en/about-us.
43. https://www.joh.cam.ac.uk/library/library_exhibitions/schoolresources/exploration/scramble_for_africa.
44. https://www.nytimes.com/2019/10/14/world/europe/catalonia-separatists-verdict-spain.html.
45. https://www.theguardian.com/world/2019/oct/19/artur-mas-catalonia-independence-too-far-too-fast.
46. https://www.nfl.com/news/colin-kaepernick-explains-why-he-sat-during-national-anthem-0ap3000000691077.
47. https://www.nfl.com/news/donald-trump-on-kaepernick-find-another-country-0ap3000000692256.
48. https://www.law.cornell.edu/supremecourt/text/74/700.
49. See Fonkem Achankeng (2015) (ed.) *Nationalism and Intra-State Conflicts in the Postcolonial World.*
50. See Tuso (n.d.).
51. https://www.newyorker.com/magazine/2011/01/17/death-of-the-tiger.

52. https://www.brookings.edu/testimonies/protecting-the-good-friday-agreement-from-brexit/.
53. https://www.theguardian.com/commentisfree/2019/oct/23/spanish-state-repression-catalonia-democracy-basque?CMP=share_btn_fb&fbclid=IwAR2OAJzox40xPQy8XdpFpx60SEY_-ng6Dn3lOC2B-fDbkpdXSWR1gfhsPvU.
54. https://english.elpais.com/spain/2021-06-22/spanish-government-approves-pardons-for-nine-jailed-leaders-of-2017-catalan-secession-attempt.html.

## Bibliography

Anderson, B. 1991, orig. 1983. *Imagined Communities: Reflections on the Origin and Spread of Nationalism*. London: Verso.

Biehl, J., and P. Locke, eds. 2017. *Unfinished: The Anthropology of Becoming*. Durham, NC: Duke University Press.

Fonkem Achankeng, M., ed. 2015. *Nationalism and Intra-State Conflicts in the Postcolonial World*. Lanham, MD: Lexington Books.

McKittrick, D., and D. McVea. 2002. *Making Sense of the Troubles: The Story of the Conflict in Northern Ireland*. Chicago: New Amsterdam Books.

Scott, J.C. 1990. *Domination and the Arts of Resistance: Hidden Transcripts*. New Haven, CT: Yale University Press.

Tamir, Y. 2019. *Why Nationalism*. Princeton: Princeton University Press.

Whitfield, T. 2014. *Endgame for ETA: Elusive Peace in the Basque Country*. Oxford: Oxford University Press.

Wimmer, A. 2018. *Nation Building: Why Some Countries Come Together While Others Fall Apart*. Princeton: Princeton University Press.

Zulaika, J., and W.A. Douglass. 1996. *Terror and Taboo: The Follies, Fables, and Faces of Terrorism*. London: Routledge.

CHAPTER 4

# Cultural Genocide, Genocide, and Amerindian Genocide

*The following narratives are excerpts from legal depositions describing the genocide in Guatemala. I collected them from an immigration lawyer friend in 2006. All names are pseudonyms to protect those who told their stories. As such, these are harrowing accounts and demonstrate how horrific the genocide was in Guatemala, a civil war lasting from 1960 to 1996, but the worst years of the genocide were 1980–1983. These legal deposition narratives express the atrocities committed by both the Guatemalan military and the Guatemalan guerrillas.*

### Deposition: Carlos

*I saw my mother and sisters and I think they all kept screaming. The women were only there for a short time, then they were sent back to \_\_\_\_\_. As they were sent back, my mother tried to come to me but the soldiers wouldn't let her. They hit her with their rifle butts and kicked her and she was forced to keep going ... Then they took us in front of the juzgado [military judge] and we saw what the other groups had already seen. I saw a lot of men from \_\_\_\_\_ and a few women, about sixty in all, who had all been tied up. Their hands were tied between their back and their feet were tied as well. They were all lying stomach down on the ground. Some were dead. Some were alive. I saw other men from \_\_\_\_\_ who were killing some of the group. They were hacking at their bodies with machetes. They were hitting them on the neck and the head. The blood was running everywhere like water. About half seemed to be* dead. All of these people were surrounded by soldiers who were ordering other people from _____ to do the killing ... I knew the faces of all of those who were killed, some of them were my father's relatives ... After three days the [Guatemalan military] soldiers left for _____ . They [Guatemalan military] killed everybody there. They [Guatemalan military] gathered all the women and children together in a house and burnt them and the house down to the ground..

## DEPOSITION: VICTOR

But around 1980, everything changed. My uncle, _____, lived in _____. One night in 1980, armed men [guerrillas] came to his door and commanded them that he give them food. Then stores began to be robbed at night and those people went to more houses at night. We called these people the "men who came at night." They told everybody the same thing. They said they were too poor, that they were guerrillas who would take care of the soldiers ... things got worse with the guerrillas. They would come at night and go house to house in all the nearby villages— _____, _____, _____, and others farther away— trying to persuade people to join them. They came to my house in _____, but I would see them or hear them at night because our house was located very near the main road going from _____ to _____ and other villages and towns to the east in the Department of _____. Around that time I heard that some guerrillas had come to _____ at night and carried off three men I knew: _____, _____, and _____. When they did not come back that night, their families went looking for them the next morning. Eventually their bodies were located and two had been killed by machete. _____ and _____'s arms were chopped off and they had been struck so hard in the neck that their heads were barely attached to their necks and body. I know because I went to their wakes that were held that night after they had been found ... When the soldiers [Guatemalan military] came to our area it was around 4:00 in the morning. I was sleeping but was awakened by loud, powerful sounds I had not heard before. I went outside and saw the soldiers passing by in trucks. A jeep carrying a big machine gun went by first, followed by five trucks and another jeep. It was easy to tell the difference between the soldiers and guerrillas because the soldiers wore camouflage uniforms and wore better boots and had Galil rifles ... About a half hour later I began to hear gunfire. The shooting went on for a long time. We heard shots fired and people screaming ... There *were men and women and children who had been killed, I knew them all. There were people dead in their doorways, bleeding. There were people who lay dead in their houses and in their fields. Three of my cousins had been killed ... The next day many of us began to dig graves. We dug holes all day on the land of the various family members who died. There was no celebration or service because everyone was too afraid. This happened in 1981, but I can't remember which month.*

### Deposition: Ines

*About four months later it happened to me ... I was out beyond the fields gathering food. I was bending over to pick up a bush when I was grabbed from behind by someone. Before I could do anything I had been pushed down on my back. I started to scream and a man put his hand on my mouth. I could barely breathe because he was so strong. He stuffed a scarf in my mouth so I couldn't scream any more. I saw there was more than one man. One of them grabbed my hands and another one tried to grab my head. The man who had grabbed me started to take his belt off. Then he undid pants and pushed them down and his shirt was loose. The man holding my arms was laughing. I was trying to scream but the man behind me was holding my head and keeping the scarf in my mouth and all along he was laughing. I saw that they were three soldiers. They were dressed in army uniforms that were camouflage; they all had guns; they had rifles and pistols. They looked like they were Spanish (Ladinos) men. They were talking to me but I didn't understand what they were saying. Two of them had moustaches and heavy sideburns.*

*While the first soldier was taking down his pants, the other soldier was yanking off my clothes. He put his hand inside my dress and grabbed my underwear and tore them off. The other soldier grabbed my wrapped skirt. He pulled off the tie and it the skirt fell underneath me. Then the first soldier raped me. He had a moustache and sideburns. While the first solder was raping me they all were laughing. When the first soldier finished, the second soldier who had been holding my arms climbed on top of me. He didn't have as much facial hair as the first. The first soldier went and held down my arms. When they had me there on the ground I was shaking so much that they must have thought I was resisting them. They laughed at me. I did try to push them away but I realized there was nothing I could do because when they were on top of me they were so heavy.*

## Deposition: Felipe

*About the third or fourth month of the guerrilla's occupation, my father was still afraid even though he began to spend more time at home at night ... around that time the guerrillas must have decided to kill my father ... I was asleep one night when the door was broken down and many guerrillas burst into the house. I started to cry but couldn't do anything but stay in my bed, which was in the middle of a long room. My parents slept on one side of the room and my grandparents on the other side. When the guerrillas burst in it was hard to see since it was so dark and the only light came from flashlights they carried. It was so dark that I couldn't tell if they wore masks or not. They went over to my father's bed and started to beat him. I couldn't see it but I could hear them hitting him with their fists and I heard him crying ... I heard the guerrilla who was in charge telling the others to go get rope to tie us up ... they used one long rope to tie us all up so it took them a long time. I could see the light behind me while they tied my hands but I still couldn't see them. They took a rag they had brought and wrapped it tightly around my mouth and around my head ... when they finished with us they started to hit my father again. I could hear them hitting his face and his body; I could hear them kicking him with their boots. It seemed that my father was already hurt badly because his responses to their hitting him were weaker ... No one came to help us until it began to get light outside ... When our relative saw that we were tied up he ran to get a machete to untie us. He took the rags off our mouths and we asked him if he had seen my father ... Then my grandfather saw the boot marks of the guerrillas in the ground heading out to a field near our house. He started following the path and we ran behind him. He followed the path for about a half mile when he said, "there he is." We saw my father's body from a distance and ran to see if he was alive. We saw him, then, and we saw that his head had been cut off from his body and that his body was badly beaten ... Someone went back to our house to get a sheet. My grandfather and the man who had found us put my father's body on the sheet and carried him back to our house ... That night we had the wake. Not very many people came because they were afraid.*

## Deposition: Miriam

*Then, looking at me, he said, "then we are going to take her." I was terrified. I thought they were going to kill me ... the camp was located somewhere in the municipality of _____. The guerrillas there spoke many different [Mayan] languages. A _____ Indian and a man who spoke Spanish were the ones in charge. Most were dressed in green uniforms. The others wore civilian clothes ... The women guerrillas ordered me and the other women who cooked to do different things. I always knew I was a prisoner. There were always guards around the camp and they kept a close watch on us ... then things got even worse. One morning one of the other cooks, whose name was _____, and I were walking together to the place where we went to the latrine. It was about one hundred meters outside the camp ... This time, one of the guards grabbed _____ and pulled her aside. I heard _____ say to me, "be careful." Before I could do anything I felt something coming close to me and it was the other guard who had come up behind me. He grabbed me by my upper arm and spun me around and pushed me down with him on top of me. He got up on his knees and ripped off my blouse and pushed the waist of my skirt up. I didn't have any panties. I was trying to push him away and I was screaming when he put his hand over my mouth and said to me, "if you're going to scream, I can say that you are running away and I can kill you." He also said angrily if I told anyone what he was doing he would kill me. He was very mad. I stopped screaming and I tried to push him away but I couldn't because he was so strong. My arms were caught between him on top of me and my chest and I couldn't push him away. Then he raped me. As soon as he was finished with me, the only thing I could think about was to get away from him and the other guard as fast as I could. I ran towards the camp, trying to hold the ripped blouse together. I looked behind me as I ran and could only see the guard who raped me watching me ... About two weeks later I was raped again. I had to go to the latrine area alone in the afternoon. There were two different guards there. Before I could go to the bathroom one of them grabbed me from behind by my hair and pulled me down on my back. The same guard pulled my hands over my head and pinned them to the ground as the other guard came in front of me, flipped my skirt up and raped me. They didn't say anything.*

Photograph of urban Amerindian housing in Manaus, Brazil (author's photograph).

## 4 CULTURAL GENOCIDE, GENOCIDE, AND AMERINDIAN GENOCIDE 93

Photograph of urban Amerindian housing in Manaus, Brazil (author's photograph).

94   J. P. LINSTROTH

Photograph of urban Amerindian housing in Manaus, Brazil (author's photograph).

Photograph of Brazilian President Jair Bolsonaro.

## Introduction

Upon reflecting on these previous accounts of the Guatemalan genocide and the legal deposition narratives we might correctly ask like Beatriz Manz (2002: 300): "How, then, does one conduct research on grief? If terror continues to pierce the grief, how does one enter that desperate place and then interpret what respondents are saying? What methodology does one employ? ... In many Guatemalan villages, diverse, often contradictory, memories coexist concerning relations with the insurgent forces. What dynamics shape and reshape these multiple narratives? Over time, memories of the same events sometimes evolve into mirror images of each other when viewed from the recollections of those inside and outside the country." Truly, it is difficult to write about genocide and to elaborate on human suffering. Nonetheless, researchers too may bear witness to such atrocities in the past as well as ongoing atrocities and thereby aid in addressing the wrongs done. As Victoria Sanford (2008: 569) asserts about the Guatemalan genocide: "Moreover, the evidence suggest that we can and should make connections between practices and discourses of violence in the past and the present." Hence, this chapter is about making those connections of violence past and present perpetrated against indigenous peoples by interweaving narratives and understanding current genocidal practices.

As Alexander Laban Hinton (2002: 1) explicates: "With the rise of the nation-state and its imperialist and modernizing ambitions, tens of millions of 'backward' or 'savage' indigenous peoples perished from disease, starvation, slave labor, and outright murder. Sixty million others were also annihilated in the twentieth century, often after nation-states embarked upon lethal projects of social engineering intent upon eliminating certain undesirable and 'contaminating' elements of the population." Indeed, as the previous chapter considered how ethno-nationalist minorities like Basques and Catalans and to some extent Northern Irish Catholics challenge the nation-state, here in relation to genocide, it is the state through its agents of power that perpetrates atrocities amounting to genocide. Minorities in this sense are wiped out because of the extreme prejudices against them for varying socio-economic, socio-historical, and socio-political reasons. States in this regard may go to war with their own peoples. Yet, often, as is the case of indigenous peoples, they are not recognized as "people" but as subhuman to be done away with.

Here in this chapter mostly I try to make sense of the genocide being perpetrated against Brazilian Amerindians, especially because of the negligent policies of Brazilian President Jair Bolsonaro and his administration, and the repercussions this has had for illegal mining and illegal logging activities leading to many indigenous deaths. Additionally, however, I discuss the genocide against the Sentinelese Jarawa people, against the Uighurs of Western China, and those genocidal practices against Native peoples of the Americas, particularly Brazil, but also in Canada and in the United States. My portrayal too touches upon the Aboriginal peoples of Australia and their experiences of genocide there. This chapter is also critical of the Brazilian government's handling of Coronavirus (COVID-19) in relation to Brazilian Amerindians. Even so, the chapter is not all-encompassing and should not be seen as the final word about such horrendous practices in these regions around the globe.

What this chapter attempts to address are the following questions: "Why does one group of human beings set out to eradicate another group from the face of the earth? What are the origins and processes involved in such mass murder? How do we respond to the bodily, material, and psychological devastation it causes? How might we go about predicting or preventing it in the twenty-first century?" (Hinton 2002: 1). Furthermore, I agree with Alexander Laban Hinton that anthropologists are uniquely positioned to address these questions because we work in the communities where such violence takes place and/or speak with victims who are survivors of such violence (Hinton 2002: 1). As such, this chapter elaborates on the genocides happening now in our world whether in the Andaman and Nicobar Islands, or Western China, or the United States, or Canada, or Australia, or Brazil—genocide is going on now. This chapter then aims to bring about awareness and a sense of urgency and, ultimately, if possible, the prevention of such outrages and wrongs.

## PROTECTING THE MOST VULNERABLE FROM GENOCIDE

Ghosts of European colonialism still haunt us today even in the twenty-first century. This was evident from the untimely death of American John Allen Chau, 26, from Washington state on November 16, 2018 at the hands of Sentinelese Jarawa people from the Andaman Islands.[1]

The last days of Mr. Chau are reminiscent of the novel *At Play in the Fields of the Lord* (1965) by late naturalist Peter Mathiessen, where everything goes wrong for the Christian missionaries, as they did for Chau. This young American was naively determined to eradicate what he called "Satan's last stronghold" in the world and paid for it with his own life.

There are only about one hundred Sentinelese Jarawa people left.[2] They are fiercely independent, rejecting contact with outsiders and culturally remaining intact. Jarawa are small-statured and ebony-complexioned, and thought to be remnants of people who originally migrated thousands of years ago from Africa and settled in the Andaman Islands east of India and west of Myanmar. For the most part, the Indian government has been successful in preventing interlopers from accessing their island. Chau paid some local fishermen to reach these remote Jarawa people.[3]

As these tribal people have managed to remain isolated, they are also highly susceptible to viral contagion, even from the common cold and flu.

As an anthropologist who writes about indigenous issues, I am aware how much European colonialism is an ever-present issue in the minds and memories of many indigenous peoples because of the horrifying genocide wreaked upon them.

Indeed, there are very few "uncontacted" indigenous peoples remaining in our globalized planet. The majority of uncontacted Natives may be found in the Amazon region in the borderland areas of Bolivia, Brazil, and Peru.[4] Anthropologists are continually worried about the safety of such vulnerable people because of their lacking immunity to Western-borne illnesses and threats from outsiders as tourists, illegal loggers, and gold miners encroaching upon their territories.

In assessing the situation of isolated people like the Sentinelese Jarawa of the Andaman Islands as well as the isolated Amerindians in the Amazon, we need to return to the history of Western thought and Western civilization for explaining the problems associated with contact in relation to indigenous peoples and Europeans.

We may begin with the Abrahamic religions' origin story of Adam and Eve, who bit from the forbidden fruit of knowledge in the biblical Old Testament and were ejected from Eden by Yahweh. The symbolism is fairly clear. The Garden of Eden represents idyllic nature or the thousands of years when humankind spent hunting and gathering until the Neolithic Revolution about 12,000 years ago with the domestication of plants and animals.[5] This was the so-called transition to civilization, eventually producing states, writing, hierarchies and class systems, organized religion, slavery, mass warfare, science, astronomy, mathematics, and genocide. It was a knowledge supposing humankind was somehow separate from nature and humans were superior to nature—at least to Western minds in the Judeo-Christian tradition.

What is more, in the "Age of Exploration," Europeans believed they had to "civilize" non-Western people and bring them God's word and convert Natives to European ways. As such, along with killing and torturing Natives, Europeans made it a practice of saving indigenes from their supposed state of nature, ignorance, and savagery.

When the Portuguese first landed in Brazil in 1500, Pêro Vaz de Caminha wrote King Manoel I: "They seem to be such innocent people that, if we could understand their speech and they ours, they would immediately become Christians. For it appears that they do not have or understand any faith."[6] Salvation of Natives indeed became one of the primary projects of the conquest.

Such religious proselytizing supposes, like Mr. Chau, Native peoples have no minds and no wills of their own and are devoid of religious thought. They are rather Native objects and vessels who require filling with the true faith brought to them by force, if necessary—why would God give the means of force to the colonizers unless He wanted them to convert the Natives?

Witness accounts from the Spanish conquest such as those of Bartolomé de las Casas describe how devastating the violence against Indians was, such as during the invasion of Peru: "I affirm that with my own eyes I saw Spaniards cut off the nose, hands, and ears of Indians, male and female, without provocation, merely because it pleased them to do it, and this they did in so many places that it would take a long time to recount."[7]

Similarly, here is an eyewitness account by Captain Nicholas Hodt of a 1861 massacre of Navajo (*Diné*) in present-day Arizona: "The Navahos, squaws, and children ran in all directions and were shot and bayoneted. I succeeded in forming about twenty men ... I then marched out to the east side of the post; there I saw a soldier murdering two little children and a woman. I hallooed immediately to the soldier to stop. He looked up, but did not obey my order."[8]

The arc of history of this protracted genocide, from massacres like "Wounded Knee" against the Sioux in 1890, or more recently, the effects of development in the Brazilian Amazon during the 1960s, is long and collectively never forgotten by descendants of the victims. In every case, Aboriginal peoples are subsequently plagued by a sense of loss of their identities, homelands, ways of life, cultures, resulting often in alcoholism, domestic violence, drug abuse, and suicide.

Unbeknownst to most Americans, Hitler partially based his ideas of the concentration camp and extermination of European Jews on Native American reservations and our racial policies in the United States.[9] Americans systematically conquered original peoples and justified the ensuing genocide with the idea of "Manifest Destiny," a term coined by journalist John O'Sullivan, meaning the divine right to settle the continental United States from "sea to shining sea." The Natives were just part of the natural landscape and in the way.[10]

Genocide continues happening now in Brazil with the persecution of the Guarani-Kaiowá on ranch lands in Mato Grosso do Sul. Even more worrying is that newly elected Brazilian President Jair Bolsonaro promises to persecute Brazilian Amerindians for their lands.[11]

Like the Sentinelese Jarawa who voluntarily choose to be isolated, the Mashco-Piro people of Western Peru live by choice without contact. As anthropologist Glenn Shepard, of the Museu Emilio Goeldi of Brazil, explains: "Isolated Amazonian groups have not remained stuck in the Stone Age since time immemorial. Rather, they have resorted to 'voluntary isolation' in modern times in order to survive."

"Civilization" is an ambivalent outcome at best for indigenous peoples. At this late date, it is likely that we can learn much more from them than the reverse. After all, their lifeways would sustain for unknown millennia, whereas climate chaos, nuclear annihilation, resource depletion and contamination—products of conquering empires—are supplanting genocide with societal suicide. Time to listen instead of preaching, time to slow down, consume much less, and respect all peoples and our planet.

## Will Ethnocide in Western China Become Genocide?[12]

At this moment, China has as many as 1 million Uighurs, Kazakhs, and other Muslim minorities held in concentration camps in Xinjiang Uyghur Autonomous Region (XUAR) in northwestern China. This has been ongoing for some time now and is beginning, finally, to be noticed.[13]

This unfolding tragedy is well known to the United Nations as well as to influential governments such as the United States. Thus far, little is being done to prevent the Chinese from carrying out its concerted efforts in imprisoning and politically indoctrinating its Muslim populations. It is so objectionable that Badger Sportswear of North Carolina announced it stopped purchasing imports from that region of China due to credible reports of mass forced labor.[14]

The Chinese government is spending huge amounts of money in Xinjiang Province, where these ethnocidal horrors are taking place. These so-called re-education camps have been analyzed by the Australian Strategic Policy Institute (ASPI). The ASPI examined twenty-eight camps in Xinjiang but stated there may be as many as 1200 across the entire region. Since 2016, the ASPI found an increase in growth of these camps to almost 470 percent.[15]

In 1981 the Chinese signed onto and ratified the International Convention on the Elimination of All Forms of Racial Discrimination (CERD), but these camps clearly violate that law.[16] Chinese officials also heavily police the region, using surveillance cameras and security checkpoints, biometric data collection, voice recordings, and requiring identification cards of its mostly Uighur population in Xinjiang. According to the most recent estimates, there are most likely 11,000,000 Uighurs and 1.6 million Kazakhs living in the Western Chinese Province of Xinjiang.[17]

Perhaps the best and most extensive report about the current situation in Xinjiang is by "Human Rights Watch" (September 2018). One Uighur refugee, Tohti, is quoted as saying: "What they want is to force us to assimilate, to identify with the country [China], such that, in the future, the idea of Uyghur will be in name only, but without its meaning."[18] From the Human Rights Watch Report we learn the Chinese government has arbitrarily detained its Muslim-minority population, and not only this, these Turkic Chinese Muslims have been abused, tortured, and deprived of fair trials. The Chinese want to eliminate basic freedoms of religion among this population for practicing Islam. The re-education of these Turkic Muslims is meant to Sino-assimilate or "Sinicize" them with Chinese identities, scrubbing them of their religious identity.

Two other refugees told Human Rights Watch: "[The guards] told us that Uyghurs and Kazakhs are the enemies of China, and that they want to kill us, and make us suffer, and that there's nothing we can do about it."[19] Another stated: "[A detainee] showed me his scar from being hung from the ceiling. He didn't have any religious materials, but after being hung for a night, he said he would agree to anything." Others had died while in detention and their families were not allowed to bury the dead with Islamic blessings or ceremonies and were forced to bury their loved ones under military watch.

Aside from the political aspects of Chinese social control, how do we understand this type of discrimination in relation to modern world history?

Humans are highly complex and for the most part racism is entirely a social construct, usually involving essentializing entire populations and persecuting them *en masse*, virtually always with a veneer of rhetoric to make it all acceptable unless we actually look. The histories are shameful. Thus, we saw all non-Europeans referred to as, what Rudyard Kipling euphemistically called them, the "white man's burden";[20] Jews and Gypsies sent by Germans to labor camps with sayings such as Work is Freedom; land stolen from Native tribes in the name of "progress"; Tutsis slaughtered by Hutus to "protect" themselves from a minority; Japanese-American families rounded up into compounds in Western United States during World War II to secure the homeland; and millions of Armenian civilians killed by Turkey a century ago to punish traitors, and other horrific chapters in our human story.[21] Almost all the terrible responses in the modern era that target innocent civilians are massive overreactions to violent attack. In China, those attacks from Islamic extremists were in 2013 and 2014 and have been the official justification for mass incarceration since then.[22]

The magnitude of China's efforts to incarcerate its Turkic Muslim-minority populations is happening in an unprecedented way, which we have not seen since Nazi Germany and the imprisonment of Jews throughout Europe. As usual, there is an official rationale and a public relations effort, including the approval of the Saudi Crown Prince Mohammed bin Salman, aka MBS, which "proves" that China's systematic persecution of Chinese Muslims for religion is not its sole rationale.[23]

How many more Muslim Chinese minorities need to be imprisoned before we say no more? When should the UN Security Council act in concert against China? When should the United States begin imposing economic sanctions upon China for its human rights abuses in Xinjiang, northwestern China?

We know from our human history that it almost always takes outside pressure to bring regimes back from the brink of genocide. Yet, we also need to be aware of our own Western Islamophobia and Western populist rhetoric and in general "China Bashing" according to anthropologist Dru Gladney and instead build bridges and helpful ties with China too.[24]

## Why Indigenous Lives Should Matter

In the United States, we live in a "post-genocide" society, whether or not we are cognizant of this fact or not. What do I mean by that? In order for the United States to have fulfilled its so-called Manifest Destiny—the divine right to conquer the lands west of the Mississippi River—we needed to wipe out the remaining Native Americans living on Western lands. The idea was coined by journalist John O. Sullivan in 1845 when he stated: "In the spirit of hostile interference against us, for the avowed object of thwarting our policy and hampering our power, limiting our greatness and checking the fulfillment of our manifest destiny to overspread the continent allotted by Providence for the free development of our yearly multiplying millions."[25]

Today, unfortunately, many indigenous peoples are still broken because of this past genocidal history. Native Americans were put on reservations, their lands were stolen, and their cultural heritage was dismissed and eradicated through the boarding school system.[26]

Those Natives currently living on reservations do so 40–60 percent below the poverty line.[27] Also, Native Americans are also 82 percent more likely to die from suicide than Caucasians and 2.3 times more likely to die from diabetes than whites. Further, Natives are also likely to have endemic alcoholic problems.[28] Statistically, more than a quarter of American Indian and Alaska Natives are more likely to live in poverty, more than double the general population, and more likely to experience violence and traumatic events than other populations.[29]

On Pine Ridge Reservation among the Lakota and Oglala Sioux with a population of about 20,000, there are 11,000 cans of beer consumed per day and 4 million cans per year from nearby Whiteclay, Nebraska. As one Lakota-Sioux woman described it: "Whiteclay is a hole … It's been based on liquid genocide for generations."[30] As such, trauma causes alcoholism, and to many Sioux people, the 1890 Wounded Knee Massacre at Pine Ridge, has been an ever-occurring trauma and was highlighted by the American Indian Movement (AIM) occupation in 1973 as protest to the past violence as well as Bureau of Indian Affairs' (BIA) inequities.[31]

Yet, the United States has not been alone in its maltreatment of its indigenous populations. For example, Australia, Brazil, and Canada, have similar histories of genocide against their Aboriginal peoples. In the cases of Australia and Canada, like the United States, are only recently coming to terms with their genocidal histories. On the other hand, Brazil is still massacring its indigenous peoples in favor of agro-businesses, cattle ranching, hydro-electric dam construction, timber extraction, mining and oil operations, and other development schemes in Amazonia.

There is a psychological pattern which follows on from massacres of indigenous peoples, which is suffering from alcoholism, child neglect, domestic violence, and sexual abuse. Moreover, there is increasing evidence demonstrating an epigenetic association of transgenerational trauma, that is traumatized parents genetically passing on trauma effects to their children. The trauma of the external is internalized, scarring populations for years.[32]

This was the case among the Oombulgurri people in northwestern Australia and the "Forrest River Massacre" of 1926 when thirty Aboriginal Oombulgurri people were murdered by white settlers.[33] The remaining population suffered from alcohol abuse, child neglect, domestic violence, sexual abuse, and suicide. The history of Aboriginal massacres throughout Australian history may be characterized as "conspiracies of silence." The countless tragic murders were covered up, bodies burned, evidence falsified, not discussed, or witnesses just disappeared, which became known as the "Great Australian Silence," according to Australian anthropologist William Stanner, and "a cult of forgetfulness."[34] Some of the knowledge about these massacres have been passed on from Aboriginal oral histories through the generations while material evidence remains scarce.

According to the Centre for 21st Century Humanities at Newcastle University, Australia, there were conservatively about 14,387 Aborigines and Torres Strait Islanders murdered between 1788 and 1930 in 522 massacres in Central and Eastern Australia and Torres Strait Islands.[35] At least fifty-one of these massacres occurred as reprisals for "killing or theft of livestock or property."[36] Yet, other estimates suggest there were at least 60,000 Aborigines murdered.[37] There were possibly some 1 million Aborigines living in Australia prior to European contact, and by 1901 had been reduced to over 100,000 First Nations people.[38] Originally, Aborigines spoke perhaps 250 languages, of which about 145 languages are still spoken today and of which 110 are critically endangered.[39]

Only now have Australian officials begun apologizing for such atrocities. Even raising a monument about past massacres has been difficult for survivor Aboriginal families such as the one at Waterloo Bay, when about 200 Wirangu and Kokatha people were killed near Elliston, South Australia.[40]

But there have also been some tearful reconciliations as well. Descendants of white militia-soldiers responsible for massacres as well as Aboriginal victim-descendants have gathered to commemorate the murders of men, women, and children lost from the Dharawal, Gandangarra, and Muringong Nations in the Appin Massacre of 1816, near Sydney.[41]

Elsewhere in the Northern Hemisphere, First Nations people at the Cat Lake Reservation declared a state of emergency in Northern Ontario, Canada, because of excessively poor housing conditions—mold, leaky roofs, and undrinkable water. Native children also suffer from skin ailments and facial sores. One tribal member died from respiratory-related problems, causing much outrage. "The government's complacency is usually at the cost of our people's lives. There's just no will to fix the problem," stated a member of the provincial parliament for Kiiwetinoong in northern Ontario, including Cat Lake Reservation.[42] In all about 700 First Nations people live at Cat Lake Reservation. Fortunately, the Canadian government has responded by sending aid in the amount of about $10 million but some Natives have commented the problem is endemic throughout Canada and not limited to Cat Lake Reservation.

On another indigenous Canadian reservation, the Six Nations Reservation (Mohawk, Cayuga, Onondaga, Oneida, Seneca, and Tuscarora) of the Grand River in Ontario near Toronto, the multinational corporation Nestlé is extracting millions of liters of drinking water from reservation lands, while the Native peoples themselves do without.[43] Most Native peoples living on this reservation do not have running water while Nestlé sells the water from their land. It is one of many ironic tragedies associated with indigenous peoples and the first world.

On the other hand, in the Southern Hemisphere of the Americas, in Brazil, indigenous peoples there are fighting for recognition and struggling against new directives of President Jair Bolsonaro to limit Amerindian rights and eradicate tribal lands. Peoples such as the Waimiri-Atroari have asked the government to recognize their genocide during the construction of Highway BR-174 beginning in 1970.[44] On the other hand, the Uru-Eu-Wau-Wau, an Amerindian group of only about 120 people, are fighting against outsiders encroaching on their lands for tin mining, timber extraction, and farmlands delimiting their lands.[45]

Brazil's President Bolsonaro has proclaimed indigenous peoples are like "animals in zoos" and he favors development projects prospecting for precious minerals on Native lands.[46] Nevertheless, Brazil's 1988 Constitution prevents mining and commercial farming on Amerindian lands without congressional approval. Bolsonaro appears to be adamant in ignoring the 1988 Constitution. For Native Brazilians, it is a desperate situation. Many indigenous peoples believe they are fighting for their lives. In fact, in central Brazil, the Kayapó people are readying themselves for warfare with Bolsonaro. One Kayapó elder chief stated: "We are ready to go to war against any misstep from President Bolsonaro … He wants to reduce our land, he wants to end our traditions, and we are warriors defending our rainforest, our river, and our culture."[47]

The Swiss-Brazilian photographer Claudia Andujar, who along with French-anthropologist Bruce Albert and other Brazilian anthropologists and shaman-chief Davi Kopenawa, helped demarcate Yanomami lands in the early 1980s, and together, they have carefully documented the current genocide of Yanomami people from gold prospectors (*garimpeiros*).[48] Additionally, oil companies and agribusinesses are vying for Yanomami lands, while Bolsonaro openly encourages such disastrous and illegal incursions.

So, what is to be done? First, we must recognize how indigenous peoples have been dehumanized and how such dehumanization has led to genocide. Moreover, we must recognize many indigenous peoples live in areas of the world needing protection for the sake of our environment and our planet. The Brazilian Amazon is just one good example. Second, we need to recognize the needs for a healing process to begin for past atrocities against Native peoples. On the other hand, indigenous peoples themselves must be recognized as having the right to decide for themselves appropriate ways to remember genocides against them. So, truth and reconciliation commissions should be established to be able to heal and listen to truth telling. Likewise, apologies should be official and made by governments and reparations should be established for survivor-descendant victims.

Reconciliation begins with apologizing, with truth-telling, and with commemorating the wrongs done. As the great Hunkpapa-Lakota Sioux Chief Sitting Bull purportedly said: "Let us put our minds together and see what life we can make for our children."

## Preventing Brazilian Indigenous Genocide and Protecting the Amazon

On the first day of the year 2019, Jair Bolsonaro was inaugurated as the thirty-eighth President of Brazil. One of his first official acts as a newly inaugurated president was doing away with demarcation of indigenous territories in Brazil. All of us living on this planet should be fearful of this act.

Bolsonaro transferred the responsibility of demarcation of indigenous lands to the Brazilian Ministry of Agriculture and placed the National Indian Foundation (FUNAI, *Fundação Nacional do Índio*) under its jurisdiction. It is FUNAI's responsibility to protect the nation's Indians and yet the Ministry of Agriculture is traditionally known to protect the interests of big business, especially soy farmers and cattle ranchers. Both are powerful lobbying groups in Brazil and likewise partly responsible for destroying the Amazon and its people. In effect, FUNAI is no more under the Bolsonaro administration.

We should also realize this is not only a fulfilled campaign promise of Bolsonaro but a realized fear for the legitimation of genocide against Brazilian indigenous peoples and also the imminent destruction of the Brazilian Amazon. It is also important to note that 60 percent of the Amazon is under Brazilian jurisdiction.

At the end of November 2018, a United Nations Convention on Biological Diversity was held in Egypt. It was there many of the world's Amazonian indigenous leaders proposed a 200-million-hectare corridor stretching from the Atlantic Ocean to the Andes mountains along the great meandering Amazon River and its tributaries in order to protect the world's largest rainforest and its incredibly varied fauna and flora. Such an ecological plan would protect not only the forest and its wildlife but its many indigenous peoples and their lands. What is more, such a scheme may have the long-term benefit of preventing climate change and global warming from becoming inevitable realities.

To understand the immensity of such a proposed biodiversity corridor, think of an area the size of Mexico and 500 different Amazonian indigenous nations with their wide array of cultures living within it. Ponder for a moment that 10 million species of animals, insects, and plants exist within the Amazon rainforest. Almost 80 percent of the world's biodiversity is to be found on indigenous lands and Native territories are some of the most biodiverse on earth.

Now more than ever we should be taking such environmental propositions very seriously for the fate of humankind. The proposal to protect the Amazon with a "sacred corridor of life and culture" was presented by COICA (Coordinator of Indigenous Organizations of the Amazon River Basin, *Coordinadora de las Organizaciones Indígenas de la Cuenca Amazónica*) at the UN conference.

Yet, Brazilian President Bolsonaro and newly elected Colombian President Iván Duque Márquez, along with other powerful business leaders, most likely will not consider such a plan because of economic interests for developing the Amazon for energy (e.g., hydro-electric dam projects and oil prospecting), mining (e.g., excavating gold), resource exploitation (e.g., timber extraction) and agri-businesses (e.g., cattle ranching and soy farming). The UN biodiversity agreement was signed in Beijing, China, in 2020.

President Bolsonaro has infamously likened indigenous peoples residing on protected territories in Brazil to "animals in zoos" (*como animais em zoo*). When humans dehumanize other humans, and equate them with non-human animals, we know psychologically such rhetoric allows for genocide. This was evident from the Rwanda genocide when Hutu heard racist radio messages about Tutsi equating them to cockroaches, among other things. Such directed racism allowed for the near Tutsi extermination, ranging between 500,000 and 1,000,000 killings in 1994. Similarly, Hitler's propagandists relentlessly compared Jews to rats. We know those results.

In a recent 2018 report commissioned by the Climate and Land Use Alliance (CLU), *Impacts on Extractive Industry and Infrastructure on Forests: Amazonia*, the following was stated: "large-scale infrastructure development, in particular road building and hydropower, have induced human settlement, forest clearance and an aggressive expansion of the agricultural frontier across substantial parts of Amazonia. The synergies between agriculture and infrastructure are important, particularly in the Legal Amazon. The scale of future changes in forest cover will depend on where and how infrastructure investments move forward."

There are presently about 850,000 Natives in Brazil. Bolsonaro believes they should be forcibly assimilated and integrated into Brazilian society along with Afro-slave descendants or Quilombolas living in the hinterland.

Three prominent Brazilian indigenous leaders, Davi Kopenawa Yanomami, Sônia Bone Guajajara, and Raoni Metuktire, have written a letter to the world to express their alarm. Their peoples live in different areas of the Brazilian Amazon.

The Yanomami people have been mostly isolated, living in Brazil and Venezuela, numbering some 35,000 people. Since the 1980s, Yanomami have been subject to massacres from Brazilian gold miners (*garimpeiros*) who have also brought disease and mass death. The Guajajara people live in the state of Maranhão and number some 19,000 people. During the 1960s through 1980s, there have been concerted efforts to develop and illegally settle on their lands. The Kayapó live in the states of Mato Grosso and Pará and number some 9000 people. Since the late 1980s, they have been fighting hydroelectric dam projects on their lands. The ongoing Belo Monte Dam will flood vast areas of Kayapó territories and have a very lasting negative impact upon the survival of these people by limiting fishing and massively destroying both fauna and flora.

Davi Kopenawa, Sônia Guajajara, and Raoni Metuktire stated in their letter:

> A genocide is unfolding in our country, Brazil. Our government is destroying us, indigenous peoples, our country's first people. In the name of profit and power, our land is being stolen, our forests burned, our rivers polluted and our communities devastated. Our uncontacted relatives, who live deep in the forest, are being attacked and killed … This is the most aggressive attack we have experienced in our lifetimes. But we won't be silenced. We do not want the riches of our land to be stolen and sold. For as long as we can remember, we have looked after our lands. We protect our forest as it gives us life … Please tell our government that our land is not for stealing.[49]

We should heed their warning and not allow the Brazilian government to sanction such a genocide against Brazilian Indians and simply remain silent. It is time to speak up.

Not only are nearly 1 million Brazilian indigenous lives at stake, but the Amazon rainforest as a world natural resource is in certain jeopardy without protective measures. The "sacred corridor" plan proposed by COICA at the 2018 UN Biodiversity Conference is a good beginning to ensure 2 million square kilometers of rainforest land along the Amazon River and its vast tributaries be preserved and safeguarded for future generations.

Let's begin by helping and protecting these people and the Amazon before it is too late.

## The Politics of Denial, the Brazilian President, and the Fate of Amazonia

With the murder of the Amerindian, Paulo Paulino Guajajara, on November 1, 2019, by Brazilian illegal loggers, was clear evidence of genocidal practices against Brazil's indigenous population continuing today. Paulino's people, *O Povo Guajajara*, are some of the most numerous Native peoples in Brazil, numbering nearly 30,000 and living in the Amazonian state of Maranhão in northeast Brazil. Paulo Paulino was also a member of the self-designated group, "Guardians of the Forest" (*Guardiões da Floresta*), who patrol their enormous indigenous reserve, *Araribóia*, some 1595 square miles (4130 square kilometers), almost twice the size of Rhode Island, in order to protect the forest against illegal loggers and illegal poachers.

According to CIMI (*Conselho Indigenista Missionario*, Catholic Indigenist Missionary Council) in 2018, the murder of indigenous peoples grew by 20 percent from the previous year to 135 cases and in the previous thirty-years there have been 1119 homicides of Brazilian Native peoples.[50] Most of these murders occurred in the Brazilian states of Roraima and secondarily in Mato Grosso do Sul. Such incidents in their majority are driven by soy farmers (*fazendeiros*) and cattle ranchers (*rancheiros*) and should be alarming to everyone around the globe. *Fazendeiros* and *rancheiros* do not want "Indians" (*Índios*) on their lands, or near their lands, and land-grabbers want to take indigenous lands for themselves, as illegal-loggers and goldminers wish to exploit Native lands. Moreover, invasions on indigenous reservations in Brazil have doubled from the year prior with as many as 153 documented cases by CIMI from illegal goldminers (*garimpeiros*), illegal loggers, land-grabbers, and poachers.[51] Even worse, the crimes against Brazilian indigenous peoples are rarely prosecuted.[52] As the indigenous kinswoman to the murdered Indian, and leader, Sonia Guajajara, remarked: "The indigenous genocide of Brazil is legitimized by the discourse of the president [Bolsonaro]."[53]

As such, the genocide happening now against indigenous peoples in Brazil has received relatively little attention outside the country. Anthropologists, like myself, fear this genocide happening against Brazilian indigenous peoples will likely endure in the long term because of the rhetoric of Brazilian President Jair Bolsonaro and his economic development policies for Amazonia.

Furthermore, adding to these tragedies we know that the Brazilian *Patanal* (wetlands) was burning at an incredible rate in 2019.[54] These conflagrations are similarly colossal as the record-breaking fires in the Brazilian Amazon over the course of 2019. In the Brazilian state of Mato Grosso do Sul the fires are said have consumed an area of at least 50,000 hectares (193 square miles) or about the size of the Island of Guam already. In November 2019, there was allegedly a 31-mile (50-kilometer) fire advancing across the Brazilian wetlands (*Patanal*). According to reports these fires began on October 25, 2019 and have increased because of dry conditions and high winds.

And aside from these man-made environmental disasters in Brazil, there have been others still. On January 25, 2019, the *Brumadinho* Dam in Minas Gerais state collapsed, killing at least 250 people in a giant mudslide releasing tons of toxic waste from an iron-ore mine nearby.[55] It was Brazil's worst industrial accident to date, proving how Brazilian business regulations are severely lacking. Ironically, a similar dam disaster occurred in Minas Gerais years earlier in November of 2015, when the *Mariana* Dam collapsed, which also released toxic sludge from an iron-ore mine, killing nineteen people, but completely contaminating the Rio Doce, causing an unprecedented environmental disaster at the time.[56]

Equally, there are the planned and ongoing hydro-electric dam constructions in the Brazilian Amazon, such as the Belo Monte Dam along the Xingu River which would flood thousands of kilometers of indigenous lands and adversely affect the livelihoods and well-being of numerous indigenous peoples inclusive of the Arara, Araweté, Asurini, Juruna, Kayapó, Parakanã, and Xikrin, as well as negatively affecting the immense biodiversity in the region.[57] In addition, dam constructions are planned for the Upper Madeira River, the Jirau and San Antônio dams. Like the Belo Monte Dam, the ones along the Madeira River will disastrously affect Apurinã, Cassupá, Jiahui, Karipuna, Karitiana, Katawixi, Mura, Oro Ari, Oro Bom, Parintintin, Pirahã, Salamãi, Tenharim, Torá, and Urueu Wau Wau indigenous peoples and the biodiversity of this lower region of the Amazon.[58]

In July of 2019, the Yanomami territories in the northern Brazilian Amazon, bordering and including those lands in Venezuela, were invaded by an estimated 20,000 illegal goldminers (*garimpeiros*), polluting the Rio Branco with mercury, and spreading disease to the Yanomami people.[59] In 1992 Yanomami land reserves in Brazil were designated as a protected park covering some 37,000 square miles (nearly 100,000 square kilometers), an area a bit bigger than the state of Indiana. Such recent invasions are reminiscent of the *garimpeiro* incursions of the 1980s, causing mass deaths among the Yanomami from the *garimpeiro* spread of "white" diseases such as measles, for which indigenous peoples living in remote areas have little immunity.

Organizations such as the "Society for the Anthropology of Lowland South America" (SALSA) have sent open letters about the unprecedented fires in Brazilian Amazonia, stating: "Since taking office earlier this year, President Jair Bolsonaro and the 'ruralist' parliamentary block have sought to open indigenous lands up to mining and logging operations; have slashed the budgets and oversight potential of environmental agencies; have backed an 'economic liberty' suite of policies for agribusiness; have vowed that the government will not demarcate 'one more centimeter' of indigenous land in Brazil, and have taken steps to try to decertify (rob) existing indigenous reserves. The parliamentary assault on indigenous peoples and on Amazonian ecosystems is vast, coordinated, and has been decades in the making ... As anthropologists who have the privilege of working with the originary peoples of Amazonia, we also have the obligation to condemn the racist rhetoric and genocidal policies pursued by the current Brazilian government" (dated August 25, 2019).[60]

When Brazilian President Jair Bolsonaro addressed the United Nations Assembly on September 24, 2019, he unfortunately disseminated a dangerous propaganda message about the Yanomami living on rich mineral reserves by declaring: "In these reserves, there is plenty of gold, diamond, uranium, niobium, and rare earths, among others." Thereby, encouraging the types of egregious invasions by the thousands of *garimpeiros* illegally invading Yanomami territories and underlining how such few Indians live on such immense reserves of land. Such treacherous rhetoric gives a "green light" to land-grabbers, illegal-loggers, illegal-miners, and poachers to invade Native Brazilian lands with impunity. What is more, Bolsonaro's political oratory has provided greater impetus for soy farmers and cattle ranchers to burn more land for their crops and livestock.

In sum, President Bolsonaro practices a politics of "denial," by denying that man-made catastrophes such as the fires in Amazonia, or now in the *Patanal* (wetlands), or the genocide against indigenous peoples are anything but real. In the mind of Bolsonaro and many of his supporters, the man-made environmental disasters occurring in Brazil are concocted by the fake media, by communists, by NGOs, and by foreign conspirators—all supposedly willing to undermine Brazil's sovereignty and its national authority to deal with such issues alone.

In fact, in his UN speech, Bolsonaro also remarked: "The Amazon is not being destroyed nor consumed by fire, as the media is falsely portraying." He also avowed: "Brazil reaffirms its unwavering commitment to the highest human rights standards, with the promotion of democracy and freedom—of expression, of religion, and of press."

It is with a heavy heart that I state this but Brazil's human rights record points to the contrary of President Bolsonaro's hyperbolic pronouncements. Aside from the increased violence against indigenous people and a notable increase in man-made environmental disasters, as I mentioned above, Brazil has a horrendous record in "freedom of expression" of its press and in "human rights standards" in general as recounted by organizations as Amnesty International and Human Rights Watch. As their separate reports have detailed, there are presently in Brazil excessive and notorious examples of assaults on the media, police abuses, domestic violence, gender discrimination, harassment of educators, and violence against environmental activists.[61]

As the indigenous leader, Executive Coordinator of APIB (Brazil's Indigenous Peoples Articulation, *Articulação dos Povos Indígenas do Brasil*), and kinswoman of murdered Paulo Paulino, Sonia Guajajara, exclaimed recently: "We no longer want to be statistics; we want measures from the government, the bodies that are increasingly being scrapped [like the National Indian Foundation, FUNAI, *Fundação Nacional do Índio*], and thereby precisely not able to protect the very people who are paying with their lives for doing the work that is the responsibility of the state. We demand urgent justice!"[62]

## Genocidal Disease (COVID-19) as It Is Happening in Amazonia

Back in 2009 with a Fulbright Foreign Scholarship and as a Visiting Professor at the Universidade Federal do Amazonas (UFAM), I conducted ethnographic fieldwork in the Amazonian and Brazilian city of Manaus of over 2 million people among urban Amerindians there. The urbanized Native peoples living in Manaus, the capitol of Amazonas State, may number as many as 50,000 or more nowadays. Of this urban Amerindian population, I worked with and studied the Apurinã, Kambeba, Kokama,

Munduruku, Mura, Sateré-Mawé, Tikuna, and Tukano peoples over a period of seven months.

Up until that time, I had never been exposed to such immense destitution and poverty. The Indians living in Manaus usually inhabited dwellings made mostly from pieced-together plywood and/or tin with dirt floors, no electricity, and no running water. For those dwellings with some electricity, it was stolen from a nearby electric power-pole and transformer. For some there was often a communal-well providing the community with water. Among the urban Sateré-Mawé I worked with, and on the week before I had arrived, neighbors to the community burned down the school-house building because they did not want Natives in their vicinity. Racism against these peoples continues to this day.[63] Whites (*os brancos*) living in Manaus will not recognize such urbanized Indians as indigenous peoples because they are thought to be "civilized" (*civilizados*), and therefore, no longer Indians. Of course, this is untrue and is racist. But more Indians live in Brazil's cities than they do in the interior.

And yet, nobody could have imagined a global pandemic like Coronavirus (COVID-19) affecting these Amerindian peoples in this way, so remote from the rest of Brazil, and even in this city of Manaus, the largest in the Amazon region.[64] In reality this genocidal nightmare from this disease may only likely be compared with the chickenpox, influenza, measles, and smallpox brought by Europeans more than 500 years ago to these Amerindian peoples. Anthropologists and geographers estimate those diseases may have wiped out as many as 90 percent of those early indigenous contact populations, as many as 56 million people.[65] Thus, what we witnessed in 2020 was "genocidal disease," and COVID-19 may continue its devastating destruction in these far reaches of Lowland South America and across Amazonia, exterminating Amerindian peoples. And while 2020 was truly devastating, the vaccine "is" reaching the far outposts of Amazonia, albeit slowly. Even so, the disease had a deleterious effect upon Amerindian populations. Now, in 2021, it is really a race against time.[66]

Nevertheless, in 2020, the rest of Brazil was paying attention to Manaus because of the ensuing health crisis there. While Manaus is not an entirely Amerindian-city, many Manaurans have indigenous descent in their family heritage, and elsewhere might be considered to be *caboclo* (a mixed-heritage person with both Indian and white ancestry), or *misturado* (mixed). Photographs of hundreds of freshly dug graves at the Parque Tarumã Cemetery just outside Manaus indicate the absolute devastation.[67]

Manaus's mayor, Arthur Virgílio, proclaimed in exasperation: "We aren't in a state of emergency—we're well beyond that. We are in a state of utter disaster ... like a country that is at war—and has lost."[68] In May 2020, Manaus was estimated to bury as many 4500 dead with funeral homes running out of wooden coffins in which to bury the deceased. The city has been filling trenches with the dead, three coffins stacked one atop another in rows of hundreds, until grieving families protested the practice against such mass trenches (*trincheiras*). Likewise, the health system in Manus is experiencing a complete breakdown in its ability to cope with the COVID-19 crisis.

According to Marcia Castro, Andelot Professor of Demography and Chair of the Department of Global Health and Population at Harvard University's T.H. Chan School of Public Health, in 2020 Manaus reached a "humanitarian crisis" for multiple and unfortunate reasons.[69] For one, there were not enough hospital beds for patients inflicted by Coronavirus, and as more became infected. Then, hospitals were at capacity or above capacity for receipt of such sick patients. Additionally, hospitals did not have enough ventilators for sick patients or "personal protective equipment" (PPEs) for staff. Moreover, at least 43 percent of the population living in Brazilian Amazonia did not have access to running water. Therefore, the notion of washing one's hands with soap for at least 60 seconds, as recommended by the World Health Organization (WHO), was all but impossible for many.[70] What is more, the state with the highest Gini coefficient in Brazil, or income inequality, was Amazonas State according to Dr. Castro.

Much of Manaus itself is a *favela*, or a "slum," and much of it is built from illegal housing. As such, it is an impoverished city and many of those living in Manaus are not registered, and therefore cannot receive the government pension during this health crisis. Already, those living in Manaus are susceptible to malaria and other mosquito-borne diseases and evident prior to Coronavirus. As elsewhere in the developing world, COVID-19 has exposed the inequalities and health disparities in the region.

While the COVID-19 crisis is ongoing, indigenous peoples throughout Brazilian Amazonia face threats from outside invaders, especially illegal loggers (*madeireiros ilegais*) and illegal miners (*garimpeiros*) onto their lands. In addition, Brazilian President Jair Bolsonaro has encouraged the development of the Amazon and has vowed to no longer protect indigenous demarcated lands. Because of this prevailing lax attitude from the Brazilian executive branch, yet another Brazilian Native was recently murdered, Ari Uru-eu-wau-wau, in the Brazilian state of Rondônia on April 17, 2020, by illegal loggers.[71] On the other hand, Zezico Guajajara was killed on March 31, 2020 also by illegal loggers. At the same time, illegal loggers and illegal miners are bringing Coronavirus to Brazilian Native peoples and causing the unnecessary further spread of the disease onto Native reserves as evident from statements made by indigenous people and recent videos from the Amazon.[72] As indigenous leader, Anderson Munduruku, explained: "We are very concerned with this issue of contamination of our relatives within our territory."

Furthermore, President Bolsonaro called COVID-19, a "little flu" (*gripezinha*) or "little cold" (*resfriadinho*), and encouraged the Brazilian people to continue to work and not self-isolate nor social distance against the advice of many state governors such as those from populous states like Rio de Janeiro and São Paulo.[73] On the other hand, many city-dwellers living in Manaus, who often live in over-crowded housing, are not following state government rules of self-isolation and social distancing because of President Bolsonaro, and as a result, the disease became more and more widespread across the metropolis. Adding to this are the economic consequences of Coronavirus, which will definitely cause "food insecurity" in the Brazilian Amazon, making a growing health catastrophe that much worse as it will elsewhere in the developing world.[74]

On May 3, 2020, there were a total of 6683 people infected by COVID-19 in Amazonas State with about 61 percent of these existing in Manaus and a total of 548 confirmed deaths.[75] In Brazil, there were a total of about 101,000 cases of COVID-19 and a total of about 7025 deaths and this was since cases have been reported from March 21 until May 2020.[76] According to the Manaus newspaper, *A Crítica*, epidemiologists and health professionals believed Manaus was projected to have as many as 748 deaths from COVID-19 by mid-May 2020.[77] Manaus continues to have a high prevalence of cases in 2021 even though the vaccinations have accelerated there.[78]

As Brazilian-American demographer, Dr. Marcia Castro explained: "We know social isolation works. A lot of people think that bringing the curve down is just to save lives. It is more than this. It is to prevent a collapse of the health system … and the resources are not that good in the Amazon. Once the system has collapsed, all the actions are what we call in public health the 'fire-brigade response'. You are going where the fire is burning but you are not preventing new fires from happening."[79] Of course, the other objective you need to have is testing. People need to be tested all the time to contain the virus.

Beyond Manaus, which is a Brazilian epicenter for Coronavirus and its ongoing devastation, is the disease's destruction of those Amerindians living in the interior of Brazil. As Carlos Fausto, Professor of Anthropology at the National Museum of the Federal University of Rio de Janeiro (UFRJ) mentioned in an article about Native peoples he studied in the Upper Xingu: "Not only because we have no vaccine [in 2020] and no viable treatment against this new virus, but also because we lack a government fit for the challenge. The Brazilian government is flirting with death, ignoring the obvious. 'It's like the measles from the time of my grandfather', as Kanari Kuikuro reminds us. Unburied bodies in the streets, endless deaths in the villages. We must take urgent measures to defend Indigenous peoples and their lands. We cannot see another genocide."[80]

Likewise, French Anthropologist, Bruce Albert, remarked in a recent 2020 New York Times Op-Ed: "In some ways it reminds me of the stories the Yanomami elders have told me about times when they fled to the forest in small groups to hide from the cannibalistic "Epidemic Spirit," *Xawarari*.[81] However, this time, we have become our own victims by loosening on ourselves the epidemiological consequences of this predatory hubris, just as indigenous leaders like Yanomami shaman and philosopher Davi Kopenawa have been warning us for decades. In today's hyperconnected industrial world, ecological imbalances or disease vectors that might once have affected only one corner of the planet now threaten us all. And perhaps now, as we are all now exposed to an invisible enemy for which we have no defenses, this harrowing experience of our shared fragility may stir global society to rethink its current course."

Additionally, I keep seeing notices on Facebook from indigenous acquaintances and friends of those who have succumbed to COVID-19. Here is one of these: "It is with regret that we received the news from the relative of the Ticuna Native group, Aldenor Ticuna, another indigenous teacher who died due to the proliferation of the COVID-19 virus. The family is mourning and we send our deepest feelings of condolences to them."

In some of the earliest reports about Brazilian Amerindians, such as about the Tupinambás, the Portuguese described them as "justified in their periodic migrations because they believed it 'better to change their faces and do the opposite of their grandparents' or they would die quickly" (doctoral thesis, Cristina Brandt Friederich Martin Gurgel, UNICAMP, 2009).[82]

And back then in the sixteenth century, many Amerindians tried running away from the diseases the Europeans brought. There are still innumerable uncontacted tribes living in the farthest reaches of Amazonia who need our protection, dozens of distinct and separate groups. But this disease, this COVID-19, will cause innumerable apocalyptic annihilation among Brazilian Amerindians. And we are allowing the Brazilian government to let it happen because they will not prevent the incursions of illegal loggers and illegal miners on Native Brazilian lands. If anything, the rhetoric of President Bolsonaro encourages such illegal invasions.

In sum, we are in the midst of a genocidal disease devastating Amazonian Native peoples and we must act to prevent this cataclysmic pandemic from completely wiping out some of the most vulnerable peoples on our planet. While vaccines are reaching Amazonia and the remotest of Native peoples in Amazonia, the rollout is quite slow and wholly inadequate given the potential of devastation.[83] There must be a greater sense of urgency in reaching all Amerindian peoples and vaccinating them.

## Bolsonaro's Continuous Follies and the Extermination of Brazilian Indians

It seems every time I write about Amazonia and COVID-19, another Amerindian leader has died from Coronavirus, another knowledgeable elder gone, and more tragedy compiling upon tragedy not only in the Brazilian Amazon but throughout indigenous communities in lowland South America.[84] By any standard, at least in Brazil, the Brazilian federal government's neglect of its indigenous peoples and the deleterious effects from the COVID-19 disease, are tantamount to genocide. Many observers, inclusive of anthropologists, journalists, NGOs, and jurists like Deisy Ventura, have said as much in regard to investigating those responsible for Amerindian genocide such as Brazilian President Jair Bolsonaro and his administration.[85]

On August 5, 2020, we learned about the death of the Amerindian leader Aritana Yawalapiti of the Yawalapiti people, Arawak language speakers of the Upper Xingu Region and Xingu National Park Reserve (*Teritório Indígena do Xingu*, TIX).[86] Another recent notable death of an indigenous leader succumbing to COVID-19 was Paulo Paiakan of the Kayapó people on June 17, 2020.[87] Paiakan was a loquacious and exuberant leader of the Kayapó and their rights and especially important for influencing the 1988 Brazilian Constitution and inclusion of indigenous rights. Paiakan also fought against the construction of the Belo Monte Dam, alongside fellow Kayapó Chief Raoni Metuktire and English musician Sting.[88]

Other significant indigenous deaths were educator and leader Higino Tenório of the Tuyuka people of the Alto Rio Negro on June 18, 2020, and female leader Bernaldina José Pedro of the Macuxi people on June 24, 2020, important for her knowledge of Macuxi traditions of legends, songs, and artisanal crafts, and for establishing a reserve for her people. In 2018, she briefly met with Pope Francis, giving him a letter, and pleading for his help for the Macuxi.[89]

Another renowned leader was Acelino Dace of the Munduruku people who died on June 3, 2020.[90] He also played a crucial role in demarcating his people's territories near the Tapajós River and in the Brazilian government's abandoning its project of a hydroelectric mega-dam at São Luiz on the Tapajós.[91] Yet, Dace was not alone, eight other Munduruku elders died within a few days of each other. As Bruna Rocha, archeologist at Universidade Federal do Oeste do Pará, remarked in an interview with Mongabay, "Every time an elder dies, a library is burnt."[92] Moreover, Bruna averred: "Besides being knowledge repositories on the environment, history, territory, production of specific artifacts and medicines, these elders provide political and spiritual guidance, being fundamental in the struggle for territorial recognition. They remind their peoples of who they are in a fast-changing world."

In Colombia, the indigenous actor Antonio Bolívar, known for his role in the popular movie *Embrace of the Serpent* (*El Abrazo de la Serpiente*, 2015), and one of the last Ocaina Indians, succumbed to COVID-19.[93] In the film, he portrayed an Indian in contact with a white botanist, inspired from the real-life diaries of Harvard botanist Richard Evans Schultes and German explorer, Theodor Koch-Grünberg.[94] Historically, the Ocaina people were enslaved, tortured, and killed by British rubber companies in the late nineteenth and early twentieth centuries during the Amazonian rubber boom. Yet, Bolívar was a true indigenous elder and according to those who knew him, he had profound botanical knowledge of Amazonian flora. In August 2020 in Colombia, there were 345,714 Coronavirus cases and about 11,624 deaths from the disease.[95]

Coronavirus had adversely affected indigenous peoples everywhere in Brazilian Amazonia, and worries are the disease will take many, many more

Native peoples. Even with the introduction of the vaccine, the rollout has been slow and has been slow in getting to indigenous peoples in remote areas. Especially vulnerable are the Yanomami of northern Brazilian and southern Venezuelan borderlands and the Matis of the remote Vale do Javari of western Amazonas State and those indigenous groups with very few remaining members.[96] Not to mention there are the most defenseless from such illnesses as those "uncontacted Amerindians" living in the remotest regions of Amazonia, perhaps numbering less than 1500 Indigenes altogether.[97]

Moreover, Brazilian Indians face incursions on their land from illegal loggers, illegal miners, and poachers, who likewise bring with them the possibility of carrying COVID-19. On the other hand, the Brazilian government does nothing to aid the Indians in their fight against such invaders. At the same time, cattle ranchers are mostly responsible for a rise in Amazonian forest fires, up 25 percent from the same time last year.[98]

Is it any wonder the Brazilian government has failed to act on behalf of its indigenous peoples when President Jair Bolsonaro has consistently denied the severity of COVID-19 in Brazil and cavalierly flaunted not wearing a mask in public? In fact, a Brazilian federal judge ruled near the end of June 2020, if President Bolsonaro did not wear a mask in public he faced being fined for his negligence.[99] So, it was no surprise to anyone when Bolsonaro himself tested positive for Coronavirus in early July 2020.[100]

According to Worldometer, Brazil was only second to the United States with COVID-19 cases across the globe in 2020 (while India now has taken second place in 2021) at almost 3 million infected and with approximately 97,000 deaths from the pandemic.[101] With Bolsonaro's overall unconcern for his own population, and even his own health, it is hardly surprising why the Brazilian president does not care for Brazil's indigenous peoples?[102]

In fact, President Jair Bolsonaro has gone out of his way to deny Brazilian Natives help. On July 8, 2020, Bolsonaro vetoed an aid package for Brazilian Indians to protect their communities from COVID-19.[103] The anticipated legislation was an emergency plan to provide funding for Brazilian Amerindians to combat Coronavirus with clean water, disinfectant, protective equipment, hygienic items, and supplemental hospital beds. Additionally, he denied financial support for emergency healthcare of Brazilian Indians.

According to SESAI (*Secretaria Especial de Saúde Indígena*, Special Secretariat of Indigenous Health) there were 16,840 confirmed cases of COVID-19 among Brazilian indigenous peoples and about 338 confirmed deaths of Brazilian Indians in 2020.[104] Yet, the non-governmental organization, *Articulação dos Povos Indígenas do Brasil* (APIB, Articulation of Brazilian Indigenous Peoples), estimates there were 22,656 confirmed Coronavirus cases among Brazilian Indians with 639 deaths and 148 indigenous ethnic groups infected out of 305 total Brazilian Native groups.[105] On the other hand, there was an estimated total of 896,917 indigenous people in Brazil.[106]

Coronavirus is ravaging indigenous communities across Brazil. As elsewhere, the elderly have been most adversely affected by the pandemic. In the city of Manaus, centrally located in the Brazilian Amazon with more than 2.2 million people, in April 2020, the number of people dying increased by 443 percent than the average for deaths over the last few years and its hospital system completely collapsed.[107] In August 2020, Intensive Care Unit (ICU) admittance somewhat leveled off to half capacity. Manaus had approximately 27,122 Coronavirus cases with about 1770 deaths and according to reports Amazonas State had the third highest rate of COVID-19 cases in Brazil with 1686 cases per 100,000 inhabitants by the end of June 2020.[108]

In the Peruvian Amazonian city of Iquitos, there had been about 12,000 cases and 555 deaths, and by June 2020 residents were desperate to buy oxygen canisters in order to give them to family members because hospitals were beyond capacity.[109] People were despondent and were raising money among communities to afford prices for oxygen cylinders since hospitals were overwhelmed and unable to treat the number of patients with Coronavirus. In August 2020, Peru had the third most cases of COVID-19 after Brazil and Mexico in Latin America with approximately 447,624 infected and 20,228 deaths.[110]

Still, many would argue because of the Brazilian president's overall negative, if not racist, attitude toward Brazil's indigenous peoples and his policies of trying to strip FUNAI (*Fundação Nacional do Índio*, National Indian Foundation) of its powers; allowing for invaders like illegal loggers and illegal goldminers on indigenous reserves; allowing murders of indigenous people with impunity; not fining ranchers for forest fires; agreeing to development schemes in the Amazon; and his overall deniability about the seriousness of COVID-19, the situation in Brazil is much worse than elsewhere in Amazonia.[111]

When Brazilian Supreme Court Justice Gilmar Mendes (*Supremo Tribunal Federal*, STF) declared the actions of President Bolsonaro were tantamount to genocide, this formalized the debate against the executive branch in humanitarian law.[112] Mendes in a videoconference stated, "The Brazilian Army associated itself with a 'genocide', it's not reasonable. We need to put an end to this,' referring to the administration's policies in combating the new Coronavirus pandemic," according to the Brazilian online news site Globo.com.[113] Bolsonaro likewise was against a Supreme Court decision which allowed Brazilian municipalities and states the autonomy to decide for themselves measures for social distancing and dealing with Coronavirus without interference from the federal government in accordance with the Brazilian Constitution.[114] Magistrate Gilmar Mendes later clarified his statements by saying that Brazil may be committing genocide against its indigenous people, "Understand and this is the debate" (*Então é este o debate*), citing the renowned Brazilian photographer Sabastião Salgado's open letter to President Bolsonaro on June 24, 2020.[115]

Hence, Professor of International Law Deisy de Freitas Lima Ventura, at the *Universidade de São Paulo* (USP), believed there was sufficient evidence to investigate President Bolsonaro and his administration for crimes against humanity by the International Criminal Court (ICC) at the Hague as well as within the Brazilian judicial system.[116] In an interview with the Spanish newspaper *El País*, Professor Ventura qualified what she meant by genocide happening in Brazil: First, I must say that, in regard to the population in general, I believe that the crime of extermination exists: article seven, letter B, of the Rome Statute. It is also a crime against humanity. And, in the specific case of indigenous peoples, I believe that it can be characterized as genocide, the most serious of crimes against humanity. The crime of extermination is the intentional imposition of living conditions that can cause the destruction of part of a population. What is striking, in this case, is that the example used in the text of the Rome Statute is precisely that of deprivation of access to food or medicine. Since the start of the pandemic, the federal government has assumed the behavior that it still has today: on the one hand, the denial regarding the disease and, on the other, an objective action against local governments that try to give an effective response to the disease, against those trying to control the spread and progression of COVID-19. And, from the beginning, I have said that this policy is one of extermination. Why? Because studies show us that the most affected populations are the black populations, the poorest, the most vulnerable, among which are the elderly and people with comorbidities. And, unfortunately, what we had predicted has happened. Despite the underreporting—which is consensual, since everyone agrees that there are more cases in Brazil than are recognized—the volume is impressive and there is a very clear profile of the people who are most affected by the disease. Both in the genocide of the indigenous population and in what, in my opinion, is an extermination policy regarding action in the face of the pandemic, I clearly see an intention ... Regarding indigenous people, two issues are especially relevant, among many ... The first is the debate on contact with isolated peoples. Ordinance 419 of the National Indian Foundation [FUNAI] determines that contact with isolated communities must be avoided ... In February of this year [2020], Victoria Tauli-Corpuz, UN Rapporteur for Indigenous Peoples, upon learning that an evangelical leader could lead the coordination of isolated peoples of the National Indian Foundation [FUNAI], warned of potential genocide. Therefore, genocide is far from trivial. We are talking about a United Nations rapporteur on the rights of indigenous peoples. The second point—and it is even difficult to speak about it calmly—is the law of the emergency plan to combat COVID-19 in indigenous territories.[117]

As mentioned above, President Bolsonaro vetoed the legislative emergency plan to stem the spread of Coronavirus on indigenous reserves, which prevented the Brazilian government from distributing essential supplies of food and medicine and hygienic products to Brazilian Indians. The Spanish journalist Eliane Brum then asked Professor Ventura the question, "With respect to indigenous peoples, what other elements demonstrate that there has been a genocidal crime committed against them?" and Ventura responded by asserting: "The essential difference, which makes it easier to identify genocide in indigenous populations, is the clear interest that exists in using their lands, natural resources, in eliminating the 'obstacle' that these figures represent, since they are the great guardians of the jungle, the environment, the Brazilian natural heritage. Eliminating these guardians would greatly facilitate the appropriation of their land, just look at the rate at which protected land is deforested and illegally occupied in Brazil. The motive for the crime is obvious. The age-old mystery movie question, who benefits from crime? Has a very obvious answer in this case."[118]

Furthermore, others have observed similar irresponsibility by the Brazilian government. In an open letter to President Bolsonaro and his administration, SALSA (Society for the Anthropology of Lowland South

America), wrote on June 15, 2020, describing how the Bolsonaro administration was failing Brazilian Indians and why the executive branch's actions have amounted to genocide. The letter states: Brazil's failure to protect and ensure the health and safety of its Indigenous populations—including inhabitants in remote areas of the Amazon as well as those who live in impoverished regions, such as the Northeast and also urban areas, where poverty makes Indigenous peoples particularly vulnerable—is irresponsible and grossly negligent. The current procedures and protocols outlined in SESAI (Special Indian Health Service of the Ministry of Health) COVID-19 Contingency Plans do not conform to WHO Guidelines and Recommendations and furthermore violate the 1988 Constitution, ILO Convention 169, and the United Nations Declarations on the Rights of Indigenous Peoples to which Brazil is signatory. Brazil's current policies concerning the health and protection of its Indigenous citizens are translating into nothing less than genocide … According to APIB [*Articulação dos Povos Indígenas do Brasil*, Articulation of Brazilian Indigenous Peoples], the incidence of Indigenous COVID-19 mortality is more than twice that of the national population. The state's negligence, its inability and unwillingness to protect the health and safety of the nation's Indigenous Peoples, has led to the high rate of infection and mortality among Brazil's Indigenous population. The state itself should acknowledge that this is unacceptable."

In sum, the prevailing question is whether or not President Bolsonaro and his administration will modify their relationship with Brazil's indigenous population and take active measures to protect Brazilian Indians? One indigenous leader, Álvaro Fernandes Sampaio Tukano, who is sixty-seven years old, of the Tukano people, and General Chief of the Terra Indígena Balaio, from the Municipality of São Gabriel da Cachoeira, of the Alto Rio Negro in the State of Amazonas, explained his view of the COVID-19 crisis on August 4, 2020: "We are tired of living in this world of injustice and here comes more government politicians and more Coronavirus. Because we don't have a job, we don't have a good education, we are not trained, we have no minimum conditions to face any pandemic. Even so, thanks to traditional knowledge, prayers and shamanism, many of our elders have helped us treat everyone's health. So, most of the Indians who caught Coronavirus in the villages survived, escaped death by taking medicine from the forest, doing their shamanism and we continue to defend those territories that the world needs … Those indigenous people who went to be treated in non-indigenous hospitals died.

They died because they did not believe in our medicines, in the way we treat, they lost their traditions and when there is this loss of traditions, we are very dependent on the system and this system is expensive for the treatment of our health. This is how we think and we are making this observation for our children, to maintain this ancient knowledge and to live in a dignified way in our territories, to maintain traditions. It is clear that this knowledge is not recognized in the official information. Many people die, we are not being visible and this data does not enter official government data. But the absolute majority, who had coronavirus escaped, thanks to the traditional medicines of the indigenous peoples."[119]

## THE GENOCIDE WE ARE ALLOWING IN AMAZONIA

The fact of the matter is that genocide against indigenous peoples in Brazil is widespread and affects all tribes in some way. Moreover, because of the animosity of Brazilian President Jair Bolsonaro toward Amerindians, stating they have too much land, has allowed for illegal mining and illegal logging on Native lands and all sorts of other atrocities, inclusive of indigenous murders.[120] Nowhere is this worse than the Yanomami territory on the borderlands between Brazil and Venezuela, a tribal reserve park the size of Portugal (9.6 million hectares or 24 million acres) in which about 27,000 Yanomami live in approximately 360 villages.[121]

The Yanomami in 2021 are facing a humanitarian crisis, not known to them since the 1990s when these Natives were devastated by miner invasions on their lands.[122] Now, again, there are at least 20,000 illegal gold miners (*garimpeiros*) on Yanomami lands bringing with them disease, malaria and COVID-19, and polluting the river ways of the Yanomami territory with mercury and other poisons from illicit mining operations. "Brazil has 566 indigenous areas, which occupy a territory of 1.17 million square kilometers – equivalent to the [Brazilian] states of Mato Grosso and Tocantins put together. According to data from the 2010 Census, the last one made by IBGE, 517.4 thousand out of the 817.9 thousand Brazilian Indians live in these reserves."[123]

In a recent report published by the Brazilian Instituto Socioambiental, "Xawara: Tracing the Deadly Path of COVID-19 and Government Negligence in the Yanomami Territory" (2020), outlines how unjust the Brazilian government's response to COVID-19 and the gold miner incursions on Yanomami lands have been over the last couple of years since Bolsonaro took office.[124]

In a statement by Yanomami and Ye'kwana leadership, they state:

> But today our land has been invaded by 20,000 miners! They are bringing COVID-19 with them, and infecting our communities. This year [2020] they murdered two Yanomami! Again we see a huge mining invasion and with it come epidemics, as occurred in the past. It is illegal mining that is bringing this new xawara (epidemic) into the forest. Increasingly COVID-19 is infecting us, we see many people falling ill with coronavirus symptoms. But that is not all! The invaders also bring malaria, lots of malaria! Throughout the territory the communities are being infected, even where malaria had disappeared. Mining goes hand in hand with xawara and this is our overriding concern: COVID-19 and malaria are attacking people. This is why we are dying. If it continues like this, our population will shrink. This is very serious! ... This COVID-19 xawara is a type of revenge wreaked by planet Earth, it is a warning to non-indigenous society that they are not caring for it. The Earth is crying for help. This is what the shamans say: mother Earth is angry and sick, she is asking non-indigenous people to stop destroying the planet.[125]

In the last *garimpeiro* invasion in 1993, sixteen Yanomami were murdered by gold miners, known today as the Haximu massacre.[126] The massacre was ruled a genocide by the Brazilian Supreme Federal Court and convicted four gold prospectors of the murder of sixteen Yanomami Indians. In the attack, the gold miners allegedly shot the elderly as well as women and children and struck a baby with a machete.[127]

"Between 2019 and 2020, in the first years of the Bolsonaro administration, illegal mining and deforestation in the TIY [Yanomami Indigenous Territory] grew exponentially.[128] According to the Imazon Deforestation Alert System (SAD), in the period August 2019–July 2020, the TIY was among the ten areas under most pressure from deforestation in the Brazilian Amazon. Between August and September 2020, the TIY retained this grim ranking." And while the National Indian Foundation (FUNAI) and the Federal Police (PF) have conducted operations in the Yanomami territories against illicit mining, it has not been enough to deter the enormous influx of illegal gold miners.

Such mining invasions are serious and this is why the threat of genocide is so severe. For example, "from mid-1987 to January 1990, the mining invasion and the spreading epidemic of malaria and respiratory diseases caused the death of around a thousand Yanomami, 14% of their population in Roraima."[129] Today, the Yanomami and Ye'kwana face a similar situation with COVID-19 and malaria infections. According to the

Instituto Socioambiental report, there have been at least 949 cases of COVID-19 with thirteen deaths out of a population of only 26,785 Indians.

Anthropologist Bruce Albert puts the situation among the Yanomami this way: "The State's negation of the Yanomami deaths and their dead from COVID-19, both in the epidemiological statistics and the secret biosafety burials, not only alludes to a sinister colonial experience, but also other more recent official strategies of collective amnesia in Brazil's recent history, such as the 'disappearance' of bodies and the names of victims during the military dictatorship. In fact, seizing the dead of others to erase them from collective memory and negate the process of mourning by their family members has always been a mark of a supreme stage of barbarity based on contempt and the ethnic and/or political negation of the Other."[130]

In June 2021, wildcat miners have become completely brazen by attacking Yanomami and Munduruku villages as well as federal police.[131] On the other hand, President Bolsonaro has openly called for legalizing mining on indigenous reserves, something which is currently unconstitutional. On May 14, 2021, Bolsonaro told supporters: "It is not right to want to criminalize the gold miner in Brazil" (*Não é justo querer criminalizar o garimpeiro no Brasil*). Such comments have allowed gold prospectors to act with impunity on indigenous lands, burning villages, threatening indigenous leaders, and even in some cases murdering Natives.[132]

In the Tapajos River Basin region of southern Amazonia in Pará State is the homeland of the Munduruku people who number nearly 14,000 and who have faced continual death threats from illicit miners. Like the Yanomami their rivers are being destroyed by the miners:

> On May 26, [2021] a major Federal Police operation to remove illegal gold miners from Munduruku Indigenous Territory turned violent, as armed miners first attacked a police outpost and then turned their fury upon the Munduruku themselves, attacking a village, firing shots, and targeting key leaders. Two houses were set ablaze, according to a statement from the Munduruku's Ipereg Ayu Movement.[133]

It is clear from the rhetoric of President Jair Bolsonaro himself, the Bolsonaro administration is not interested in indigenous rights or the lives of Brazil's small Amerindian population. Bolsonaro wishes to develop the

Amazon at their expense. Bolsonaro has no issue with miners or loggers or others who wish to rape the indigenous lands of Brazil. To him, the Indians are just an impediment to Brazilian progress much like the motto of the Brazilian flag: *Ordem e Progresso* (Order and Progress), a positivistic anachronism of a bygone era.

Contrary to the thinking of Bolsonaro, Brazil's Amerindian peoples have agency and they are fighting for their rights regardless if the federal government supports them or not. Because of this and because of the urgency of recent events, new massacres are bound to happen in Yanomami territories, on Munduruku lands, and elsewhere in Amazonia.

Likewise, as long as Bolsonaro is president nothing much will change for the Yanomami or the Munduruku and other Native peoples in Brazil. This is why it is so important to support organizations such as Survival International and Amazon Watch and others to put pressure on the Bolsonaro administration in Brazil for the sake of these remaining indigenous peoples.

## Conclusion

This chapter began by discussing the issue of so-called uncontacted indigenous peoples and how vulnerable they are to the outside world. Uncontacted peoples choose to remain isolated and we should respect their collective volition for doing so. Most vulnerable, as I explained are those in the Andaman and Nicobar Islands, as well as in the remote Amazonian regions of Bolivia, Brazil, Ecuador, Paraguay, Peru, and Venezuela, and some isolated peoples in Papua New Guinea, Malaysia, and perhaps Central Africa. More needs to be done to protect these vulnerable groups lest we lose them. As Scott Wallace (2011: 224) explains: "Even many sympathetic to the plight of persecuted Indians view the term *uncontacted* as a misnomer that discredits their cause, conjuring images of Stone Age savages inhabiting a kind of fictional Lost World … The isolation, even from other tribes, appears to be a relatively recent phenomenon, born of the violent imposition of the White Intruder." Let us hope there is enough positive governmental intervention and international concern to prevent unwanted intruders into their remote territories.

In Western China, Uighur, Kazakh, and other Muslim minorities are being persecuted by the Chinese and placed in concentration camps. Some estimate there are at least 1 million Uighur, Kazakhs, and other Muslim Chinese in these camps. The Chinese call these concentration camps, "re-education camps," while there are well-regarded reports such as from Human Rights Watch (2018) which expose the barbarities occurring in them. The mass incarceration of Chinese Turkic Muslim populations in Xinjiang, China, is to many not only evidence of mass ethnocide happening but tantamount to genocide as well.

What we realize too is that ongoing genocide does not have to be limited to massacres and actual violence but may be carried onward through structural violence as well through the results of past genocidal practices resulting in alcoholism, domestic abuse, sexual abuse, depression, suicide, and endemic health issues in indigenous populations. After the United States massacred its Native populations they were placed on reservations and then their cultures were mostly eradicated through the school boarding system, the latter practice also was carried out in Canada. The proper term is "ethnocide."

Recently, in June 2021, there were mass graves found at former residential Native schools in Saskatchewan and British Columbia Provinces. In Canada, since the nineteenth century, there were more than 150,000 First Nations children forced into attending Christian and state-funded Native residential boarding schools where they were to be assimilated into Canadian society.[134]

Similar patterns of genocidal trauma are encountered in Australia with similar mental health and physical health repercussions. In some places in Australia white descendants of soldiers and family members of Aboriginal survivors have gathered at sites where massacres have occurred to reach some forms of reconciliation with the genocidal past.

In Brazil and elsewhere in Lowland South America, Native peoples are threatened by development schemes which threaten genocide. As David Maybury-Lewis (2002: 48) declared: "Nowadays indigenous peoples frequently find themselves threatened by a particular aspect of modern 'civilization,' namely 'development'. It is all too often argued by governments and development planners that indigenous peoples 'must not be allowed to stand in the way of development.'" This has been particularly evident for Brazilian President Jair Bolsonaro and his administration and the wish to delimit and delegitimize Amerindian demarcated lands as well as undermining indigenous rights and the very livelihoods of indigenous peoples throughout Brazil. As Maybury-Lewis (2002: 43) argued: "The defining characteristic of indigenous peoples is not therefore priority on the land but rather that they have been conquered by invaders who are racially, ethnically, or culturally different from themselves. Accordingly, indigenous peoples are those who are subordinated and marginalized by alien powers that rule over them. It follows that they are relatively powerless, and so they become prime targets for genocide." Nevertheless, Brazilian Indians are fighting back and struggling for recognition. As evident in this chapter, illegal logging and illegal mining as well as ranching have threatened the very existence of Amerindians throughout Brazil while the Bolsonaro administration has actively worked against Native rights and, from Bolsonaro's rhetoric, encouraged nefarious activities against indigenes.

What is more, the Bolsonaro administration's lackadaisical attitude toward COVID-19 has exacerbated the effects from the disease on Brazil's Native populations. By not acting soon enough, and by allowing for the health system in Manaus to collapse, are evidence enough that President Bolsonaro and his administration allowed for Coronavirus to spread more widely than necessary. Moreover, there is now (as of 2021) an ongoing Brazilian Senatorial investigation regarding Bolsonaro's handling of the COVID-19 crisis in Brazil, which by present day estimates has killed more than 533,546 Brazilians.[135] Furthermore, by allowing illegal loggers and illegal miners to invade indigenous lands in Brazil, the Bolsonaro administration has turned a blind eye to the plight of Native peoples.

In sum, more needs to be done to raise awareness about ongoing genocides throughout the world and more concerted efforts need to be exerted on the behalf of indigenous peoples everywhere. As Totten, Parsons, and Hitchcock (2002: 84) make clear: "Governments must live up to their obligation to protect indigenous peoples and not compromise their rights under the weight of so-called progress, economic growth, or nationalism. Finally, all institutions, whether states, corporations, nongovernmental organizations, or indigenous support groups, need to work together to promote the rights not just of indigenous peoples but also of all human beings."

## Notes

1. https://www.theguardian.com/world/2019/feb/03/john-chau-christian-missionary-death-sentinelese
2. https://www.survivalinternational.org/tribes/sentinelese
3. https://www.outsideonline.com/outdoor-adventure/exploration-survival/john-allen-chau-life-death-north-sentinel/
4. https://www.survivalinternational.org/uncontactedtribes

5. https://www.nationalgeographic.com/culture/article/neolithic-agricultural-revolution
6. https://www.jstor.org/stable/29742027
7. See Herma Briffault's translation of Bartolomé de Las Casas' *The Devastation of the Indies: A Brief Account* (1974).
8. See Iverson (2002). *Diné: A History of the Navajos*
9. https://indiancountrytoday.com/archive/hitler-studied-us-treatment-of-indians
10. https://www.americanyawp.com/reader/manifest-destiny/john-osullivan-declares-americas-manifest-destiny-1845/
11. https://www.nationalgeographic.com/environment/article/brazil-president-jair-bolsonaro-promises-exploit-amazon-rain-forest
12. It should be noted that professor and anthropologist Dru Gladney has discussed this issue extensively about the oppression of the Uyghur people and other minorities within China. Here is an example of one of his talks on the issues surrounding Chinese persecution of minorities: https://china.usc.edu/whats-stake-xinjiang
13. https://www.nytimes.com/2019/03/02/world/asia/china-muslim-detention-uighur-kazakh.html
14. https://hongkongfp.com/2019/03/04/camps-factories-muslim-detainees-say-china-using-forced-labour/
15. https://xjdp.aspi.org.au/explainers/exploring-xinjiangs-detention-facilities/
16. https://www.ohchr.org/en/professionalinterest/pages/cerd.aspx
17. https://www.aspi.org.au/report/uyghurs-sale
    https://xjdp.aspi.org.au/explainers/exploring-xinjiangs-detention-facilities/
18. https://www.hrw.org/report/2021/04/19/break-their-lineage-break-their-roots/chinas-crimes-against-humanity-targeting
19. https://www.hrw.org/report/2021/04/19/break-their-lineage-break-their-roots/chinas-crimes-against-humanity-targeting
20. http://historymatters.gmu.edu/d/5478/
21. https://www.historyplace.com/worldhistory/genocide/index.html
22. https://www.nytimes.com/2014/05/23/world/asia/deadly-attack-in-western-china.html?module=inline
23. https://www.worldpoliticsreview.com/articles/27556/will-mbs-defense-of-china-s-uighur-crackdown-backfire-in-saudi-arabia
24. https://china.usc.edu/whats-stake-xinjiang
25. https://www.americanyawp.com/reader/manifest-destiny/john-osullivan-declares-americas-manifest-destiny-1845/
26. https://en.wikipedia.org/wiki/American_Indian_boarding_schools

27. http://www.nativepartnership.org/site/PageServer?pagename=naa_livingconditions
28. https://www.ncbi.nlm.nih.gov/pmc/articles/PMC4035872/
    https://minorityhealth.hhs.gov/omh/browse.aspx?lvl=4&lvlid=33
    https://americanaddictioncenters.org/alcoholism-treatment/native-americans
29. https://www.ncbi.nlm.nih.gov/pmc/articles/PMC2567901/
30. https://www.theguardian.com/society/2017/sep/29/pine-ridge-indian-reservation-south-dakota
31. https://en.wikipedia.org/wiki/Wounded_Knee_Occupation
32. https://www.ncbi.nlm.nih.gov/pmc/articles/PMC5977074/
33. https://www.theguardian.com/australia-news/2019/mar/08/a-very-tragic-history-how-the-trauma-of-a-1926-massacre-echoes-through-the-years
34. https://en.wikipedia.org/wiki/William_Edward_Hanley_Stanner
    https://theconversation.com/indigenous-lives-the-cult-of-forgetfulness-and-the-australian-dictionary-of-biography-86302
35. https://c21ch.newcastle.edu.au/colonialmassacres/introduction.php
36. https://www.theguardian.com/australia-news/2019/mar/04/the-killing-times-the-massacres-of-aboriginal-people-australia-must-confront
37. https://www.theguardian.com/australia-news/postcolonial-blog/2018/jun/08/australias-frontier-war-killings-still-conveniently-escape-official-memory
38. https://en.wikipedia.org/wiki/History_of_Indigenous_Australians
    https://www.theguardian.com/australia-news/2019/mar/04/as-the-toll-of-australias-frontier-brutality-keeps-climbing-truth-telling-is-long-overdue
39. https://aiatsis.gov.au/publication/35167
40. https://www.theguardian.com/australia-news/2019/mar/07/its-like-a-big-dark-cloud-has-lifted-the-town-dragged-into-reconciliation-photo-essay
41. https://www.theguardian.com/australia-news/2019/mar/01/when-glenda-met-sandy-descendants-of-massacre-survivor-and-soldier-unite-in-grief
42. https://www.theguardian.com/cities/2019/mar/08/beggars-in-our-own-land-canadas-first-nation-housing-crisis
43. https://www.theguardian.com/global/2018/oct/04/ontario-six-nations-nestle-running-water
44. https://amazoniareal.com.br/o-genocidio-dos-waimiri-atroari-um-possivel-reconhecimento-historico/

https://nypost.com/2019/03/08/amazon-tribe-accuses-brazilian-military-of-genocide/
45. https://www.bbc.com/news/av/world-latin-america-48845015
https://pib.socioambiental.org/en/Povo:Uru-Eu-Wau-Wau
46. https://www.theguardian.com/world/2019/mar/04/we-are-fighting-brazils-indigenous-groups-unite-to-protect-their-land
47. https://www.ft.com/content/7a0a661c-558b-11e9-91f9-b6515a54c5b1
https://pib.socioambiental.org/en/Povo:Mebêngôkre_(Kayapó)
48. https://www.nybooks.com/daily/2019/04/17/claudia-andujar-witness-to-the-yanomamis-last-struggle/
49. https://assets.survivalinternational.org/documents/1686/davi-sonia-raoni-letter-eng.pdf
50. https://g1.globo.com/natureza/noticia/2019/09/24/numero-de-assassinatos-de-indigenas-cresce-20percent-no-brasil-em-2018-aponta-relatorio.ghtml
51. https://www.theguardian.com/world/2019/oct/02/war-for-survival-brazils-amazon-tribes-despair-as-land-raids-surge-under-bolsonaro
52. https://www.theguardian.com/world/2019/nov/02/brazilian-forest-guardian-killed-by-illegal-loggers-in-ambush
53. https://www.theguardian.com/world/2019/nov/02/brazilian-forest-guardian-killed-by-illegal-loggers-in-ambush
54. https://www.bbc.com/news/world-latin-america-50257684
55. https://www.bbc.com/news/world-latin-america-50310768
56. https://en.wikipedia.org/wiki/Mariana_dam_disaster
57. https://www.survivalinternational.org/about/belo-monte-dam
58. https://www.survivalinternational.org/about/madeira-dams
59. http://www.salsa-tipiti.org/wp-content/uploads/2019/08/PIAC-Statement-on-Miners-Invading-Indigenous-Lands-in-Brazil-AUG2019.pdf.pdf
https://news.mongabay.com/2019/07/yanomami-amazon-reserve-invaded-by-20000-miners-bolsonaro-fails-to-act/
60. http://www.salsa-tipiti.org/wp-content/uploads/2019/08/PIAC-Letter-re-Fires-in-Amazonia-Aug2019-.pdf.pdf
61. https://www.amnesty.org/en/countries/americas/brazil/report-brazil/
https://www.hrw.org/world-report/2019/country-chapters/brazil
62. https://apiboficial.org/2019/11/02/nota-de-repudio-e-pesar-pelo-assassinato-do-guardiao-paulo-paulino-guajajara/
63. https://www.academia.edu/16432733/Urban_Amerindians_and_Advocacy_Toward_a_Politically_Engaged_Anthropology_Representing_

Urban_Amerindigeneities_in_Manaus_Brazil_in_Book_Indigenous_Studies_and_Engaged_Anthropology_2015_
64. https://www.bbc.com/news/world-latin-america-52139875
65. https://www.sciencedirect.com/science/article/pii/S0277379118307261
66. https://www.reuters.com/article/us-health-coronavirus-indigenous-trfn/vaccine-rollout-a-war-against-time-for-amazon-indigenous-groups-idUSKBN29V2DV
    https://www.reuters.com/article/us-brazil-coronavirus-indigenous-trfn/slow-rollout-of-covid-19-vaccine-in-brazil-leaves-indigenous-at-risk-idUSKCN2AW2DV
67. https://www.theguardian.com/world/2020/apr/30/brazil-manaus-coronavirus-mass-graves
68. https://www.theguardian.com/world/2020/apr/30/brazil-manaus-coronavirus-mass-graves
69. https://brazillab.princeton.edu/news/covid-19-and-amazonias-future
70. https://www.who.int/southeastasia/news/detail/15-10-2020-handwashing-an-effective-tool-to-prevent-covid-19-other-diseases
71. https://apiboficial.org/2020/04/25/murders-invasions-and-coronavirus/?lang=en
72. https://g1.globo.com/fantastico/noticia/2020/04/19/audios-e-videos-revelam-detalhes-de-esquema-de-grilagem-dentro-de-terras-indigenas.ghtml
73. https://www.euronews.com/2020/04/06/a-little-flu-brazil-s-bolsonaro-playing-down-coronavirus-crisis
    https://www.theguardian.com/world/2020/mar/23/brazils-jair-bolsonaro-says-coronavirus-crisis-is-a-media-trick
74. https://www.theguardian.com/global-development/2020/apr/21/millions-hang-by-a-thread-extreme-global-hunger-compounded-by-covid-19-coronavirus
75. https://www.acritica.com/channels/coronavirus/news/com-621-novos-casos-am-bate-recorde-diario-de-infectados-pela-covid-19
76. https://www.google.com/search?safe=strict&client=safari&source=hp&ei=c6yvXqf9EZGWtQXQ8ZW4DA&q=Brazil+deaths+covid-19&oq=Brazil+deaths+covid-19&gs_lcp=CgZwc3ktYWIQAzoFCAAQgwE6AggAOgUIABDEAjoGCAAQFhAeUJ4EWO5BYNdDaANwAHgAgAG-NAYgBqBOSAQQyMC41mAEAoAEBqgEHZ3dzLXdpeg&sclient=psy-ab&ved=0ahUKEwjngomJwZnpAhURS60KHdB4BccQ4dUDCAw&uact=5
77. https://www.acritica.com/channels/coronavirus/news/am-deve-registrar-ate-segunda-quinzena-de-maio-748-mortes-por-covid-19-aponta-estudo

78. https://www.thelancet.com/article/S0140-6736(21)00183-5/fulltext
    https://www.washingtonpost.com/world/2021/07/16/brazil-coronavirus-manaus/
79. https://brazillab.princeton.edu/news/covid-19-and-amazonias-future
80. http://somatosphere.net/2020/the-measles-from-the-time-of-my-grandfather-amazonian-ethnocide-memories-in-times-of-covid-19.html/
81. https://www.nytimes.com/2020/04/27/opinion/yanomami-covid-brazil.html
82. http://repositorio.unicamp.br/bitstream/REPOSIP/309188/1/Gurgel_CristinaBrandtFriedrichMartin_D.pdf
83. https://www.reuters.com/article/us-health-coronavirus-indigenous-trfn/vaccine-rollout-a-war-against-time-for-amazon-indigenous-groups-idUSKBN29V2DV
    https://www.reuters.com/article/us-brazil-coronavirus-indigenous-trfn/slow-rollout-of-covid-19-vaccine-in-brazil-leaves-indigenous-at-risk-idUSKCN2AW2DV
84. https://www.counterpunch.org/2020/05/07/genocidal-disease-as-it-is-happening-in-amazonia/
85. http://www.iea.usp.br/pessoas/pasta-pessoad/deisy-ventura
    https://elpais.com/internacional/2020-07-25/hay-indicios-significativos-para-que-autoridades-brasilenas-incluido-bolsonaro-sean-investigadas-por-genocidio.html?fbclid=IwAR15sYJo-vSVO0-WFxnFlJxY4AB19oRGzQA1aottI-WUEjE03jZYXcy-lN4
    https://en.wikipedia.org/wiki/Jair_Bolsonaro
86. https://www.socioambiental.org/pt-br/noticias-socioambientais/aritana-yawalapiti-grande-lutador-e-articulador-de-mundos
    https://pib.socioambiental.org/en/Povo:Yawalapiti
    https://en.wikipedia.org/wiki/Xingu_Indigenous_Park
87. https://www.socioambiental.org/pt-br/noticias-socioambientais/morre-paulo-paiakan-grande-lideranca-kayapo
    https://pib.socioambiental.org/en/Povo:Mebêngôkre_(Kayapó)
88. https://www.bbc.com/news/world-latin-america-53087933
    http://raoni.com/biography.php
    https://www.biography.com/musician/sting
89. https://amazoniareal.com.br/morre-o-grande-educador-higino-tenorio-lider-do-povo-tuyuka-vitima-do-novo-coronavirus/
    https://pib.socioambiental.org/en/Povo:Tuyuka
    https://www.nytimes.com/2020/08/03/obituaries/bernaldina-jose-pedro-dead-coronavirus.html
    https://pib.socioambiental.org/en/Povo:Macuxi
90. https://news.mongabay.com/2020/06/every-time-an-elder-dies-a-library-is-burnt-amazon-covid-19-toll-grows/

https://pib.socioambiental.org/en/Povo:Munduruku
91. https://www.theguardian.com/world/2016/apr/22/brazil-amazon-dam-project-suspended-indigenous-munduruku-sao-luiz-do-tapajos
92. https://ufopaedu.academia.edu/BrunaRocha
    https://news.mongabay.com/2020/06/every-time-an-elder-dies-a-library-is-burnt-amazon-covid-19-toll-grows/
93. https://www.newyorker.com/news/daily-comment/the-death-of-antonio-bolivar-an-indigenous-elder-in-the-amazon-rainforest
    https://www.imdb.com/title/tt4285496/
    https://es.wikipedia.org/wiki/Ocainas
94. http://botlib.huh.harvard.edu/libraries/Nash/schultes.htm
    https://en.wikipedia.org/wiki/Theodor_Koch-Grunberg
95. https://www.worldometers.info/coronavirus/
96. https://pib.socioambiental.org/en/Povo:Yanomami
    https://pib.socioambiental.org/en/Povo:Matis#Sources_of_information
97. https://www.survivalinternational.org/tribes/uncontacted-brazil
    https://www.nationalgeographic.com/history/article/disaster-looms-indigenous-amazon-tribes-covid-19-cases-multiply
98. https://www.nationalgeographic.com/history/article/disaster-looms-indigenous-amazon-tribes-covid-19-cases-multiply
    https://www.theguardian.com/environment/2020/jul/17/dramatic-footage-fuels-fears-amazon-fires-could-be-worse-than-last-year
99. https://www.theguardian.com/world/2020/jun/23/brazilian-judge-tells-bolsonaro-to-behave-and-wear-a-face-mask
100. https://news.yahoo.com/brazilian-president-jair-bolsonaro-tests-144500440.html
101. https://www.worldometers.info/coronavirus/
102. Brazil, now in 2021, has nearly 600,000 deaths attributed to COVID-19.
    https://www.worldometers.info/coronavirus/
103. https://www.cnn.com/2020/07/08/americas/brazil-jair-bolsonaro-coronavirus-intl/index.html
104. https://painelcovid19.socioambiental.org/indigenas/casos/
105. https://covid19.socioambiental.org
106. https://www.iwgia.org/en/brazil.html
107. https://brazilian.report/liveblog/coronavirus/2020/07/05/has-the-worst-of-the-coronavirus-crisis-passed-in-manaus/
108. https://brazilian.report/liveblog/coronavirus/2020/06/30/manaus-mayor-arthur-virgilio-hospitalized-with-covid-19/
109. https://www.google.com/search?safe=strict&client=safari&sxsrf=ALeKk01a5pD9heSEKQmryxnTqzTMF7Ulag%3A1596691270418&source=hp&ei=RpMrX-_wFtGGsAXK4ZGQDw&q=iquitos+

coronavirus&oq=iquitos+&gs_lcp=CgZwc3ktYWIQARgAMgcIABAU
EIcCMggILhCxAxCRAjICCAAyAggAMggILhDHARCvATICCAAy
AggAMgIILjICCAAyAggAOgQIIxAnOgQILhAnOg4ILhCRAhCL
AxCkAxCoAzoOCC4QsQMQgwEQxwEQowI6CAgAELEDEIMBOg
UIABCxAzoFCC4QsQM6DgguEJECEIsDEKgDEKQDOggIABC
RAhCLAzoHCCMQ6gIQJzoHCC4Q6gIQJzoHCC4QJxCTAjoL
CAAQsQMQgwEQiwM6DgguELEDEMcBEKMCEIsDOggIABCxAx
CLAzoICC4QkQIQkwI6BQgAEIsDOhEILhCxAxCDARDHARCjAh
CLAzoLCC4QsQMQkQIQkwI6BAgAEAo6BAguEApQkAFY-xRgsi
5oA3AAeACAAZoBiAHeCZIBBDAuMTGYAQCgAQGqAQdnd3
Mtd2l6sAEKuAEC&sclient=psy-ab
https://www.cnn.com/2020/06/05/americas/peru-coronavirus-oxygen-shortages-intl/index.html
110. https://www.worldometers.info/coronavirus/
111. https://www.culturalsurvival.org/news/why-are-there-so-many-isolated-indigenous-peoples-infected-covid-19
https://www.survivalinternational.org/articles/3540-Bolsonaro
https://news.mongabay.com/2019/06/brazils-congress-reverses-bolsonaro-restores-funais-land-demarcation-powers/
https://news.mongabay.com/2020/05/brazil-opens-38000-square-miles-of-indigenous-lands-to-outsiders/?fbclid=IwAR1LtFPq_CKv12xFo5BOxzq3TyXdmIiVOZLnFfnS074bHkCMNwW8r5kULBY
112. https://en.wikipedia.org/wiki/Gilmar_Mendes
113. https://g1.globo.com/politica/blog/cristiana-lobo/post/2020/07/15/pazuello-liga-para-gilmar-mendes-apos-conselho-de-bolsonaro.ghtml
114. https://perma.cc/63CA-MNBS
115. https://www.theguardian.com/world/2020/may/03/eve-of-genocide-brazil-urged-save-amazon-tribes-covid-19-sebastiao-salgado
https://www.nexojornal.com.br/expresso/2020/07/15/Governo-Bolsonaro-e-genoc%C3%ADdio-da-hipérbole-aos-alertas-no-exterior
https://secure.avaaz.org/community_petitions/po/presidente_do_brasil_e_aos_lideres_do_legislativo__ajude_a_proteger_os_povos_indigenas_da_amazonia_do_covid19/?cZZUvqb&utm_source=sharetools&utm_medium=copy&utm_campaign=petition-994813-ajude_a_proteger_os_povos_indigenas_da_amazonia_do_covid19&utm_term=ZZUvqb%2Bpo
116. https://elpais.com/internacional/2020-07-25/hay-indicios-significativos-para-que-autoridades-brasilenas-incluido-bolsonaro-sean-

investigadas-por-genocidio.html?fbclid=IwAR15sYJo-vSVO0-WFxnFlJxY4AB19oRGzQA1aottI-WUEjE03jZYXcy-lN4
https://www.icc-cpi.int
117. https://elpais.com/internacional/2020-07-25/hay-indicios-significativos-para-que-autoridades-brasilenas-incluido-bolsonaro-sean-investigadas-por-genocidio.html?fbclid=IwAR15sYJo-vSVO0-WFxnFlJxY4AB19oRGzQA1aottI-WUEjE03jZYXcy-lN4
https://www.icc-cpi.int/NR/rdonlyres/ADD16852-AEE9-4757-ABE7-9CDC7CF02886/283503/RomeStatutEngl.pdf
https://www.ohchr.org/en/issues/ipeoples/srindigenouspeoples/pages/victoriataulicorpuz.aspx
118. https://elpais.com/internacional/2020-07-25/hay-indicios-significativos-para-que-autoridades-brasilenas-incluido-bolsonaro-sean-investigadas-por-genocidio.html?fbclid=IwAR15sYJo-vSVO0-WFxnFlJxY4AB19oRGzQA1aottI-WUEjE03jZYXcy-lN4
119. https://racismoambiental.net.br/2020/08/04/covid-19-e-os-povos-indigenas-no-brasil-entrevista-com-lideranca-indigena-alvaro-tukano/
https://pib.socioambiental.org/en/Povo:Tukano
120. https://www.gazetadopovo.com.br/wiseup-news/bolsonaro-raised-the-issue-do-natives-own-too-much-land-in-brazil/
121. https://www.theguardian.com/global-development/2021/may/27/brazil-aerial-photos-reveal-devastation-by-goldminers-on-indigenous-land
122. https://www.socioambiental.org/sites/blog.socioambiental.org/files/nsa/arquivos/coy_ingles_r03_2020117.pdf
123. https://www.gazetadopovo.com.br/wiseup-news/bolsonaro-raised-the-issue-do-natives-own-too-much-land-in-brazil/
124. https://www.socioambiental.org/sites/blog.socioambiental.org/files/nsa/arquivos/coy_ingles_r03_2020117.pdf
125. https://www.socioambiental.org/sites/blog.socioambiental.org/files/nsa/arquivos/coy_ingles_r03_2020117.pdf
126. https://www.survivalinternational.org/articles/3298-haximu-survivors
127. https://www.survivalinternational.org/news/1786
128. https://www.socioambiental.org/sites/blog.socioambiental.org/files/nsa/arquivos/coy_ingles_r03_2020117.pdf
129. https://www.socioambiental.org/sites/blog.socioambiental.org/files/nsa/arquivos/coy_ingles_r03_2020117.pdf
130. https://www.socioambiental.org/sites/blog.socioambiental.org/files/nsa/arquivos/coy_ingles_r03_2020117.pdf
131. https://www.theguardian.com/world/2021/may/28/brazil-wildcat-miners-police-indigenous-amazon

132. https://www.terra.com.br/economia/nao-e-justo-querer-criminalizar-o-garimpeiro-no-brasil-defende-bolsonaro,4d0610fbcd42caa042d239ccba4a942anxlbufg4.html
133. https://amazonwatch.org/news/2021/0602-mounting-violence-by-brazils-criminal-miners-endangers-indigenous-leaders
134. https://www.theguardian.com/world/2021/jun/24/canada-school-graves-discovery-saskatchewan
135. https://www.worldometers.info/coronavirus/country/brazil/; https://www.bbc.com/news/world-latin-america-57773540; as of September 23, 2021, there are nearly 600,000 deaths in Brazil due to Coronavirus.

## Bibliography

Hinton, A.L., ed. 2002. *Annihilating Difference: the Anthropology of Genocide*. Berkeley: University of California Press.

Iverson, P. 2002. *Diné: A History of the Navajos*. Albuquerque, NM: The University of New Mexico Press.

Manz, B. 2002. Terror, Grief, and Recovery: Genocidal Trauma in a Mayan Village in Guatemala. In *Annihilating Difference: The Anthropology of Genocide*, ed. A.L. Hintion, 292–309. Berkeley: University of California Press.

Maybury-Lewis, D. 2002. Genocide Against Indigenous Peoples. In *Annihilating Difference: The Anthropology of Genocide*, ed. A.L. Hinton, 43–53. Berkeley: University of California Press.

Sanford, V. 2008. ¡Si Hubo Genocidio en Guatemala! Yes! There Was Genocide in Guatemala. In *The Historiography of Genocide*, ed. D. Stone, 543–576. New York: Palgrave Macmillan.

Totten, S., W.S. Parsons, and R.K. Hitchcock. 2002. Confronting Genocide and Ethnocide of Indigenous Peoples: An Interdisciplinary Approach to Definition, Intervention, Prevention, and Advocacy. In *Annihilating Difference: The Anthropology of Genocide*, ed. A.L. Hinton, 54–91. Berkeley: University of California Press.

Wallace, S. 2011. *The Unconquered: In Search of the Amazon's Last Uncontacted Tribes*. New York: Crown Publishers.

CHAPTER 5

# Racial Trauma and Racism

*The narratives below are all exemplars of biographical knowledge from episodic memories in relation to racism as experienced by Guatemalan-Mayan immigrants living in South Florida. Following these, there are narratives of racism as experienced by Brazilian urban Amerindians.*

In order to understand "racism" as a subject of study, it is not "only" important to analyze its causes, but likewise to consider its effects. In other words, and unfortunately, the results of racism often result in "trauma" of those who have experienced it. Elsewhere I wrote about how racism may have everyday qualities, or be diachronic, because some populations experience it every day in their lives.[1] While some episodes of racism are particularly acute and therefore racist, experiences may also be experienced as synchronic, or particular to an instant in time, or particular instances in time.

Many ethnic groups such as the indigenous peoples I studied, both urban Amerindian groups within Brazil, and Guatemalan-Mayan Indians in South Florida, have memories of racist experiences which may be postulated as having both diachronic and synchronic qualities—ongoing in their lives and particular to certain episodes in their lives. Therefore, racism and trauma should be viewed as complementary understandings in the way memories are formed from such deplorable, devastating, shocking, surprising, and even disgusting experiences for the individual subjected to hate, whether those experiences are prolonged, or singular.

My research about racism is tied to memories and perceiving how memories form identities. An individual's memories, if they have had racist *experiences, may inform how an individual may comprehend society. In other words, many indigenous peoples like the ones I studied, have extreme distrust of "white society" and "white people," whether these are Brazilian urban Amerindians or Guatemalan-Mayan Indians. Indigenous distrust in white society for peoples of the Americas extends over 500 years. Moreover, because racism against indigenous peoples is concurrent and recurrent, their trauma has been exacerbated over time as well and it is trauma they live with and have had to adapt to over a long period of time.*

\*\*\*

Guatemalan-Mayan Immigrant Interviews About Racism

*In terms of my Mayan informants and interviewees, Maria, Lorena and Sergio, (pseudonyms) all of them experienced some forms of racism in their lives and such memories about racism may be characterized as "episodic memories of discrimination."*[92] *Moreover, racism itself is a social mode of structural violence. Racism embodies ways of acting and/or speaking which are characterized by hate toward others, often ethnic and/or religious minorities, in order to keep others, ethnic minorities, oppressed by the dominant society, whether this is conscious or inadvertent.*

*Thus, structural violence (or structures of violence) is a form of violence, as not only actions, whether speech or real physical acts, but those barriers within society preventing others from education, employment, or habitation, and/or access to the dominant society. Structural violence may extend not only toward ethnic or religious minorities but also toward gender minorities such as those from the LGBT community. Historical structures of discrimination like these are part of the exclusionary practices which may in fact define dominant societies. Not only did Guatemalan-Mayas experience such discrimination in their home country in Guatemala from the Ladino (or majority white population) but they newly experience it among other Hispanic-Americans in the United States and among whites in general from American society. What is more, the rhetoric against immigrants became worse under the Trump administration, especially those from El Salvador, Guatemala, and Honduras but also Mexico. Yet, the irony of course is that many of these immigrants initially began migrating to the United States because of American foreign policy in their respective countries, especially the proxy wars which were fought under the Reagan administration in the 1980s against communism in Central America.*

\*\*\*

Interview: Maria

There are scholarships but they were given to the Ladinos, and not to Mayan people, even though they [Mayan] had good points [grades] they [the government] always want that the Mayas are always down and continue being peasants, and housewives because they [the government] are the ones who want to control the country ... the ladinos are descendant from the Spanish, that are not Mayan, they don't have Mayan blood, they have Spanish blood because they are the descendants, that is the Hispanic or Spanish, I don't know, I think all the Hispanic are descendants from the Spanish, right, they come from Spain, so those are the ones who are in Guatemala.

***JPL: You mentioned that you are not Latin nor Hispanic, could you explain to me then, how do you perceive yourself?

Maria: I am a Mayan, I have my own language, my own culture, rituals, clothes, we don't dress like that [western], well, we have to do it because is cheaper and because our clothes are not sold over here.

***

### Interview: Lorena

I tried belonging to La Unidad, which was the Latina club on campus, I went to one or two meetings and I was just like, I've never really truly have identified myself as Latina, I mean I happen to be from Latin America, but I've always identified myself as Mayan, as a Guatemalan Mayan with indigenous background, so being there in La Unidad I was just like this is so strange, I can't relate to any of these women, and so instead I also had friends who were Native American, Hopi, especially Hopi and Cherokee, and we decided to expand the Native American club on campus and it was, there weren't many of us, but we did that, and that was a lot of fun, because I could relate to them on so many levels, because there is so much we have in common with the Native Americans.

***

### Interview: Sergio

Grade school was pretty difficult, especially, uhm, trying to learn the language and not using the language correctly. Uhm, we were ridiculed a lot, uhm, interestingly, we weren't really ridiculed by the Americans or African-Americans, we were ridiculed by the Mexicans and Latinos—Spanish people. Uhm, in hindsight, the reason why is 'cause we were trying to learn Spanish first and our Spanish was broken, ah, so then they would ridicule us regarding that. That was really a blow to the ego, 'cause, you know, you think you're saying it right but then someone points out that you're saying it wrong but they do it in a manner that, uhm, it's bad and it's a step backwards instead of forwards. So, once we got past that, now it became English, became the *obstacle too ... When I say that, it's uhm, it was okay to go out there and use the English language, and even though you got ridiculed you still felt good because they understood what you were saying, they might laugh at you but they understood what you were trying to say and the majority of the time they would correct us but it was done in a way that we didn't take it as an insult compared to when we were learning Spanish and then all kinds of Spanish people would just laugh at us and ridicule us.*

**\*\*\*JPL: What about now, what is it like being here?**

**Sergio:** *Now, it's, you know, now you're in the real world and now you're not secluded, you're not protected and racism, discrimination—it's an everyday ... it's a part of everyday life. You learn to live with it, uhm, we come from a culture of where we're a passive people. We're not in your face, we're not vocal, so when we are mistreated we accept it but we try to play the role of—ok, these people are uneducated, they just don't know what they're talking about ... they're quick to categorize you as something—"ok, this guy, he's a landscaper, he's (mumbles)." But they don't know the credentials I have but I not going to sit here and be like "don't judge me 'cause you don't know me," I'm just wasting my time with that individual and there's more productive things that I can do for society in different avenues, different areas.*
\*\*\*

*The following quotes are from the indigenous people I engaged with, studied, and worked with in 2009. The Brazilian urban Amerindians I engaged with came from eight distinct indigenous groups: Apurinã, Kambeba, Kokama, Munduruku, Mura, Sateré-Mawé, Tikuna, and Tukano.*[3] *These are excerpts from interviews with Brazilian urban Amerindians about racism.*
\*\*\*

Brazilian Urban Amerindian Interviews About Racism

*My urban Amerindian informants, Paulo, Davi, Yolanda, Iliana, Raquel, Alberto, Neva, Estefania, and Lara, (pseudonyms), likewise experienced discrimination throughout their lives as had my Guatemalan-Maya informants. The reasons are different but nonetheless there are similar patterns to urban Amerindian discrimination as the Guatemalan-Mayas.*
\*\*\*

**Interview with Paulo (twenty-nine years old, *Tuxaua*, a leader of one group of Sateré-Mawé in Manaus, March 23, 2009):**

*Other Indians when they arrived in that epoch [1960s-1970s] hid their Indian identity, but we never negated our race as Indians, we always remained Indians, never negating our race ... we kept learning and this struggle to be indigenous, we learned about the law ... behind this struggle and our struggle is always Tupana [God].*

\*\*\* JPL: How do you view the "white" world (*os brancos*)?

Paulo: *In this world to each their own, no help ... there is no help, individualism, the indigenous world is not like this. It is organized another way to help one's relatives.*

\*\*\*JPL: How do you view discrimination in Manaus?

Paulo: *You feel sad, it hurts the spirit, it makes you sad ... but given time and once you better understand it, it makes you want to fight harder ... you use it as a medium to fight. They say to us: "what are you doing here, living in the slums, you are Indians ...," but we have our artisanal crafts, and our culture, the tucandeira dance ... so we began inviting the public [to the tucandeira], especially public schools. There were few people at first but this increased to more. Those people who discriminated against us began to think differently. Now they begin to value the Sateré-Mawé culture. We do this to demonstrate the Sateré-Mawé culture, for people to understand it. It has become much better but it [discrimination] still exists.*
\*\*\*

### Interview with Davi (twenty-seven years old, Sateré-Mawé, March 24, 2009)

*They say the Indians belong in the forest, this is what they tell us [commenting on discriminatory remarks he has heard].*
\*\*\*

### Interview with Yolanda (twenty years old, Sateré-Mawé, March 24, 2009)

*There was a time when we were very discriminated against ... Yes when we were in school, they [other students] used to call us names and the neighbors too but not now, no ... the white man does not think about people.*
\*\*\*

### Interview with Iliana (twenty-three years old, Sateré-Mawé, March 25, 2009)

*When I was little there was discrimination at school. We heard things like "there are the Indians, they belong in the forest," and with the teacher too ... One time I was told by a teacher: "Indians are not worth anything," people saying things like that to me. Those are the things I remember.*
\*\*\*

### Interview with Raquel (twenty-seven years old, Munduruku, married to a Sateré-Mawé, March 30, 2009)

*Our children are very discriminated against when they go to school, especially when they go to school painted [adornment during their festivities] and this causes shame ... then after a while we started having our festival [tucandeira ritual] here ... then they discriminated against us less.*

\*\*\*

Interview with Iliana (April 15, 2009) [describing the incident which occurred at Lago Azul on March 11, 2008; the Indians occupied a piece of land near Manaus as homesteaders. They were called "invaders" and were forced off the land by the Brazilian Military Police.]

*At that moment I was angry ... I was pregnant with child and holding my baby when they [military police] started pushing me ... I was angry because they [military police] were choking my husband with a baton ... they hit me on the arm and started pushing me ... they [military police] said to me: "You are not an Indian, what are you doing here?" "You are not an Indian." They [military police] said the people [Indians] were "civilized," and that people [Indians] were invaders ... They [military police] came to throw us off the land. I was angry when they hit my arm ... they told us to leave ... that photo appeared in the newspaper [referring to a photo of the incident] ... this occurred on 11 of March, 2008 ... they need to respect the Indians and what they say ... I remember crying ... we had stayed there 10 days.*

\*\*\*

Interview with Alberto (fifty-two years old, Apurinã, May 4, 2009) [he describes how he was hit when he was young by non-indigenous people in Manaus trying to survive in the city. His father had died and his uncle left him in the city during his adolescence to fend for himself and find his way.]

*I, I suffered ... In Apurinã [culture] when they do not like you they leave you ... They [his uncle and other kin] took me to the white city [Manaus], all to each his own ... In the streets they called me dog and hit me, paff! ... Listen, I suffered a great amount ... I learned how to work. I did not know where to go ... what happened to my father and grandfather, they suffered too [also, relates to the oppressive work during the Rubber Boom era and the work of his grandfather.] ... Now it is better and today people in the street treat me with respect ... I have a presence in front of white people ... many people think of the Apurinã as in the past [referring to past discrimination] ... To remember is suffering, a lot of suffering, you do not know which road to take ... during my adolescent years I went through a lot of suffering ... For me things have gotten much better with work, family, learning.*

\*\*\*

**Interview with Neva (twenty-six years old; identifies as being Kokama with her husband's group; her mother is Apurinā and father is caboclo, May 13, 2009)**

*Unfortunately, there still exists prejudice today ... In the past we were like Blacks, now no. It is very awful prejudice and very ugly also ... we are also prejudiced by the government [FUNASA] because we do not get proper health care from them ... Marriages between Indians and Indians is good because the whites do not understand our culture unfortunately.*

\*\*\*

**Interview with Estefania (twenty-two years old; Kokama; her father is Mura, mother is Kokama, May 13, 2009)**

*I see discrimination as really awful because we are Indians. Discrimination is ugly ... discrimination is a big thing. These things are opening how people are thinking. There are more opportunities today ... the whites discriminate against the Indians still.*

\*\*\*

**Interview with Lara (nineteen years old; Tukano, May 29, 2009)**

*When I was a child there was a lot of discrimination at the school. Classmates did not look at me in a nice manner while in school but things have begun to change as I have been involved in the indigenous movement ... [asked her to explain a personal incident]. When I was in the primary, public state school, there was a teacher who knew I was indigenous. She was a traditional teacher, a white teacher. She told me I did not understand anything because I did not speak Portuguese very well. So, she did not treat me very well and neither did my classmates. Then there were fights with my classmates and then after that I did not identify with being indigenous. When I learned Portuguese, it was better ... it happened when I was 9 years old.*

Photograph of Sateré-Mawé tuxaua (chief), an urban Amerindian in Manaus, Brazil (author's photograph).

5 RACIAL TRAUMA AND RACISM   147

Photograph of Dr. Martin Luther King, Jr. Monument in Washington, D.C. (author's photograph).

Photograph of Malcolm X.

Photograph of George Floyd Memorial in Minneapolis, Minnesota.

## INTRODUCTION

The previous narratives from Guatemalan-Mayas and Brazilian urban Amerindians demonstrate how memories of racism are tied to certain traumas which live on in the mind from structural or symbolic violence. As I explained in a previous article, "Mayan Cognition, Memory, and Trauma" (2009), memories of this type differ in category and kind from flashbulb memories because they may have episodic qualities, which reveal specific periods of time of being injured and offended over a prolonged time frame. Such memories are more semantic in character as well because such memories are ways of knowing about discrimination and oppression which are carried forward from experiential episodes or "schema" in the case of the home country of Guatemala to the host country of the United States for the Guatemalan-Mayan immigrants. On the other hand, such ways of knowing about discrimination and racism are part of adapting to city life for the Brazilian urban Amerindians who moved from the interior to urban centers like Manaus. (Although some informants were born in Manaus too.)

In my view, structural violence is a type of violence which may have everyday qualities and become norms in people's lives as it has for Guatemalan-Mayan Indians and Brazilian urban Amerindians. Such memories of racism are based upon what Scheper-Hughes (1992: 225) has called "routines of humiliation and violence." These are associated with discrimination, prejudices, racism, stereotyping, and labeling, which as a whole demean individuals and collectives. Because such oppression may be so pervasive for individuals and collectives they in turn may have permanent consequences.

Discrimination and racism may create situations of social exclusion whereby individuals are excluded from mainstream society and life because of their ethnicity, religion, and/or sexual preference. Pierre Bourdieu (1977: 237) has asserted that "symbolic violence" is a "form of domination which, transcending the opposition usually drawn between sense relations and power relations, communication and domination, is only exerted *through* the communication in which it is disguised." As evident from the Guatemalan-Maya and Brazilian urban Amerindian narratives and their experiences with racism, we understand how repetitive and routinized discrimination may be and how such routines therefore become the very structures of exclusion in society or "structural or symbolic violence." Such experiences of exclusion become social norms and therefore memories of racism have structurally violent and semantic qualities. As Harvey Whitehouse (2000: 8) argues: "Semantic memory results from strengthening over time of such repertoires, such that the organism is able to classify and model experiences on the basis of common features, in other words, to develop schemas for recurrent experiences."

Moreover, such memories of racism allude to different forms of time. It is my viewpoint that a conception of time in relation to biographical ethnography is essential for defining how, for example, Guatemalan-Mayan immigrants and Brazilian urban Amerindians, relate to their pasts, and how we as researchers may explain differing forms of memory, both episodic and semantic. Elsewhere, and following Alfred Gell (1992: 52), I explained how diachrony and synchrony are not formulations of two kinds of time but are really just one (Linstroth 2002: 169). In other words, specific episodes of discrimination have synchronic qualities in memory but because discrimination may last over a long period of time and may have everyday qualities, these are part of diachronic memories as well. All such memories may form part of an individual's inventory of experiential racism relating to specific episodes and/or experiencing such racism every day and for a long time. Earlier (Linstroth 2009), I explained such memory forms may be termed "synchronic trauma" and "diachronic trauma," as synchronic relates to specific traumatic memories of racism and diachronic trauma relates to long-term trauma of racism over time.

"For biographical purposes, placing these time episodes into a chronological sequence and by referring to cognitive formations of memory as having synchronic qualities—their childhood, the period of migration, the burning of the village, the killing of an uncle, etc.—places specific episodes of trauma as being characterized by another mental framework than the mentality of everydayness of semantic forms. Thus, we may wish to explain why semantic forms of structural violence, by contrast, are part of the identity of the [Guatemalan-Mayan] immigrant experience" and/or Brazilian urban Amerindian experience "and the long-term history of suffering by a people through inter-ethnic conflict. Long-term trauma of this kind experienced through discrimination, social segregation and oppression, I will call here "diachronic trauma." Such forms of trauma are not limited to one generation but may affect subsequent generations, and may form structural aspects of violence in society. We know this through studies of children of Holocaust survivors, who also suffer from varying forms of trauma.[4] These memory forms of trauma are diachronic because of enduring effects on the individual's psyche from everyday happenings rather than specific episodes. Such distinctions of time and the particular forms of suffering and trauma explained here are fundamental for differentiating memory types" (Linstroth 2009: 169).

Additionally, we may expound on this discussion to include what Maurice Bloch (1998: 110) has stated that "Adult humans construct a multiplicity of narratives of different types appropriate to different contexts." Yet, while I agree with this statement, I disagree with Bloch (1998: 102) when he asserts that he finds it is "totally unacceptable … the notion that cognition of time and other fundamental categories is constructed through narratives and that consequently an examination of narratives will reveal directly a particular group of peoples' concepts of the world they inhabit." Certainly, trauma as it relates to time, especially through episodic and semantic memories reveal how a cognition of time is possible, exposing a certain knowledge about in this instance racism. "How else are we to make sense of these narratives and memory forms in relation to time if not to structure them through a cognition of time, episodic versus every day?" (Linstroth 2009: 170). Understanding relationships of time associated with memory forms provides us with a window into the differences between synchronous episodes and diachronic persistence as foundations of ontological identity which may be fashioned from discrimination and racism and thereby underlining how both types of memory form overall memories in an individual's lifetime.

Aside from the biographical narratives describing episodes of racism in the lives of Guatemalan-Mayan immigrants and Brazilian urban Amerindians, this chapter broadens the discussion of racism to include current affairs in the United States and beyond—former President Trump's racist rhetoric, the murder of George Floyd and other unfortunate African-American deaths at the hands of police, racism against Native Americans, and the racialized issues surrounding COVID-19 in Brazil.

\*\*\*

In this chapter, I discuss what I will call the "politics of racism" in relation to recent events and episodes. By the "politics of racism," I mean not only how race is a social construct but how racism forms part of the construction of the political landscape, especially from the populist rhetoric of political leaders (see Chap. 1.). Specifically, with the advent of prior President Donald J. Trump of the United States and President Jair Bolsonaro of Brazil, both men represent a kind of populist bigotry. Both men shocked through their rhetoric in their respective countries causing many problems. The former, Trump, targeted Latin American immigrants,

Congresswomen of color, the handicapped, women in general, minorities, and political enemies, and the latter, Bolsonaro, targeted indigenous peoples, homosexuals, women, political enemies, and neglected the severity of Coronavirus in Brazil. (Hence, the reason why some have given Bolsonaro the moniker, the "Trump of South America.")

This chapter also develops and expounds upon how COVID-19 may be associated with structural violence. Why are some countries in the developing world across Latin America, Asia, and Africa less equal and less able to cope with a worldwide pandemic like Coronavirus than others in the developed world, namely, for example, in Europe, the United States, Australia, New Zealand, and Japan. Why do we have such stark inequalities in our world today and how does a disease like Coronavirus underline such inequities.

Another aspect of this chapter makes clear other injustices, such as the death of George Floyd and how racism has persisted in policing, not only against African-Americans but against Native Americans as well. Issues of race in the United States have been at the forefront of people's minds ever since the death of Floyd but not only limited to Floyd but the unjust deaths of so many other African-Americans at the hands of the police and/or because of white supremacists, such as the tragic case of Ahmaud Arbery.

Indeed, the rise of Donald J. Trump to the U.S. presidency has made many to question how we went from the first Black president to one so bigoted as Trump? To many Trump's ascendency to the presidency was a surprise. As Ibram Kendi (2016: ix, xi) summarizes: "Trump's election left many Americans in shock, in search of serious answers to serious questions. How could a Donald Trump follow Barack Obama into the presidency? How could the candidate of angry bigots, the Klan's candidate, the stop-and-frisk candidate, the candidate of border walls, the candidate that said a Latino judge can't be objective and that 'African Americans and Hispanics' live in 'hell'—how could this birther theorist follow the first Black president? How could Trump rise when Obama's rise seemed to make it impossible? … If Barack Obama came to embody America's history of racial progress, then Donald Trump should come to embody America's history of racist progress. And racist progress has consistently followed racial progress."

Cornel West (1993: 155–156) through his own writing has anticipated the issues raised by this chapter when he states: "Race is the most explosive issue in American life precisely because it forces us to confront the tragic facts of poverty and paranoia, despair and distrust. In short, a candid examination of *race* matters takes us to the core of the crisis of American democracy. And the degree to which race *matters* in the plight and predicament of fellow citizens is a crucial measure of whether we can keep alive the best of this democratic experiment we call America."

Of course, race "matters" not only in the United States but across the globe. As this chapter will validate, racism is played out in different contexts and among different peoples, whether in the United States, Brazil, or in the developing world, or whether for African-Americans or Native Americans, or other subalterns. Our very humanity depends upon how we as human beings from varying societies across our world treat fellow human beings with dignity and respect.

## A Racist President and Racist Trauma

When an American person of color hears—"go back to where you came from"—those very words epitomize racism. They are white code for "you do not belong here." And "you are not white" and therefore "you are not us"; and as such, you are not part of this country, the United States, which should be white.

Yet, when the President of the United States remarked with racist rhetoric, more specifically, when former President Donald J. Trump used the bully pulpit through racist tweets—how as a country were we moving toward "making America great again"? And by the way, "make America great again" (MAGA) is racist code for "make America white again" (MAWA), which was reiterated by House Speaker Nancy Pelosi (D-California).[5]

This is the era we live in. How is this an example for our children and their future? What America is this? Why is this tolerable today? Why were Republicans mostly silent about the president's discriminatory comments?

On July 16, the U.S. House of Representatives approved a resolution, 240-187, censuring the previous president's racist tweets and stated it: "Strongly condemns President Donald Trump's racist comments that have legitimized and increased fear and hatred of new Americans and people of color."[6]

Remember Charlottesville, Virginia in 2017? On July 15, 2019, a Virginia judge sentenced, a self-proclaimed neo-Nazi, James Fields, to life plus 419 years for killing Heather Heyer and injuring more than two dozen others by ramming his car through a crowd in Charlottesville on August 12, 2017.[7] The night before there was an organized neo-Nazi and white supremacist rally, where young men carrying torches, held a vigil of hate, and chanted: "blood and soil" and "Jews will not replace us!"[8] The following day, former President Donald J. Trump, declared: "I've condemned many different groups. But not all of those people were neo-Nazis, believe me. Not all of those people were white supremacists by any stretch. Those people were also there because they wanted to protest the taking down of a statue of Robert E. Lee ... and you had some very bad people in that group, but you also had people that were very fine people, on both sides."[9]

Excuse me Mr. previous President, if you are chanting, "Jews will not replace us!'—you are not among the fine people in this country protesting for legitimate issues and for the betterment of humanity. You are shouting racist rants. Also, isn't it ironic Mr. President that General Robert E. Lee himself never wanted any statues built in his image or to commemorate the Civil War in any way?[10]

Here was what prior President Donald J. Trump tweeted on Sunday, July 14, 2019: "So interesting to see 'Progressive' Democrat Congresswomen, who originally came from countries whose governments are a complete and total catastrophe, the worst, most corrupt and inept anywhere in the world (if they even have a functioning government at all), now loudly ... and viciously telling the people of the United States, the greatest and most powerful Nation on earth, how our government is to be run. Why don't they go back and help fix the totally broken and crime ... These places need your help badly, you can't leave fast enough."[11]

It is remarkable these words came from the President of the United States. Certainly, we have had racist presidents in our history, perhaps, Andrew Johnson, Woodrow Wilson, and Richard Nixon, prominently come to mind. Moreover, we have had slave-owning presidents, such as George Washington, Thomas Jefferson, and Andrew Jackson.[12]

Yet, we live in the twenty-first century, and before Trump, we elected our first African-American president in Barack Obama. Even so, former President Donald J. Trump began his presidential bid by declaring Obama was not born in the United States, the so-called Birther Movement.[13] Where were Republicans reproaching this overt racism? What about Republicans such as Senator John McCain in the 2008 presidential election correcting audience members about whether or not then Senator Barack Obama was a U.S. citizen: "No ma'am, no ma'am, he is a decent family man, who I just happen to have disagreements with" (about whether or not Obama was an Arab).[14]

Trump's tweets on Sunday, July 14, 2019, were not just about anyone but directed at four freshman U.S. Congresswomen—all women of color. Additionally, all of them are citizens of the United States. So, Trump's history of racist rhetoric, first denying U.S. citizenship to former President Barack Obama, was extended to four U.S. Congresswomen along the same veins of racist ranting. These targeted U.S. Congresswomen in question are: Representative Alexandria Ocasio-Cortez (D-New York), Representative Ilhan Abdullahi Omar (D-Minnesota), Representative Ayanna Pressley (D-Massachusetts), and Representative Rashida Tlaib (D-Michigan). Only Omar was foreign-born in Somalia but she lived most of her life as a refugee in the United States and is a full U.S. citizen.

So, where all of these U.S. Congresswomen come from is the United States, not some foreign country. But in the mind of former President Trump, their ethnic origins defined them, whether these are: African-American, Palestinian-American, Puerto Rican-American, or Somali-American—somehow, they are "not" American because they are "not" white? These women are alleged to come from sh**hole countries, just because they are women of color. When in fact, they all come from the United States. Mr. previous President your racist ranting and racist tweeting is making the United States a sh**hole country by elevating racism as acceptable discourse. Why should white supremacist and neo-Nazi hateful communications become normalized ways we talk about difference?

The four U.S. Congresswomen held a press conference on July 15, 2019, refuting the president's racist remarks.[15] These four women directly explained why prior President Trump's tweets were and are harmful, not only to them, but for the country as a whole. Then, the House of Representatives led by Nancy Pelosi (D-California), passed a resolution rebuking former President Trump.

Let me be clear and go further. I have been writing about racism for a decade now as a social and cultural anthropologist. I teach students how and why racism is a destructive social construct. And, let me repeat, "racism discourse," in all of its multiple forms, is very, very damaging, hurtful, and dangerous.

In 2009, I wrote an article, titled: "Mayan Cognition, Memory, and Trauma," which was partially about the mental health damages caused by memories of racism, specifically against Mayan-American immigrants.[16]

I believe one of the central arguments of that essay is still pertinent today. It is the idea that racism, and memories of racism, have traumatic effects upon an individual over time. In the article, I theorized such memories may be characterized as "synchronic trauma" and "diachronic trauma." In other words, memories of racism occur at specific times but also may be carried forward over time and may be constant over time. An individual may remember when someone said, for example, "go back to where you came from" and remember who said it, when they said it, and where they said it. That racist remark may always be remembered throughout an individual's lifetime.

Likewise, an individual may experience racism as an everyday occurrence. Racism may be part of one's experience at school, or at work, or during leisure. When individuals are harmed by racism, then racism itself may be part of what is called "structural violence." This is to say, for example, when racism prevents individuals from getting good jobs, from attending good schools, or from having fair pay—all become structures of violence which are engrained in society. Racism, in this sense, may be a barrier, and therefore, transforming into those structures of violence for prevention.

Racism is violent in the real sense too because its discourse may be violent in nature. It may threaten real violence. It is also violent through the real actions which supports it systemically, such as the slavery of African-Americans in the South prior to the Civil War, or the lynching of African-Americans during the Jim Crow South, or the genocide of Native Americans, or more recently, the mass shootings at synagogues, or attacks of mosques.[17]

Former President Trump was reckless. Regardless, of the political gains he may have wished to have for the presidential elections in 2020 against his rival democratic opponents, his racist rhetoric may have far lasting consequences for the children of this country. It is the normalization of racism and racist discourse which may have caused the most harm. I truly worry about my nieces and nephew and what world they may inherit because of such racism as acceptable and customary.

On July 17, 2019, previous President Trump held another MAGA political rally and incited the attending crowd by falsely declaring Congresswoman Ilhan Omar supported Al-Qaeda and deceitfully charged her with being an anti-Semite, as the crowd yelled: "Send her back! Send her back!"[18]

As Americans, we should all remember the immortal words of our founders in the Declaration of Independence: "We hold these truths to be self-evident, that all men are created equal, that they are endowed by their

Creator with certain unalienable Rights, that among these are Life, Liberty and the pursuit of Happiness."[19]

And finally, we need to remember the immortal words of Dr. Martin Luther King, Jr. in his acceptance speech for the Nobel Prize for Peace: "I refuse to accept the view that mankind is so tragically bound to the starless midnight of racism and war that the bright daybreak of peace and brotherhood can never become a reality ... I believe that unarmed truth and unconditional love will have the final word."[20]

## WHAT ABOUT THE AMERINDIANS DURING THE CORONAVIRUS PANDEMIC?

Most of us were preoccupied with quarantining, and whether or not we would have jobs to go back to in 2020 in the midst of the Coronavirus pandemic. In truth, it took months. Therefore, it was difficult to imagine how Coronavirus (COVID-19) could wreak more economic or mortal havoc elsewhere, but it did, especially in the "developing world." Imagine, cities like Dhaka, Karachi, Lagos, Manila, Port-au-Prince, or Brazilian *favelas* (slums), and/or refugee camps in the Middle East—places where social distancing was all but impossible. Imagine throughout Africa, Asia, and Latin America, where they did not have access to enough ventilators they needed, not enough testing kits, not enough masks nor rubber gloves, and other protective equipment, nor the types of health care systems, and amounts of money in order to combat Coronavirus (COVID-19).[21] Now, in 2021, the question is whether or not the developing world are able to get enough vaccines and have their populations vaccinated prior to an impending epidemiological crisis in such countries.

Now imagine peoples and areas of the world, much, much more vulnerable to Coronavirus (COVID-19) than other populations because of their lack of immunity to respiratory illnesses. Such peoples are Brazilian Amerindians. Many anthropologists, epidemiologists, physicians, and public health experts, are sounding the alarm. Indigenous populations like those in Brazil were and are particularly vulnerable and have been so for more than 500 years with the invasion of Europeans onto their lands and the spread of European diseases such as influenza, measles, and smallpox.[22] Even more worrisome are the isolated Natives who have no contact with the outside world and modern society. In Brazil, there are as many as 170 such isolated indigenous groups without outside contact living in the Amazon.

In 2009, I spent about seven-months in the Amazonian city of Manaus with a population of more 2 million in Amazonas State as a Fulbright scholar, visiting professor, and anthropological researcher, conducting an anthropological study on urban Amerindian peoples there. It is the most populous city in the Brazilian Amazon with more than 2 million inhabitants and it is the city where most Brazilian Amerindians living in Brazil's interior Amazon will try to go for hospital and medical care. But the distances are frequently great. For example, the distance between São Gabriel de Cachoeira, a largely indigenous-city of almost 41,000 in the Upper Rio Negro area, and Manaus, is about 850 kilometers (528 miles).[23] By airplane it is about four hours, and by ferry boat the distance is about three days. By then, if one travels by boat, it might be too late for most Indians who try to make the journey with those stricken by the illness. São Gabriel de Cachoeira does not have the hospital facilities nor the medical care for such a deadly contagion.

Some have stated that much of the indigenous peoples in the Amazon, and elsewhere, might become wiped out from the virus since medical care for most communities in the interior is so remote. To make matters even worse, President Jair Bolsonaro of Brazil, has flat out denied the severity of Coronavirus (COVID-19), and has called it a "little flu," a "measly cold," and a fake-media con.[24] In fact, Bolsonaro has criticized various state governors in Brazil, especially São Paulo State and Rio de Janeiro State governors, two of the most populous ones, for quarantining residents in their states and also closing the beaches. In 2020, there was even a concerted effort to "impeach" Bolsonaro, even among his governor and legislative supporters, who are contradicting his numerous ignorant and lackadaisical pronouncements about his non-scientific views on COVID-19.[25] Bolsonaro's rhetoric is quite dangerous, akin to similar reckless and uninformed declarations about Coronavirus as those of Mexico's President Andrés Manuel López Obrador.[26] Both Latin American leaders are putting their populations at mortal risk by not taking the Coronavirus pandemic seriously. On April 9, 2020, there were 15,927 confirmed cases of Coronavirus and 800 deaths from the disease in Brazil, the most in Latin America. [27] (Today, in September 2021, Brazil has almost 600,000 dead from Coronavirus only second to the United States.)[28]

Regardless, in Brazil, the country's indigenous population, who make up approximately 0.6 percent of the nation's some 211 million inhabitants, are at extreme risk from COVID-19.[29] The situation is truly dire and urgent because if more and more indigenous people become infected, mortality rates among Native peoples could get out of control. In 2020, only a few Amerindian individuals became infected but this drastically changed as the disease progressed and began taking more and more Native lives. Moreover, the government does not count indigenous peoples living outside demarcated Indian lands and therefore has underreported Indian deaths as a result.[30] (Now, in 2021, the problem is getting enough Natives vaccinated and unfortunately the rollout to do so has been quite slow.)

Many Brazilian Amerindian communities and indigenous reserves throughout Latin America closed themselves off from outsiders in 2020 for fear of contagion from this pandemic virus.[31] Many Amerindian peoples are in fact barricading roads leading to their community reserves for dread of contamination from Coronavirus. Furthermore, the aforementioned indigenous city, São Gabriel de Cachoeira, was on complete lockdown in 2020 by disallowing any boat traffic entering or leaving the city and suspending all flights.[32]

I want to be clear about this. We may be witnessing the worst genocide from a disease not experienced by indigenous peoples in the Western Hemisphere since the first European contacts with Native peoples more than 500 years ago. Coronavirus (COVID-19) has the potential of devastating Amerindians in Brazil and Amerindians elsewhere in lowland South America at levels never seen before in the modern era.

In the early days of the disease in 2020, there was an adolescent Yanomami boy, aged 15, who was gravely ill with Coronavirus and died. There were six other known cases of Amerindians with the disease in the Brazilian states of Amazonas, Pará, and Roraima.[33] Aside from the Yanomami boy, there were four cases attributed to the Kokama Indians, another of an eighty-seven-year-old Borari woman, and a forty-five-year-old man from the Baré tribe. These were the early stages of infection but the pandemic among Brazilian Indians grew much worse in 2020 to present day.

As worrisome are invaders on Brazilian indigenous reserves, such as the illegal goldminers (*garimpeiros*) on Yanomami lands. If such illegal goldminers are not forcibly removed by the Brazilian and Venezuelan governments, they may unnecessarily bring COVID-19 to Yanomami people and wipe out entire villages in the process and annihilate the remaining few

Yanomami people. Also, on April 2, 2020, there was news of yet another Guajajara Indian who was assassinated by illegal loggers (*madeireiros ilegais*) invading the Guajajara Native Reserve, the fifth such murder of these tribespeople within six months.[34]

Already, Brazilian President Bolsonaro has a horrendous record on human rights with racist proclamations against Brazilian Indians, as well as racist remarks against other minorities such as contra Brazilian Afro-descendent populations, and against those from the Brazilian LBGT community. Not long ago, Bolsonaro declared: "Increasingly, the Indian, is becoming human, just like us" (*Cada vez mais, o índio é um ser humano igual a nós*)—a truly ignorant observation about Brazil's indigenous population.[35]

Thus, experts have written open-letters expressing their concerns, such as the Society for the Anthropology of Lowland South America (SALSA).[36] In an open letter from SALSA on March 22, 2020, the organization stated: "SALSA is therefore deeply concerned about the dangers that the coronavirus (COVID-19) pandemic poses to the indigenous peoples of Brazil, especially isolated peoples, who are among the most vulnerable … Thus SALSA considers any unwarranted attempt to approach immunologically vulnerable people in the midst of such an unpredictable pandemic, especially without the input and participation of experienced field agents, to be reckless and potentially catastrophic, and urges Brazilian and international authorities to treat any lethal consequences of such approach as murder or genocide."

As the Brazilian indigenous Krenaki-leader Ailton Krenak avowed: "What I have learned over the decades is that everyone needs to wake up, because for a time it was just us, the indigenous peoples, who were threatened with a complete rupture or extinction about the meaning of our lives as human beings. Yet today, we are all facing a sense of immediacy from the Earth not willing to support our demands."[37]

As such, I am very, very worried about the urban Amerindian people I worked with a decade ago in Manaus, Brazil, namely, the Apurinã, Kambeba, Kokama, Munduruku, Mura, Sateré-Mawé, Tikuna, and Tukano, urban Amerindian peoples. And unlike popular mythology, just because such Indians have migrated to cities, does not detract from their indigeneity, nor does it mean they are more immune to such grave respiratory illnesses as Coronavirus (COVID-19). These are Natives living in the margins of Amazonian cities like Manaus and because of their extreme poverty, are that much more vulnerable to susceptibility for contracting the virus.

I can only hope that the Brazilian government will aid these urban Amerindians as well. But the situation is so potentially catastrophic because the present political climate of the Bolsonaro administration is ignoring the rights of Brazil's indigenous people.

May all of the Amerindians stay healthy and safe and may they continue in the struggle (*luta*) for their rights. As a Sateré-Mawé chief (*tuxaua*) frequently said to me in his own language: *Waku Sese*! (*Tudo Bem*! All Well!)—indeed, may all be well for all of you my Amerindian friends!

## CORONAVIRUS, POVERTY, AND STRUCTURAL VIOLENCE

As a nation, obviously, there are so many things we can do better. There always will be. Yet, what the Coronavirus (COVID-19) pandemic has made all too apparent is how we have not appropriately dealt with poverty in the United States. This is not just about the former Trump administration or even the present Biden administration, it is about all past presidential administrations and past congressional sessions which have largely ignored the issue in favor of corporate concerns, or more lucrative economic programs, and/or private interests. At times, poverty has been on the governmental agenda, and at times, some legislation has been passed. But in all honesty, why has poverty not been a more major issue to tackle?

Way back in 1964, President Lyndon B. Johnson promoted legislation, which became known as a "War on Poverty."[38] In reality, Johnson's vision was a continuation of President Franklin Delano Roosevelt's "New Deal" and Johnson's policies were effective with the "Economic Opportunity Act" (1964), "Food Stamp Act" (1964), "Elementary and Secondary Education Act" (1965), and "Social Security Act" (1965, initiation of Medicare and Medicaid). Poverty decreased and people's lives improved from this legislation. We can also thank the "Civil Rights Movement" and leaders like Dr. Martin Luther King, Jr. for pushing President Johnson to do something. Also, highly influential was Michael Harrington's seminal book, *The Other America: Poverty in the United States* (1962).[39]

Even so, here we are today. As prior New York Governor Andrew Cuomo stated in 2020: "It always seems that the poorest people pay the highest price. Why is that? Why is that? Whatever the situation is. With the natural disaster Hurricane Katrina, the people standing on those rooftops were not rich white people. Why? Why is it the poorest people always pay the highest price?"[40] These are crucial questions and they need to be asked. It is indeed unfortunate that it takes a pandemic to ask them and to underline the issues of health disparities and issues surrounding poverty in general in the United States.

The renowned French sociological-theorist Pierre Bourdieu, in *Outline of a Theory of Practice* (1972), explained social forms of domination, such as poverty, as "symbolic violence."[41] Other researchers like anthropologist Nancy Scheper-Hughes expanded the understanding in her classic monograph *Death Without Weeping: the Violence of Everyday Life in Brazil* (1992), with an interpretation of "structural violence" whereby populations, such as the impoverished people she studied in Northeast Brazil, experienced everyday "routines of humiliation and violence."[42] In turn, I elaborated on these theorists to understand racism against Mayan refugees and their experiences of "discrimination, prejudice, racism, stereotyping, and labeling" in my article "Mayan Cognition, Memory, and Trauma" (2009).[43]

Similarly, if we examine issues of "structural violence" in association with Coronavirus (COVID-19), we find ethnic minorities, especially African-Americans and Hispanic-Americans, are more susceptible to illnesses and pandemics because of numerous socio-economic factors. As neurologist and primatologist Robert Sapolsky discusses in his acclaimed book *Why Zebras Don't Get Ulcers* (1994), how measuring the correlation between poverty and health is not simply just about the "socioeconomic status (SES) gradient" but about "feeling poor."[44] As Sapolsky asserts: "Cardiovascular measures, metabolism measures, glucocorticoid levels, obesity in kids. *Feeling* poor in our socioeconomic world predicts poor health … subjective SES is built around education, income, and occupational position (in other words, the building blocks of subjective SES), plus satisfaction with standard of living and feeling of financial security about the future."

Given that in general African-Americans and Hispanic-Americans are more likely to have lesser education and lower incomes than whites in the United States, also predicts some of the factors for structural violence in American society against these minorities.[45] Equally, another factor, which is "gender inequality," compounds the problems associated with health in our society. As the editors Amy Schulz and Leith Mullings (2006) argue in their book *Gender, Race, Class & Health: Intersectional Approaches*: "The malleability of race, gender, and class as socially constructed categories as well as the obdurate nature of inequalities structured around these concepts in the United States" are thus central to understanding why "structural violence" persists and why the correlation to poverty and health are still present in American society.[46]

In statistical terms, it is remarkable just how many socio-economic disparities exist in the United States compared with other "First World" and developed nations, especially since we are the wealthiest. According to the Center for Economic and Policy Research (CEPR), the United States has no national policy for paid sick leave and "zero" paid sick days leave for cancer treatment or influenza recovery, whereas Luxembourg and Norway have fifty for cancer and five for the flu.[47]

Moreover, among African-Americans and Hispanic-Americans their health risks are more notable. The National Partnership for Women and Families (NPWF) and the NAACP, estimate approximately 40 percent of "7.3 million Black workers" are unable to earn even a single paid sick day.[48] And, because of this, African-Americans are more often than not forced to choose "between their health and the health of their families and their economic security" if they fall ill, or have to care for an ill family member. The statistics are very similar for Hispanic-Americans. On the other hand, Latinos represent the largest labor force among ethnic minorities within the United States, approximately 15 million, like African-Americans, and are more than likely not able to earn any paid sick days according to UnidosUS and NPWF.[49]

Of course, health disparities should include the most marginalized in our society, namely, the homeless and the imprisoned populations. According to the "National Coalition for the Homeless": "Homelessness and poverty are inextricably linked. Poor people are frequently unable to pay for housing, food, childcare, health care, and education."[50] In a 2016 report from the U.S. Department of Housing and Urban Development (HUD), on any given night as many as about 550,000 people experienced homelessness in 2016 in America.[51] Homeless populations in general are likely to have pre-existing conditions which make them particularly vulnerable to Coronavirus as well.[52] Therefore, the need among the homeless is great, which means "providing food, sanitary devices and stations, port-a-potties and shower trucks to keep homeless individuals safe" are paramount for disease prevention.

Furthermore, jails and prisons are exceptionally susceptible to a pandemic like Coronavirus (COVID-19) and are like "petri dishes" because inmates are trapped with nowhere to go and where social distancing is altogether impossible.[53] According to a 2020 *New York Times* article:

"America has more people behind bars than any other nation. Its correctional facilities are frequently crowded and unsanitary, filled with an aging population of often impoverished people with a history of poor health care, many of whom suffer from respiratory problems and heart conditions."[54]

Additionally, there are many complications for considering early release programs both at the federal and at the state level. Let alone the prison employees who have likewise contracted the disease. In all, there are about 2.3 million incarcerated people in the United States, and in 2020 both prison staff and inmates in the states of Florida, New York, Michigan, Pennsylvania, Texas, and Washington tested positive for COVID-19.[55] The "Prison Policy Initiative" elaborates on five reasons how the criminal justice system might lessen the pandemic: (1) reduce numbers in local jails; (2) reduce numbers of inmates in federal and state prisons; (3) eliminate face-to-face meetings with people in the criminal justice system; (4) make correctional healthcare more humane; (5) allow families of inmates freer communication access.[56] As of 2021, the justice system has accomplished many such initiatives, especially early release for non-violent criminals.[57]

And finally, according to the Urban Institute, many poor people live in overcrowded housing, making social distancing impracticable and unmanageable and likewise negatively affecting educational outcomes for children.[58] Moreover, the average African-American household incomes are $40,165 in comparison to $65,845 for white households and in keeping with statistics from the U.S. Census and the Office of Minority Health (OMH).[59] While African-Americans also have lower life expectancies, Hispanics have the highest uninsured rates of any ethnic group within the United States, and in keeping with OMH statistics, 19.4 percent of Hispanics in comparison to 9.6 percent of whites were living in poverty.[60]

When President Lyndon B. Johnson declared an "unconditional war on poverty" in his State of the Union speech in 1964, he remarked: "It will not be a short or easy struggle. No single weapon will suffice. But we shall not rest until that war is won. The richest nation on earth can afford to win it. We cannot afford to lose it."[61] Those astounding words spoken by President Johnson fifty-seven years ago should also resound with us today with as much urgency as they did then, and maybe even more so with the growing economic crisis.

## Malcolm or MLK?

In 2020, the world witnessed a murder of an innocent Black man, George Floyd, what many, including Jesse Jackson, called a "public lynching" in broad daylight, at the hands of a white policeman, Derek Chauvin.[62] It was a brutal killing by the manner in which Minneapolis policeman, Chauvin, pressed his knee into Floyd's neck, slowly and viciously forcing the life out of Floyd for almost nine minutes. On the other hand, Chauvin's fellow officers, by not coming to Floyd's aid, were complicit to the crime. There was no need for Chauvin to have subdued Floyd in such a cruel and purposeful way until Floyd could no longer breathe, especially since Floyd had already been restrained. Nor, did Floyd have any weapon. Nor had he committed any crime warranting such force. In a video captured by a teenager, Floyd could be heard stating he could not breathe, and calling out for his deceased mother. Since 2014, there have been other police killings of African-Americans with no consequences for the police officers involved.[63]

All of the circumstances surrounding these African-American deaths at the hands of the police were suspicious at best, Floyd being the latest victim. There was Eric Garner on Staten Island, New York (2014), Michael Brown in Ferguson, Missouri (2014), Laquan McDonald in Chicago, Illinois (2014), Tamir Rice in Cleveland, Ohio (2014), Walter Scott in North Charleston, South Carolina (2015), Freddie Gray in Baltimore, Maryland (2015), Jamar Clark in Minneapolis, Minnesota (2015), Alton Sterling in Baton Rouge, Louisiana (2016), Philando Castile in St. Paul, Minnesota (2016, SP twin-city to Minneapolis), Stephon Clark in Sacramento, California (2018), Botham Jean in Dallas, Texas (2018), and Breonna Taylor in Louisville, Kentucky (2020), and finally, Floyd in Minneapolis.[64] The fact these murders took place all over the United States points to a "systemic issue" in policing in our country, a system valuing white privilege over people of color, fifty-seven years after the passage of the Civil Rights Act of 1964, and even after the recent introduction of body cameras.[65] In reality though, such police use of excessive force betrays a "societal systems failure," not just policing as will be explained. Fortunately, bystanders have captured many of the questionable circumstances of these deaths with cell-phones.

Garner was put in a deadly choke-hold by one officer who was never convicted. Garner's crime selling "loosie cigarettes" (single cigarettes). Then there was Brown who allegedly took something from a convenient store and was walking in the middle of the street. He scuffled with a police officer and was shot and left on the pavement for hours. Then there was McDonald who supposedly threatened an officer with a knife but the video evidence proves otherwise. Then, Rice who was only twelve years old was carrying a toy pellet gun when he was shot and killed. Elsewhere, Scott who was stopped for a broken taillight and because he ran away was shot five times. Then, Gray who was carrying a knife when he was detained and after being handcuffed and shackled, he was found in a police van after almost an hour with his spine nearly severed. On the other hand, Jamar Clark was shot in a suspicious situation. Then, Sterling who was selling DVDs outside a convenient store and when officers detained him, they shot him. Then, there was Castile who was in a car with his girlfriend and her baby-daughter. As Castile reached for his wallet, the officer shot him seven times. On the other hand, Stephon Clark, a victim of mistaken identity, and in his grandmother's driveway, and after running, was shot twenty times by police because his cell phone was mistaken as a gun. Also, Jean was an innocent victim, the officer entered his apartment thinking it was her own and thinking Jean was a burglar. So, Jean was shot in his own apartment. Taylor likewise was shot in her own apartment because police entered upon suspicion of drugs without prior warning. Taylor was shot eight times. And then, on Memorial Day, May 25, 2020, George Floyd, who was forty-six years old, was murdered by a white policeman.

In 2019 alone, 1099 people have been killed by the police in the United States. The top five cities with the worst police homicides against African-American males in the United States are: Reno, Nevada; Oklahoma City, Oklahoma; Santa Ana, California; Anaheim, California; and St. Louis, Missouri.[66] Furthermore, 99 percent of killings by police between 2013 and 2019 never resulted in any convictions of any police officers. Also, Black people are three times more likely to be killed by police than white people are.[67]

As Cornel West has rightly pointed out, American democracy is in real trouble, especially for perpetuating a system of inequality, not only for its minority populations but in the disparities of wealth distribution.[68] Why are we propping up a system favoring billionaires, just interested in tax cuts and not progressive reform? We need a national healthcare system. State university education should be free. According to Cornel West: "Any society that refuses to eliminate or attenuate dilapidated housing, decrepit school systems, mass incarceration, massive unemployment and underemployment, inadequate healthcare and its violations of rights and liberties is undesirable and unsustainable."[69] So, business as usual is not going to work. The United States cannot expect to maintain a corrupt system without breakdown, without people saying enough, without mass civil disobedience. It is just untenable.

This is not simply a question of a few "bad apple cops" as the National Security Advisor, Robert O'Brien said.[70] Nor is it just about policing. Many police do a very difficult job well. Nonetheless, it is a systems problem, the whole system, our whole American democracy and American society, need reforming if we are ever able to be sustainable for the future. Moreover, this social movement has proven that all ethnicities and identities can come together—Black, white, Hispanic, Asian, Native, LGBTQ—and struggle against the problems associated with whole system.[71]

What is more, the election of prior President Donald J. Trump was the culmination of the problems in our society.[72] He was elected because of the overall symptomatic issues disparaging our American democracy today, especially the notion of fear of the "Other"—the immigrant, the African-American, or simply put, the "non-white." It is a frail system and it will not survive unless we can address the real inequalities of our society, whether these are rooted in economics, racism, xenophobia, education, housing, or healthcare. In fact, all are interrelated.

Hence, the title of this particular essay in this book posed a question: "Malcolm X or Dr. Martin Luther King, Jr.?"[73] The question was posed to highlight the need to return the better ideals of our Civil Rights past (1954–1968) and because the murder of George Floyd inspired some soul searching.[74] Therefore, it is right to ask what heroes we may look up to and who do we turn to for guidance in a context all the more ironic because little has changed from more than fifty years ago until now in regard to the disparities Americans face today. We saw how Coronavirus (COVID-19) unfairly affected both African-Americans and Hispanic-Americans because a majority of these minorities for many reasons could not self-isolate.[75] Nor do many of them have adequate healthcare or the type of housing to social distance. Many of these minorities, African-Americans and Hispanic-Americans, had to work in the service economy to feed their families and could not stay home.

So, "Malcolm or MLK?"—and the answer is we need both voices now more than ever. The murder of George Floyd brings to the fore all the historical racism and all the unfair police-targeting African-Americans face daily. We need voices like Malcolm X, who see the bullshit for what it is and who can wake people up to the realities of what is happening around them and to them. And we need voices like Dr. Martin Luther King, Jr. who will lead us toward real peaceful change and reform. We need both Malcolm and MLK as guiding lights—we always have. We need voices who spoke up against racism and who spoke out for social justice and because they did so, they were murdered too.

Moreover, we need our society not only to have an MLK Holiday once a year but to have a Malcolm X holiday day too. We need to recognize Black voices who speak the truth and who speak the truth to power. So, Malcolm X deserves a monument near the National Mall in Washington DC as much as that of MLK exists there now.[76]

Let's listen to what both Malcolm X said before he was assassinated in 1965 at only thirty-nine years old and Dr. Martin Luther King, Jr. said before he too was assassinated in 1968 at the same age, and let's appreciate them both. The former a Muslim and the latter a Christian. Both voices as different and important as Booker T. Washington and W.E.B. Du Bois.[77]

Let's celebrate their memories by demanding our lawmakers in the U.S. Congress to pass meaningful legislation and let's hope the new Biden administration will be allowed to pass its agenda toward such reforms.

Here are some memorable quotes from these two American Civil Rights heroes.

\*\*\*

"We must learn to live together as brothers or we will perish together as fools."
**Dr. Martin Luther King, Jr.**[78]

"You can't separate peace from freedom because no one can be at peace unless he has his freedom."
**Malcolm X**[79]

"The time is always ripe to do what is right." **Dr. Martin Luther King, Jr.**[80]

"Usually, when people are sad, they don't do anything. They just cry over their condition. But when they get angry, they bring about a change." **Malcolm X**[81]

"Change does not roll in on the wheels of inevitability, but comes through continuous struggle."
**Dr. Martin Luther King, Jr.**[82]

"There was police brutality and there was atrocity, and the press was just as atrocious as the police. Because they helped the police to cover it up by propagating a false image across the country." **Malcolm X**[83]

"Darkness cannot drive out darkness; only light can do that. Hate cannot drive out hate; only love can do that." **Dr. Martin Luther King, Jr.**[84]

"We need more light about each other. Light creates understanding, understanding creates love, love creates patience, and patience creates unity." **Malcolm X**[85]

"Nothing in the world is more dangerous than sincere ignorance and conscientious stupidity."
**Dr. Martin Luther King, Jr.**[86]

"Every defeat, every heartbreak, every loss, contains its own seed, its own lessen on how to improve your performance next time." **Malcolm X**[87]

"He who accepts evil without protesting against it, is really cooperating with it."
**Dr. Martin Luther King, Jr.**[88]

"You're not supposed to be so blind with patriotism that you can't face reality. Wrong is wrong, no matter who does it or says it." **Malcolm X**[89]

"The function of education is to teach one to think intensively and to think critically. Intelligence plus character—that is the goal of true education."
**Dr. Martin Luther King, Jr.**[90]

"I believe that there will be ultimately a clash between the oppressed and those who do the oppressing. I believe there will be a clash between those who want freedom, justice, and equality for everyone and those who want to continue the system of exploitation. I believe there will be that kind of clash, but I don't think it will be based on the color of the skin."
**Malcolm X**[91]

"Injustice anywhere is a threat to justice everywhere." **Dr. Martin Luther King, Jr.**[92]

"I'm for truth no matter who tells it. I'm for justice, no matter who it is for or against. I'm a human, first and foremost, and as such I'm for whoever and whatever benefits humanity as a whole." **Malcolm X**[93]

"I have decided to stick with love. Hate is too great a burden to bear."
**Dr. Martin Luther King, Jr.**[94]

\*\*\*

As Sam Cooke (1963) once sang: "A Change Is Gonna Come."[95] It really has been a long time waiting for change to come, but we need change, and we need it NOW!

## Why Race Is Everything in America!

The issues of "race" and "racism" have been with us since the founding of our august republic. Unfortunately, they are perniciously still with us today. They were the reason we fought the Civil War (1861–1865) and have mired our history throughout. There is no period in our history, the history of the United States, when "race" has not been significant in some profound way.

For many reasons too, the American Civil War is still with us today. It is still with us in every racial conflict we have had since. It is still being fought, perhaps unknowingly by many African-Americans, who have experienced "structural violence" in some way, whether in terms of wanting better education, better housing, or a better job, or even rights for a normal life. And it is still with us today when African-Americans are targeted unfairly by law enforcement.

Practically everyone in the United States has by now seen the gruesome video of alleged murder of a forty-six-year-old African-American man, George Floyd on Memorial Day, May 25, 2020, by a white Minneapolis policeman, Derek Chauvin.[96] The policeman, Chauvin, kneeled onto the neck of Floyd for almost nine minutes while Floyd was handcuffed and immobile and until Floyd was lifeless. On the other hand, other Minneapolis police officers at the scene kept Mr. Floyd immobile and failed to prevent policeman Chauvin from choking out Floyd.[97] It took four days for Minneapolis prosecutors to charge Derek Chauvin with third-degree murder and second-degree manslaughter and days more for charges to be brought against the other three officers.[98] Both the Federal Bureau of Investigation (FBI) and the Minnesota Bureau of Criminal Apprehension (BCA) likewise investigated the incident.[99] What makes the alleged killing of Floyd even more egregious and even more tragic was the flimsiness of the necessity to use such police force against Floyd. Nor is it even clear if Floyd supposedly used a counterfeit $20 bill to buy cigarettes at a local eatery and grocery store, which is why police officers were alerted to the scene in Minneapolis. What is very clear to most people is that Floyd's death was absolutely unnecessary. Moreover, Floyd was unarmed at the time of his detention not posing a threat to anyone. Above all, why should a man, any man, have to die for $20 dollars?

As African-American political activist and television commentator, Van Jones remarked on CNN: "What we saw was a lynching. That is what a lynching is. We saw a white man deprive a Black man of his life in public with the entire community staring, you know, horror struck. Now the world witnessed a lynching. There have been lynchings happening in America for hundreds of years. Umm ... this is what we have lived with."[100]

Any familiarity with U.S. history, verifies Van Jones' statement. About 3446 lynchings of African-Americans have been documented as occurring in the United States between 1882 and 1968 according to the Tuskegee Institute.[101] In reality too, slavery continued well after the Civil War (1861–1865) and following Reconstruction (1863–1877), and following the passage of the 13th (slavery abolishment), 14th (equal protection of citizenship under law), and 15th (right to vote) Constitutional Amendments.[102] Slavery continued through Southern practices of "share-cropping" by forcing former slaves into indentured servitude; through Southern practices of "chain gangs" by forcing African-American men into forced-labor imprisonment following false detentions; and through "Jim Crow Laws" (1870s–1964), informal ways of enforcing racial segregation between Blacks and whites and through "Black Codes," formerly "slave codes," laws disallowing citizenship rights of African-Americans.[103]

In fact, it took one hundred years after the Civil War for African-Americans to have their rights restored through the Civil Rights Movement (1954–1968) from luminaries like Dr. Martin Luther King, Jr. and Malcolm X, among many others.[104] Yet, in terms of policing with all the talk of police reform over the past fifty-seven years since the passage of the Civil Rights Act of 1964 has much been done?[105] Well, in my view, not enough has been done. Just examine the recent case of Breonna Taylor, a twenty-six-year-old African-American emergency technician, who was a victim of a no-knock search warrant, whereby the Louisville police forcibly entered her apartment and shot her at least eight times on March 13, 2020.[106] Or what about the latest tragic case on June 12 of Rayshard Brooks, a twenty-seven-year-old African-American man, who fell asleep at a Wendy's drive-thru in Atlanta, Georgia.[107] Allegedly, he was drunk and failed a sobriety test. Brooks then supposedly tussled with the police and took a police-taser and as Brooks was running away and pointing the taser at the police, Brooks was shot in the back. Why was "any" violent force used against Brooks in the first place for being drunk and falling asleep in a drive-thru? This is worth repeating, he fell asleep in his car and he was shot and killed.

As a result of Breonna Taylor's death, Louisville Metro Council voted on a ban of no-knock search warrants in Louisville, Kentucky, and as a result of Brooks' death, the Atlanta police chief resigned.[108] The anger and outrage in our country are real. Racism is evil. People are taught to be racists. It is a social construct which is learned but it can be unlearned as well.

Even so, examine the tragic case of Ahmaud Arbery, another victim of a modern white lynching on February 23, 2020, Ahmaud was only twenty-five years old, an African-American man who was out for a casual jog in a suburban neighborhood near Brunswick, Georgia, along the coast, and was hunted down and shot by two white men, a son and a father, Travis McMichael and Gregory McMichael, the latter a former police officer.[109] It took authorities seventy-four days for them to arrest the McMichaels and charge them with murder, along with an accomplice Roddie Bryan who filmed the murder on his cellphone. As in the case of Floyd, the damning cellphone video shows the murder of Arbery but ironically the racist McMichaels used it to show off their crime and their pride in hate of Blacks. Allegedly, Travis McMichael stood over Arbery's body and said, "F***-in N***-er!"—obviously, deep-seated and overt racism.[110]

I have been to Brunswick, Georgia and visited those beautiful coastal areas with grey-moss bedecking and hanging on oak trees and its sleepy hamlets on those marshy islands. The same area where Arbery died. It reminds me how in many places and almost anywhere in the United States you may find overt racism. I am equally reminded of white privilege. Often times, just because you are white, other whites, "racist whites," might just assume you are just as racist as they are. The so-called wink-wink and nod-nod kind of people. I remember visiting a plantation in southern Georgia, and as our tour guide gave us our paid-for-tour, the white guide began talking about Blacks in a very derogatory way as if I not only understood what he was saying but also automatically agreed with his point of view. Obviously, I did not. I was disgusted and embarrassed by his disparaging remarks and really angered by them. I remember telling this white plantation guide off in some way. That was about fifteen years ago. It reminded me then that the "Jim Crow South" was not as remote as I hoped it should be.

Another incident occurred while I was an Anthropology graduate student in Tallahassee, Florida. I visited a middle school in the area to explain something about culture and so on to school kids. The white teacher took me aside and began explaining to me that the Black kids she taught are like "little monkeys," she literally said that! And she asked me if they evolved differently or something absurd along those lines. I think I turned red and told her she was full of it, and walked off really angry and really upset.

Racism of the overt kind is more ubiquitous than many people imagine or are willing to admit to. It is evident in articles like the recent one, titled: "Reflections from a Token Black Friend" by Ramesh Nagarajah, wherein white people are mostly unwilling to admit to their own biases and racism.[111]

For my Master's degree in Cultural Anthropology at Florida State University, I took a class, called "Contemporary Folk Relations." For my final paper, I conducted some preliminary fieldwork at a Black Baptist church in southern Georgia. I will never forget the experience. I interviewed many African-Americans involved in the church. I also learned a couple of years later many of the same Black Baptist churches in the area had been torched out of racism and racist hate against Blacks in southern Georgia—more unnecessary violence against Black people.[112] In any event, on one evening, one of the church deacons invited me to his house. It was there that I interviewed this African-American man who had experienced the worse kinds of racism I had ever heard anywhere up until that time. This man in his 80s was a World War II veteran and an airman from the famed Tuskegee Airmen squadron.[113] I learned his father had been a sharecropper and his grandfather had been a slave. I learned he earned his university degree from Florida A&M University.[114]

And as we continued sitting together in his darkened kitchen and as I listened to his story, I was in tears. He told me how with a university degree, the only job he could ever hold was as a janitor at the nearby university. He was not offered anything else. Even though he had been a renowned Tuskegee Airman, and even though he had a university education. It did not matter. His Blackness was a stigma.

That is racism in America and was twenty-eight years ago when he told it to me. It is still true enough today. In many ways, it transformed me and opened my eyes to what racism really is. Racism is a sickness. It objectifies people. It dehumanizes people. And it unfairly oppresses people for their phenotype, mostly for the color of their skin or other Afro-descendant characteristics in the case of African-Americans. If you are familiar with the novel *Invisible Man* (1952) by Ralph Ellison, you know what I mean.[115] Or worse, if you have experienced these things yourself. As Ellison wrote: "I am invisible, understand, simply because people refuse to see me. Like the bodiless heads you see sometimes in circus sideshows, it is as though I have been surrounded by mirrors of hard, distorting glass. When they approach me, they see only my surroundings, themselves or figments of their imagination, indeed, everything and anything except me."

Black people for too long have been invisible in our society. Not only are they unseen, but for too long have been unheard as well. They have been passed over for jobs, or not allowed to live in certain neighborhoods, or turned away, and so on. This is the very definition of "structural violence," those structures in societies, keeping people invisible and oppressed.

I do not wish to generalize about the African-American experience, because there are as many different African-American experiences as there are different African-American people and, above all, these are "American stories." Racism is an American story, even though it is everywhere in the world. American racism has its own malignant history. But we have to rid ourselves of this sickness called "racism" once and for all in America. We need a sea change—the type of civil rights legislation we saw in the 1960s under President Lyndon B. Johnson.

Likely, U.S. Congressional legislation in regard to policing will not be enough, especially if it is only for chokeholds and neck-holds, or for restraining individuals.[116] Some Congressional Democrats, however, have proposed not only banning chokeholds but limiting military weaponry to police, defining lynching as a federal hate crime, establishing a police misconduct registry, and limiting qualified immunity for police officers.[117] Maybe like the President LBJ administration, not only do we need a new "War on Poverty," but we need a "War on Racism as well?"[118]

Fifty-four years ago, in July 1967, America erupted in riots, similar to today in places like Newark, New Jersey, Minneapolis, Minnesota, Detroit, Michigan, and Milwaukee, Wisconsin.[119] At the time, African-Americans also believed not enough was being done for "civil rights," and like then, the overwhelming frustrations led to tragic violence. In 1968, the riots across the country were even more out of control because of the death of Dr. Martin Luther King, Jr.[120] Yet, the irony of course, is the same "structures of violence" in our urban metropolises remain, and in many ways, continue unaltered—unemployment, educational deficiencies, racial bigotry, and police brutality.

Coming to terms with our social divisions, especially over racism, means understanding our long history of racial discrimination and our long history of racial violence. Moreover, it may take another president who is willing to address such issues and unite our country once more. Even so, violence is never the answer.[121] As Dr. King once proclaimed in a 1957 sermon in Montgomery, Alabama: "Darkness cannot drive out darkness; only light can do that.[122] Hate cannot drive out hate; only love can do that." Even so, Dr. King also said in 1966, "We have got to see that a riot is the language of the unheard.[123] And what is it that America has failed to hear? It has failed to hear that the economic plight of the Negro poor has worsened over the last few years ... The mood of the Negro community now is one of urgency. That we aren't going to wait. That we have got to have our freedom. We have waited too long ... I hope that we can avoid riots because riots are self-defeating and socially destructive." King's words as pertinent today as when he first spoke them.

Yet, in my view, Wesley Lowery, in an article in *The Atlantic*, titled: "Why Minneapolis Was the Breaking Point," summed up the current #BlackLivesMatter (BLM) movement best when he states: "Racism is not to blame, the thinking popular among at least some conservatives goes. It's the people fighting racism who are the problem. If everyone could just stop talking about all of this stuff, we could go "back" to being a peaceful, united country. No one seems to be able to answer when, precisely, in our history that previous moment of peace, justice, and racial harmony occurred."[124]

## WHY NATIVES IN THE UNITED STATES SUPPORT #BLACKLIVESMATTER

If you speak of historical events seared on Native American minds, unspeakable traumas, the "Indian Removal Act" (1830), the "Trail of Tears" (1838–1850), the "Sand Creek Massacre" (1864), and even, the "Wounded Knee Massacre" (1890), perhaps come to the forefront, among a plethora of genocidal acts against Native peoples too numerous to count.[125] In 2020, the effects of Coronavirus (COVID-19) on tribal nations across the United States and the consequences of the absolute neglect of former President Donald J. Trump and his administration of Native peoples who were losing more people per capita to the disease than most countries, were particularly bad.[126]

With the murder of the African-American man, George Floyd in 2020, Native Americans want to be included in on the conversation about race, especially since historical indigenous genocide is hardly discussed in the media today.[127] Not only must the United States confront the horrors of slavery and its long history of racism against Black people, but such discussions must include Native peoples as well who were wiped out by the same white American mindset. Some of this colonial mentality was couched in a utopian dream of white settlement known as "Manifest Destiny."[128] A dream in which all of the American West was open to settling from divine providence wherein the American dream could be fulfilled and huge swathes of mythical land was devoid of its indigenous peoples.

Presently, indigenous peoples in the United States like African-American and Hispanic-American minorities were also left behind by COVID-19 and were more adversely affected than whites. Some Native nations in our country are still feeling the effects of Coronavirus and in 2020 many Native reservations were on lockdown because of the disease.

In recent statistics from the end of May 2020 in New Mexico, Native Americans contracted COVID-19 at a rate of 57.6 percent of the total state population, the highest of any ethnic group within the state.[129] On the other hand, Native peoples, those from the Apache, Navajo, and Pueblo, and other tribal nations, are only 9.6 percent of New Mexico's overall population, proving how much Coronavirus has affected indigenous peoples in Southwestern United States. Moreover, the previous Trump administration made the disbursement of funds from the CARES (Coronavirus Aid, Relief, and Economic Security) Act to Tribes almost impossible and bogged down in bureaucracy and unnecessary red-tape.[130]

Furthermore, the prior Trump administration, specifically the Treasury Department, threatened "not" to allocate CARES Act funds to Native Nations.[131] Regardless, a federal judge ordered the remainder of CARES Act funds to be disbursed to Tribes by June 17, 2020, a balance of approximately $679 million.[132]

A curfew was in effect for the Navajo Nation where twenty-two new cases of COVID-19 were reported on June 15, 2020, and its total of 319 deaths and a total of 6672 cases from Coronavirus. This is out of a population of about 300,000, an infection rate much more than most countries around the world.[133]

Beyond Coronavirus, Native peoples have their own issues with law enforcement and a long history of police abuse among their communities, which is why so many indigenous peoples in the United States support the #Black Lives Matter (BLM) Movement.[134]

There are places in the United States where Native Americans are just as discriminated against and targeted like African-Americans by law enforcement and just because they are Natives.[135] Hence, if the "original sin" in the United States was slavery, then what was genocide against Native peoples in our country called? Both slavery of African-Americans "and" the genocide against indigenous peoples in the United States are therefore entwined original sins. Moreover, Black Civil Rights leaders like Stokely Carmichael (Kwame Ture) (1941–1998), All-African People's

Revolutionary Party (A-APRP), knew this too and supported Native civil rights.[136] Black leaders knew this when Native peoples had their own civil rights struggles in 1973 and occupied "Wounded Knee" on the Pine Ridge Reservation through the efforts of the American Indian Movement (AIM) in a standoff against the Federal Bureau of Investigation (FBI) during President Nixon's administration.[137]

Today, Native peoples, such as those from the Sioux Nation often have a difficult time finding housing outside of reservations in states like South Dakota, or problems getting served at restaurants, or obstacles in buying a car.[138] Or in states like Montana, South Dakota, North Dakota, and Wyoming, are targeted by police as African-Americans often are in large metropolises in places like Chicago, Los Angeles, or New York City, and across most cities in the USA.

As one Native Blackfeet author, activist, and lawyer, Gyasi Ross, on MSNBC explained: "The hallmark of racism against Native Americans in the United States is that nobody knows about it … We suffer violent crime at the highest rates in this country, nobody knows it. We die at the hands of law enforcement and nobody knows it. We get expelled and suspended from schools according to 2014 Department of Education statistics at the highest rate which later on leads to having contact with the criminal justice system, which nowadays are calling schools the prison pipeline for Native people and Black people and nobody knows it. So, there is a common narrative there among Native people and Black people. It's different because the circumstances within our communities are different and the circumstances in the way that it is policed is different and everybody is catching hell. That is the point."[139]

American Native peoples are also fighting oil pipelines and fracking on indigenous lands. As *The Guardian* reported (June 10, 2020): "Today, the US Bureau of Land Management is considering a plan, known as the Mancos-Gallup Amendment, which could lease land in the region for some 3,000 new wells—many of which would be for fracking oil and gas. The plan would expand drilling into some of northern New Mexico's last available public lands, threatening the desecration of sacred Native artefacts near Chaco Canyon while bringing in a swath of new public health risks to a place that's already reeling from one of the worst Covid-19 outbreaks in the world."[140] Canadian Aboriginal peoples are also protesting against the construction of oil pipelines such as the proposed pipeline across British Columbia through the Wet'suwet'en Nation's territory.[141] And like their U.S. indigenous brothers and sisters, Canadian Aboriginals face overt racism as well and are protesting against the systemic racism they have been subjected to in Canada.[142]

The late Dennis Banks (1937–2017), an American Indian Movement (AIM) co-founder, was from Minneapolis, and he helped to found American Indian Movement in the Twin Cities because of police brutality back in 1968.[143] In a recent opinion article by Levi Rickert of the Prairie Band Potawatomi Nation, recalled interviewing Banks about the founding of AIM. Rickert wrote: "The effort to fight police brutality in the American Indian community was the impetus of AIM … He [Dennis Banks] said that AIM founders were fed up with the large number of urban American Indians being rounded up each weekend, beaten and then hauled off to jail in paddy wagons. Often, they were made to do manual labor as part of their punishment."[144]

So, historical ties of racism and struggle, and even the history of protests against police brutality, while both the African-American and Native American civil rights movements are quite different, likewise demonstrate their similarities. AIM began in Minneapolis and expanded. The recent Floyd Movement is expanding from Minneapolis too.

Native Americans are also advocating for symbols of genocide such as statues remembering those perpetuating indigenous genocide to be taken down and removed. Many Native activists have been advocating for their removal for years.[145] However, since the Floyd murder, activists are dismantling such statues in places like California and New Mexico as well as protesting the "white-washing" of this genocidal history.

One indigenous scholar, emeritus professor Tink Tinker (wazhazhe, Osage Nation), Clifford Baldridge Professor of American Indian Cultures and Religious Traditions of Iliff School of Theology in Denver, Colorado, shared his thoughts about the matter on Facebook: "Let's be clear. Statues & monuments have already erased history! We have seen Native history, African history in the Americas, & other POC [People of Color] histories persistently erased in favor of elevating eurochristian history & White supremacy on the continent. Whether it is the brutality of the Spanish eurochristians in the southwest (Oñate, de Vargas, & their missionaries); the Doctrine of (Christian) Discovery conquistadores of the north (Washington, Jefferson, Marshall, et al); or the diehard Christian slavery defending confederate 'heroes' of the south, all of them function to erase history even as they elevate the history of Whiteness. That history is only important as a means for maintaining the status quo of White eurochristian superiority. Time to let it go & create a history that is inclusive of all of us."[146]

Above all, this should be a time for peace and reconciliation as well. It is time for "dialogue" on many issues of conflict, whether in the past or the present. Most Native peoples are aware of the destruction of "Mother Earth," our environment, and the effects of climate change. Our era of the Sixth Extinction is also known as the "Anthropocene."[147] The Cartesian dynamic of separating body from nature seems to be another unnecessary holdover of colonialism whereby nature is meant to be conquered and not cared for. This is what Julie Morley has called the "Cartesian Sleep."[148]

Chief Arvol Looking Horse, nineteenth generation and keeper of the Sacred Pipe, Lakota Dakota Nakota Sioux Nations, remarked: "My grandmother on her deathbed said if the people don't start to straighten up, you shall be the last bundle keeper ... I am going to pray for global peace and global healing ... I carry the message of the 'White Buffalo', the prophecy of mending the 'Sacred Hoop'. That sacred hoop of the nation was broken at Wounded Knee ... We signed a treaty with the U.S. government over a hundred years ago. It was broken at Wounded Knee 1890 ... We're survivors of Holocaust, massacres in the name of progress. They put our people on 'concentration camps'. It's called a reservation but back then it was a concentration camp. The military came and took our children, five, six years old [referring to Native boarding schools]. If you don't let go of your children, they shot your children right in your arms, so much abuse ... we rode horseback from the 1980s until 1993, we did the ceremony. We prayed there would be no more Wounded Knees throughout the world. But the way things are going. The way things are doing right now, looks not that way ... Mother Earth she has a fever. Man has gone too far, disrespect everything. Sacred sites have been destroyed. Eagles are flying into trash pits [municipal landfills]. When I go outside our community into the world, this is a strange world that can't succeed ... We have come to a time and a place of great urgency. Even scientists are saying we are at the point of no return ... People are so spiritually disconnected. We need to reconnect with the Spirit. Mother Earth is the Spirit. Mother Earth is the source of life, not a resource. We are at the crossroads but there is hope."[149]

## Conclusion

At the beginning of this chapter, I analyzed the traumatic experiences of racism against Guatemalan-Mayan immigrants and Brazilian urban Amerindians. As Didier Fassin and Richard Rechtman (2009: 275) elucidate: "Trauma has come to give new meaning to our experience of time.

It marks both the psychic and the metaphorical trace of what has passed: a psychic trace to which trauma neurosis, and more recently post-traumatic stress disorder, bear witness, giving grounds for the intervention of psychologists and psychiatrists; a metaphorical trace that is invoked in the demands of descendants of slaves and native peoples, victims of massacres and genocides, calling for legislation or for reparations." Even while I concur with Fassin and Rechtman (2009: 284) that "trauma today is a moral judgement," their analyses fall a bit short by not representing the "primary agency" of social actors themselves, "especially non-Western peoples in relation to Western societies" (Linstroth 2015: 136). "By this I mean the manner in which traumatized peoples such as Indians, whose traumatization through discrimination and racism, also instigates in them to become 'intentional beings' in using experiences of trauma as a mode of provocation against Brazilian white oppressors [or for Guatemalan-Mayan immigrants the oppression of Hispanic-Americans or white society in general in the United States]. What I am arguing is that stigmatizing trauma in the form of discrimination and racism actually reinforces indigenous identities. It makes them intent on overcoming defamatory remarks and malicious treatment by Brazilian white society as well as creating a counterpoint in which to establish their difference and ethnicity" (Linstroth 2015: 136). The same may be said for the Guatemalan-Mayan immigrants, at least my informants, who used their traumas from racism to overcome and better themselves in American society.

Furthermore, in my view the cognition of trauma is very real, and contra Fassin and Rechtman (2009) does exist in the "psyche, the mind, and the brain" because of the harmful and injurious attributes associated with racism and structural violence as I explained earlier. While trauma may be a moral judgment, it is also very real for victims of violence, whether survivors of warfare, genocide, or racism. Among indigenous peoples like Guatemalan-Mayan immigrants and Brazilian urban Amerindians, racism is very real. As Jonathan Warren (2001: 280) reminds us: "During the past five centuries, the racial hierarchies that European discoveries birthed in Latin America have changed little. The descendants of indigenous people, whether they self-identify as Indian or not, remain economically, politically, and socially marginalized. In many countries, the state of racism can be compared to apartheid in South Africa or Jim Crow in the United States."

In the rest of the chapter, I discussed what I called the "politics of racism," how racist ideas are attached to the political landscape such as the racist rhetoric of politicians like previous U.S. President Donald J. Trump and Brazilian President Jair Bolsonaro, and what repercussions their racist rants and populist bombast have had for the United States and Brazil. Even so, the "politics of race" is broader. As Michael Hanchard (2000: 180) explains: "The struggles between dominant and subordinate racial groups, the politics of race, help constitute modernity and modernizing projects across the globe. It uses racial phenotypes to assess, categorize and judge persons as citizens and noncitizens. Racial politics operate not only in a polity's defining moments but in the ongoing process of its re-creation. It permeates the minutiae of daily life: nervous, furtive glances are exchanged in elevators, men and women are rendered suspects without ever having committed a crime; not yet socialized by racist practices, white children run gleefully into the arms of their parents' racial others as their parents watch nervously. This is racial politics between whites and blacks in the late-twentieth century [and now in the twenty-first century]."

It is clear that former President Trump shares the view of some white Americans in general concerning white supremacist racial views about minorities. According to Eduardo Bonilla-Silva (2014), it is a type of racism "without the self-perception" of being racist. It is: "A racial ideology, a loosely organized set of ideas, phrases, and stories that help whites justify contemporary white supremacy; they are the *collective representations* whites have developed to explain, and ultimately justify, contemporary racial inequality. Their views, then, are not just a 'sense of group position' but *symbolic expressions of whites' dominance*" (Bonilla-Silva 2014: 302). Corresponding with this belief system are the racial disparities "income, wealth, and education," which consequently point to the view that there is something wrong with the minorities themselves and with further evidence of such "minorities' overrepresentation in the criminal justice system or on death row (Bonilla-Silva 2014: 302). This likewise includes Black and Latino underperformance on standardized exams as evidence something is wrong with minorities, "maybe even genetically wrong" (Bonilla-Silva 2014: 302). Unfortunately, because former President Trump used the bully pulpit to express such views, his racist rhetoric was that much more damaging because his views aligned with white supremacist views. Trump populist bigotry thereby underlined an ideology which expressed white insecurity by blaming the minorities for being the so-called problem.

Like Trump, Brazilian President Jair Bolsonaro likewise used the public forum to declare his populist racism whether against indigenous peoples or other minorities. By contrast to the United States, Afro-Brazilians are mostly "silent" in the face of white supremacy in Brazil (Winddance Twine 2005: 150–153). This makes confronting the populist bigotry of Brazilian politicians like Bolsonaro all that more difficult. In fact, "[r]acism, racial discrimination, and racial inequality have persisted in Brazil more than one hundred years after the end of slavery" (Telles 2004: 239). Perhaps most damaging of all have been Bolsonaro's racist rhetoric against indigenous peoples, stating, for example, "The Indian is becoming human, just like us," suggesting Native peoples are animals, which has allowed for the exacerbation of Coronavirus among Brazil's Native population.

In the United States, and in general, minorities have been adversely affected by COVID-19, evident from the income inequalities of African-Americans and Hispanic-Americans, wherein many Blacks could not afford not to work and wherein many Latinos did not have healthcare in proportion to whites. Moreover, in housing projects throughout the United States during the height of the pandemic in 2020, social distancing was all but impossible for many African-Americans and Hispanic-Americans. The structural violence surrounding Coronavirus of 2020 to present was made obvious on many fronts and revealed the inequities of those living at the poverty line or below it. As much as African-Americans and Hispanic-Americans have been more adversely affected by Coronavirus than whites, so too have been indigenous minorities in Brazil compared to the wider Brazilian population. The mishandling of COVID-19 in Brazil by the Bolsonaro administration has led many to speculate we are witnessing a genocide in Brazil against Native peoples there.

In this chapter, I also articulated why we need more black voices like Malcolm X and Dr. Martin Luther King, Jr. and why it is striking today following the death of George Floyd how bereft we are of such voices. Nevertheless, the anger about Floyd's killing was very real and multi-ethnic as seen in protests across the United States. One wonders today if the same urgency as in the 1960s may be communicated in a post-Civil Rights era with lasting repercussions. As Cornel West (1993: 58) avowed: "What stood out most strikingly about Malcolm X, Martin Luther King, Jr., Ella Baker, and Fannie Lou Hamer was that they were always visibly upset about the condition of black America. When one saw them speak or heard their voices, they projected on a gut level that the black situation was urgent, in need of immediate attention. One even gets the impression that their own stability and sanity rested on how soon the black predicament could be improved." Indeed, without such luminary voices in the

Black community, it is difficult to see how the Floyd movement and #Black Lives Matter will have lasting effects, especially if no legislative measures are passed to curb police power and racial profiling, whether by eliminating police qualified immunity and/or the power of police unions.

According to Anne Warfield Rawls and Waverly Duck (2020: 1-2): "Racism does not usually take an obvious form that we can see and prevent; rather it masquerades as the most ordinary of daily actions: as unnoticed and ever-present as the air we breathe … racism is coded into the everyday social expectations of Americans … that create vast amounts of hidden unconscious—Tacit Racism—which most Americans are not aware of … Race divisions pose a *clear and present danger* to the nation and its democratic institutions." The same may be said for every country across the globe where ethnic strife and racial conflicts raise their ugly heads, sometimes resulting in genocide (see Chap. 4).

After all, and as mentioned, "*Race is not a biological fact.* It is a social convention, a 'social fact' (a fact by social agreement)" (Warfield Rawls and Duck 2020: 2). Unfortunately, people are defined often by their phenotypes as we are all more genetically similar than not. Many of us have a surprising amount of mixed genetic heritage as well. As Ashley Montagu (1997: 41) maintains: "The idea of 'race' represents one of the most dangerous myths of our time, and one of the most tragic. Myths are most effective and perilous when they remain unrecognized for what they are." One of the prevalent myths concerns so-called the "Myth of Black criminality and violence is as much a fiction as the myth of White superiority. Just as there is no White Race, there is no Black Race" (Warfield Rawls and Duck 2020: 3).

In this chapter, I also tried to make sense of why "race is everything in America" and discussed instances when I myself was directly confronted with "racist" dialogue and "racist" talk. As such we must struggle to be anti-racist and it is an ongoing battle we find not only in American society but in every society across the globe (as evident in Chap. 4). "But racism is one of the fastest-spreading and most fatal cancers humanity has ever known. It is hard to find a place where its cancer cells are not dividing and multiplying. There is nothing I see in our world today, in our history, giving me hope that one day antiracists will win the fight, that one day the flag of anti-racism will fly over a world of equity. What gives me hope is a simple truism. Once we lose hope, we are guaranteed to lose. But if we ignore the odds and fight to create an antiracist world, then we give humanity a chance to one day survive, a chance to live in communion, a chance to be forever free" (Kendi 2019: 238).

Lastly, in the chapter, I discussed why Native Americans support the #Black Lives Matter movement and how and why Native peoples have been victims as well in American society. Native Americans experienced genocide and as such have recently wanted to remove the symbols of genocide against them in the form of monuments and statues which celebrate conquerors (*conquistadores*), among some examples. Likewise, Native peoples are protesting against fracking and oil pipelines on indigenous lands. We also know that Native Americans in some places in the United States are just as targeted as African-Americans for crime. Hence, in my view, any discussion about racism in America must also include not only African-Americans but other minorities as well (see Chap. 6 for a discussion about racism against Asian-Americans).

In trying to solve such issues of racism, we know protesting is not enough. As Ibram Kendi (2016: 510) argues: "But protesting racist policies can never be a long-term solution to eradicating racial discrimination—and thus racist ideas—in America [and elsewhere in the world]. Just as one generation of powerful Americans could decide or be pressured by protest to end racial discrimination, when the conditions and interests change, another generation could once again encourage racial discrimination. That's why protesting against racist power has been a never-ending affair in America."

Therefore, the solution is one of power. We must ensure that anti-racist policies are put in place through laws and legal actions and by ensuring that anti-racist people are put in power. Perhaps, we should be hopeful like Ibram Kendi (2016: 510–5111) that this is possible as well. "There will come a time when racist ideas will no longer obstruct us from seeing the complete and utter abnormality of racial disparities. There will come a time when we will love humanity, when we will gain the courage to fight for an equitable society for our beloved humanity, knowing, intelligently, that when we fight for humanity, we are fighting for ourselves. There will come a time. Maybe, just maybe, that time is now" (Kendi 2016: 511).

## Notes

1. Linstroth, J. P. (2009). 'Mayan Cognition, Memory, and Trauma'. In *History and Anthropology*, Vol. 20, No. 2, pp. 139-182.
2. Linstroth (2009)
3. These quotes were previously published in: Linstroth, J. P. (2015b). 'Urban Amerindians and Advocacy: Toward a Politically Engaged

Anthropology Representing Urban Amerindigeneities in Manaus, Brazil' in Paul Sillitoe (ed.), *Indigenous Studies and Engaged Anthropology: The Collaborative Moment*, pp. 115-145.
4. Bar-On and Chaitin (2001)
5. https://thehill.com/homenews/administration/453108-trump-hits-pelosi-for-racist-statement-saying-maga-means-make-america
6. https://apps.npr.org/documents/document.html?id=6200155-House-Resolution-Condemning-Trump-Comments
7. https://www.reuters.com/article/us-virginia-protests/neo-nazi-faces-sentencing-in-murder-of-protester-in-charlottesville-virginia-idUSKCN1UA0TV
8. https://www.youtube.com/watch?v=EiAT2IEzJAc
9. https://www.politifact.com/article/2019/apr/26/context-trumps-very-fine-people-both-sides-remarks/
10. https://www.pbs.org/newshour/nation/robert-e-lee-opposed-confederate-monuments
　https://www.snopes.com/fact-check/robert-e-lee-confederate-monuments/
11. https://twitter.com/realDonaldTrump?ref_src=twsrc%5Egoogle%7Ctwcamp%5Eserp%7Ctwgr%5Eauthor
12. https://www.msnbc.com/hardball/watch/jon-meacham-trump-joined-andrew-johnson-as-most-racist-president-in-american-history-63903301513
13. https://www.politifact.com/factchecks/2016/sep/16/donald-trump/donald-trumps-pants-fire-claim-he-finished-obama-b/
14. https://time.com/4866404/john-mccain-barack-obama-arab-cancer/
15. https://www.msnbc.com/mtp-daily/watch/full-squad-press-conference-in-response-to-trump-s-attacks-63899205762
16. https://www.tandfonline.com/doi/full/10.1080/02757200902887964?scroll=top&needAccess=true
17. https://en.wikipedia.org/wiki/List_of_synagogue_shootings
　https://en.wikipedia.org/wiki/List_of_Islamophobic_incidents
18. https://www.realclearpolitics.com/video/2019/07/17/trump_maga_rally_crowd_chants_send_her_back_to_rep_ilhan_omar.html
19. https://www.archives.gov/founding-docs/declaration-transcript
20. https://www.nobelprize.org/prizes/peace/1964/king/26142-martin-luther-king-jr-acceptance-speech-1964/
21. https://www.nytimes.com/2020/04/09/world/coronavirus-equipment-rich-poor.html?action=click&module=Top%20Stories&pgtype=Homepage
22. https://www.elespectador.com/ambiente/si-el-covid-19-afecta-a-los-indigenas-por-que-nos-afectara-a-todos-article-911046/

https://www.theguardian.com/world/2020/mar/30/south-america-indigenous-groups-coronavirus-brazil-colombia
https://www.theguardian.com/global-development/2020/apr/02/brazil-confirms-first-indigenous-case-of-coronavirus-in-amazon
23. https://www.rome2rio.com/s/Manaus/São-Gabriel-da-Cachoeira
24. https://www.theguardian.com/commentisfree/2020/mar/31/the-guardian-view-on-jair-bolsonaro-a-danger-to-brazilians
https://www.nytimes.com/2020/04/01/world/americas/brazil-bolsonaro-coronavirus.html
25. https://www.nytimes.com/2020/04/01/world/americas/brazil-bolsonaro-coronavirus.html
26. https://www.theguardian.com/commentisfree/2020/mar/31/the-guardian-view-on-jair-bolsonaro-a-danger-to-brazilians
https://www.theguardian.com/commentisfree/2020/apr/02/brazil-message-world-our-president-wrong-coronavirus-jair-bolsonaro
https://www.vox.com/2020/3/26/21193823/coronavirus-mexico-andres-manuel-lopez-obrador-health-care
27. https://www.gov.br/saude/pt-br
28. https://www.statista.com/statistics/1093256/novel-coronavirus-2019ncov-deaths-worldwide-by-country/
29. https://indigenas.ibge.gov.br/graficos-e-tabelas-2.html
30. https://news.mongabay.com/2021/05/study-brazil-govt-undercounts-indigenous-deaths-from-covid-19-by-half/
31. https://g1.globo.com/mt/mato-grosso/noticia/2020/03/23/liderancas-indigenas-bloqueiam-acessos-a-aldeia-para-prevencao-do-coronavirus-em-mt.ghtml
https://www.theguardian.com/world/2020/mar/30/south-america-indigenous-groups-coronavirus-brazil-colombia
32. https://www.socioambiental.org/pt-br/noticias-socioambientais/cidade-mais-indigena-do-brasil-sao-gabriel-da-cachoeira-se-isola-contra-a-covid-19
33. https://oglobo.globo.com/brasil/adolescente-yanomami-em-estado-grave-um-dos-7-casos-de-coronavirus-entre-indigenas-no-brasil-24358870
https://www.theguardian.com/world/2020/apr/08/coronavirus-indigenous-communities-brazil-yanomami
34. https://www.bbc.com/news/world-latin-america-52135362
35. https://g1.globo.com/politica/noticia/2020/01/24/cada-vez-mais-o-indio-e-um-ser-humano-igual-a-nos-diz-bolsonaro-em-transmissao-nas-redes-sociais.ghtml

36. https://www.salsa-tipiti.org/covid-19/covid-19-related-concerns/covid-19-for-isolated-indigenous-peoples/
37. https://br.noticias.yahoo.com/covid-19-o-que-os-povos-indigenas-podem-ensinar-ao-mundo-poscoronavirus-184718585.html
38. https://www.washingtonpost.com/news/wonk/wp/2014/01/08/everything-you-need-to-know-about-the-war-on-poverty/
39. https://www.amazon.com/Other-America-Poverty-United-States-ebook/dp/B007BP3VLW/ref=sr_1_1?dchild=1&keywords=the+other+america&qid=1586643511&s=books&sr=1-1
40. https://www.msnbc.com/11th-hour/watch/ny-gov-cuomo-on-coronavirus-why-do-the-poorest-pay-the-highest-price-81813573665
41. https://www.amazon.com/Outline-Practice-Cambridge-Cultural-Anthropology-ebook/dp/B00D2WQ1YW/ref=sr_1_1?dchild=1&keywords=outline+of+a+theory+of+practice&qid=1586651224&sr=8-1
42. https://www.amazon.com/Death-Without-Weeping-Publisher-University/dp/B004QTM2IE/ref=sr_1_2?dchild=1&keywords=death+without+weeping&qid=1586651173&sr=8-2
43. https://www.tandfonline.com/doi/abs/10.1080/02757200902887964
44. https://www.amazon.com/Why-Zebras-Dont-Ulcers-Stress-Related/dp/B0096EB9UG/ref=sr_1_2?dchild=1&keywords=why+zebras+don%27t+get+ulcers&qid=1586651296&sr=8-2
45. https://www.apa.org/pi/ses/resources/publications/minorities
https://www.bls.gov/spotlight/2018/race-economics-and-social-status/pdf/race-economics-and-social-status.pdf
46. https://www.amazon.com/Gender-Race-Class-Health-Schulz-dp-0787976636/dp/0787976636/ref=mt_paperback?_encoding=UTF8&me=&qid=1586652660
47. https://cepr.net/documents/publications/paid-sick-days-2009-05.pdf
48. https://www.nationalpartnership.org/our-work/resources/economic-justice/paid-sick-days/african-american-workers-need-paid-sick-days.pdf
49. https://www.nationalpartnership.org/our-work/resources/economic-justice/paid-sick-days/latino-workers-need-paid-sick-days.pdf
50. https://nationalhomeless.org/about-homelessness/
51. https://www.hudexchange.info/resource/5178/2016-ahar-part-1-pit-estimates-of-homelessness/
52. https://thehill.com/changing-america/respect/poverty/492272-homeless-population-uniquely-vulnerable-to-coronavirus
53. https://www.nytimes.com/2020/03/30/us/coronavirus-prisons-jails.html
54. https://www.nytimes.com/2020/03/30/us/coronavirus-prisons-jails.html

55. https://www.prisonpolicy.org/reports/pie2020.html
56. https://www.prisonpolicy.org/blog/2020/03/27/slowpandemic/
57. https://www.cjinstitute.org/corona/
58. https://www.urban.org/urban-wire/americas-housing-getting-more-crowded-how-will-affect-children
59. https://www.minorityhealth.hhs.gov/omh/browse.aspx?lvl=3&lvlid=61
60. https://minorityhealth.hhs.gov/omh/browse.aspx?lvl=3&lvlid=64
61. https://www.youtube.com/watch?v=f3AuStymweQ
62. https://www.charlestonchronicle.net/2020/06/02/the-murder-of-george-floyd-was-a-lynching-in-broad-daylight/
63. https://www.nytimes.com/2020/05/31/us/george-floyd-investigation.html
    https://www.cbc.ca/news/world/police-killings-recent-history-george-floyd-1.5593768
64. https://www.cbc.ca/news/world/police-killings-recent-history-george-floyd-1.5593768
65. https://www.history.com/topics/black-history/civil-rights-act
    https://www.justice.gov/opa/pr/justice-department-awards-over-23-million-funding-body-worn-camera-pilot-program-support-law
66. https://mappingpoliceviolence.org
67. https://mappingpoliceviolence.org
68. https://www.theguardian.com/commentisfree/2020/jun/01/george-floyd-protests-cornel-west-american-democracy
69. https://www.theguardian.com/commentisfree/2020/jun/01/george-floyd-protests-cornel-west-american-democracy
70. https://thehill.com/homenews/administration/500328-national-security-adviser-blames-a-few-bad-apples-says-theres-not
71. https://www.theguardian.com/us-news/2020/may/29/george-floyd-killing-protests-police-brutality
72. https://www.esquire.com/news-politics/politics/news/a49415/america-waiting-for-donald-trump/
73. https://en.wikipedia.org/wiki/Malcolm_X
    https://en.wikipedia.org/wiki/Martin_Luther_King_Jr.
74. https://www.history.com/topics/black-history/civil-rights-movement
75. https://news.harvard.edu/gazette/story/2020/04/health-care-disparities-in-the-age-of-coronavirus/
76. https://www.bostonglobe.com/opinion/2019/03/08/time-for-malcolm-monument-too/ePKHddvjVdV923tNwL5miI/story.html
    https://www.nps.gov/mlkm/index.htm

77. https://en.wikipedia.org/wiki/Booker_T._Washington
    https://en.wikipedia.org/wiki/W._E._B._Du_Bois
78. http://dailyorange.com/2019/01/syracuse-dr-martin-luther-king-jr-s-messages-resonate-half-century-later/
79. https://www.usatoday.com/story/news/nation-now/2015/02/21/malcolm-x-anniversary-death/23764967/
80. https://swap.stanford.edu/20141218230016/http://mlk-kpp01.stanford.edu/kingweb/popular%5Frequests/frequentdocs/birmingham.pdf
81. https://www.oxfordreference.com/view/10.1093/acref/9780191866692.001.0001/q-oro-ed6-00007024
82. https://www.birminghamtimes.com/2015/01/marin-luther-king-jr-black-history-quotes/
83. http://historymatters.gmu.edu/d/7041/
84. https://www.youtube.com/watch?v=522wcqUlS0Y
85. https://www.aljazeera.com/opinions/2020/2/21/malcolm-x-is-still-misunderstood-and-misused/
86. https://ncte.org/blog/2017/01/martin-luther-king-jr/
87. https://www.malcolmx.com/quotes/
88. https://www.seattletimes.com/opinion/mlk-speaks-powerfully-to-us-in-2019/
89. https://books.google.com/books?id=ShfNyQrAa-YC&pg=PA149#v=onepage&q&f=false
90. https://projects.seattletimes.com/mlk/words-education.html
91. https://themilitant.com/2019/09/21/there-will-be-a-clash-between-the-oppressed-and-the-oppressors/
92. https://www.africa.upenn.edu/Articles_Gen/Letter_Birmingham.html
93. https://genius.com/Malcolm-x-chapter-19-1965-annotated
94. https://parade.com/252644/viannguyen/15-of-martin-luther-king-jr-s-most-inspiring-motivational-quotes/
95. https://www.youtube.com/watch?v=wEBlaMOmKV4
96. https://www.youtube.com/watch?v=wEBlaMOmKV4
    https://www.cnn.com/2020/05/28/us/video-george-floyd-contradict-resist-trnd/index.html
97. https://www.cnn.com/videos/us/2020/05/29/george-floyd-kneeled-on-by-three-officers-video-vpx.cnn
98. https://www.youtube.com/watch?v=mj7WuDI0hJY
    https://www.cnn.com/2020/06/03/us/george-floyd-officers-charges/index.html
99. https://en.wikipedia.org/wiki/Murder_of_George_Floyd
100. https://www.cnn.com/videos/tv/2020/05/28/lead-panel-1-live-jake-tapper.cnn

101. https://web.archive.org/web/20160313030351/http:/192.203.127.197/archive/bitstream/handle/123456789/511/Lyching%201882%201968.pdf
    https://web.archive.org/web/20180510151602/https:/lynchinginamerica.eji.org/report/
    http://192.203.127.197/archive/handle/123456789/511?show=full
102. https://www.amazon.com/Civil-War-Volumes-1-3-Box/dp/0394749138/ref=sr_1_1?dchild=1&keywords=the+civil+war&qid=1590815469&s=books&sr=1-1
    https://www.amazon.com/Reconstruction-Updated-Unfinished-Revolution-1863-1877/dp/0062354515/ref=sr_1_2?dchild=1&keywords=reconstruction&qid=1590815387&s=books&sr=1-2
103. https://www.amazon.com/Deep-South-Anthropological-Southern-Classics/dp/1570038155/ref=sr_1_13?dchild=1&keywords=sharecropping+in+the+south&qid=1590815222&s=books&sr=1-13
    https://www.amazon.com/Slavery-Another-Name-Re-Enslavement-Americans/dp/0385722702/ref=pd_sbs_14_2/145-6776557-5404837?_encoding=UTF8&pd_rd_i=0385722702&pd_rd_r=f75418c9-b89e-4511-8af6-ba61f25ef377&pd_rd_w=YjNMo&pd_rd_wg=LkwWs&pf_rd_p=12b8d3e2-e203-4b23-a8bc-68a7d2806477&pf_rd_r=PNAKATEHNNE89ZH9J8R0&psc=1&refRID=PNAKATEHNNE89ZH9J8R0
    https://www.amazon.com/Twice-Work-Free-Labor-Political/dp/1859840868/ref=pd_sbs_14_4/145-6776557-5404837?_encoding=UTF8&pd_rd_i=1859840868&pd_rd_r=ea72ec3a-9652-42b4-937d-05a191cbd2ce&pd_rd_w=tFnsi&pd_rd_wg=OKTn8&pf_rd_p=12b8d3e2-e203-4b23-a8bc-68a7d2806477&pf_rd_r=8265WG57GV6P1H9FXXKP&psc=1&refRID=8265WG57GV6P1H9FXXKP
    https://www.amazon.com/Stony-Road-Reconstruction-White-Supremacy/dp/0525559531/ref=sr_1_3?dchild=1&keywords=jim+crow&qid=1590815056&s=books&sr=1-3
104. https://www.history.com/topics/black-history/civil-rights-movement
105. https://www.ourdocuments.gov/doc.php?flash=true&doc=97
106. https://en.wikipedia.org/wiki/Killing_of_Breonna_Taylor
107. https://www.ajc.com/news/crime%2D%2Dlaw/man-shot-killed-atlanta-police-wendy-drive-thru/rUUFN6yfvgsevgIc2Q7ZkJ/

108. https://www.cbsnews.com/news/no-knock-warrant-ban-breonnas-law-louisville-city-council/
https://www.ajc.com/news/crime%2D%2Dlaw/man-shot-killed-atlanta-police-wendy-drive-thru/rUUFN6yfvgsevgIc2Q7ZkJ/
109. https://bittersoutherner.com/2020/ahmaud-arbery-holds-us-accountable
110. https://en.wikipedia.org/wiki/Killing_of_Ahmaud_Arbery
111. https://humanparts.medium.com/reflections-from-a-token-black-friend-2f1ea522d42d
112. https://www.hsdl.org/?view&did=1410
113. https://www.pri.org/stories/2015-07-02/fire-last-time-1990s-wave-145-church-burnings-map
114. https://en.wikipedia.org/wiki/Tuskegee_Airmen
115. https://www.famu.edu
116. https://www.amazon.com/Invisible-Man-Ralph-Ellison/dp/0679732764
117. https://www.aclu.org/feature/police-practices
118. https://www.pbs.org/newshour/politics/whats-in-the-justice-in-policing-act
119. https://www.washingtonpost.com/news/wonk/wp/2014/01/08/everything-you-need-to-know-about-the-war-on-poverty/
120. https://www.usnews.com/news/national-news/articles/2017-07-12/50-years-later-causes-of-1967-summer-riots-remain-largely-the-same
121. https://www.blackpast.org/african-american-history/martin-luther-king-assassination-riots-1968/
122. https://apnews.com/article/be7faf7879724e8da237cb6c7f72d58c
123. https://vimeo.com/24614519
124. https://www.youtube.com/watch?v=_K0BWXjJv5s
125. https://www.theatlantic.com/politics/archive/2020/06/wesley-lowery-george-floyd-minneapolis-black-lives/612391/?fbclid=IwAR2fMfwiExd09iQD5phRscgRD9XxHiTNFAQMdQ-FHbZhtyrTaDBhTmBp_Uo
https://blacklivesmatter.com
126. https://guides.loc.gov/indian-removal-act
https://www.history.com/topics/native-american-history/trail-of-tears
https://www.smithsonianmag.com/history/horrific-sand-creek-massacre-will-be-forgotten-no-more-180953403/
https://www.britannica.com/event/Wounded-Knee-Massacre
127. https://www.theguardian.com/us-news/2020/may/26/native-americans-coronavirus-impact

128. https://www.msnbc.com/am-joy/watch/george-floyd-protests-supported-by-native-american-communities84612165852?fbclid=IwAR2zks1Sry1SfBtFdMCfr9PpcACTox71vLWQz4CO73-iNX6Jb6LRITL985A
https://www.voanews.com/usa/nation-turmoil-george-floyd-protests/native-americans-want-be-included-race-talks?fbclid=IwAR2mFdzik_ljdQ7sC11YPdl-t2IBUElmhV7I7IsqRAqHgSAlAyuHQ82ifzI
129. https://en.wikipedia.org/wiki/John_L._O%27Sullivan
130. https://cvprovider.nmhealth.org/public-dashboard.html
131. https://www.indianz.com/News/2020/05/26/we-must-remain-diligent-and-prepared-cor.asp
132. https://www.indianz.com/News/2020/06/04/an-utter-disaster-trump-adminsitration-t.asp
133. https://nativenewsonline.net/currents/federal-judge-orders-distribution-of-remaining-cares-acts-relief-funds-to-tribes
134. https://www.navajo-nsn.gov/history.htm
https://www.navajo-nsn.gov/News%20Releases/OPVP/2020/Jun/FOR%20IMMEDIATE%20RELEASE%20-%2022%20new%20cases_3207%20recoveries_and%20no%20new%20deaths%20related%20to%20COVID-19%20reported%20as%20daily%20curfew%20is%20still%20in%20effect.pdf
https://www.ndoh.navajo-nsn.gov/COVID-19
135. https://blacklivesmatter.com
136. https://www.sdstandardnow.com/home/tim-giago-writes-that-in-rapid-city-sd-there-are-many-ways-to-put-a-knee-on-the-oyates-neck?fbclid=IwAR0n8SgSG2H6cXOOfLet1dRYNMrQC4Our02YcGdZ5C14i-123lvJX96RYEQ
https://www.counterpunch.org/2015/10/29/do-indian-lives-matter-police-violence-against-native-americans/
137. https://www.youtube.com/watch?v=MojDoeloUTc
https://en.wikipedia.org/wiki/Stokely_Carmichael
138. https://friendsofpineridgereservation.org
https://www.history.com/this-day-in-history/aim-occupation-of-wounded-knee-begins
139. https://www.sdstandardnow.com/home/tim-giago-writes-that-in-rapid-city-sd-there-are-many-ways-to-put-a-knee-on-the-oyates-neck?fbclid=IwAR0n8SgSG2H6cXOOfLet1dRYNMrQC4Our02YcGdZ5C14i-123lvJX96RYEQ
http://plainshumanities.unl.edu/encyclopedia/doc/egp.na.107
140. https://blackfeetnation.com
https://en.wikipedia.org/wiki/Gyasi_Ross

https://www.msnbc.com/am-joy/watch/george-floyd-protests-supported-by-native-american-communities-84612165852?fbclid=IwAR2zks1SrylSfBtFdMCfr9PpcACTox71vLWQz4CO73-iNX6Jb6LRITL985A
141. https://www.theguardian.com/us-news/2020/jun/10/new-mexico-fracking-navajo-indian-country
142. https://globalnews.ca/news/6634179/indigenous-consent-pipeline-protests/
http://www.wetsuweten.com/culture/
143. https://globalnews.ca/video/rd/25e423ac-5dbe-11ea-b7b6-0242ac110004/?jwsource=cl
https://www.theguardian.com/world/2020/jun/14/canada-systemic-racism-history
144. https://en.wikipedia.org/wiki/Dennis_Banks
145. https://nativenewsonline.net/opinion/why-black-lives-matters-movement-resonates-with-american-indians
https://www.pbpindiantribe.com
146. https://www.theguardian.com/environment/2020/jun/24/protests-target-spanish-colonial-statues-new-mexico
147. https://www.iliff.edu/faculty/tink-tinker/
148. https://www.amazon.com/Sixth-Extinction-Unnatural-History/dp/1250062187/ref=sr_1_1?dchild=1&keywords=the+6th+extinction&qid=1592380924&s=books&sr=1-1
https://en.wikipedia.org/wiki/Anthropocenehttps://oneandallwisdom.com/sentience-by-julie-j-morley/
149. https://bsnorrell.blogspot.com/2020/05/chief-arvol-looking-horse-world-peace.html
https://indiancountrytoday.com/archive/important-message-from-keeper-of-sacred-white-buffalo-calf-pipe?redir=1
https://www.youtube.com/watch?v=liqYx7VvopQ
https://www.youtube.com/watch?v=llVm4F84PpE
https://www.history.com/news/how-boarding-schools-tried-to-kill-the-indian-through-assimilation

## Bibliography

Bar-On, D., and J. Chaitin. 2001. *Parenthood and the Holocaust.* Jerusalem: Yad Vashem Publications, Search and Research, Lectures and Papers 1.

Bloch, M. 1998. *How We Think They Think: Anthropological Approaches to Cognition, Memory, and Literacy.* Oxford: Westview Press.

Bonilla-Silva, E. 2014. *Racism Without Racists: Color-Blind Racism and the Persistence of Racial Inequality in America*. 4th ed. Lanham, MD: Rowman & Littlefield Publishers, Inc.

Bourdieu, P. 1977. *Outline of a Theory of Practice*. Cambridge: Cambridge University Press.

Fassin, D., and R. Rechtman. 2009. *The Empire of Trauma: An Inquiry into the Condition of Victimhood*. Princeton: Princeton University Press.

Gell, A. 1992. *The Anthropology of Time: Cultural Constructions of Temporal Maps and Images*. Oxford: Berg.

Hanchard, M. 2000. Black Cinderella? Race and the Public Sphere in Brazil. In *The Idea of Race*, ed. R. Bernasconi and T.L. Lott, 161–180. Indianapolis, IN: Hackett Publishing Company, Inc.

Kendi, I.X. 2016. *Stamped from the Beginning: The Definitive History of Racist Ideas in America*. New York: Bold Type Books.

———. 2019. *How to Be an Antiracist*. New York: One World.

Linstroth, J.P. 2009. Mayan Cognition, Memory, and Trauma. *History and Anthropology* 20 (2): 139–182.

———. 2015. Urban Amerindians and Advocacy: Toward a Politically Engaged Anthropology Representing Urban Amerindigeneities. In *Indigenous Studies and Engaged Anthropology: The Collaborative Moment*, ed. Paul Sillitoe, 116–145. Surrey, UK and Burlington, VT: Ashgate Publishers Limited.

Montagu, A. 1997. *Man's Most Dangerous Myth: The Fallacy of Race*. 6th ed. London: Altamira Press.

Scheper-Hughes, N. 1992. *Death Without Weeping: The Violence of Everyday Life in Brazil*. Berkeley: University of California Press.

Telles, E.E. 2004. *Race in Another America: The Significance of Skin Color in Brazil*. Princeton: Princeton University Press.

Warfield Rawls, A., and W. Duck. 2020. *Tacit Racism*. Chicago: The University of Chicago Press.

Warren, J.W. 2001. *Racial Revolutions: Antiracism and Indian Resurgence in Brazil*. Durham, NC: Duke University Press.

West, C. 1993. *Race Matters*. New York: Vintage Books.

Whitehouse, H. 2000. *Arguments and Icons: Divergent Modes of Religiosity*. Oxford: Oxford University Press.

Winddance Twine, F. 2005. *Racism in a Racial Democracy: The Maintenance of White Supremacy in Brazil*. New Brunswick, NJ: Rutgers University Press.

CHAPTER 6

# Environment, Humanism, Science, and Tolerance

*This book was written in part to create a more respectful and tolerant world in which to live in. Tolerance extends to not only peoples of different ethnicities and peoples from different religions, but those with different sexualities, as in the LBGT (Lesbian Bisexual Gay and Transsexual) community, as well. In part, I felt compelled to write about tolerance toward the LBGT community in response to a family member who believes that being "gay" is a personal choice and not something one is born with. This family member, who in many ways is very zealous in their religious beliefs, has no clue about the science of same-sex relations, nor cares to know. They believe that being gay or being part of the LBGT community is akin to accepting a life of Sodom and Gomorrah, rather than understanding the biological components of such identities. In other words, society often places values upon what is considered to be "normal," not only in the United States, but really everywhere. Even though as a socio-cultural anthropologist I believe one's sexuality may be variable according to cultural attributes, cultural traditions, and cultural norms, just as much as gender is socially constructed; nonetheless, one cannot discount the biological factors of sexual identity as well. Moreover, while I am of the opinion that religious beliefs and their variations should be protected; regardless, such views should be filtered if they become "intolerant" or if such views promote "intolerance." Religious views cannot necessarily supplant facts such as evolution either. Many religions, for many reasons, try to represent the world and depict the reasons for life and the why reasons of life. However, this does not make such views so, nor does it make such religious*

© The Author(s), under exclusive license to Springer Nature Switzerland AG 2022
J. P. Linstroth, *Politics and Racism Beyond Nations*,
https://doi.org/10.1007/978-3-030-91720-3_6

*views factual. Even if a religion imagines life as it should be, it does not often account for life as it is, nor explain nature as science knows it to be, especially for religious beliefs based upon religious texts 1000 or more years old, and so on. Nor can magical thinking supplant reality, however convincing such religious views may be to their adherents. For example, our earth is "not" 6000 years old, or even, 10,000 years old according to some Christian viewpoints.[1] Rather, the earth is at least 4.5 billion years old and there is plenty of geological evidence to demonstrate why this is factual. What is more, the theory of evolution is provable in varying ways, for example, DNA mutations, fossil evidence, vestigial organs, domestic animal breeding, and so on.*

*While I have previously published on gender, such as my book* Marching Against Gender Practice: Political Imaginings in the Basqueland *(2015) and the article "Gender as a Category for Analysis of Conflict" (2010), I did not previously emphasize the "biological aspects and identities" associated with those identifying with the LBGT community.[2] Therefore, I believe it is necessary to explain how biological interpretations of sexualities and gender may complement socio-cultural views, and as such, they must be discussed for more complete understandings of both gender and sexualities and their expressions in humans.*

*For these reasons, in 2020, I asked several people if they would not mind answering a few questions about "being gay" in hope to understand how "intolerant thinking" may be so devastating to the individual. (I had three respondents.) Furthermore, I wanted to comprehend how religion may be harmful rather than helpful in individual psychological development.*

*In order to understand the "gay community," I reached out to as broad a net as I could—affinal kin, friends, former students, and colleagues I know in Florida and elsewhere in the United States. It is "not" meant to be a complete sampling of "gay people." One could argue I did not reach out to Lesbians, or Transgender people, or Bisexuals, or Transvestites, or Asexuals, and so on. So, in advance, I apologize for this. However, I tried to capture the general suffering, and trauma from "being gay" from this very diverse, LGBTQ community. I was looking for qualitative answers which would describe what it was like "growing up gay" and what it was like to be discriminated against as a "gay person." Furthermore, and as I analyze the issue through science, the academic discussion which follows provides a broader perspective. Also, the book is not only about the gay community but more about "intolerance" and "discrimination," and how society, broadly speaking, overcomes such narrowmindedness and prejudice and hate. The following are responses to my queries from self-identified three gay men.*

\* \* \*

### Sean, Fifty-Eight Years Old

*The following are therefore questions sent to a friend of a friend who is by their own admission "gay" and their ensuing answers to my queries. For the purposes of research for this book, I used a pseudonym for the subject's name in order for them to remain anonymous and in order to protect their identities. For these purposes, I will call him "Sean," a 58 year old male, from New York City, New York. As such, Sean answered a series of questions I sent them via email. (Self-identifies as Caucasian as well.)*

**Question 1: What was it like growing up gay? (Explain.)**

*I was raised in a very conservative fundamentalist Christian home. There was a lot of love in it, but there was also a loathing of anything that deviated from the norm. Homosexuality was a particularly despised deviation. I remember that my pastor father once said that he thought that homosexuality was "the unforgiveable sin" since he had never known a homosexual who had ever changed. It never occurred to him or others who taught the same thing that sexual orientation might be immutable.*

*Obviously, there was a lot of self-loathing in me as I came to understand that I was gay. Reconciling being gay and being Christian never entered my young mind. All I wanted to do was change my orientation.*

**Question 2: When did you first realize you might be gay? And what were those feelings like?**

*I think I first realized I was gay sometime in elementary school. I remember having crushes on other little boys, although I would never have thought of them like that (romantically). They were more like intense friendships. These feelings were actually quite dreadful to me because of my religious upbringing. I was terrified of what I was feeling and full of self-loathing for being "sinful" or "defective."*

**Question 3: Was religion an influence in your life and did it confuse your feelings about being gay in any way? If so, why?**

*As to the why question, I fully believed that God hated sin and sinners, and being gay was (perhaps) the worst kind of sin. There was a strong message from my pastor father and his church that being gay was worse than being a murderer, largely because gay people kept repeating the sin over and over again. The idea that I might be gay was so abhorrent to me that it became my primary motivation in life to change my orientation.*

**Question 4: Have you read any scientific studies on homosexuality and what do you think of them?**

*Early in my coming out, I did read some studies that helped me to understand myself better. But I never read any extensively, and I don't read them now. I came to understand my own lived experience as being authoritative. This was consistent with the experience-based nature of my early religious upbringing. In other words, while interesting, I don't need anyone else to validate my experience and I have absolutely no interest in trying to convince anyone else of the validity of my own experience.*

Question 5: How have your views on homosexuality changed over the years, and if so, why?

*They have changed a lot. It was a matter of survival. While I was never suicidal in my behavior, I did have suicidal thoughts early on in the coming out process. I had begged God to change me. I had been through years of so-called reparative therapy. I did not change and God did not seem to answer any of my prayers. The conclusion I then drew was that God hated me.*

*In order to survive, I had to change the way I thought/believed. I later came to see this experience of change as being part of my spiritual, as well as psychological, growth. I came to see God at work in it. Coming out is an integral part of my spiritual journey.*

Question 6: Do you think society is more accepting of homosexuality now than in the past? (If so, why? Or, if not, why not?)

*It is more accepting. The world has changed a great deal in my lifetime (I am 58). I am legally married to my husband—something I could have never dreamed of as a young adult. It's astounding, really.*

Question 7: How might society become more tolerant? What does tolerance mean to you?

*In order for American society to be more tolerant, the influence of right-wing politics and religion must wane. The Trump years have caused the opposite to happen. Hateful and exclusionary thinking has been given permission to rear its head, even among the highest reaches of government and society. It's frightening. And I fear it could get worse. Lately I have been wondering where in the world we could immigrate to if things in the US got really bad.*

*For me, tolerance is very simple: doing unto others what you would have them do unto you. Also, I do not need others to approve of me. But I do need them to tolerate me; to practice tolerance.*

*But it is an over-reach to say that the whole world has changed or that the battle is done. Anti-gay bias is still very strong in many parts of this country and the world. And the positive changes that have been made are tenuous at best. A major crisis of any kind could see the advances made by gay people evaporate. Or worse.*

Question 8: What does it mean to be gay to you?

*To be gay is to be attracted to members of your own sex. I do not attach any political meaning to it.*

Question 9: If you have traveled, do you believe views on homosexuality are different in different countries you have visited? (Or, if not traveled outside the United States, in different states in the United States?) Please explain.

*I have been to countries where homosexuality is far more accepted and countries where it is forbidden to act on your desires or sexual impulses. The degree of acceptance seems to be attached to the wane of religious practice (Christian and others). The United States seems to be somewhere in the middle, but conservative religion still plays a significant role in intolerance.*

*[The last question, number 10, asked if he wanted to add anything. And he did not answer that one.]*

\* \* \*

### Chad, in His 40s

*Some of the participants wished to have their names used. One of these is Chad Luke Schiro, a man in his 40s, originally from New Orleans [He did not want to reveal his exact age]. His answers here are edited and excerpted. (Self-identifies as Caucasian as well.)*

Question 1: What was it like growing up gay? (Explain.)

*On the surface, it was a very simple, fun, loving childhood. Beneath, however, I lived a private nightmare. We knew no gay people. I'd never met or seen a single one until high school. When I did finally see a gay man, he was pointed out to me as a freak and a predatory degenerate. No one could find me out. I would never allow this to happen. In spite of the fact that I was this obviously effeminate child, this was all buried incredibly deep inside.*

Question 2: When did you first realize you might be gay? And what were those feelings like?

*When I was 6 or 7, my older brother (he was 9) told me that when he went to hang with my Father and uncles that they said I was gay. He said that it was bad and they all talked about it. I already knew that I didn't relate to the men in my family. This made it much worse. To this day, I still avoid the men in my father's side of the family. A boy at school, when he began calling me gay, soon affirmed this. I was a straight A student. He was from a "trashy" family and had been held back a grade. He had a sister a few years older who I'm sure told him this. It stuck with me throughout school and was incredibly traumatizing. It also deeply manipulated any sense of pride I might have had* in being "gay." I wouldn't realize until much later that this was manifesting incredible amounts of self-hatred. I was incredibly intuitive and began to sense when anyone had "clocked me." I could feel the men in my family silently conveying discomfort in conversation. This led to the subconscious belief that even my closest friends somehow thought very little of me. My voice would give me away, so I wouldn't speak. Even my voice became buried. This would take years of undoing, and it's still a daily process.

**Question 3: Was religion an influence in your life and did it confuse your feelings about being gay in any way? If so, why?**

*Yes. 14 years of Catholic school, and I was good at it. Like Pavlov's dog, I knew exactly what to do to get the desired response and I was loved and awarded and applauded by all of my teachers. I won bible study contests, played guitar in the church choir and knew the laws of Catholicism much more clearly than any of my peers. I knew that I could have the gay thoughts and impulses, but if I ever acted on them I'd then have to confess to the priest to avoid hell. It's pretty fucked up. Looking back, it was the perfect way for Catholics to allow for gay men and women to exist in oppression.*

**Question 4: Have you read any scientific studies on homosexuality and what do you think of them?**

*Early on I read all of the literature put out by PFLAG [Parents, Family, and Friends of Lesbians and Gays]. It was all incredibly helpful to me. A friend of mine gave me the introductory packet to give to my Mother. His mother was an educated psychologist and raised him as an openly gay, evolved son. The pamphlets never made it to my Mom, but they allowed me to be a better parent myself and assisted in my articulation of my coming out. Although I don't know where I'd learned them, I knew the American Psychiatric Association's views on homosexuality. Not long after I came out, I began working as a professional dancer in New York. I gathered pieces of gay history from plays like Angels In America and The Normal Heart, the Broadway community had been decimated by AIDS in the 80's, and I arrived in NY in the mid/late 90's. The Actor's Union and the nonprofit, Broadway Cares/Equity Fights AIDS would hold several enormous fundraisers throughout the year for people living with the disease. I learned a great deal from their history. In my early career, I was uninsured and would go to GMHC, Gay Men's Health Crisis, for regular HIV testing. I'd always read pamphlets and periodicals there. It was still a horrifying time to be a gay man in NYC. I've also read books like, Quentin Crisp's "The Naked Civil Servant", "The Velvet Rage" and others on homosexuality itself. When the internet came along, it changed everything. It was really a patchwork approach to education. Many Dr.'s volunteer and older gay men were more helpful. I was also much more likely, at an early age, to have a conversation or read a pamphlet or the gay magazines on the stand inside of every gay bar than to read scientific studies. I now have a good friend who writes for POZ.com. his articles are always two steps ahead of what's happening in the Dr.'s office. I rely on open dialogue with friends, and I chose to put my insurance dollars toward seeing my General Practitioner at one of the most diverse and important LGBTQ clinics in NYC. I believe that my dollars pay for those who can't pay, and the staff there are incredibly educated and open to any and all questions. This is crucial to LGBTQ health.*

**Question 5: How have your views on homosexuality changed over the years, and if so, why?**

*I'm an LGBTQIA [Lesbian Gay Bisexual Transgender Queer Intersex Asexual] Plus writer and activist. I now fight for the rights of my Transgender friends. This country prides itself on having come a long way. Considering where we started, we have not. We're still ruled by morality, religion, and major manipulation of Right To Life voters who don't truly understand what's on the ballot. Single-issue voters, even if they believe that gay people are great, are still keeping us from achieving equality.*

**Question 6: Do you think society is more accepting of homosexuality now than in the past? (If so, why? Or, if not, why not?)**

*Accepting, but not supportive. There's a difference. We're only ten percent of the general population, and not enough LGBTQIA people drill the facts to their families and friends. It's not always fun, but it's the only way. I think Trump was the first time an entire new generation of queer people saw their families, who claim to support their rights and full equality, vote against them. We can't study or scream the truth loudly enough. It takes making people you love feel uncomfortable, and it's a lot easier to say pass the mashed potatoes and keep the conversation neutral. It also means asking a traumatized community to be healed enough to repeatedly dive head first into their trauma. Trust me. It's beyond exhausting. It can be maddening. I do it for those who came before me and died for my freedom.*

**Question 7: How might society become more tolerant? What does tolerance mean to you?**

*Tolerance is bullshit. You tolerate an experimental drug or an edgy bipolar coworker or family member, because they have a disorder. The LGBTQ community is perfect. We are not a mental disorder or a risky experiment. Science is the only answer, and religion in this country is in direct opposition to science. For me this means education. The American Psychiatric Association* declared homosexuality a normal variance in sexual orientation in 1973. It's 2020. Let that sink in, but that fact should be on the lips of every single LGBTQIA person. We also need to tell our religious family and friends that tolerance is not enough. Many of them see it as harmless to financially and spiritually support religions whose policies do not support us. It's not enough to say you don't believe all of your Church's doctrine. If you're walking in every week and giving them your "Amen" and your money, you are supporting every word of their doctrine. Be vocal. Ask your priest questions weekly. Write to the Pope monthly. All you need to do is ask the Ali Forney Center for homeless LGBTQIA youth in NYC what the number one cause of homelessness is for our youth. It's religion. LGBTQIA people make up 10% of the population, yet 40% of homeless youth identify as LGBTQIA. Religion is the number one cause of this disparity. I believe that people want to be better than that. They can understand that, but they need the information. In the age of smart phones and sound bites, we cannot scream it loudly enough.

**Question 8: What does it mean to be gay to you?**

At best, it means having your eyes open to not just your own truth. It means taking the personal experience of being born into a less than perfect, and less than truthful, society and applying it to everything. In 2020, more than ever, it means correlating the lapses in truth in doctrine and law and applying them toward justice. "Correlating" is the most important word for me. I thought about what Harvey Milk asked when he told us that remaining closeted wasn't an option. "You MUST come out." We're out now, but people gay and straight equate this with freedom. We are far from free. Being gay in 2020 means building on the legacy of the giants upon whose shoulders we stand. For most of us, this is much less physically dangerous than it used to be. The path forward is also far less obvious. This is why we must correlate our experience of oppression with every other disenfranchised group. LGBTQIA people are only 10% of the population, but what we share with every other oppressed minority is a common oppressor. "The Women's March," the "Black Lives Matter" movement, and the movement toward full equality for Transgender and Nonbinary populations all share a common enemy, therefore, being gay in 2020 means understanding the histories of other historically disenfranchised groups and speaking out and standing up and showing up for them. This is the only way we can ask them to do the same for us. This is the power of true intersectional existence. Not just social media or entertainment photo ops, but a life of true intersectional diligence. It's the responsibility of knowing and standing with and for your neighbor, and it's also the incredible opportunity to deeply know ourselves.

*It's also the very personal journey of continually asking myself who the hell I am. Being raised and rewarded to do and say the perceived "right" thing is the enemy of building a strong sense of self. Being gay in 2020 means daring to know myself and act as my individual self even when I know that it might be endlessly easier to conform to the most homogenous version of gay life yet. There are categories of gays. You're either a "Chelsea Gay" guy or a "twink" or a "bear" or "Wall Street Gay" or "Nonbinary."[8] I used to feel like I didn't belong to any of these groups. This was the mental trap of not believing I belonged in my own family. Being gay, for me, means honoring who I am today and working to believe that I fit in everywhere.*

[Skipping Question 9]

Question 10: Explain something about homosexuality not asked with these questions. Is there anything more you would like to add, or you would like others to know about homosexuality? (Explain.)

*The biggest and most allusive aspect of homosexuality for me is self-hatred. Because many of us will always have an outside enemy (They've existed throughout history and will continue through existence.) many LGBTQ people don't take the time or have the time to look inward. Like the concept of intersectional strength, it's complicated and take time to understand, but it may be even more frightening. Acknowledging self-hatred requires strength and an existing structure of queer support. It requires moving through deeply buried feelings, and powerfully engrained beliefs. Because of this, it can also be dangerous to unlock. Whether it's a network of close friends or an expert therapist, one must be supported to do this work. For me, this monster lives in the realm of illogical thoughts and feelings. They're the direct result of my formative years. For this reason, I equate religious views against homosexuality with child abuse, conversion camps and the horrific lobotomies and shock therapies of the 1940's and 50's.*

\* \* \*

### Robert, Forty Years Old

*Another respondent was Robert, who at the time of the interview was forty years old and also self-identifies as Chinese-American. He grew up in Hong Kong but now lives in South Florida. Robert is a pseudonym he chose for the interview.*

Question 1: What was it like growing up gay? (Explain.)

*My experience growing up has informed me a little about sexuality in general. Having been educated in a single-gender environment since before* puberty, and having grown up in a restrictive family environment, I had very little knowledge or even desire towards the opposite sex. On the other hand, the single-gender environment at school has allowed me to recognize my romantic inclinations towards boys my own age. However, the hyper-competitive academic culture of Hong Kong means that I had no free time for any type of socialization. Tutors and academic coaches occupied every single bit of free time outside of school.

In a broader cultural context, growing up in Hong Kong as a gay kid is quite different than growing up in other parts of the world. While it was a British colony (at the time), I was not aware of any instances where police and the government actively persecute members of the LGBT community (although as of this writing, gay marriage remains illegal). Being gay (or the act of homosexuality can be considered "gross" by my peers, but there are no large scale political and societal opposition to LGBT people. In addition, there are LGBT celebrities in pop culture as far as I can remember, but the culture in which I grew up prizes privacy and discretion, and the dating lives of celebrities are well hidden despite being common knowledge or social assumptions (i.e., the so-called "glass closet").

**Question 2: When did you first realize you might be gay? And what were those feelings like?**

I flirted with girls when I was a child, but by the age of 12–13 I became fascinated with men. I find myself drawn to sights and pictures of shirtless men, while the naked female form did not provide me with the same joy that my peers seemed to have. I never quite questioned my feelings, but I never expressed them publicly or verbally. Given my sheltered and regimented upbringing, I barely had time to discover my sexuality let alone discuss it with a trusted adult.

It would not be until my college years that I fully explored my sexuality and my sex life, save a couple instances of experimentations. (I will not share the circumstances of those instances due to privacy and potential legal issues.)

**Question 3: Was religion an influence in your life and did it confuse your feelings about being gay in any way? If so, why?**

The simple answer is "no." My family was never religious in any significant manner. We participated in Chinese traditional rites (e.g. venerating ancestors, cleaning the tombs of our dead relatives, visiting various Taoist/Buddhist temples, etc.) but religion is not part of our daily lives. In terms of education, I attended religious schools, first with private kindergarten and primary school (Baptist), then a secondary school run by the Jesuits. The choice of these schools was fundamentally based on the quality of education they offer, *since they were considered superior to public schools. During my time in secondary school, I attended mass once or twice every academic year, but religion was not foisted on us like some religious schools in the United States. Study of the bible was strictly relegated to comparison to other religions.*

*Since religion figured so little in my upbringing, I never considered it to be a factor in my discovery of my sexuality. It was only when I moved to the United States that I realized the power of conservative religious groups and their assault on LGBT youth development.*

**Question 4: Have you read any scientific studies on homosexuality and what do you think of them?**

*As a social scholar and researcher, I have consumed a lot of articles about homosexuality and the LGBT community. Serious scientific research, done with the scientific method and uncolored by religious or political biases, have consistently shown that homosexuality is natural and same-sex attraction is at least partly influenced by genetics.*

*On the other hand, I am very concerned when conservative and religious organizations use pseudoscientific jargon to promote their biased views by cloaking their bigotry with scientific language. A notable example is Regnerus' study of "New Family Structure" that was poorly conducted and reviewed.[4] It was cited by conservative organization to show that children who are raised by same-sex couples were disadvantaged in life when the actual data did not support that conclusion. This type of so-called scholarship is the equivalent of fake news in social science and research circles and are designed to confuse the results of proper scholarship as well as a cloak of respectability for bigotry.*

**Question 5: How have your views on homosexuality changed over the years, and if so, why?**

*As a 40-year old, I lived through some of the most eventful periods of LGBT history. From being classified as automatic AIDS victims to the realization of marriage equality, LGBT people have come a long way dismantling some of the worst structural injustices and prejudices that were prevalent when I was born. When I first realized my sexuality, coming out was a major event in one's life, as it is a symbol of shedding the hetero-normative constraints of social expectations was groundbreaking. By the time I "came out" in college in the late 90s, being gay was not without stigma, but it was certainly not groundbreaking in a liberal college environment in Boston. Now living in South Florida amid a large LGBT community, my sexuality is simply a personal detail, not unlike being Asian or being short. In sum, my views of my own sexuality and others' have changed over the years. What was once a life changing event for some is now a simple fact of life.*

**Question 6: Do you think society is more accepting of homosexuality now than in the past? (If so, why? Or, if not, why not?)**

*Yes, and No. While there are many parts of the developed world that are more understanding and accepting of homosexuality, there are still many parts that hold contrary views, including some fairly advanced nations such as Singapore. Those who cling on to bigotry often cite religious reasons to disapprove of alternative sexual identities, while others simply cling on to the notion of tradition. From time to time, when we are discussing travel, I have to remind my husband that some locations are simply "verboten" for us to visit due to their views on sexuality, which might lead to official disapproval, judicial punishments, or extrajudicial violence. I am also reluctant to spend money in countries who refuse to acknowledge LGBT rights. Furthermore, there seems to be a backlash against LGBT rights in some parts of the United States and other countries where conservative politicians continue to use the community as a scapegoat.*

*On the other hand, there is a momentum towards equality in general, even though there are some setbacks in Eastern Europe and the United States. Taiwan (the Republic of China) recently became the first country to legalize same-sex marriage in East Asia, and around the world there have been incremental improvements.*

*Personally, my residency in the United States have been largely located in very liberal urban areas along the coast, and my experience is that attitudes towards homosexuality has markedly improved during my decades in this country. In the past, those who espouse bigotry have largely relied on twin prongs of personal distaste (the idea that homosexuals are "gross") and religious disapproval (especially Judeo-Christian values) to enact discriminatory policies and/or excuses to celebrate homophobic violence. These attitudes are now largely relegated to fringe groups and hate groups (although they have seen a resurgence under the Trump administration). Public views of alternative sexualities have improved according to numerous studies and polls, and outright bigotry is no longer acceptable in mainstream political discourse. The fact that "social conservatives" have to change their rhetoric over time to justify their views in order to gain support from the public (e.g. from labeling homosexuals as abnormal or diseased or arguing the lack of ability of LGBT couples to raise children) reflect the fact that most of the public is no longer accepting of their old ideas.*

**Question 7: How might society become more tolerant? What does tolerance mean to you?**

*Tolerance is a complicated concept, and we must not equate tolerance as support. Tolerance is the absence of adverse action against those who do not conform to a persona's worldview, while acceptance is the embrace of alternative worldviews.*

*Therefore, in the context of homosexuality and the LGBT community, tolerance means the lack of discrimination, bigotry, and violence against my community. By that definition, society has become more tolerant. Homosexual acts can no longer be criminalized under the law thanks to the Lawrence [v. Texas] Case in 2003, and states can no longer bar marriage between same-sex partners.[5] On the other hand, there is still much to be gained, including freedom from discrimination in many states that continue to allow LGBT people to be discriminated against in everyday life.*

*To make society more tolerant, we must change societal attitudes towards LGBT people. Education and legislation can only do so much, however, as many would hold on to ingrained values of the past. Time is an important factor, as older generations give way to a more tolerant generation of leaders who are more likely to accept and tolerate sexual diversity.*

**Question 8: What does it mean to be gay to you?**

*To be gay is to be attracted to people of the same gender. Nothing more, nothing less. That said, like every other minority community, there are certain values that we uphold and certain customs that are more accepted within our community that is not widely embraced outside.*

**Question 9: If you have traveled, do you believe views on homosexuality are different in different countries you have visited? (Or, if not traveled outside the United States, in different states in the United States?) Please explain.**

*I grew up travelling extensively with my family, but I was not able to explore any sexuality-related topics back then. As an adult I have traveled within the United States and Europe (including the UK). I find Europe to be most welcoming to LGBT people, but I can find the same level of tolerance and acceptance in most major American cities where there are concentrated LGBT populations. In general, I would say that more cosmopolitan regions are more accepting of my community, and the better educated the population is, the more welcoming they are.*

**Question 10: Explain something about homosexuality not asked with these questions. Is there anything more you would like to add, or you would like others to know about homosexuality? (explain.)**

*If there is one thing left unsaid in this survey, it is that LGBT people are as diverse as society itself. We come from all societal classes, and all races and nationalities. We are scholars, shopkeepers, cowboys, and factory workers. We are billionaires and the poor. Therefore, like any study of minority groups, there is a certain amount of generalization that cannot apply to every member of our community.*

Photograph of LGBTQ Pride flag

## Introduction

The previous narratives of three gay men, Sean, Chad, and Robert (all pseudonyms), encapsulate in a limited but qualitative way, what it means to grow up gay and to be gay. I begin the chapter with these narratives to prove how biological forces (genetics) mold in important respects one's social identity. As a social and cultural anthropologist, I know too that gender and sexuality are mutable. In a previous encyclopedic entry, I proved why this is so (Linstroth 2010). As I stated: "Sexual difference is not an obvious one of bifurcation or sexual dimorphism in human society, or as exclusive to heterosexuality, because of the variability of interpreting bodies and bodily functions among non-Western peoples ... [and Western peoples alike]" (Linstroth 2010: 227). The individual, as such, may have "conflicting and multivalent potential of agency and individuality" and these are varied both in Western and in non-Western societies (Linstroth 2010: 227). For example, in some parts of Papua New Guinea there were societies where ritual homosexuality was practiced and where young initiate-men were induced to perform fellatio and drink semen of other older men in order to become heterosexual men (see Herdt 1981). On the other hand, in some parts of rural Albania, some women take on the role of men and become men, in manner and dress, and swear virginity their entire lives for these transformed male gender roles (see Young 2000). Human gender constructions and sexuality constructions are as varied as the societies of their origins and likewise variable from individual human behavior as well.

Moreover, this chapter is supposed to inspire how science may lead to more tolerance. For instance, through better understandings of the biological bases for Lesbian, Bisexual, Gay, Transgender (LBGT) constructions may help in some manner with the social acceptance of same-sex or alternative sexual identities beyond the hegemonic constructions of the hetero-male and the hetero-female. What I am arguing for here is an understanding of what Maurice Bloch (2012: 183) calls the "implicit." By this he means how people: "Reconstruct in their own minds the implicit that lies behind the explicit that they can observe from the behaviours and words of those with whom they are in interaction. What lies behind [mental] concepts and schemas gets known by a process of minute, very rapid and continual mind reading. This is a mutual colonisation of minds" (Bloch 2012: 183).

In other words, to understand what Sean, Chad, and Robert say it means to be gay, we need to not only examine their words and their explicit social constructs of "being gay," but likewise examine the implicit biological bases for being so. Thus, the social interrelates with the biological and as such they are elided with one another to form a complex whole. Thus, this complex whole, or what it means to be human, signifies: "that the social, sexual, and reproductive characteristics of the human species means that we go in and out of each other's bodies in at least three different ways, and that this implies an indeterminacy of the level of relevant differentiation" (Bloch 2013: 17).

To analyze the narratives of Sean, Chad, and Robert, one might say the questions posed allowed them to explain in their own words their self-realizations for being gay from childhood and how this changed into adulthood through full acceptance. Their narratives also relate to the fact that society may still be oppressive of the LBGTQ community and what this means. This was very much apparent in two of the respondents (Sean and Chad) in regard to religion and how much religious belief and religious thought were oppressive to earlier childhood understandings of being gay (the former Protestant and the latter Catholic). It is unfortunate how much religion influences society into wrong thinking, especially with respect to biological factors which may be beyond an individual's particular control. Beyond their narratives, and because I discussed trauma in Chap. 5, I will not elaborate on this conceptualization here in regard to some of their childhood memories, I now turn to the biological for an explication of what it means to be gay.

In Bruce Bagemihl's (1999) book *Biological Exuberance: Animal Homosexuality and Natural Diversity*, he documents 300 species of mammals and birds which exhibit homosexual and transgender behaviors. In documenting the polysexual and polygendered animal world, we find that humans are not alone in homosexual, same-sex, and transgendered behaviors in the animal kingdom but many, many other non-human animal species share these characteristics as well. As Bagemihl (1999: 6) remarks: "Sexual and gender variance in animals offer a key to a new way of looking at the world, symbolic of the larger paradigm shifts currently underway in a number of natural and social sciences. The discussion is rooted in the basic facts about animal homosexuality and nonreproductive heterosexuality." Hence, humans are just one among numerous animal species who exhibit homosexual and transgendered behaviors.

More specifically, in Jacques Balthazart's (2012) book *The Biology of Homosexuality*, we have more exact reasoning why from the "implicit" perspective, the genetic disposition of the individual, why a person is homosexual or transgendered or identifies with another varied sexual identity. We know, for example, that hormones act upon the hypothalamus and thereby imprint upon the individual in the embryonic stage (Balthazart 2012: 154–155). Embryonic sex steroids likewise act upon brain structures which may help vary an individual's sexual orientation (Balthazart 2012: 155). According to Balthazart (2012: 155–156): "Homosexuality is not simply a different sexual orientation; it is accompanied by complex physical, functional, and behavioral changes. Homosexuality therefore affects not only a particular aspect of sexual behavior but also multiple sexually differentiated traits that are not related to sexuality." Another physical characteristic is the size of the "sexually dimorphic nucleus of preoptic area (SDN-POA)," which is larger in heterosexual men than women and for male homosexuals the same general size as the female's (Balthazart 2012: 156). Likewise: "The genetic contribution to sexual orientation is most likely multigenic and therefore very difficult to identify" (Balthazart 2012: 157).

Moreover, and this is significant for those supposing there are social factors in creating homosexuality (or other identifiers to LBGTQ) in childhood and adolescence, do not exist. "In contrast, the alternative explanations of homosexuality that are based on psychoanalysis, psychology, or sociology are perhaps attractive at first glance, but the rare quantitative studies that were conducted to test them provide, to our knowledge, no support" (Balthazart 2012: 157). In sum, "It seems undeniable that the balance between biological and cultural factors that may explain homosexuality very much favors the biological factors acting predominantly during embryonic life. Human (and animal) homosexuality is the result of an interaction between hormonal and genetic embryonic factors with perhaps a minor contribution of postnatal social and sexual experiences" (Balthazart 2012: 158).

\* \* \*

In this chapter, in addition to the above analyses of the narratives of Sean, Chad, and Robert and what it means to be homosexual, I will promote a kind of tolerance through neurobiology and primatology. Particularly, I explore how crucial specific structures in the brain are in influencing human behavior such as the amygdala as a fear and anger center and why neurochemicals such as oxytocin enhance in-group and out-group behaviors. There is also the insular cortex (insula) and how moral disgust may be related to physical aversion to tastes and smells, which may then inform attitudes about Latino immigrants, for instance (see Sapolsky 2017: 398). Furthermore, I investigate non-human primate behaviors and what such behaviors tell us about being human.

Additionally, this chapter debates some of the issues surrounding the destruction of the Brazilian Amazon and the negligence of Brazilian President Jair Bolsonaro's administration for allowing such devastation. The massive fires in Amazonia are ongoing crises of mega-proportions and evident as of this writing in July 2021 wherein according to several scientists carbon-release for the first time is more than carbon-capture.[6]

Moreover, this chapter will establish why the developing world is having difficulties in curbing mortality and spread of Coronavirus and why race should not in any way be associated with diseases like COVID-19. The latter harkens back to the Middle Ages when Jews were rounded up and systematically murdered for the Plague across Europe in what became known as pogroms.

Lastly, I assert why history and science should be propagated for the purposes of enlightenment as candles in the dark. Hence, what I attempt to do is relate how fake news is nothing new as evident from the witch hunts in England during the sixteenth and seventeenth centuries and how people use social networks to circulate and promulgate nonsense. As Charles Kadushin (2012: 202) maintains: "Social networks are driven by motivations, expectations, and cognitive limitations. They are influenced by and responsive to social norms and institutions. Through repeated interactions, new norms and institutions are created." What I elaborate on is the correlation of social networking pasts with the present such as the fake news promoted by the former President Donald Trump about winning the 2020 presidential election and what this means for our democracy in the United States in general. Thus, in the United States social networks have been created around mass media promotion through such outlets as CNN, MSNBC, and FOX News, whereas in sixteenth- and seventeenth-century England, information about witches was promulgated through pamphlets.

How we as people in the United States and across the globe advocate for tolerance and mindfulness will be up to us as this chapter illustrates.

## Teaching Tolerance

I believe it is important to remind ourselves of tolerance and mindfulness. As an educator and anthropologist, I teach about the history of racism both at the high school level as an honors history teacher and at the college level as an adjunct professor. What is particularly important for me is explaining origins of our racist history. First, I explain why "race" is entirely a social construct, not biological, and second, I explain how humans have socially created such an egregious construct throughout history.

There are, no doubt some biological aspects concerning how humans go about "othering" unrelated fellow humans. For example, we may turn to Jane Goodall's studies of chimpanzees and understand proto-genocidal behavior through the manner in which related male-chimps conduct border patrols around their territories. (We share 96 percent of our DNA with chimpanzees.)[7]

Yet, defining someone by their melanin or skin color and their physical traits is completely arbitrary at best. On the whole, we are all more genetically similar than we are different. People are taught to believe in "Us" versus "Them" dichotomies. They are taught those people are different than us and therefore we need to treat them differently. The prominent primatologist and neurologist, Robert Sapolsky, claims these differences are often exacerbated by a brain chemical, oxytocin, and a brain region, the amygdala.[8]

We humans, who are present today, are products of an evolutionary history over the last roughly 200,000 years. Over the last 200 years humanity has increased on the magnitude of almost 8 billion people and is rapidly growing still.[9] Our crowded planet creates an ever more urgent need for the promotion of tolerance because of our finite ecological resources.

We are all products of a global colonial history which saw the forced subjugation of millions of peoples in Africa, Asia, and the Americas, now the developing world, by Europeans powers. Our great history in the United States has been mired by African slavery and continual oppression of African-Americans long after the abolition of their bondage as well as the genocide of Native Americans and near-extinction of these varied peoples across our lands.

Global economic, political, and social inequalities still exist today and have their historical antecedents in European colonialism. According to the Center for Strategic & International Studies (CSIS), over the last few years, we have not faced this level of "forced migration" since World War II. By 2016, 66 million people had been forcibly expelled from their homelands because of violence.[10] This number includes 22.5 million people who are refugees and about 40 million people who are "internally displaced persons" (IDPs) with 3 million people seeking asylum. The most vulnerable of these forced migrants are women and children.[11]

In 2015, according to the UN International Organization for Migration (IOM), there were 244 million international migrants or about 3 percent of the world population.[12] This is the stark reality of the world we live in today. So, when we talk about "caravan invasions" we should keep this in mind. It is understanding why these people are vulnerable and why they have left their home countries seeking better lives. The same may be said of many of our ancestors who left Ireland and Southern Europe and Eastern Europe in order to reach Ellis Island in the late nineteenth and early twentieth centuries.

We in America are on the whole a welcoming people and we have integrated the ethnic diversity of our humanity in the United States for a long time, perhaps more so than any other country. In fact, many of our ancestors faced the same kind of racism new immigrants do today. Pause and think about that for a moment. Xenophobic rhetoric is nothing new but it is no less insidious for those who have to confront it.

Of course, it does not have to be this way. We can remind ourselves of our long history of racism and try preventing it. We can learn to empathize with new immigrants and understand their many struggles as well as those of our ancestors who came before us. Let's dispel some myths about forced migrants. First, forced migrants are "not" terrorists. They are themselves victims of violence and trauma. Second, most forced migrants will never return to their homelands. These people are refugees. They have been forced to move from their home countries because of warfare, gang fighting, civil conflict, and genocide. In fact, they may not have a home to go back to at all.[13]

Such refugees may not return, because if they do, they would be killed. Think of the civil war in Syria, or Rohingya refugees from Myanmar, or the civil war in Yemen, or the continuing conflicts in Afghanistan and Iraq, or war in Darfur, Sudan, or the drug wars in Mexico, or gang savagery in El Salvador and Honduras—and these are only a few current examples.

These people are less fortunate than many of us in the United States as we have not experienced a civil war on our soil since 1865. People come here because we have democratic ideals which have been the envy of the world for more than 200 years and to live the "American Dream" for a better life for themselves and their children just as our ancestors before them.

Tolerance should likewise extend to the LGBTQ community as well. I have mentors and friends from this community and as such their sexual orientations have to do with biology and "not" a chosen lifestyle according to some Christians. When you hear things like—"they were born this way." Well, it is true. Their brains are wired differently than heterosexuals which has been well founded in the scientific establishment. Some of this has to do with prenatal development and testosterone exposure within the womb. In neurological studies, further evidence is found in the manner by which the hypothalamus develops. The hypothalamus is the region which determines both reproductive behavior and individual responses to sexuality. Another area of the brain determining sexual orientation is the amygdala and more complexly the connectivity between different brain hemispheres.[14]

Moreover, if the neuroscientific studies do not convince you, then turn to the animal kingdom. According to Bruce Bagemihl's (1999) book *Biological Exuberance: Animal Homosexuality and Natural Diversity*, at least 450 species other than humans have exhibited same-sex behaviors through affection, courtship, pair-bonding, parenting, and sex. Some of the animals on this long list are: bats, dolphins, ducks, elephants, giraffes, lions, penguins, non-human primates, and sheep. And yes, even dogs and cats!

So, please stop with the intolerance. Think about your place in the world and think about the vulnerability of others. Think why some people may not be as fortunate as you and why some are fleeing from real crises and real wars and real threats and real traumas. Remember humans are biological and social animals and some of us have same-sex preferences and some of us do not. Understand humans are not unique in the animal kingdom in this regard either.

To use Buddhist terminology, "be mindful." Be mindful of yourselves and of others. Allow love to give you empathy and allow love to make the world a more peaceful place and accept people for who they are and not who you think they should be.

## PRIMATES ARE US: BEING SELF, BEING OTHERS

Whether celebrating Christmas, Hanukkah, Kwanzaa, or another sacral rite, we cherish our holidays and traditions though they continually evolve. It is also time to focus on much needed empathy. We think of Santa Claus wearing all-red—first from Coca-Cola ads; modern Christmas tree lighting originating from pagan tree worship, Roman Saturnalia rituals, and arboreal decorations in seventeenth-century Germany; or the curious coincidence of the celebrated date of the birth of Jesus so close to winter solstice. And Christmas gift exchange from the offerings of the three Magi—gold, frankincense, and myrrh—now a major commercial enterprise.

Hanukkah is based upon the Maccabean Revolt (167–160 BC), when the Second Temple in Jerusalem was rededicated.[15] As the Rabbis waited for more holy oil, they were able to light the Temple with one lamp lasting eight days—a full week more than available lamp oil allowed. Now, Hanukkah is celebrated with presents on each commemorative day, eating latkes, and playing dreidel.

These are origins of some of our most wonderful celebrations, some ancient and some "invented traditions," as British scholars Eric Hobsbawm and Terence Ranger explained, ever evolving. We are social animals defining ourselves through rituals and relations to others. As an anthropologist, I try raising questions like: What makes us uniquely human? Or follow-up ones, such as how may we become more empathic to others? Who we are has as much to do with what we inherit as it does with our social environments.

From analyzing the origins of our monotheistic religions, we know they arose in desert environments where other animals are scarce. Polytheistic religions are common where life is abundant. Our Judeo-Christian-Islamic religions developed in isolation from other non-human primates (monkeys, lemurs, primates) and thus also influenced our views about nature and it in relation to us. In other words, we did not see ourselves in other primate species as happens in Amazonia and their Native myths about monkeys and humans, for example.

Significant here is this interplay between the biological and the social—the exclusion of either in our analysis being a significant omission. As the eminent cognitive anthropologist Maurice Bloch elucidates, we may think of interactive exchanges between people as the "transactional social," in contrast to conscious and overt social symbols perpetuated by rituals and ritualistic behavior, which is the "transcendental social."[16] Our social life is so complex that the prefrontal cortex, the brain part responsible for controlling our sociality, most likely developed last in our evolution.

Enormous strides have been made in the neurosciences since the 1970s. Only in the last few years have we begun to understand the many and varied nuances of cognition and neurology associated with human conduct. Some of the more interesting questions about human behavior in recent years have been raised by primatologists like Frans de Waal and Robert Sapolsky. While we are told we diverged on the evolutionary tree from other primates perhaps 5 million years ago, we are much like non-human primates, especially in our tendency to bond and share.

According to de Waal in his book *Age of Empathy: Nature's Lessons for a Kinder Society*, monkeys raised in isolation of other monkeys will develop severe mental and social impairments.[17] Likewise, humans have the same needs. This was proven by the results of Romanian orphanages under the communist Ceaușescu regime. Under Ceaușescu abortion was illegal, resulting in thousands of children being abandoned at state orphanages.[18] By the early 1980s, the conditions in Romanian orphanages were deplorable with rampant abuse and child neglect. As de Waal describes, Romanian "orphans were incapable of laughing or crying, spent the day rocking and clutching themselves in a fetal position ... and did not even know how to play."[19]

Our sociality is an important part of who we are and how we develop into adulthood and how we socialize with others. On the whole, humans have an enormous capacity for empathy as well—that is, imagining others' pain and feelings as our own.

Our empathy is so attuned as to be sometimes expressed with social altruism and not unique among animals as the late great Oxford evolutionary biologist, William Hamilton, proved quite well. Altruism here means that the benefit of the recipient of deeds outweighing the benefits of someone doing the deeds. Think about NYC firemen on 9/11 entering the World Trade Center Towers after the airplanes had collided with both buildings in order to save those who were stranded there.

Indeed, the empathy involved in feeling another's pain is quite ingrained in human cognition, even empathy for the pain of non-human animals. Yet, being altruistic and being empathic do not necessarily have to be interrelated as altruistic impulses may be carried out for group survival and not necessarily as feeling another's pain or preventing another's pain.

In the animal kingdom, according to Sapolsky, consoling a victim from aggression may elicit sympathy from other group members as happens among chimpanzees, crows, dogs, elephants, ravens, and wolves. In our neural wiring, the brain region known as the "anterior cingulate cortex," aside from activating from real pain, according to Sapolsky, is also triggered from abstract social and emotional suffering by anxieties, revulsion, social rejection, and shame.[20] This is also where our empathic feelings emerge for others, elaborated in Sapolsky's recent book *Behave: The Biology of Humans at Our Best and Our Worst*.

Feeling empathy is much easier among those we consider to be "ingroup" people, those most familiar to us and who we identify with, and much less so for strangers. Because it is the anterior cingulate cortex which elicits empathy, its anatomical position also indicates its long evolutionary history. Empathic brain pathways also pass through the insula and amygdala, resonating with emotions from others' facial and bodily expressions and familiar voices.

Surprisingly, as Sapolsky argues, empathy is most often also tied to "self-interest" as dopamine is released in the brain and we feel good about giving to others. Therefore, our chemical reward systems are activated when we are voluntarily giving to others and are not asked to do so.

Charles Dickens's novella *A Christmas Carol* (1843) plays upon our empathic sensibilities for the less fortunate, a morality tale of not only inherent inequalities in capitalism but also the psychological underpinnings about the unease in allowing others' suffering. And so, just as the main character, Ebenezer Scrooge, found redemption and was transformed into a more sympathetic person, we too might learn to become more empathic toward others, especially the less fortunate, in the next holiday season but also, if we are to evolve, year round.

As empathy is more of a natural proclivity for helping family and friends, we may try moving beyond our centers of comfort by embracing strangers in need and making the world a better place.

## Mother of Us All

When many of us celebrate Mother's Day, we recognize it as a day to commemorate and contemplate how wonderful our mothers are and to acknowledge their love—past and present. Additionally, as inhabitants of this planet, we should be encouraged to commemorate the "mother of us all," our Mother Earth, and our place in it as human beings.

Worryingly, the "Intergovernmental Science-Policy Platform on Biodiversity and Ecosystem Services" (IPBES) released a preliminary report on May 6, 2019, about the current alarming rate of extinction for nearly 1 million species heading for demise—what scientists are calling the "Sixth Extinction"—from the UNESCO (United Nations Educational, Scientific, and Cultural Organization) headquarters in Paris, France.[21]

Why the "Sixth Extinction," you might ask? Well, there have been five mass extinctions of life on earth over millions of years of evolution.[22] While our understanding of "extinction events" is somewhat incomplete from the fossil record, paleontologists generally agree at least five such events occurred on a massive scale.

The first happened around 450 million years ago with the "Ordovician-Silurian Extinction Event" which wiped out almost 70 percent of life on earth.[23] Imagine the Earth being dominated by shallow seas and life commanded mostly by squid-like creatures (*cephalopods*), snail-like animals (*gastropods*), clam-like creatures (*pelecypods*) and trilobites (a segmented-insect-like swimming *arthropod*), corals (*coelenterates*), and sponges (*Porifera*). In another 100 million years, there was the "Late Devonian Extinction" (360 m.y.a), which some paleontologists believe lasted for as long as 20 million years, causing again approximately the same loss of life among clam-like, snail-like, and segmented-bodied insect-looking creatures.[24]

Approximately, 100 million years later was the "Permian-Triassic Extinction" (250 m.y.a.), also known as the "Great Dying," or the worst extinction in Earth's geological history, killing off about 90 percent of Earth's animal species.[25] It was when only about 5 percent of sea creatures survived and almost all trees were eradicated. During this period, there were strange reptilian-mammalian-like creatures roaming the planet. Some are known as "synapsids," canine-looking lizards with sailfish fanned-backs, and dog-sized "dicynodonts" with turtle-like beaks and males sporting large toothy-fangs along with the *Lystrosaurus*, a flat-faced pygmy-hippo-like animal with protruding tusks, and the *Dinogorgon*, a ten-foot-long, Sabertoothish-looking reptile. Among paleontologists, it is still a mystery as to the direct culprit to this massive extinction. Some believe the atmosphere may have been poisoned by volcanic gases and a prevalence of acidic rains.

With continent separating, intensive volcanic activity, and Pangea rifts, came the "Triassic-Jurassic Extinction" (200 m.y.a.) when almost three-fourths of Earth's species were wiped out. This was a time of giant salamander-like vertebrates called *Metoposaurus* and *Temnospondyls*, large-skulled crocodilian-salamander-like, perhaps amphibious beasts, wandering around primordial swamps.[26]

Then after almost 140 million years (66 m.y.a.) was perhaps the most famous extinction, the end of the "dinosaur" era, the "Cretaceous-Paleogene Extinction." When those beasties made famous by Michael Crichton's novel *Jurassic Park* (1990), and Steven Spielberg film adaptation, were resuscitated: *Tyrannosaurus rex*, *Triceratops*, *Ankylosaurus*, *Parasaurolophus*, and *Argentinosaurus*. In all likelihood, a giant asteroid struck the Earth at the tip of the present-day Yucatán Peninsula, known as the "Chicxulub Crater."[27]

Of course, "megafauna," from the last "Ice Age" in the transition period from the Pleistocene to Holocene around 13,000 (BCE), became extinct, such as: Mastodon (*Mammut americanum*), Woolly Mammoth

(*Mammuthus primigenius*), Giant Ground Sloth (*Megatherium*), Saber-toothed Tiger (*Smilodon*), and Woolly Rhinoceros (*Coelodonta antiquitatis*). Nevertheless, the Holocene extinction continues to the present. Some climatologists and paleontologists distinguish the present era as a time shift named the "Anthropocene" as beginning with the "Agricultural Revolution" around 15,000 years ago, or more recently with the first successful test of the nuclear bomb in 1945.[28] Doing so, underlines the advent of human causation of climate change and the irreversible role of *Homo sapiens* affecting the planet.

In returning to the recent IPBES report, it characterizes the drivers of the so-called Sixth Extinction for numerous combined reasons.[29] For example, "75 per cent of global food crop types, including fruits and vegetables and some of the most important cash crops such as coffee, cocoa and almonds, rely on animal pollination." Alarmingly, insect pollinators like bees are dying out on an unprecedented scale, a fact known for some time with causation from a variety of factors such as ubiquitous usage of "pesticides and fungicides" and from pathogenic viruses and "parasitic mites" in beehives.[30]

Furthermore, coastal ecosystems and coral reefs have been devastated across the planet. Such habitat losses create greater risks to human life from flooding and hurricanes through the lack of natural barriers.[31] According to IPBES statistics: "Seventy-five per cent of the land surface is significantly altered, 66 percent of the ocean area is experiencing increasing cumulative impacts, and over 85 percent of wetlands (area) has been lost."[32]

More specifically, according to the IPBES World Team of Scientists, Sandra Diaz, Josef Settele, and Eduardo Brondízio, et al.: "Human actions threaten more species with global extinction now than ever before. An average of around 25 percent of species in assessed animal and plant groups are threatened, suggesting that around 1 million species already face extinction, many within decades, unless action is taken to reduce the intensity of drivers of biodiversity loss."[33]

This prestigious scientific team points to five major drivers to today's extinction, which are: (1) land and sea alterations from human management; (2) widespread exploitation of organisms; (3) unprecedented climate change; (4) large-scale pollution; (5) pervasive invasions from alien species into new habitats. As biological beings, we are dependent on the Earth and its wellbeing. If Nature is in peril, and it is, we are in dire jeopardy as well. Our survival as a species on this planet is wholly dependent on the survival of other species and the ecosystems which support them.

If anyone doubts the veracity of species extinction, and whether or not losing only one species really makes any difference, take the example of "re-introductions" of grey wolves (*Canis lupus*) to Yellowstone National Park in 1995 and the evidence for ecosystem habitat renewal and transformation.[34] In scientific terms this is called a "trophic cascade."[35] According to the likes of Ripple and Beschta (2004), it begins from the top of the food chain, with leading predators such as grey wolves, and trickles down the food pyramid with the culling of herbivores such as elk (*Cervus elaphus*), thereby allowing for recuperation of flora as willows (*Salix spp.*), for example, and over time, even modifying the course of rivers. It is a natural knock-on effect with healthier elk populations and tree species recoveries such as aspens (*Populus tremuloides*), while also resulting in the return of beavers (*Castor canadensis*) to the park.

There are some artists who have captured our chaos and our propensity for self-destruction better than others. In my view, a prominent one is the cinematographer, Ron Fricke with his avant-garde time-lapse photography, resulting in kaleidoscopic journeys around the world, depicting varieties of human religions and human experiences, as well as disturbing examples of human violence and colossal destruction, and stunning visions of nature and the natural world, in juxtaposition with mind-numbing human exploitation.[36] His best works are: *Koyaanisqatsi* (1982, a Hopi word for "life out of balance"), *Baraka* (1992, a Hebrew word meaning "blessing" and in Arabic "God's life force"), and *Samsara* (2011, a Sanskrit word meaning "cyclical change" or "life cycle"). Such visual mnemonic devices demonstrate to popular audiences just how precarious the human predicament really is, and necessary—beyond scientific reports and warnings from United Nations umbrella organizations.

As the eminent and emeritus Harvard biologist, E.O. Wilson once stated about the ultimate irony of humanity's evolution: "that in the instant of achieving self-understanding through the mind of man, life has doomed its most beautiful creations."[37] Yet, we should not fail to lose hope. As Elizabeth Kolbert (2015) remarked in her book *The Sixth Extinction: An Unnatural History*: "Another possibility—considered by some to be more upbeat—is that human ingenuity will outrun any disaster human ingenuity sets in motion."[38]

Certainly, we must take such reports as the one from IPBES seriously—not only pondering the existential threat we have created for ourselves, and not because the peril extends to other species, but because the peril is for the very fate of humanity itself, and whether or not our own extinction inevitable.

## The Science and Politics Behind the Brazilian Amazon Mass Fires[39]

In order to understand the science behind the recent mass burning of the Brazilian Amazon, we must put this man-made catastrophe in context with Brazilian politics. Hence, when Jair Bolsonaro became President of Brazil in January 2019, his developmental policies for the Brazilian Amazon and his negative views of its indigenous inhabitants in effect transformed Brazilian Amazonia into a worsening ecological disaster.

In recently released statistics by the Brazilian National Institute for Space Research (*Instituto Nacional de Pesquisas Espaciais*, INPE) for the estimations of the Brazilian Amazonian forest fires represented an almost 30 percent increase in mass conflagrations from 2018 to 2019, whereby 9762 square kilometers (circa 3769 square miles) were burned in 2019 or an equivalent land mass of a little bit more than the island of Cyprus.[40] The overall devastating effects of these mass fires cannot be overstated.[41] The Amazonian riverine system is by far the largest river system in the world with more than 1000 tributaries, seventeen of which are more than 1600 kilometers long. The Amazon Basin itself is more than 6.9 million square kilometers as a whole. It is colossal and massive, covering 40 percent of South America. In the Amazon region, there are as many as 390 billion individual trees consisting of more than 16,000 tree species.[42] Two-thirds of Amazonia exists within Brazil, and within it, scientists believe there exists at least some 2.5 million insect species, 4000 plant species, 5600 fish species, 1300 bird species, 430 mammalian species, 1000 amphibian species, and 400 reptilian species.[43] As such, the environmental costs would be extremely high if the largest and the most unique and the most complex terrestrial biome were to be lost from man-made destruction.

Environmental experts who have studied Amazonian rainforest destruction believe at least 80 percent of its present devastation are the result of the actions of Brazilian cattle-ranchers.[44] These ranchers (*rancheiros*) were most likely the culprits of the mass conflagrations in Brazil in 2019.

Furthermore, we may point to the economic development policies of President Jair Bolsonaro who wants to open up the Brazilian Amazon to investors and those willing to develop the region. Bolsonaro's political rhetoric is thereby implicitly allowing for illegal loggers, illegal miners, poachers, and illicit land-grabbers to invade indigenous lands and in some cases murder Amerindian peoples. A Brazilian Native, Paulo Paulino Guajajara, was killed on November 1, 2019 by illegal loggers on his tribe's land of *Araribóia*, an area twice the size of the U.S. state of Rhode Island or 4130 square kilometers in the Amazonian state of Maranhão.[45] The indigenous people of the Guajajara are some of the most numerous in Brazil, accounting for some 30,000 Amerindians. Paulo Paulino Guajajara belonged to his tribal group's "Guardians of the Forest" (*Guardiões da Floresta*) who patrol their tribal lands in order to protect them from illegal invaders, such as the ones responsible for his murder.

The Brazilian Catholic Indigenist Missionary Council (*Conselho Indigenista Missionario*, CIMI) estimated that in 2018 murders of Brazilian indigenous peoples increased by 20 percent from 2017, with as many 135 cases, and over the last thirty-years, it found that there have been some 1119 homicides against Brazilian Amerindians.[46] In the majority, most of these murders occurred in the Brazilian states of Roraima and Mato Grosso do Sul. This is an ongoing genocide and Brazilian *rancheiros* wish to clear their lands of its indigenous inhabitants as well as burn Amazonian rainforest land in order to create more land for cattle grazing. The same may be said for many Brazilian soy farmers and many other Brazilian farmers (*fazendeiros*). Often times, gunmen are hired to eradicate the Native peoples on cattle and farm lands.

It is remarkable today, at the beginning of the twenty-first century, such a genocide in Brazil is still occurring. There are so few Brazilian Amerindian peoples left in the country, only about **896,917** according to the latest 2010 IBGE report (Brazilian Institute of Geography and Statistics, *Instituto Brasileiro de Geografia e Estatistica*).[47] Of these, Brazilian Indians belong to about 255 distinctive ethnic groups which in turn correspond to about 0.47 percent of the total Brazilian population.[48] Of the almost 1 million Brazilian Natives, half of them live in the interior in the country on **600** indigenous reservations and others among them live elsewhere. Even more precarious are the uncontacted Amerindian groups who are thought to number some 100-distinct ethnic-groups in the thousands living near the Bolivian, Brazilian, and Peruvian borderlands. (Some live in Venezuela and Paraguay as well.)[49]

Moreover, President Bolsonaro's political rhetoric favoring Brazilian Amazonian economic development is not only a detriment to the environment but also an existential threat to indigenous peoples. Bolsonaro's dangerous proclamations have in effect given a "greenlight" for permitting illegal loggers, illegal miners, illegal land-grabbers, and poachers to invade indigenous lands for their own benefits. Yet, if the mass fires in the Amazon, and the Patanal (Brazil's wetlands) continue to be tolerated by the Brazilian government, in the long term, the damage done to this most biodiverse region of the world, may become irreversible.

One needs to better imagine the scale of the possible carbon releases by such an ecological disaster as the mass burnings of the Amazon have endured to the present. To give one example, one large Amazonian-tree may store as much as 3–4 tons of $CO_2$ according to Oxford University scientist Erika Berenguer, who is associated with Oxford's Environmental Change Institute (ECI).[50] By comparison, the Amazon rainforest as a whole may process as much as 18 billion tons of carbon per year.[51]

As stated by renowned environmental scientist, Philip Fearnside: "Brazil's Amazonian deforestation in June 2019 was 88 percent greater than for the same month in 2018, and deforestation in the first half of July [2019] was 68 percent above that for the entire month of July in 2018."[52] The evidence is clear, more needs to be done, and the world needs to pay attention before it is too late. Further, environmental activists such as Greta Thunberg are right to endure in their calls for raising the alarm bells about the current environmental crisis.[53]

Even so, it must be recognized that the Brazilian government of President Jair Bolsonaro has unnecessarily accelerated and exacerbated Amazonian deforestation and Brazilian indigenous genocide. Organizations such the "Society for the Anthropology of Lowland South America" (SALSA) have sent an open letter (dated August 25, 2019) about the mass conflagrations in Brazil.[54] In it, they stated: "Since taking office earlier this year, President Jair Bolsonaro and the "ruralist" parliamentary block have sought to open indigenous lands up to mining and logging operations; have slashed the budgets and oversight potential of environmental agencies; have backed an "economic liberty" suite of policies for agribusiness; have vowed that the government will not demarcate "one more centimeter" of indigenous land in Brazil, and have taken steps to try to decertify (rob) existing indigenous reserves. The parliamentary assault on indigenous peoples and on Amazonian ecosystems is vast, coordinated, and has been decades in the making … As anthropologists who have the privilege of working with the originary peoples of Amazonia, we also have the obligation to condemn the racist rhetoric and genocidal policies pursued by the current Brazilian government."

In 2019, the famous Brazilian indigenous leader Ailton Krenak was quoted as saying: "Future generations will have to be increasingly empowered to secure a place to live. Agribusinesses cannot go out consuming everything.[55] Mining companies cannot go out consuming everything. In this way, there will come a time when they will consume everything up, including themselves ... The protected areas—the lands of the *quilombos* [isolated Brazilian afro-communities], Native lands—are places we think need to be preserved as a common good for everyone. But they are bulldozing everything ... They point fingers at others, but they are the true vandals—these miners and ruralists [ranchers and farmers]. They think they can undo everything and take it all away. Yet, this is stupid. A vital part of nature is burning which eliminates any common future we might have together."

## Bolsonaro Fiddles While the Amazon Burns

Of course, the title of this subsection conjures up images of the Emperor Nero (37–68 AD) fiddling while ancient Rome burned, and for many reasons, this myth was a historical falsehood. Fiddles did not exist in 64 AD when a great fire ravaged ancient Rome, but stringed instruments did nonetheless, like the *cithara* and *lyre*.[56] Moreover, Nero himself was not responsible for the conflagration. He was away at his villa but quickly returned to Rome to deal with the crisis. Even so, the myth supports the notion that Nero was an idle and an incompetent governor. Regardless of whether or not he was responsible for Rome's burning, to many, Emperor Nero, was incapable of leading the empire. Nero was overly self-indulgent and had more thespian ambitions than political ones.

This historical analogy I think is therefore an apt one in association with present day Brazil. Not only had Brazilian President Jair Bolsonaro mishandled the forest fire crisis in the Brazilian Amazon, where hundreds of thousands of hectares of rainforest lands were smoldering, but Bolsonaro's policies on the environment and with respect to indigenous peoples have considerably worsened the disaster in 2019.[57] Furthermore, Bolsonaro could be doing much more but is not and will not. Bolsonaro's policies in relation to the environment, his policies for wishing to develop the Brazilian Amazon, along with his negative views about the fate of Brazilian indigenous peoples—all point to a level of incompetence, indifference, and neglect toward the Amazon Basin on an unprecedented scale in Brazil, not seen since the military-dictatorship era (1964–1985).[58]

The Amazon rainforest is not only a national treasure for Brazil but also a natural patrimony site for the world. It would seem that President Jair Bolsonaro would rather blame non-governmental organizations (NGOs) for instigating the fires throughout the Amazon region and the country's interior, by all accounts, baseless claims, than accuse Brazilian ranchers and farmers (*rancheiros e fazendeiros*) as the likely culprits. These Brazilian ranchers and farmers are likewise some of his biggest financial supporters of his presidency. To make matters even worse, President Bolsonaro also claimed his government did not have the resources to fight the blazes across the Amazon and the country's interior with firefighters and fire prevention assets in 2019.[59]

The Amazon rainforest is the biggest in the world, with by far the largest riverine system with over 1000 tributaries, of which seventeen are more than 1000 miles long, and in total the Amazon Basin is 6.9 million square kilometers in size—absolutely colossal and enormous—covering 40 percent of the entire South American continent.[60] It is estimated the Amazon region has as many as 390 billion individual trees from some 16,000 tree species. Most of the Amazon, two-thirds of it, exists within Brazilian borders. Additionally, it is thought there are as many as 2.5 million species of insects living within its rainforests. In terms of other biodiversity within the Amazon basin, scientists widely agree it contains roughly 40,000 plant species, 5600 fish species, 1300 bird species, and more than 430 mammalian species, some 1000-amphibian species, and over 400 reptilian species. Environmental experts believe that cattle ranching was responsible for 80 percent of Amazonian deforestation in 2019.[61]

According to the Brazilian census (IBGE) in 2010, there are about 896,917 Brazilian Amerindians of which there are approximately 255 distinct ethnic groups and corresponding to about 0.47 percent of the total Brazilian population.[62] Among these peoples, 150 indigenous languages are spoken. Of the nearly 1 million Brazilian Indians, about half of them still live in the interior of the Amazon Basin, and elsewhere in Brazil's interior and apart from urban populations on over 600 indigenous reserves (cited in Linstroth 2015).[63] More so, there are still about 100 uncontacted Amerindian groups, living in remote borderland areas of Brazil, Peru, and Bolivia, (some in Venezuela and Paraguay) and number in the thousands.[64]

Therefore, protecting "the most" biodiverse ecosystems on our planet, the Amazon Basin, is absolutely urgent. The blazing fires across the Brazilian Amazon and across central Brazil were destroying forest lands in alarming rates in 2019. And because President Bolsonaro stated the Brazilian government did not have adequate resources in which to stem the raging infernos in Brazil's Amazon, elicited the necessity of other nations to lend vital aid and technology for firefighting.

According to the Brazilian National Institute for Space Research (*Instituto Nacional de Pesquisas Espaciais*, INPE), these devastating conflagrations have increased by 84 percent since the beginning of 2019 for a total of some 75,336 registered bushfires detected through satellite monitoring.[65] Likewise, widespread fires across the Brazilian Amazon Basin in 2019 accounted for an 85 percent increase in fire outbreaks since 2017. Likewise, the estimated rate of deforestation of the Amazon then was at a football field per minute.[66] In the Brazilian Amazon Basin, according to the Brazilian Environmental Agency, IBAMA (*Instituto Brasileiro do Meio Ambiente e dos Recursos Naturais Renováveis*), on August 21, 2019, there were 568 new recorded fire outbreaks for a current total of 1181 forest fires across the Brazilian nation.[67]

These apocalyptic and blazing infernos are the direct result of President Bolsonaro's greenlight deregulation policies in allowing loggers, miners, and ranchers to exploit the Amazon Basin with impunity, not only putting in danger the most biodiverse region on the planet, but likewise endangering those able to act as its guardians—Brazil's indigenous peoples.

On Monday, August 19, 2019, São Paulo's skies ominously blackened with dark clouds, causing the Brazilian capital city to be in night-time conditions, when day became night during the afternoon.[68] As one of my Brazilian friends living in São Paulo explained to me: "We thought it was going to be a really, really bad storm and we were waiting for a huge rainfall when it turns out to be billows of smoke from fires in the Amazon." The Amazon region is some 2700 kilometers away from the capital, São Paulo, and because of this, some Brazilian meteorologists suggested the excessive smoke clouds came from fires in nearby Paraguay.[69] On the other hand, the Brazilian Environmental Minister Ricardo Salles declared the "pollution clouds" (*nuvem de poluição*) over São Paulo's skies on August 19, 2019, were none other than "fake news" and "environmental sensationalism" from the media.[70]

Such deflections and scapegoating seemed to be right out of former President Donald Trump and his administration's political playbook. Whether we examine President Bolsonaro blaming non-governmental organizations (NGOs) for starting fires in the Amazon because of withholding federal funding for them, especially environmental groups which Bolsonaro views as his enemies, or the Brazilian Environmental Minister impugning the media for "fake news" because of smoke pollution in São Paulo—were both Trumpian politico-playbook tactics. Then, it therefore seemed foreign governments, such as the one in Brazil, looked to the U.S. government, not so much as a harbor of democratic ideals, but rather as political-directive signaling for redirecting blame from internal problems.

What is more tragic are the real implications beyond politics. The Amazon Basin burned while President Bolsonaro fiddled around, even stating there were no resources in which to combat the smoldering infernos across the country. While President Bolsonaro denied Amazonian deforestation as exaggerated and fake, and even as "lies," the numbers collected by scientists attested to a different picture. According to renowned environmental scientist, Philip Fearnside: "Brazil's Amazonian deforestation in June 2019 was 88 percent greater than for the same month in 2018, and deforestation in the first half of July [2019] was 68 percent above that for the entire month of July in 2018."[71]

As distinguished scientists, Frances Seymour and Nancy Harris, of the World Resources Institute (WRI) summarized what needs to done to prevent deforestation, they asserted in the prestigious journal, *Science* (2017): "For tropical forest protection to become a viable political proposition for elected officials, financial and market incentives must be augmented by increased public awareness of the many benefits that forests provide, locally as well as globally. Building such awareness through better communication of the science is an essential complement to our increasingly sophisticated understanding of why tropical forests are being destroyed."[72]

As the prominent anthropologist, Margaret Mead (1968), once remarked: "Our humanity rests upon a series of learned behaviors, woven together into patterns that are infinitely fragile and never directly inherited."[73] Indeed, we must all unlearn harming the environment and all learn how to protect it for the sake of our children and our children's children. The time is now and it is a pressing emergency.

## Why the Developing World Cannot Flatten the Curve with Coronavirus (COVID-19) and Beyond

The "developing world" is often left behind in the medical treatment of epidemics and other diseases, whether these are HIV-AIDS, Cholera, Black Fever, or Tuberculosis, and so on. These are the countries, what previous President Trump once called "sh\*\*hole" countries, those in the southern hemisphere, below the Equator. To this day, they are still exploited by the first world for their natural resources and for their cheap labor through beneficial trade agreements with the first world, namely with the United States, Canada, Europe, Japan, Australia, and New Zealand. As medical anthropologist and physician Paul Farmer stated: "The idea that some lives matter less is the root of all that is wrong with the world."[74]

In other words, when we speak of epidemics, and even pandemics like Coronavirus (COVID-19), we must understand that medical care is unequal in our world today. We must understand that "power structures" control who gets medical care and who does not. We must understand that so-called First World nations will be treated for Coronavirus and in all likelihood the "developing world" will be left behind. Of course, this also includes the unequal distribution of vaccines worldwide as of 2021 according to the World Health Organization (WHO).[75]

All you have to do is travel to Haiti, or rural India, or Uganda, or a favela in Brazil, or a Palestinian refugee camp in Lebanon, and there you will encounter why such inequalities are all too evident. It does not have to be this way. However, what we know is that in our post-colonial world, the same sorts of inequities from the colonial world have remained, and most probably will continue to remain for the foreseeable future.

In his well-regarded book *Pathologies of Power: Health, Human Rights, and the New War on the Poor* (2005, p. 6), Paul Farmer argues: "The most basic right—the right to survive—is trampled in an age of great affluence, and … that the matter should be considered the most pressing one of our times. The drama, the tragedy, of the destitute sick concerns not only physicians and scholars who work among the poor but all who profess even a passing interest in human rights. It's not much of a stretch to argue that anyone who wishes to be considered humane has ample cause to consider what it means to be sick and poor in the era of globalization and scientific advancement."[76]

We live in an age of extreme inequity. In the United States alone to reach the income of the top 1 percent would mean earnings of at least $500,000.[77] When measuring varying regions and countries' Gini coefficient of income, that is, the measure of income inequality, Latin America and Africa have the highest income inequalities. For example, Latin America and the Caribbean have a Gini of 48.82 percent, whereas Africa has a Gini of 44.26 percent, in comparison to the United States and Canada with a Gini of 37.07 percent.[78] The top five countries with the highest Gini coefficients are: "1) Lesotho (0.632); 2) South Africa (0.625); 3) Haiti (0.605); 4) Botswana (0.605); and 5) Namibia (0.597)."[79]

Given this, why are first world nations not responding more to the needs of developing nations and to lessen these disparities? The simple answer is that it is not in the interest of the first world to do so. Allowing for international mining concessions, international oil exploration, and labor exploitation, and many other private corporate interests, has become the norm for multinational corporations. Such economic leverage over developing countries and corporate power over leaders of such so-called Third World nations, provide needed cash flows to these emerging nations. Thereby, such relationships of power, similar to the colonial past, have continued unequal forms of dominance and control.

Hence, when we speak of this "new" pandemic, the health care structures in the developing world simply do not exist for dealing with Coronavirus (COVID-19). Who will be building new hospitals in rural India, or Gambia, or Zimbabwe, or Haiti? Who will donate respiratory machines for those who succumb to Coronavirus? Who will be providing test-kits to the most vulnerable in the developing world, and most importantly, who will care?

In 2018 statistics, East and Southern Africa is the region most affected by HIV/AIDS in the world and home to those with the largest population living with HIV/AIDS.[80] This total, equals some 20.6 million people, and in the same year, 800,000 new people contracted the disease. While those dying of AIDS decreased by 61 percent, the World Health Organization (WHO), stated it was not near where it needed to be to decrease infection and mortality rates as a whole.[81]

Another horrendous disease, is Leishmaniasis, which mostly affects impoverished populations, such as those in the Sudan. The disease in the Sudan is known as "Kala-Azar" or "Black Fever." In one form of the disease, "Visceral Leishmaniasis," if left untreated is fatal in 95 percent of the cases.[82] Symptoms of this illness are high fever, weight loss, enlargement of the spleen and the liver, and anemia. Aside from Sudan (and South Sudan), it occurs in Brazil, elsewhere in East Africa, and India. The parasite is transmitted by a sand fly. And again, treatment for the disease is not equal for those living in Africa, compared to health care in the first world.

Hence, when we hear about "Flattening the Curve" from a popular 2020 *New York Times* article, and how washing hands, and social distancing, and self-isolating, will mitigate Coronavirus (COVID-19), and thereby limit deaths from the disease as well as lessening contagion, does "not" in my view apply to the "developing world" whatsoever.[83] How will third world epidemiological curves flatten if they cannot and do not receive equitable health care as we have in the first world? What countries will step forward to mitigate the spread of Coronavirus to the developing world—to Africa, Asia, and South America?

President Biden has recently stated in September 2021, the United States will donate an additional 500 million vaccines to the rest of the world, bringing the total to 1.1 billion vaccine shots for lower- and middle-income countries.[84] Yet, there needs to be a broader coalition to do so and such efforts should be coordinated by the World Health Organization. The question is will Coronavirus be controlled sooner by such efforts or will there be a lag in such rollouts of vaccines.

What I am talking about here is "structural violence," that is those structures which keep in place the inequalities which exist in our world today. Such inequalities are power structures by keeping the developing world, impoverished, and by disallowing equal access to health care, which as Paul Farmer maintains, should be a given right for everyone.

In another well-received book by Paul Farmer (1999, p. 5), *Infections and Inequalities: the Modern Plagues,* he asserts: "Disease emergence is a socially produced phenomenon, few have examined the contribution of specific social inequalities. Yet such inequalities have powerfully sculpted not only the distribution of infectious diseases but also the course of health outcomes among the afflicted."[85]

Will the first world even care about "flattening the curve" for the developing world? And when will the news media ever discuss the morbidity rates of the Global South in regard to Coronavirus (COVID-19), instead of solely focusing on how we in the First World are self-isolating, and self-sacrificing? Will we be able to flatten the curve of COVID-19 across the globe with new vaccine rollouts for the developing world or will the developing world inevitably fall behind as it does so for HIV-AIDS and Black Fever?

## Why a Race Is Not a Virus and a Virus Is Not a Race

It is dangerous rhetoric indeed when former President Donald J. Trump called Coronavirus (COVID-19), the "Chinese Virus" in 2020.[86] Even if the intent was political and meant to communicate to Beijing that the U.S. military was not responsible for the spread of the disease within China, contrary to a conspiracy theory there.[87]

The labeling by prior president of Coronavirus (COVID-19) as "Chinese" has unnecessarily allowed for the entry of prejudice and racism into an epidemiological discussion about the consequences of a deadly pandemic and an increasingly growing tragedy for the United States and the rest of the world. Consequently, a couple of days later, former President Trump seemingly retracted his previous remarks by stating: "It seems there could be some nasty language toward our Asian-Americans, and I don't like that at all. These are incredible people and they love their country."[88]

Thus, as most know, a virus is not tied to any particular ethnic group or race. Nor does it have any religious origins. A virus is entirely agnostic and mindless. Its aim is contagion and replication, and has biologically evolved to attach itself to the most hosts possible. Even so, throughout human history ignorance has persisted and people have paired diseases with ethnic groups and particular populations. And if not disease, then other tragedies and unusual events.

Of course, the prior president was not alone in linking Coronavirus (COVID-19) to China, or simply relating to it as solely a "Chinese Virus." Ever since the pandemic has spread across the United States, racial incidents against Asian-Americans have been on the rise and have been widely reported across the country. In the initial stages of the spread in 2020, "Chinatowns" in many large cities such as San Francisco and New York City, were notably avoided.[89] The ignorance about disease and race in popular mythology link the two together—even though nothing could be further from the truth.

As one woman, Trang, explained in a *2020 USA Today* interview: "There have been a lot of people who just use this fear to justify racism against Asian people and to scapegoat Asian people for their fear of Coronavirus."[90] As such, there is so much misinformation and so many urban myths among the general population, which has caused more unwarranted racial attacks against Asian-Americans. The FBI, in fact, has warned of an increase in hate crimes against Asian-Americans.[91]

Likewise, many have used Coronavirus to validate their own racist views. The New York Attorney General has launched a hotline for New Yorkers to report hate crimes associated with COVID-19.[92] Additionally, the Asian Pacific Planning and Policy Council and Chinese for Affirmative Action, following its launching on March 19, 2020, "has received more than 1000 reports from people in thirty-two states detailing verbal abuse, denial of services, discrimination on the job or physical assaults" according to a recent *Los Angeles Times* article.[93]

Unfortunately, throughout history, people have made similar mistakes by associating particular ethnic groups with epidemics. In the Middle Ages, for example, Jews were widely scapegoated for causing the "Great Plague." As the "Black Plague" had spread across Western Europe by 1349 AD, massacres of Jews increased on massive scales, "pogroms," in such places as Aragon, Spain, and Flanders, Belgium as well as Jewish communities in Frankfurt, Mainz, and Cologne in Germany.[94] Thousands of Jews were burnt at the stake, or were tortured into falsely confessing about poisoning city-wells.

In 1918, the influenza outbreak which caused as many as 50 million deaths worldwide was known as the "Spanish Flu," and in all likelihood, was a misnomer. Scientists are still uncertain of the flu's origins. It may have been spread from pig farms in the Midwest of the United States to U.S. military camps and then on to the killing grounds of World War I in Western Europe and elsewhere. It became known as the "Spanish Flu" because the Spanish media was free to report on the disease.[95]

In relation to Asian-Americans in the United States, there is a long history of racism associated with disease. In 1900, in Honolulu, Hawaii, the Board of Health burned Chinatown there to the ground for fear of the spread of the plague whose residents included "3,000 Chinese, 1,500 Japanese, and 1,000 Native Hawaiian residents."[96] Similarly, in Reno, Nevada, its Board of Health Department demolished that city's Chinatown because the area was viewed as "unclean" and "immoral," making room for land development.

Aside from disease, there has been a long history of "Nativist" views against Asian-Americans with the "Chinese Exclusion Act" of 1882, which prohibited Chinese laborers from entering the United States, and a similar act, known as the "Gentleman's Agreement of 1907," limiting Japanese migration to the United States. Moreover, following the Japanese attacks on Pearl Harbor, Hawaii, in 1941, mostly Japanese-Americans living in the states of California, Oregon, and Washington were relocated to internment camps during World War II.[97]

Regrettably, the past xenophobia and racism experienced by many Asian-Americans still persists and has considerably worsened because of Coronavirus (COVID-19) and the pandemic's association to their ethnicities. In fact, many Asian-Americans are wrongly blamed for the virus.

Trump initially insisted that his labeling Coronavirus the "Chinese Virus" was "not" racist because it indicated, according to him, its geographical location and country of origin. Whereas health experts, historians, and even the World Health Organization (WHO) emphasized how unhelpful it is to label a disease by its geographic locale. Such associations become blurred with particular ethnic groups and may lead to xenophobic violence, as evident in recent reports and in the past.[98]

Former presidential candidate Andrew Yang stated in a *New York Times* interview about Trump's use of the term as his way: "to distract from his administration's slow response to Coronavirus."[99]

The National Association of School Psychologists (NASP) has likewise perceived these negative associations of the disease and its association with racism. On its website, it informs parents how they might speak to their children about Coronavirus (COVID-19) and the current stigma of Asian-Americans related to it.[100] As NASP states: "Though the initial spread of COVID-19 occurred in China, it is important to inform children in a developmentally appropriate manner that the disease is linked to a geographic location and not to a race or nationality. People who identify as Asian-American or Pacific Islander (AAPI) are currently being subjected to racism related to the COVID-19 virus."

As Cornel West once observed in his renowned book *Race Matters* (1993: 6): "To engage in a serious discussion of race in America, we must begin … with the flaws of American society—flaws rooted in historic inequalities and longstanding cultural stereotypes. How we set up the terms for discussing racial issues shapes our perception and response to these issues."

In my view too, we must recognize the "structures of violence" in society which have kept minorities oppressed. Until we deconstruct such barriers and reshape the public rhetoric, fears and scares will persist. Ethnic groups will be unfairly scapegoated.

As a society, we are better than this. We all deserve a United States of America where everyone is invited to the table and everyone participates in our democracy, even through great crises, as the one now, and not bumbling from unfounded fears.

## HISTORY AND SCIENCE AS CANDLES IN THE DARK

On Saturday, November 7, 2020, we watched Joseph R. Biden, Jr. become the 46th President of the United States through a legitimate electoral process whereby he reached past the electoral college threshold of 270 electoral votes with 279 votes. After Pennsylvania and Nevada finally counted their votes, it was clear Biden and Harris were the winners, and even though votes were still being officially counted in other states. The final electoral vote tally was Joe Biden's 306 to Donald Trump's 232.[101]

Regardless, it is also historic because Kamala Harris became the first woman vice-president and the first African-American and Asian-American vice-president. At least half the country, those who voted for Biden/Harris, breathed a sigh of relief, and knew at least for a while, "fake news," "presidential lies," "presidentially driven conspiracies," and efforts to delegitimize U.S. institutions would be forgotten, or in any case, not take center stage for some time. Maybe, just maybe, things would return to a kind of normalcy, not seen for four years.

Then again, on Fox News they were promoting former President Trump's lies about the election is "not" over?! Moreover, Trump was tweeting: "I WON THIS ELECTION, BY A LOT!" All in caps.[102] On this date, November 7, 2020, it was difficult to imagine how President Trump could gain the electoral votes he needed to win the presidential election. But millions of those who voted for Trump believed the election was somehow stolen and made illegitimate by the Democrats, a true political fantasy created by the president himself and perpetuated by his followers. As if the Democrat donkey symbol also grew a unicorn horn on the day of election and Biden and Harris became fantastical figures out of a Harry Potter novel and magically stole the election because of their secret magic powers and because of the magic cabal they are part of. Such were the conspiracy theories of Trump and his supporters.

For many, Biden/Harris may not have been their first choices, especially many on the liberal left. Of course, we must consider half the country who voted for Trump as well and we must somehow reconcile with these Americans too. More than 70 million Americans voted for Trump and because of this we must hope Biden/Harris will bring the country together and will bring the Trump voters into the fold of American democracy and treat them as our fellow Americans, which they are.

For these reasons, I wish those Republican-Americans who voted for Trump could read this. I know most will not simply because they do not read the same media outlets or consider others' political points of view. Nor do they most likely read many academic books (as most people don't).

As a people, we have to contemplate how much media is to blame for our current divisions in this country. This media manipulation goes well beyond the "manufacturing consent" promoted by Edward Herman and Noam Chomsky (1988) because neither Herman, nor Chomsky anticipated Facebook, or Twitter, or Instagram, or Snapchat, or WhatsApp, or TikTok, and the overall influences of the Internet, and twenty-four-hour cable news.[103] One simply needs to watch the Netflix documentary *The Social Dilemma* (2020) to realize how dangerous social media has become for the health of American politics and American democracy.[104] Social media and twenty-four-hour news media are completely toxic, regardless if you are comparing Fox News with MSNBC, or any other media outlet, or those media sources promoting conspiracy theories and alternate forms of realities. What we know scientifically is that people aggregate around similar ideas.

These social media manipulations are really hazardous and treacherous for many reasons. Many of us are not even cognizant how political and social manipulations affect us and affect us in very negative ways. It is important, therefore, to examine how our brains create enemies and foes without realizing neural chemistry is at play, nor how certain cerebral mechanisms are activated.

The title of this section is an intellectual nod to Carl Sagan and his perspicacious book *The Demon-Haunted World: Science as a Candle in the Dark* (1996) because I believe we must look not only to our history for answers but to science as well.[105] So, when we see political triggers, say, "Trump" flags, or MAGA hats, or to others, as Biden/Harris signs—our brains react to these signals because of our social predispositions and because symbols mean things to human primate-brains. What part of the brain is tied to "fear and anxiety," the amygdala, and what part of the brain is tied to "aggression," again the amygdala. Is it any wonder when politicians promote fear mongering among the population, in turn, for some, fear turns toward aggression? What about the insular cortex activating when we are confronted with something we find morally disgusting, the same region of the brain responsible for processing gustatory disgust such as aversion to rotten meat. In Robert Sapolsky's book *Behave: The Biology of Humans at Our Best and Worst* (2017), he explains how cerebral regions and neural chemistry help to manipulate human behavior.[106]

Now examine the hormone "oxytocin," which enhances human social behavior. On the one hand, oxytocin may heighten feelings of compatibility, positivity, and trust, on the other hand, it may increase feelings of belligerence, hostility, and exaggerate unconscious biases. Some researchers such as Merolla et al. (2013) in their article "Oxytocin and the Biological Basis for Interpersonal and Political Trust" in fact proved that subjects intranasally stimulated with the peptide oxytocin were generally more trusting of the government.[107] So, not only must we consider how media influences how we think, but we also need to consider what effects it has on our brains. Thus, being cognizant of such effects may help us, if we are able, to limit how we are being controlled, directed, and swayed.

If we examine, not only why we are social beings, because humans are essentially primates who thrive on social bonding, but how certain ideas which make up our environment likewise contribute to our social networks. Therefore, such social networks cause us to be attracted to like-minded people with like-minded ideas. Notions of theorizing about social networks have been around for a while. Perhaps a better explanation is Charles Kadushin's (2012) book *Understanding Social Networks: Theories, Concepts, and Findings*.[108] In other words, humans take socializing, just as everything else humans do, to completely new heightened levels which would baffle any non-human primate. Perhaps more accessible, are the social network theories explored in a PBS documentary *Networld* (2020) and narrated by historian Niall Ferguson.[109]

Fake news is nothing new either. For example, the idea of witch-hunting spread virally throughout Europe during the Counter-reformation (1545–1648), a resurgence of Catholicism in response to the Protestant Reformation. In England between 1645 and 1647 many women were accused of witchcraft and publicly executed.[110] The hysteria over so-called witches in England was exacerbated by the printing press which promoted falsehoods through books and pamphlets, especially across Cambridgeshire, a center for Puritanism. The historian Sir Hugh Trevor-Roper expertly explained the social madness in his book *The European Witch-Craze of the Sixteenth and Seventeenth Centuries and Other Essays* (1956).[111] As Trevor-Roper states: "The European witch-craze of the sixteenth and seventeenth centuries is a perplexing phenomenon: a standing warning to those who would simplify the stages of human progress. Ever since the eighteenth century we have tended to see European history, from the Renaissance onward, as the history of progress, and that progress has seemed to be constant … But when we look deeper, how much more complex the pattern seems!" (p. 90). "Some 40,000 people, mostly women, were put to death on bogus charges."[112] It would seem our current age is rife with irrationality as well with all the so-called fake news and conspiracy theories floating around digital social networks and other media sources.

In Carl Sagan's book *The Demon-Haunted World*, he writes: "Even a casual scrutiny of history reveals that we humans have a sad tendency to make the same mistakes again and again. We're afraid of strangers or anybody who's a little different from us. When we get scared, we start pushing people around ... We can be manipulated into utter senselessness by clever politicians ... The framers of the Constitution were students of history. In recognition of the human condition, they sought to invent a means that would keep us free in spite of ourselves." (pp. 397–398). In our world today, many Americans do not believe in anthropogenically driven climate change. Nor do many Americans believe in the science and epidemiology for controlling COVID-19.

Additionally, it is amazing to me how divided we are as a society today around the concepts of so-called liberalism and conservatism without understanding the real meanings of these ideas, or their history, or even how we use them as convenient political and social labels. The reality is far more complex.

During this election cycle when I saw trucks with monster tires roaring up the road with Trump flags, I wondered how many had wondered how these same trucks had replaced the confederate flag with the Trump flag. Also, any time I saw a red MAGA hat, "Make America Great Again," I saw hate. I saw the letters transpose into "I Am A Racist." I wondered how many others thought this too?

Moreover, we all know political parties just as any other aspect of society, transform. We know the Republican Party of Abraham Lincoln is not the same as it is today, nor for that matter is the Democrat Party. In thinking about this, we need to somehow comprehend how the Republicans now because of former President Donald Trump represent the working class, especially working-class white men. And for those of us who are educated and wish to support a more enlightened society, it is with these working-class Americans intellectuals need to dialogue and find ways out of the current impasse of mutual hate between the political parties. Otherwise, we are on the brink of civil war again. Perhaps, realizing how much media is to blame for our national polarization will help in addressing these conflicts prior to mutual self-destruction. Of course, this is ironic since Donald Trump is supposedly a billionaire and is seemingly more out for himself than the working blue-collar people he purportedly represents.

In returning to liberalism and conservativism, aside from thinking about politics along a linear continuum as left of center or right of center, we should well remember that our founding fathers for their age were radicals. They believed in liberal ideas which supported freedom and liberty and democratic values which were unpopular in Europe among the ruling classes. The Declaration of Independence was derived from the likes of English philosopher John Locke and his *Two Treatises of Government* (1689). Locke asserted when describing man in the state of nature: "A state also of equality, wherein all the power and jurisdiction is reciprocal, no one having more than another; there being nothing more evident than that creatures of the same species and rank, promiscuously born to all the same advantages of nature and the use of the same faculties, should also be equal one amongst another without subordination or subjection ... The state of nature has a law of nature to govern it, which obliges every one; and reason, which is that law, teaches all mankind who will but consult it that, being all equal and independent, no one ought to harm another in his life, health, liberty, or possessions."[113] Thomas Jefferson re-wrote these ideas into the Declaration as: "We hold these truths to be self-evident, that all men are created equal, that they are endowed by their Creator with certain unalienable Rights, that among these are Life, Liberty, and the Pursuit of Happiness."[114]

So too, we need to have a better comprehension how a history of communist scares has led us in wrong directions in the United States. The supposed threats from the Russian Revolution of 1917 inspired the "Palmer Raids" between 1919 and 1920. At least 3000 were arrested, especially targeting Italian-immigrants and Eastern European Jewish-immigrants.[115] Furthermore, after World War II, U.S. Senator Joseph McCarthy of Wisconsin went on an anti-communist crusade, charging many Hollywood movie stars and intellectuals as belonging to the communist party.[116] There was no evidence for such accusations and McCarthy eventually was discredited. Many people had their reputations damaged and many lost their jobs from the baseless indictments. These so-called communist scares worry me because they may be repeated again.

Here in South Florida, for example, many in the Hispanic-American community were led to believe a Biden/Harris administration would convert the United States into a communist country. The word "socialism" to many Hispanics here in South Florida, as elsewhere in Latin America, especially the exiled Cuban-American and Venezuelan-American communities, is a dirty word. It conjures up communist leaders like Cuban Fidel Castro and Venezuelan Hugo Chavez and communist regimes in South America.

Fox News commentator Tucker Carlson likewise spouts this nonsense by claiming the United States is becoming more like China from COVID-19 restrictions and millions of Americans believe him.[117] What is more, Dr. Anthony Fauci has been vilified by the likes of Fox News commentators such as Carlson because of advocating for epidemiological controls to stem the increase of Coronavirus.[118]

Yet, most Americans are apparently unaware of their own history it would seem in relation to socialism. President Franklin Delano Roosevelt (1882–1945), our 32nd president, also known as FDR, saved capitalism through his socialist programs according to renowned historian H. W. Brands in his superb biography *Traitor to His Class: the Privileged Life and Radical Presidency of Franklin Roosevelt* (2008).[119] Roosevelt, the only U.S. president to have been elected four times led the nation through the "Great Depression" (1929–1939) and led the country through most of World War II (1939–1945).[120] Roosevelt was a great American and to many considered one of our greatest presidents of all time. FDR realized more needed to be done than his predecessor, Herbert Hoover (1874–1964), in regard to the economy and as soon as FDR was sworn in as president, he acted toward saving the nations' banks.[121] Today, because of Roosevelt's economic saving programs we have the Social Security Administration, the Federal Deposit Insurance Corporation (FDIC), and the Securities and Exchange Commission (SEC). Because of all FDR did in his first one hundred days in office, all modern presidential critics and supporters, likewise judge an administrations' accomplishments in its first one hundred days as well. Moreover, Franklin Roosevelt restored the confidence of the American public by having weekly fireside chats over the radio, explaining to the American people what he was doing and what his plans were. While it may be more accurate to state that the American economy improved dramatically because of World War II, many believed, including many in his administration, that FDR had indeed saved capitalism.[122] One may likewise state that FDR also saved democracy through his leadership as president during World War II.

While it is no small feat that President Joseph Biden has defeated incumbent Donald J. Trump for a second term, disallowing presidents a second term has happened several times in our past, beginning with our second President John Adams (1735–1826).[123] Ten presidents in all have failed in trying to be re-elected for a second term and with Trump being the eleventh.[124] Thomas Jefferson, by the way, ran a nasty campaign against Adams and Adams lost to Jefferson's unfair propaganda and false claims disseminated in political pamphlets across the colonies.[125] John Adams' presidential son President John Quincy Adams (1767–1848) also failed to gain a second term and so did "the Little Magician" President Martin Van Buren (1782–1862); and while Grover Cleveland (1837–1908) failed to win a second term his first try, he did earn another term after defeating Benjamin Harrison (1833–1901), the president who had defeated him for his second term the first time. Thus, Harrison became another one-termer. President William Howard Taft (1857–1939), the hand-picked acolyte of Theodore Roosevelt, was also unsuccessful in achieving another term. Also, in part because Teddy Roosevelt ran against him as a third-party candidate with Teddy's self-created "Bull Moose Party." Then there was Herbert Hoover, the predecessor of FDR. In more recent years, President Gerald Ford was not re-elected, probably because Ford pardoned President Richard Nixon and neither was his successor President Jimmy Carter (1924–present) re-elected. Also, George H.W. Bush (1924–2008) did not manage a second term, and now twenty-eight years later, Trump has lost a second presidential tenure.

What is worrisome to many observers, including myself, is that former President Donald J. Trump has tried to de-legitimize the U.S. presidential elections and as such undermine our democracy. More sadly, millions of Americans follow what Trump says, no matter how fabricated, ludicrous, wrongful, or deceitful. In fact, Trump had 88.8 million followers on Twitter. Therefore, it was so alarming when prior President Trump proclaimed on national television at the White House on November 5, 2020, the following: "If you count the legal votes, I easily win. If you count the illegal votes, they can try to steal the election from us. If you count the votes that came in late, we're looking at them very strongly but a lot of votes came in late. I've already decisively won many critical states, including massive victories in Florida, Iowa, Indiana, Ohio, to name just a few. We won these and many other victories despite historic election interference from big media, big money, and big tech. As everybody saw, we won by historic numbers and the pollsters got it knowingly wrong. They got it knowingly wrong."

Regardless, the Republicans, Trump himself, and Trump's supporters have yet to provide concrete evidence of any fraudulence in the 2020 presidential election. Even Karl Rove, George W. Bush's chief campaign strategist, remarked in *The Guardian*: "Stealing hundreds of thousands of votes would require a conspiracy on the scale of a James Bond movie. That isn't going to happen. Let's repeat that: that isn't going to happen."[126] On the other hand, Republican governor of Maryland Larry Hogan declared: "But to make accusations of the election being stolen and widespread fraud without providing any evidence, I thought was really bad for our democratic process and it was something I had never seen in my lifetime."

In his acceptance speech, on November 7, President Joe Biden avowed: "It's time to put away the harsh rhetoric. To lower the temperature. To see each other again. To listen to each other again. To make progress, we must stop treating our opponents as our enemy. We are not enemies. We are Americans. The Bible tells us that to everything there is a season—a time to build, a time to reap, a time to sow. And a time to heal. This is the time to heal in America. Now that the campaign is over—what is the people's will? What is our mandate? I believe it is this: Americans have called on us to marshal the forces of decency and the forces of fairness. To marshal the forces of science and the forces of hope in the great battles of our time."[127]

Let us hope President Joe Biden and Vice-President Kamala Harris can unite the United States and bring Americans together again. Let us all try to remember the lessons from history and science. Similar to Biden's acceptance speech, Carl Sagan asserted in his book *The Demon-Haunted World*: "But if the citizens are educated and form their own opinions, then those in power work for *us*. In every country, we should be teaching our children the scientific method and the reasons for a Bill of Rights. With it comes a certain decency, humility and community spirit. In the demon-haunted world that we inhabit by virtue of being human, this may be all that stands between us and the enveloping darkness" (p. 408).

Let history and science be candles in the dark.

## Conclusion

In my view, through scientific awareness and knowledge, we may be able to have a more tolerant world to live in. This chapter began with the narratives of Sean, Chad, and Robert, and their understandings about what it means to grow up gay and be gay as well as how society treats them today. And since this book is about varying minorities, it is fitting to address the LBGTQ community as well. Here in this chapter, I have tried to demonstrate in part and through science how we may better understand LBGTQ sexualities and gendered identities.

Thus, science also allows us to understand ourselves aside from the qualitative measures and beyond ethnographic paradigms expressed here. For example, I explained that "otherness" and "othering" are in part explained through neurology and neurobiology. The anterior cingulate cortex (ACC) is one area of the brain which registers empathy, particularly empathizing with other people's pain (see Sapolsky 2017: 528). On the other hand, the cerebral organ the amygdala is responsible for not only aggression but anxiety and fear as well (Sapolsky 2017: 34), whereas the insular cortex (insula) activates not only for some disgusting taste or smell but for imagining something repellant like eating a cockroach (Sapolsky 2017: 41). These areas of the brain may be stimulated when thinking about people who are deemed socially abhorrent such as some views about Latino immigrants or gay people or other minorities. The brain may elicit these emotive centers for various so-called moral reasons or unreasonable-judgements even though these brain centers actually evolved to warn us about fears about predators or nauseating foods and so on.

There is also the neurochemical oxytocin which enhances "Us" versus "Them" emotions and thoughts. As Robert Sapolsky (2017: 117) explains: "Oxytocin, the luv hormone, makes us more prosocial to Us and worse to everyone else. That's not generic prosociality. That's ethnocentrism and xenophobia. In other words, the actions of these neuropeptides depend dramatically on context—who you are, your environment, and who that person is." Our brains create "Us" versus "Them" scenarios with rapid speed. "Fifty-millisecond exposure to the face of someone of another race activates the amygdala, while failing to activate the fusiform face area as much as same-race faces do—all within a few hundred milliseconds. Similarly, the brain groups faces by gender or social status at roughly the same speed" (Sapolsky 2017: 388). In fact, "Oxytocin exaggerates Us/Them-ing" (Sapolsky 2017: 389).

Interestingly as well, children also dichotomize Us/Them based on phenotypes like skin color. Non-human primates likewise dichotomize in-group ape faces for a particular troop say as opposed to out-group faces of those from another troop (Sapolsky 2017: 392–393). According to Sapolsky (2017: 393 and 398): "Us/Them-ing typically involves inflating the merits of Us concerning core values—we are more correct, wise, moral, and worthy when it comes to knowing what the gods want/running the economy/raising kids/fighting this war. Us-ness also involves inflating the merits of our arbitrary markers, and that can take some work—rationalizing why our food is tastier, our music is more moving, our language more logical or poetic ... Just as we view Us in standardized ways, there are patterns in how we view them. A consistent one is viewing Them as threatening, angry, and untrustworthy."

Aside from neurology and neurobiology, I have also argued we may learn an enormous amount about ourselves from primatology. As prominent primatologist Frans de Waal (2009: 205) declares: "Empathy is part of our evolution, and not just a recent part, but an innate, age-old capacity. Relying on automated sensitivities to faces, bodies, and voices, humans empathize from day one." We also know apes and monkeys are altruistic like humans. "For example, apes will voluntarily open a door to offer a companion access to food, even if they lose part of it in the process. And capuchin monkeys are prepared to seek rewards for others, as we see when we place two of them side by side, while one of them barters with us with differently colored tokens. One token rewards only the monkey itself, whereas the other rewards both monkeys. Soon, the monkeys prefer the "prosocial" token. This is not out of fear, because dominant monkeys (who have least to fear) are in fact the most generous."

So, why do animals help each other? "If all that matters is survival of the fittest, shouldn't animals refrain from anything that fails to benefit themselves? Why help another get ahead? There are two main theories: First, that such behavior evolved to help kin and offspring, hence individuals who are genetically related. This promotes the helper's own genes as well ... The second theory follows an "If you scratch my back, I'll scratch yours" logic: if animals help those who return the favor, both parties stand to gain" (De Waal 2005: 171). Therefore, "kindness" has its evolutionary benefits and explains in part our propensity to be altruistic. Indeed, we need more empathy and understanding if we are to address societal ills.

Our empathy should extend to "Mother Earth" as well. After all, we are very much part of the natural world of this planet as animals even if this is often forgotten. Living in the Anthropocene (Human Age), which has been dominated by human activity, has affected not only the climate of the planet but all life on earth. Undeniably, we are in an age where we are facing the so-called Sixth Extinction because many animals across the globe are worryingly endangered. The "Intergovernmental Science-Policy Platform on Biodiversity and Ecosystem Services" (IPBES) released a report stating that as many as 1 million animal species are heading for annihilation. This should worry us all.

# 6 ENVIRONMENT, HUMANISM, SCIENCE, AND TOLERANCE   245

Likewise, the Amazon rainforest and its biome are endangered as well. In this chapter, I raised the issues surrounding the massive Amazonian fires in Brazil and what effects this is having not only across Amazonia but on our planet as well. Recently, in July 2021, two important articles were published in the journal, *Nature*, which explain that the Amazon is no longer a Carbon sink, taking in more carbon than expending it.[128]

As Scott Denning (2021: 354) writes: "Atmospheric measurements show that deforestation and rapid local warming have reduced or eliminated the capacity of the eastern Amazonian forest to absorb carbon dioxide—with worrying implications for future global warming." Furthermore, since Brazilian President Jair Bolsonaro and his administration have refused to put in measures to protect against the massive conflagrations has exacerbated this ecological demise and jeopardized the lives of Native inhabitants across Brazilian Amazonia. Additionally: "The overall pattern of deforestation, warmer and drier dry seasons, drought stress, fire and carbon release in eastern Amazonia seriously threatens the Amazon carbon sink. Indeed, the results cast doubt on the ability of tropical forests to sequester large amounts of fossil-fuel-derived $CO_2$ in the future" (Denning 2021: 355). Not only is the Brazilian Amazon in peril but so are the livelihoods of indigenous peoples who live across Amazonia, especially from threats from illegal loggers, illegal miners, poachers, and ranchers.

Moreover, in our present struggle with Coronavirus, all of us should be aware how differently the developing world is coping with the pandemic. The developing world, across Latin America, Asia, and Africa, do not have the same resources to stem the tide of COVID-19. As I mentioned in this chapter, it will be very difficult for the developing world to so-call flatten the curve without the aid of first world countries like the United States, Europe, Australia, New Zealand, and Japan, or even with the aid of second-tier countries like China and Russia. Certainly, it is in the interest of all of us to have millions of vaccinations distributed where they are needed most and for this to be happening as soon as possible. The question in 2021 is will the worldwide vaccine rollouts happen fast enough or will the virus outrun our vaccination efforts?

Unfortunately, tolerance in regard to how Coronavirus is treated raises issues about racism as well, particularly how Asian-Americans have been targeted racially because of COVID-19. From the beginning of the pandemic in the United States, Asians have been unfairly the victims of attacks because of the disease. Former President Trump called the disease the "China virus," which some believe allowed for more Asians to be racially targeted. Racism against Asian-Americans has a long history in the United States as outlined by this chapter with for example the Chinese Exclusion Act (1882) and the Gentleman's Agreement (1907) with Japan as well as the internment of Japanese-Americans during World War II.

Lastly, this chapter expounded upon the issues surrounding fake news, especially when former President Donald Trump declared he had won the 2020 presidential election. Comparisons were made to the sixteenth- and seventeenth-century witch hunts in England when false news was promulgated to capture and kill those accused of witchcraft.

In all, history and science are viewed as candles in the dark to illuminate paths forward in order to avoid nonsensical logic and harmful nonsensical information. Through scientific knowledge we may learn to be tolerant and hopefully learn to create a better world in which to live in.

## Notes

1. https://www.livescience.com/46123-many-americans-creationists.html.
2. J. P. Linstroth (2015). *Marching Against Gender Practice: Political Imaginings in the Basqueland*. Lanham, MD: Lexington Books and "Gender as a Category for Analysis of Conflict" in *The Oxford International Encyclopedia of Peace*, Vol. 2, (ed.) Nigel Young, pp. 226–232.
3. https://en.wikipedia.org/wiki/LGBT_culture_in_New_York_City.
4. https://en.wikipedia.org/wiki/New_Family_Structures_Study.
5. https://www.oyez.org/cases/2002/02-102.
6. https://www.nature.com/articles/s41586-021-03629-6.
7. See Goodall (1971: 265).
8. Sapolsky (2017: 107–117).
9. https://www.worldometers.info/world-population/world-population-projections/.
10. https://www.unhcr.org/globaltrends2018/.
11. https://csis-website-prod.s3.amazonaws.com/s3fs-public/publication/180529_Ridge_ForcedMigrationCrisi.pdf.
12. https://www.un.org/en/development/desa/population/migration/publications/migrationreport/docs/MigrationReport2015_Highlights.pdf.
13. https://www.unhcr.org/en-us/displacement-in-central-america.html.
14. See Sapolsky (2017).
15. https://www.haaretz.com/world-news/.premium.HIGHLIGHT-the-revolt-of-the-maccabees-the-true-story-behind-hanukkah-1.5343197.
16. See Bloch (2013).
17. See de Waal (2009).

18. See de Waal (2009).
19. De Waal (2009: 13).
20. Sapolsky (2017: 528–534).
21. https://www.ipbes.net; https://www.vox.com/science-and-health/2019/5/7/18531171/1-million-species-extinction-ipbes-un-biodiversity-crisis.
    https://www.newyorker.com/magazine/2019/05/20/climate-change-and-the-new-age-of-extinction.
22. https://www.amazon.com/Sixth-Extinction-Unnatural-History/dp/1250062187/ref=sr_1_3?keywords=the+sixth+extinction&qid=1557958978&s=gateway&sr=8-3.
23. https://www.britannica.com/science/Ordovician-Silurian-extinction.
24. https://www.researchgate.net/publication/283569714_Relationship_among_sea-level_fluctuation_biogeography_and_bioevents_of_the_Devonian_An_attempt_to_approach_a_powerful_but_simple_model_for_complex_long-range_control_of_biotic_crises; https://www.sciencedirect.com/bookseries/developments-in-palaeontology-and-stratigraphy/vol/20/suppl/C.
25. https://www.nationalgeographic.com/science/article/permian-extinction.
26. https://www.britannica.com/science/end-Triassic-extinction.
27. https://en.wikipedia.org/wiki/Jurassic_Park_(novel); https://en.wikipedia.org/wiki/Chicxulub_crater.
28. https://www.amazon.com/Anthropocene-Very-Short-Introduction-Introductions/dp/0198792980/ref=sr_1_fkmrnull_3?crid=1AIL63U8TDGV&keywords=anthropocene+a+very+short+introduction&qid=1557957966&s=gateway&sprefix=anthropocene+a+very+short+%2Caps%2C167&s.
29. https://www.ipbes.net/sites/default/files/inline/files/ipbes_global_assessment_report_summary_for_policymakers.pdf.
30. https://e360.yale.edu/features/declining_bee_populations_pose_a_threat_to_global_agriculture.
31. https://www.nwf.org/~/media/PDFs/Global-Warming/2014/Natural-Defenses-Final-Embargoed-Until-102114-10amET.pdf.
32. https://www.ipbes.net/sites/default/files/inline/files/ipbes_global_assessment_report_summary_for_policymakers.pdf.
33. https://www.ipbes.net/sites/default/files/inline/files/ipbes_global_assessment_report_summary_for_policymakers.pdf.
34. https://www.yellowstonepark.com/things-to-do/wildlife/wolf-reintroduction-changes-ecosystem/.
35. https://academic.oup.com/bioscience/article/54/8/755/238242.
36. https://en.wikipedia.org/wiki/Ron_Fricke.

37. https://www.goodreads.com/quotes/1301484-if-there-is-danger-in-the-human-trajectory-it-is.
38. https://us.macmillan.com/books/9780805092998.
39. Recent reports and studies suggest the 2021 fires across the Amazon in Brazil have been just as bad as the 2020 fires, if not worse. See: https://news.mongabay.com/2021/06/the-brazilian-amazon-is-burning-again/; https://news.mongabay.com/2021/06/may-deforestation-in-the-amazon-hits-14-year-high/; https://news.mongabay.com/2021/07/brazils-amazon-is-now-a-carbon-source-unprecedented-study-reveals/; https://www.nature.com/articles/s41586-021-03629-6.
40. http://www.inpe.br/noticias/noticia.php?Cod_Noticia=5294.
41. https://www.counterpunch.org/2019/08/28/bolsonaro-fiddles-while-the-amazon-burns/.
42. https://rainforests.mongabay.com/amazon/amazon_wildlife.html.
43. https://rainforests.mongabay.com/amazon/amazon-rainforest-facts.html.
44. https://wwf.panda.org/discover/knowledge_hub/where_we_work/amazon/amazon_threats/unsustainable_cattle_ranching/?
45. https://www.counterpunch.org/2019/11/08/the-politics-of-denial-the-brazilian-president-and-the-fate-of-amazonia/.
46. https://g1.globo.com/natureza/noticia/2019/09/24/numero-de-assassinatos-de-indigenas-cresce-20percent-no-brasil-em-2018-aponta-relatorio.ghtml.
47. https://pib.socioambiental.org/en/List_of_indigenous_peoples.
48. https://pib.socioambiental.org/en/How_many_are_they%3F.
49. J. P. Linstroth (2015). "Brazilian Nationalism and Urban Amerindians: Twenty-First Century Dilemmas for Indigenous Peoples Living in the Urban Amazon and Beyond." In *Nationalism and Intra-State Conflicts in the Post-Colonial World*, (ed.) Michael Fonkem. Lanham, MD: p. 438, Endnote 5, https://www.survivalinternational.org/tribes/brazilian.
50. https://www.bbc.com/news/av/science-environment-48917148; https://www.eci.ox.ac.uk/about/.
51. https://www.cbsnews.com/news/amazon-rainforest-losing-its-ability-to-store-carbon/.
52. https://news.mongabay.com/2019/07/brazilian-amazon-deforestation-surge-is-real-despite-bolsonaros-denial-commentary/.
53. https://www.youtube.com/watch?v=H2QxFM9y0tY.
54. http://www.salsa-tipiti.org/wp-content/uploads/2019/08/PIAC-Letter-re-Fires-in-Amazonia-Aug2019-.pdf.pdf.
55. https://www.cartacapital.com.br/sociedade/201cse-o-bicho-avancar-vamos-encarar-de-pe201d-diz-ailton-krenak-1118/.

56. https://penelope.uchicago.edu/Thayer/E/Journals/CJ/42/4/Nero_Fiddled*.html.
57. https://www.bbc.com/news/world-latin-america-49415973.
58. https://en.wikipedia.org/wiki/Military_dictatorship_in_Brazil.
59. https://www.bbc.com/news/world-latin-america-49433437.
60. https://rainforests.mongabay.com/amazon/amazon-rainforest-facts.html.
61. https://rainforests.mongabay.com/amazon/amazon_wildlife.html. https://wwf.panda.org/discover/knowledge_hub/where_we_work/amazon/amazon_threats/unsustainable_cattle_ranching/?
62. https://pib.socioambiental.org/en/List_of_indigenous_peoples; https://pib.socioambiental.org/en/How_many_are_they%3F.
63. https://rowman.com/ISBN/9781498500258/Nationalism-and-Intra-State-Conflicts-in-the-Postcolonial-World.
64. https://www.survivalinternational.org/tribes/brazilian.
65. https://queimadas.dgi.inpe.br/queimadas/portal; https://queimadas.dgi.inpe.br/queimadas/portal-static/situacao-atual/.
66. https://www.bbc.com/news/world-latin-america-49443389.
67. http://www.ibama.gov.br/consultas/incendios-florestais/consultas-monitoramento-de-queimadas/boletins-diarios-de-monitoramento-avaliacao-do-fogo-na-amazonia-e-cerrado; https://queimadas.dgi.inpe.br/queimadas/cadastro/v1/relatorios/biomas/amazonia.pdf.
68. https://www.livescience.com/amazon-rainforest-burning-fire.html.
69. https://www.bbc.com/news/world-latin-america-49415973.
70. https://www.esquerdadiario.com.br/Para-Ministro-de-Bolsonaro-nuvem-de-poluicao-em-SP-fruto-da-destruicao-ambiental-e-fake-news.
71. https://news.mongabay.com/2019/07/brazilian-amazon-deforestation-surge-is-real-despite-bolsonaros-denial-commentary/.
72. https://science.sciencemag.org/content/365/6455/756.
73. https://en.wikiquote.org/wiki/Margaret_Mead.
74. https://www.nst.com.my/opinion/columnists/2019/06/498893/turning-sympathy-bateq-orang-asli-empathy?fbclid=IwAR26vpRyAyKLjNuzi83w1g5nKlGrecCzXIVUCkGAEtfJXqmAqmy64JIpEdk.
75. https://www.un.org/press/en/2021/ecosoc7039.doc.htm.
76. https://www.amazon.com/gp/product/0520243269/ref=dbs_a_def_rwt_bibl_vppi_i0.
77. https://www.bloomberg.com/news/articles/2019-10-16/americans-now-need-at-least-500-000-a-year-to-enter-the-top-1.
78. https://www.stlouisfed.org/on-the-economy/2017/october/how-us-income-inequality-compare-worldwide.
79. https://worldpopulationreview.com/country-rankings/gini-coefficient-by-country.

80. https://www.avert.org/professionals/hiv-around-world/sub-saharan-africa/overview.
81. https://www.hiv.gov/hiv-basics/overview/data-and-trends/global-statistics.
82. https://www.who.int/news-room/fact-sheets/detail/leishmaniasis.
83. https://www.nytimes.com/article/flatten-curve-coronavirus.html.
84. https://www.theguardian.com/global-development/2021/sep/22/joe-biden-vaccination-gap-poor-nations.
85. https://www.amazon.com/Infections-Inequalities-Plagues-Updated-Preface/dp/0520229134/ref=sr_1_5?keywords=Paul+farmer&qid=1584427731&s=books&sr=1-5.
86. https://www.cnn.com/2020/03/20/politics/donald-trump-china-virus-coronavirus/index.html.
87. https://www.nytimes.com/2020/03/13/world/asia/coronavirus-china-conspiracy-theory.html.
88. https://www.nbcnews.com/news/asian-america/trump-calls-u-s-protect-our-asian-american-community-hours-n1167241.
89. https://www.eater.com/2020/2/10/21131642/novel-coronavirus-american-chinese-restaurants-explained.
90. https://www.usatoday.com/story/news/nation/2020/03/28/coronavirus-racism-asian-americans-report-fear-harassment-violence/2903745001/.
91. https://www.abccolumbia.com/2020/03/27/fbi-warns-of-increased-hate-crimes-against-asian-americans-during-outbreak/.
92. https://www.usatoday.com/story/news/nation/2020/03/28/coronavirus-racism-asian-americans-report-fear-harassment-violence/2903745001/.
93. https://www.latimes.com/opinion/story/2020-04-01/coronavirus-anti-asian-discrimination-threats.
94. https://www.amazon.com/Mortality-1348-1350-Bedford-History-Culture-ebook/dp/B06XB23TT2/ref=sr_1_19?keywords=black+death&qid=1585800292&sr=8-19.
95. https://www.history.com/news/why-was-it-called-the-spanish-flu.
96. https://www.bloomberg.com/news/articles/2020-03-17/when-racism-and-disease-spread-together.
97. https://en.wikipedia.org/wiki/Chinese_Exclusion_Act; https://en.wikipedia.org/wiki/Gentlemen%27s_Agreement_of_1907; https://www.history.com/topics/world-war-ii/japanese-american-relocation.
98. https://www.nytimes.com/2020/03/29/us/politics/coronavirus-asian-americans.html.
99. https://www.nytimes.com/2020/03/29/us/politics/coronavirus-asian-americans.html.

100. https://www.nasponline.org/resources-and-publications/resources-and-podcasts/school-climate-safety-and-crisis/health-crisis-resources/countering-covid-19-(coronavirus)-stigma-and-racism-tips-for-parents-and-caregivers.
101. https://www.archives.gov/electoral-college/2020.
102. https://twitter.com/realDonaldTrump.
103. https://www.amazon.com/Manufacturing-Consent-Political-Economy-Media/dp/0375714499.
104. https://www.netflix.com/title/81254224.
105. https://www.amazon.com/Demon-Haunted-World-Science-Candle-Dark/dp/0345409469/ref=sr_1_1?dchild=1&keywords=carl+sagan+our+demon+haunted+world&qid=1604800143&s=books&sr=1-1.
106. https://www.amazon.com/Behave-Biology-Humans-Best-Worst/dp/0143110918/ref=sr_1_1?dchild=1&keywords=sapolsky+behave&qid=1604807666&s=books&sr=1-1.
107. https://link.springer.com/article/10.1007/s11109-012-9219-8.
108. https://www.amazon.com/Understanding-Social-Networks-Theories-Concepts/dp/0195379470/ref=sr_1_1?dchild=1&keywords=Charles+kadushin&qid=1604813220&s=books&sr=1-1.
109. https://www.imdb.com/title/tt12021664/.
110. https://www.youtube.com/watch?v=CxtU3AQpcx4.
111. https://www.amazon.com/European-Witch-Craze-Sixteenth-Seventeenth-Centuries/dp/0061314161.
112. https://www.youtube.com/watch?v=CxtU3AQpcx4.
113. https://www.amazon.com/Two-Treatises-Government-John-Locke/dp/1495323447/ref=sr_1_2_sspa?crid=3DLF7TV429PTS&dchild=1&keywords=john+locke+two+treatises+on+government&qid=1604824477&sprefix=John+Locke+two+Tre%2Caps%2C192&sr=8-2-spons&psc=1&spLa=ZW5jcnlwdGVkUXVhbGlmaWVyPUFLNFBTUkZSREpTUVQmZW5jcnlwdGVkSWQ9QTEwMjc5NjIzQkVGTldDTEY0R0xGJmVuY3J5cHRlZEFkSWQ9QTA1OTI3NzFJRjlVSk0zNkMyMlkkd2l0Z2V0TmFtZT1zcF9hdGYmYWN0aW9uPWNsaWNrUmVkaXJlY3QmZG9Ob3RMb2dDbGljaz10cnVl.
114. https://www.archives.gov/founding-docs/declaration-transcript.
115. https://en.wikipedia.org/wiki/Palmer_Raids.
116. https://www.history.com/topics/cold-war/red-scare.
117. https://www.foxnews.com/media/tucker-carlson-coronavirus-response-us-communist-china.
118. https://www.foxnews.com/media/tucker-carlson-coronavirus-response-us-communist-china.

119. https://en.wikipedia.org/wiki/Franklin_D._Roosevelt; https://www.amazon.com/Traitor-His-Class-Priviledged-Presidency/dp/0307277941.
120. https://www.history.com/topics/great-depression/great-depression-history; https://www.history.com/topics/world-war-ii/world-war-ii-history.
121. https://en.wikipedia.org/wiki/Herbert_Hoover.
122. https://www.historynet.com/15-minutes-saved-america.htm.
123. https://www.washingtonpost.com/politics/joe-biden-elected-president/2020/11/07/53ec8726-1f0b-11eb-ba21-f2f001f0554b_story.html.
124. https://www.independent.co.uk/news/world/americas/us-politics/how-many-us-presidents-lost-second-term-b1640998.html.
125. https://www.mentalfloss.com/article/12487/adams-vs-jefferson-birth-negative-campaigning-us.
126. https://www.theguardian.com/us-news/2020/nov/06/republicans-break-ranks-with-donald-trump-over-baseless-vote-claim.
127. https://www.aljazeera.com/news/2020/11/8/joe-biden-acceptance-speech-full-transcript.
128. https://www.nature.com/articles/s41586-021-03629-6; https://www.nature.com/articles/d41586-021-01871-6.

# Bibliography

Bagemihl, B. 1999. *Biological Exuberance: Animal Homosexuality and Natural Diversity.* New York: St. Martin's Press.

Balthazart, J. 2012. *The Biology of Homosexuality.* Oxford: Oxford University Press.

Bloch, M. 2012. *Anthropology and the Cognitive Challenge.* Cambridge: Cambridge University Press.

———. 2013. *In and Out of Each Other's Bodies: Theory of Mind, Evolution, Truth, and the Nature of the Social.* London: Paradigm Publishers.

Denning, Scott. 2021. Southeast Amazonia Is No Longer a Carbon Sink. *News and Views*, July 14.

Farmer, P. 1999. *Infections and Inequalities: The Modern Plagues.* Berkeley: University of California Press.

———. 2005. *Pathologies of Power: Health, Human Rights, and the New War on the Poor.* Berkeley: University of California Press.

Goodall, J. 1971, 2010 new edn. *In Shadow of Man.* Boston: Mariner Books, Houghton Mifflin Harcourt.

Herdt, G. 1981, new edn. 1994. *Guardians of the Flute: Idioms of Masculinity.* New York: McGraw-Hill.

Edward S. Herman and Noam Chomsky (1988; new edn. 1995). *Manufacturing Consent: The Political Economy of the Mass Media.* London: Vintage.

Kadushin, C. 2012. *Understanding Social Networks: Theories, Concepts, and Findings*. Oxford: Oxford University Press.

Kolbert, E. 2015. *The Sixth Extinction: An Unnatural History*. New York: Picador, Henry Holt and Company.

Linstroth, J.P. 2010. Gender as a Category for Analysis of Conflict. In *The Oxford International Encyclopedia of Peace: Volume 2 – Early Christianity and Antimilitarism – Mass Violence and Trends*, ed. Nigel Young, 226–234. Oxford: Oxford University Press.

———. 2015. Brazilian Nationalism and Urban Amerindians: Twenty-First Century Dilemmas for Indigenous Peoples Living in the Urban Amazon and Beyond. In *Nationalism and Intra-State Conflicts in the Postcolonial World*, ed. Fonkem Achankeng, 405–451. Lanham, MD: Lexington Books.

Locke, J. 1689, new edn. 1994. *Two Treatises of Government* (ed. P. Laslett). Cambridge: Cambridge University Press.

Mead, Margaret. 1968. https://libquotes.com/margaret-mead/quote/lbw9h4p.

Merolla, J.L., G. Burnett, K.V. Pyle, et al. 2013. Oxytocin and the Biological Basis for Interpersonal and Political Trust. *Political Behavior* 35, 753–776.

Ripple, William J., and Robert L. Beschta. 2004. Wolves and the Ecology of Fear: Can Predation Risk Structure Ecosystems? *BioScience* 54 (8), 755–766. https://doi.org/10.1641/0006-3568(2004)054[0755:WATEOF]2.0.CO;2.

Sagan, C. 1996. *The Demon-Haunted World: Science as a Candle in the Dark*. New York: Ballantine Books.

Sapolsky, R. 2017. *Behave: The Biology of Humans at Our Best and Worst*. New York: Penguin Books.

de Waal, F. 2005. *Our Inner Ape: A Leading Primatologist Explains Why We Are Who We Are*. New York: Riverhead Books, Penguin Group, Inc.

———. 2009. *The Age of Empathy: Nature's Lessons for a Kinder Society*. New York: Harmony Books.

West, C. 1993. *Race Matters*. New York: Vintage Books.

Young, A. 2000. *Women Who Become Men: Albanian Sworn Virgins*. Oxford: Berg.

CHAPTER 7

# Empathy, Love, and Peace

*After all the analysis on violence and trauma from racism, nationalism, terrorism, and genocide, it is in my view important to discuss ways to overcome some of the horrific experiences alluded to in previous chapters. Also, as someone who has worked in peacebuilding and peace studies for years, humanity must think about ways to see beyond the human propensity for violence and how to overcome suffering. For these reasons, I have looked to Buddhism for some of the answers to such perplexing questions.*

*In response to my questions about "love and Buddhism," one Tibetan Buddhist monk responded to all of them by stating in writing:*

*"Attachment is the near enemy of love. It's not a form of intense love, it's actually the enemy of genuine love. Genuine love does not cling. Genuine love says, 'I love you and I want you to be happy.' Attachment says, 'I love you. Therefore, I want you to make me happy.'"*

*As a result, I wanted to explore Buddhist notions of love and peace further—moreover, because Buddhism as a philosophy and religion has explored how to explain suffering, especially from the teachings of Siddhārtha Gautama, or the Buddha. Suffering is the Buddhist concept known as "dukkha." The following are excerpts from interviews I had with three Buddhist monks and one Buddhist nun about the subjects of empathy, love, peace, racism, suffering, and violence in 2020. The interviews are edited and excerpted out of brevity. I hope I have captured their essence here.*

*Furthermore, it should be noted that for two of the monks, Geshe Lama Phuntsho and Geshe Lobsang Tsultrim, their first language is "not" English and therefore the transcription of their interviews reflects this fact. Regardless, I hope the essence of what they are trying to say is reflected here.*

\* \* \*

**Bhutan Buddhist Monk Geshe Lama Phuntsho, Fifty-Seven Years Old,**
**Mahayana Tradition**
**Gaden Shartse Thubten Dhargye Ling Monastery (1st Interview)**
**Question 1: What does the concept of "love" mean to you? (Please explain in detail.)**

*So, you often hear about couples who live for each other. They love for the other person and they spend their whole lives devoting themselves to that one person. So, when one of the individuals die, or something happens, then what happens? The surviving person is lost. They don't know what to do. That is not love. That is attachment. Love is allowing the other person to be who they are. Also, you cannot give love unless you understand yourself first. You cannot be giving love without knowing love. Sometimes, people get in relationships and they believe the other person has to make them happy. In other words, the person who they fall in love with has to make them happy. That is not love. That is attachment. Then when that person they love later disappoints them, what happens? They resent the other person. Love in this case turns into resentment. You cannot give love unless you know yourself first. You cannot give love to another unless you understand self. So, they say, love is like light from moonlight shining down but then the light can be like light from the devil if it turns like this. So, attachment is not love. Attachment prevents love. This is what Buddhism believes.*

**Question 2: How is your understanding of love influenced by your Buddhist beliefs and what does love mean to you from a Buddhist perspective? (Please explain in detail.)**

*First, to be able to love, you have to have a big heart. Your intention is good. You are humble. This is what we say in Buddhism. You do not put conditions on love. If you do this, or if you do that. No, this is not love. These are conditions. They do not have to do with love. They have to do with wants. They have to do with desires. A person who loves, has a big heart. They want the other person to be happy. Also, this is because they are happy themselves. They do not place conditions on the other person. Love, true love, is unconditional.*

We know unconditional love is true love. This is part of the "Dharma" [Buddhist teachings].

Question 3: How may a Buddhist understanding of "love" improve our world and make it a better place? (Please explain in detail.)

Okay, so, first you have to be thankful. You know like, I did not make the water I drink. I did not make the air I breathe. But I am thankful for them. You know Buddhists, right? I did not pay for the house I have or build it. Someone gave me this space to live. Someone else built it. Someone else gave me the food. Someone else prepared it. But I am always thankful for these things. Okay, so let me explain it this way. You know an apple right. I mean most people just consume it. They eat it without really thinking about it. But I think about the farmer who grew it. You know the apple. It started out as a seed. And then, it grew into a tree. And, that tree had to be taken care of, it had to be watered. It needed sunshine. So, you know, an apple is not an apple. It is all these things. So, we are thankful for that. It is more than an apple it is all these things. These are all blessings. You know the water, the sun, the farmer, the apple. They are all blessings. Even the person who beats you up is a blessing. It is a lesson. And we appreciate these lessons, you see. You know I read a story recently. It was about an old man. I think he was 95 years old. And he had Coronavirus. So, when he went to the hospital, they told him he needed oxygen to keep him alive. And the oxygen would cost $500 dollars a day in the hospital. So, he said to the nurse staff and to the doctor, "Thank God, thank God for this." And, I think the doctor asked him, "But why are you thanking God?" And the old man said, "I thank God because I have lived for 95 years and all that time, the oxygen I breathed was free." It is the realization, you see, how much we take for granted. That story really moved me. I thought this is so true. There is so much we take for granted. So, it is the same for me, I live on the generosity of others, my food, my house. I wake up but I don't worry about what to wear, pick out shoes or outfit and so on. I wear same color. You see. And, meditation is very important. I live in small space. But when I meditate I create a big space. You have a wider view. You may, for example, meditate on one thing, let's say "love." You meditate on it for a while and you begin to understand many things.

Question 4: Do you believe a person can learn to love better? And, how does Buddhism help a person become a person of love and peace and therefore a better person? (Please explain in detail.)

Okay so, you have to do first thing first. You know what I mean? You have to do things for self, first, before you help others. You cannot help others without knowing self. You cannot try to bring peace to others and do this huge thing *for others without doing for yourself. Do you see? Okay, so, let me explain. Imagine you are in a storm and you get stuck in the mud. And there are others with you. But you cannot help them without getting unstuck yourself. You have to help self first. You see? Like you know you are in quicksand. And you are sinking. And there are others with you, sinking too. But you cannot help them without helping yourself first. So, you know, you somehow make it to the bank and then get out and then maybe you offer your hand or something like that. You have to help yourself first. Otherwise, you are not going to be able to help others. You see what I mean? So, after you help yourself, then you are able to spread love and peace.*

**Question 5: How may Buddhism help to create a more peaceful world and why? (Please explain in detail.)**

*Okay, so imagine this. You know you swim in the ocean and there are a lot of predators there. You have to learn how to swim there. The ocean is very, very big and there are a lot of predators. So, you must learn how to swim. But you know if you persevere, that is the only way. You must persevere. I mean you are not going to change the whole world tomorrow, right? If you set out to do this you will fail and then you get frustrated and then it will be much worse than when you started out. So, imagine being able to change one person at a time. You know if you change one person, say one person out of a thousand, well then, this makes a difference. One thing at a time. You cannot do everything at once. No, one thing at a time. Also, you have to be very, very patient. I mean think of the world. We are just a dot next to the sun, right? And then, think of the universe and then think of yourself on this little dot. You see? Very small. You see? It makes us insignificant, small, right?*

**Question 6: How does an average person become more "empathetic" and how does Buddhism help a person become more empathetic? (Please explain in detail.)**

*Okay, well, first, I don't like that word "empathy." It is. I don't know, distant, okay. To me, you know it should be love and related to love. You have to be brave to love. You have to really see them. Really feel them. You have to understand why they suffer, for example. Empathy, for me, is too, too far away. So, I don't like that word. I like the idea of "brave love." Because you have to be brave to love. This is the only way. To understand, for example, that animals, all animals have their place. Things are the way they are. But to see people, you really need to begin with love. It takes a lot of bravery to love and to love the right way. To see the right. Do you see?*

\* \* \*

Bhutan Buddhist Monk Geshe Lama Phuntsho, Fifty-Seven Years Old,
Mahayana Tradition
Gaden Shartse Thubten Dhargye Ling Monastery (2nd Interview)
Follow-up Question 1: What is your understanding of Ahimsa (Buddhist idea of non-violence) in relation to the World? (Please explain.)

*For example, a fight is somewhere going on. Then you don't want to fight. You don't want to create this fight. You try to help and get in a middle of the fight. I don't think it will work. When they are in a normal situation, when they are in a normal situation then we can talk and try to see what is going on … You have wait in the right situation … We don't have proper communication. We need proper communication. Because if you don't have proper communication then things will never be solved … If we are talking about nations or even in a family, it all starts on lack of communication … I think we need to take the time to sit down and talk or listen … We don't have the time to listen.*

Follow-up Question 2: In the world as you know, you had the conflict with the Sinhala Buddhists and the Hindu Tamils, and in Southern Myanmar you had the conflict with Buddhist monks and the Rohingya people, and even in Southern Thailand you had Buddhist monks as soldiers—what do you think of all that in relation to Buddhism?

*I always try to see from both angles. If you see from one angle side, the one is right and the other is wrong. You have to look at from both angles. We see then both are right and both are wrong … You have to see from both angles … Non-violence only comes when you are in a good situation. If you go out in the field, knowing the reality of both situations then … When you are in survival mode survival comes first. Non-violence only comes when you are in a good situation. We can just watch TV or something and complain, that's very easy but if we go out in the field, knowing the reality of both situations then we can say who is right and wrong … From a long-distance view then we are a lazy person … If we go back in history to what happened in India when the Buddhists were wiped out … you know who did it right? The Muslims but the Buddhists never said a word just practiced non-violence. I am sure there must have been someone who fought back … At that time it doesn't work with non-violence and violence. If you practice non-violence and someone tries to take over your country, it won't work if you practice non-violence … Those people* live those situations, it is like looking at something happened on the other side of the mountain.

**Follow-up Question 3: What are your views on the Buddhist concept of "dukkha" (suffering)?**

*That is a very interesting topic. That is the reason the Buddha operates on Enlightenment. When Siddhartha Gautama, the Buddha, after he achieved Enlightenment he began teaching the four Noble Truths, out of the four what did he teach first: What is suffering? Why did he want to teach something about that? He wanted us to understand the reality of being in this world, or samsara [the cycle of death and rebirth to which the material reality of this world is bound]. The reality of being born into this world. If we do not understand what we reality we are facing now, then we will never work hard to overcome the suffering. So, that is why he taught about suffering. To explain day to day life. And how life is so fragile and even though we are all going through difficulties. Even if I had this I will be happy, even if I had a stronger body I will be happy, even if I have plastic surgery I will be happy. But it never gives happiness. It relieves temporarily maybe. It is like if you stay inside and it is very cold and you are suffering because of cold. So, you go outside in the sun you feel good and the sun is warm but then you are in the sun too long and you get sunburned and you suffer from that. That will never give you happiness only it looks like happiness. ... So, for example, you have an advertisement for a beautiful car and it looks very nice. It looks very safe. I wish to have that car. What kind of action are we going to do? You need money ... Our desire to achieve the car is so strong we don't realize suffering is around ... Medicine is supposed to relieve from stomach ache but that medicine may be bad for you and worse than the actual pain. Or if you eat food because you are hungry but you eat too much that food might be poisoning you. That is also suffering. If we look at our own body. Our body is made of several elements: The earth element, the water element, the fire element, the wind or air element, and the space element. Do these elements go together, I don't think so. But it is a balance in our body. If some element is not balanced in the body then we may die. That is the suffering ... As long as we are born in this body, we cannot run away from suffering ... The reason why the Buddha is trying to teach us about suffering is because birth is a suffering. Aging is a suffering. Sickness is a suffering. Death is a suffering. These four sufferings you have no excuse whether you are rich or poor, or young or old, or handsome or ugly. You have no excuse. Whether you are powerful or you have wealth, position, or money or you have a lot of family around. You have no excuse. That is the suffering too ... But now we want more and more we think this will relieve us from suffering. But no, it increases more suffering. Everything we are trying to overcome suffering are all contaminated. But if the object or anything you are trying to pursue to give you joy and happiness and what you are trying to pursue is uncontaminated then you will truly achieve true happiness or relief from suffering.*

**Follow-up Question 5: You said in our last interview you did not like the word empathy and instead you liked the concept "brave love" can you please elaborate on that?**

*Many people who use the word empathy and I think it should be okay ... Empathy is like a distant and you are not part of my own surroundings. You are sorry for that ... But true love is like something in a family. For example, your children, your wife, your parents, your aunt, and so on .... You don't feel empathy with that you truly feel the pain. Because my children, uncle, or aunt feels pain. But empathy is not related to our own. It is too distant ... If everyone is to share the love you shouldn't discriminate. If you truly want to share the love without conditions with others. Everyone should be under the family umbrella of your love. If you are truly sharing your feelings with others ... In Buddhism there is no such thing as caste or color or race ... And even there is no discrimination between animals or humans. You have to equally respect everyone.*

**Follow-up Question 6: What do you think of the term "mindfulness" in Buddhism?**

*One thing we always say is that if you want to meditate then motivation is important. If you want to use meditation in your daily life, then mindfulness is important ... When you are doing a meditation practice your motivation is important ... If you want to apply meditation in your daily life and work, then mindfulness is important. You apply it to the law of cause and effect. What you are doing, what you are speaking, what you are acting physically ... If you don't have mindfulness then we become dominant with our own evil mind. Our mind is a tricky thing ... If someone stares at you and you get upset. You meditate on that ... Then you think I should be thinking positive about that ... You try to call on your actions, thoughts, and body and you are mindful about these.*

**Follow-up Question 7: What are your thoughts on Buddhism, love, and peace?**

*Sitting down face to face and communicating is the only way to bring peace ... Everything happening now is because of lack of communication. Sometimes it is very unfortunate that people have to go through trauma and something like that ... I think the system is so messed up ... We are taught from a young age survival. If you want to have a beautiful flower. You have to have the proper water and sunshine to expect the flower to grow. If you are only looking at the flower it is too late. If we look at people who are traumatized you go back to the origins ... This goes to how we raise children with love and care and an ethical life ... It's all about me, me, me ... When we try to do things with instant gratification ... I have experienced this in America. People do not know how to get angry. They don't want their children to be angry and cry. They don't know how to get angry. They have to learn how to overcome their anger ... This is truly important.*

\* \* \*

Tibetan Buddhist Monk Geshe Lobsang Tsultrim, Fifty-Two Years Old,
Mahayana Tradition
Diamond Light Tibetan Buddhist Group

Question 12: How do you view Buddhists, even so-called Buddhist monks involved in violence, for example past events among the Sinhala Buddhists in Sri Lanka, Buddhist actions in Myanmar against the Rohingya, or Buddhist monk-soldiers in Southern Thailand?

*They are not Buddhist. If you are Buddhist you cannot do any violence. Some people do Muslim terrorism, that's completely wrong. They are not any more Buddhists or Muslims, they use religions but they are not practitioners ... Same thing in Myanmar, some [Buddhist] monks what they say, they use Buddhist monks' clothes but in reality they are not any more Buddhists ... They are not monks. A vow means that you change your clothes and cut your hair, you have a vow and you are taking care. You do not harm others. You are no longer monks. You are not Buddhist.*

Question 3: How may a Buddhist understanding of "love" improve our world and make it a better place? (Please explain in detail.)

*First we need an understanding of world. It means we love ourselves. You think about other beings. We have to think in both sides. He loves himself too. We both have equal ways. Everything depend on others. Whether we like it or not we have to rely on others. If you do not love others you cannot survive. We call this in the monk training the compassion way. We become more peaceful. Not harm each other.*

Question 4: Do you believe a person can learn to love better? And, how does Buddhism help a person become a person of love and peace and therefore a better person? (Please explain in detail.)

*Love does not come through prayer. I am a monk. I am not interested in religion. I am not interested in that. I am interested in reality like a scientist way. Real love is really the source where we come from. Where does it come from? Your deeper understanding of those things. We talk about mind training. Training of the mind. At first to have training of the mind you have to have a good mind ... Buddhism talk about mind is not just one, the fifty-one mental factors, depend upon the power of our mental faculties.[1] We talk about changing mental factors. First, you need to know what is the nature of the mental factor. What is the cause of the mental factor, what is the effect of the mental factor? Not just religion but philosophical way. We call Buddhism science, Buddhism philosophy, Buddhism religion ... What is the right view? I am here therefore I need to be best. That is the wrong view ... There is dependent self and independent self.*

Question 6: How does an average person become more "empathetic" and how does Buddhism help a person become more empathetic? (Please explain in detail.)

*I was born in Tibet, the real Tibet. I had high school education in China. Then a Buddhist education, I got twenty years in a Buddhist monastery in South India then I come to the United States. Then share my knowledge every year. When I talk some people really interested in becoming Buddhist. We are not trying to increase the Buddhist population. We are trying to make people happy. It does not matter if you are Buddhist or not. You have to follow your own traditional way. Your own religion and faith. I teach Buddhist philosophy for the last seventeen years. First, make a normal way, a scientific way, through understanding. The Dalai Lama tells the same way.*

Question 7: What does "mindfulness" mean to you from a Buddhist perspective? And, how does a person learn to become more mindful? (Please explain in detail.)

*Mindfulness very powerful in 1960s. Westerners talk about mindfulness. But Buddhism way is a little bit different, traditional Buddhist way ... We teach kids watch your mouth, parents say watch your mouth. But we teach extra things. Watch your mind, that is mindfulness ... Crossing your legs and put your hands above your legs and meditating is not real mindfulness ... Real mindfulness is where you go, what are you eating, what are you talking, what are you thinking ... Negative mind grow up, make harm to me, make harm for others too. You have to watch negative mind. ... When positive mind grows, make positive mind increases. Your mind you can watch but other people cannot watch your mind. Other people can watch your action, speech-actions but not your mind. You can only read your mind yourself.*

*Therefore, mindfulness even in the dream level Buddhists practice even in the dream level. We watch our minds too. That means mindfulness. You need to set up and build a good motivation. What is good motivation means proper purpose. I need to make a contribution to all other beings, includes myself. Therefore, I need to practice mindfulness and a strong motivation like that.*

Question 8: How may an average person learn from Buddhism to become a person of peace without necessarily renouncing modern life? And how should an average person incorporate Buddhist practices into their lives? (Please explain in detail.)

*Today our world, every day, every year, gets more busy more stressful. We are going to get worse and worse. There is no doubt about it ... First you make happy for others, first make happy for family. First you need to be a happy person. You cannot make other people happy if you are not happy first ... If you make your family happy. One obstacle is anger ... Your family is not a happy family if you are an angry person ... First you need to understand patience. Patience is the antidote of anger. Practice forgiveness and tolerance. Tolerance, patience, and forgiveness. Your family become more happy. Then, you have chance to increase spread and flourish. You can make it bigger and bigger happy for world.*

Question 9: How do we make a more peaceful world? What can average people do to make the world more peaceful from a Buddhist perspective? (Please explain in detail.)

*First, we need ethics. Everyone needs to follow ethics and morality. And peace follows from there ... Everyone follows by law and the constitution. All the religions say no killing, no stealing, no lying. In Buddhism we talk about the ten different non-virtues[2] ... We have to take care of ethics ... There is right speech ... In Sri Lanka or elsewhere once they harm others, once they do this they break their vows, they are no longer Buddhist ... First, generosity, then ethics, third patience, fourth effort, fifth concentration, sixth wisdom. Those six needs combined. Then create love.*

Question 10: Is there an issue you would like to discuss or elaborate upon, which was not asked in the above questions? Please elaborate on anything else you would like to say about empathy, love, mindfulness, and peace? (Please explain in detail.)

*First we need to change ourselves and our perspective. If we change our perspective we can change our attitudes. If we change our attitudes then it is easier to change our emotions and our feelings. Then change our behavior. Then action become everything positive. Then formations of happiness. Those things are like stages. First we change our perspective. Right now we have wrong perspective. Then we change our perspective then we have right view. Then change our thinking and change our attitude. Our feelings then change and then emotion levels then change too. Then you will be happy. Those change behaviors. Then the formations of happiness will change. Change the structure of the mind then our brain functions will change. First change perspective, then change attitude, then change behavior, then change happiness. These are the very foundations of the key factors to change the wrong habits ... We need to change the negative thinking. To positive view and positive outlook. That is what I would like to add.*

\* \* \*

Ajahn Amaro Bikkhu (J.C. Horner), Sixty-Five Years Old (English),
Theravada Tradition
Amaravati Buddhist Monastery, Chiltern Hills, South East England
Question 1: What does the concept of "love" mean to you? (Please explain in detail.)
*My understanding in relationship to love is strongly conditioned I have been a Buddhist monk since I was twenty-one. The Greeks, for example, have several categories for love. But from a Buddhist perspective, I would divide love into different categories as well. The one I will call "possessive love," another I will call "liberative love." So, from a Buddhist perspective "possessive love," which is described by the word "pya," which means "dear." And that kind of love has always had a "self" involved in it. There is me. There is you. I love you. You love me. I belong to you. You belong to me. So, whether that love is between a parent and a child, two romantic partners, a student and a teacher, or even more broadly, say you are loving your family, or you love a particular group, say you love a particular football team, or you love Oxford University, as long as there is a possessive quality within that then there is always going to be some kind of pain associated with that. There is always going to be a sense of loss when that bond is challenged, or interrupted, or broken. So, that I would say is a kind of love. It is the most common in the human world but it necessarily brings with it a quality of pain along with it. Either the beginning, the middle, or the end, or along the way. Then that is always a part of it. "Liberative Love," the qualities we use in our Buddhist language, what we call the "Brahmaviharas" or the "sublime abidings."[8] This represents a quality of love which is essentially non-personal. So, that we talk about loving kindness, or compassion, sympathetic joy, and serenity. These*

*are qualities of mind. So, they are expansive. They are radiant. They are nonpersonal. So, we would say when the mind is fully awake, an enlightened being. Their emotional nature is colored or guided or forms into particular modes of kindness or compassion or sympathetic joy, happiness of the good fortune of others, or the quality of serenity. Being fully at peace and being attuned to things in the midst of agitation or turbulence or any kind of activity. So, for myself, when I speak about love it really divides itself into these two very different categories. And the latter kind, the "Brahmaviharas" or sublime abidings as we call them. I call them "liberative" because they are a kind of love that let's go. A love that leads to liberation. It's a love that doesn't necessarily lead to any kind of suffering whatsoever. Even with compassion, which means to suffer with. In Buddhist psychology, if there is genuine "karuna," genuine compassion, there is an appreciation of the sufferings of others but you as an individual do not suffer on the account of the suffering of others. You empathize with it. You are aware of it. But it does not create suffering in your own heart. So, by using the Buddha as an example we would say the Buddha had a greatly compassionate heart, ocean-like compassion, is a word that we use. But he did not suffer on the account of the suffering of other beings. He worked ceaselessly for forty-five years to relieve the suffering of others but he did not create suffering in himself on the account of the suffering of others. So, that quality of love, which is non-possessive, which is liberative, which is free of conceit of me and my and free of the conceits of the self's view. Then, that is a love of a very different nature.*

**Question 3: How may a Buddhist understanding of "love" improve our world and make it a better place? (Please explain in detail.)**

*I feel it is a bit presumptuous of me how Buddhism might improve the world. Other people may have very different opinions. The cultivation of these liberative kinds of love rather than possessive kinds of love would be very helpful and beneficial. Because we don't have to look very far to see how the prisons and the shelters for battered women and the hospitals are filled with the results of possessive love, not completely as there many wholesome aspects of love that are based on more possessive and personal attitudes, but a huge number of crimes, violent crimes, rape, physical assault, sexual assault, the harming of women in marital relationships, are heavily advanced by a sense of possessiveness. You know you belong to me. You should be there for me. Of course, it goes in the other direction as well. Women can have very possessive relationships to me and can be abusive and even violent towards men. Similarly, it does not depend on gender. Same-sex relationships are exactly the same. So, that you don't have to look very far to see the painful and often horrific results of possessive love. In news you see over and over again, you see people murdering their own children, murdering their families, because the marriage is broken up, the family is broken up. So that one member of the family kill themselves or their children, they kill their partner who has rejected them, or that they have become separated from. Not to be too alarmist, obviously there is not such a huge proportion of such things, but it is very regularly in the news. But if you look at that, where does that come from? Where it comes from is, if I cannot have you nobody can. I don't want anyone else to look after my children. Nobody else can bring these children in the world in such a way as I could and they are separated from me now so it is better for them to die than it is to be brought up by somebody else or away from me. Again, I do not want to make too many sweeping statements but I would say that kind of attitude comes from a sense of possessiveness, of ownership, from a profound grasping or clinging and attachment. So that the more we can relate to our loved ones, our marriage partners, our romantic partners, our children, our family members, our colleagues, and people in the world and living beings in the world with a more liberative attitude which is non-possessive and non-personal. Then, it is not a kind of emotional flattening but a rather emotional expansiveness or a maturity I would say. So, that it is a kind of love that let's go. And the degree to which that liberative quality of loving could be communicated and can be articulated in different languages and put in different psychological forms or spiritual forms or different ways of expressing that let's say within different religious, spiritual, psychological, or social traditions then that could in terms of human relations greatly improve our world. And similarly, in terms of love and the sense of self, there is a lot of conflict in the world, especially between social groups within a country or between countries depends a lot on identification. My team, my group, I am English. I am from Kent. I am a man of Kent. I am not a Kentish man, I am English. I am not the same as the Scots. Or a I'm a Theravada Buddhist. I am not the same as the Mahayana Buddhists. Or, I'm a Buddhist, I am not a Christian, or a Muslim, or a Hindu. Or, I am a man, I'm not a woman. Or, I'm a Chelsea supporter not a Manchester United supporter. Or, I'm a Liverpool supporter, not a Chelsea supporter. The way that the heart bonds with a particular group and says this is good. This is an absolute good and I am this. The degree to which that identification is seen as absolute is often the degree to which we find ourselves in conflict with the Other. So, the more that Buddhist teachings can understand that any kind of identification can only be a kind of convenient fiction. I was born in Tenterden in Kent. So, that means I am a man of Kent. What does that really mean? I am not a Kentish man. I am a man of Kent. So what? Does one have to make anything of that? To anyone outside of Kent, it is kind of meaningless from the get go. But you can focus on that. If you come from Liverpool are you a Liverpool supporter or Everton supporter? That is massively important. If you come from Madison, Wisconsin, it means nothing. If you live in Delhi, that means nothing. If you live in Beijing, Bangkok, or Tasmania, it has no meaning for you. So, to develop a scope of view. To see our own affiliations, to see our own gender, our age, our nationality, our social group, knowing that those things, they only have meaning and value as convenient fictions. Then, we can function much more easily with others. I think particularly in the terms of meditation and the development of wisdom to reflect that I don't experience "the" world. I experience my mind's version of the world. If that understanding can be really taken to heart then it means there is a greater recognition of well of course other people's worlds are going to be different. If I think I see "the" world and my seeing is 100% accurate, then necessarily I am going to be in an alienated and divided state from others. If I recognize I experience my mind's version of the world, more of a phenomenological perspective, which is very much in tune with the Buddhist perspective, that I only know my mind's version of the world. Of course, other people's version of the world is going to be radically different. Therefore, a quality of respect and appreciation and an ability to attune to others as they relate to others from a place of humility and respectfulness and kindness and sympathy rather than I am right and you are wrong. Or, I know the truth. You don't. I see the world as it is. If you see it differently, then you are deluded. You are wrong.*

**Question 6: How does an average person become more "empathetic" and how does Buddhism help a person become more empathetic? (Please explain in detail.)**

*Well, empathy I would say, "karuna," or "compassion" as we usually translate it in English. Empathy is probably a better term. It was only really developed a hundred years or so ago in the Western psychological tradition. I feel it's a closer match for the quality of "karuna." Another word for compassion in Pali is "anukampa," which literally means to resonate with or attune to.[4] Or to harmonize with. To resonate with the experience with another so that the heart appreciates or is attuned to the suffering of others, the difficulties and sufferings of others but is not suffering on account of that. In terms of how to develop more empathy, firstly I would say the capacity of to let go of self-view. To not think in self-centered terms. To not think in terms of I, and me, and my or I should or I must or I've got or I have or I haven't got or I need to get. Or I have got this or you've got that. The way the mind forms rigid concepts of self and other is a way that we divide ourselves from each other. We don't create a genuinely empathetic relationship. Even when one's livelihood is around compassion, you can be a social worker and but so obsessed with self-view, what I should be doing and I am not doing enough. I should try harder and it's my responsibility to make all of these people happy. Even if our profession is compassionate, we can still really on a genuine level lack a quality of empathy because the mind is still operating in a rigid sense of self and other. So, I say genuine empathy from the Buddhist perspective is most helpfully established by letting go of self-view. What we call "sakkaya dithi" or that sense of a rigid identification with I am the body. I am the personality.*[5] *This is all and everything that I am. And the other part of that of self-view is seeing others in rigid ways. We judge others as male and female as old and young, our teacher, our student, our parent, our child, and we relate to the category, the labeling we give to the other person. We think of my father or my mother and they are only my mother or my father but they have a life of their own. They were in the world a long time before they even met each other. They have their own minds, their own families, their own story. So, they don't exist just in the world as in father of Ajahn Amaro [referring to himself here] or mother of Ajahn Amaro but they have their own nature as living beings. So, to let go of self-view. To let go of others' rigid categorizations and as the founder of this monastery, Ajahn Samato, put it: "don't take your life personally." So, the more we can see those feelings of love and hate, of happiness and unhappiness, as natural processes. Rather than I am happy or I am unhappy or I am angry or I am joyful. Rather there is a feeling of anger it is like this. There is a feeling of joy it is like this. There is a feeling of gaining it is like this. There is a feeling of loss it is like this. Then there is a way of visioning of viewing the flow of our experience from a position of nature. Seeing things in terms of nature rather than in terms of personality. So, the process of inside meditation. Is a lot about making that shift going from a self-centered viewpoint to a nature centered viewpoint. And out of that, one of the things that emerges is that one of the things I was talking about is the phenomenological approach. We recognize that my version of the world is only this what is experienced here. Why should it be the same as your version of the world. So, when we train the mind to be more empathetic. To let go of self-view. To let go of perceptions of self and other in a rigid way. Then, one of the things that naturally arises is how could I be more important than you? How could my feelings and preferences be more important than yours? This is ridiculous. How could that be possible? That's not from an idealistic or theoretical position, it's an intuition of the heart. So, I would say developing empathy then primarily letting go of self-view and letting go of ideas how we should be or wanting to be an empathetic person, letting go of that ideal: I should be more like this or that person is really great. Or, he is really empathetic. Or, I need to be like him. I'm not good enough. I should be like him or her. She is really great. The degree to which the mind stops believing and identifying with those perceptions of self and other and is more simply attuned with the time, the place, the situation, let's go of self-view, let's go of that rigid categorization. Then empathy naturally arises. It's an automatic quality. The ways they talk about it in the Buddhist tradition is to say: "When your leg is injured then your hand doesn't have to decide whether or not it is going to help out." The leg and hand belong to the same body. So, when the leg is injured, the hand immediately reaches to protect the wound. To soothe the injury. The hand is not a separate thing. It automatically goes to where the hurt is. So, that's a good way of characterizing the quality of empathy. It is automatic. We're part of the same living body. We're part of the same organic system. So, of course, this being cares and feels for the qualities of that being. How could it not? The hand is not going to refuse or refrain to help the leg. Because it is all part of the same body. So, it all works together.*

**Question 7: What does "mindfulness" mean to you from a Buddhist perspective? And, how does a person learn to become more mindful? (Please explain in detail.)**

*Mindfulness is obviously a very key, if not central part of Buddhist practice. The Buddha said: "mindfulness is the path to the deathless, heedlessness is the path to death." The mindful never die, the heedless are as if dead already. So, he is talking about psychological life and death. So, to be mindful is to be fully alive. You are there for your own life. To be heedless is to be as if you are dead already. You're not there for your own life. So, in the Buddha's words it might sound a bit harsh. It is as if you are dead already. You're not really there for your own life. So, mindfulness is the key quality, the principal quality in many, many respects. The classic way of characterizing mindfulness is to talk about the four foundations or the four domains of mindfulness. So, mindfulness of the body, the "kayanupassana," the contemplation of the body; both your own body, other people's bodies, how the body works. And so, mindfulness of physical form and paying attention to the body whether you are sitting still, or standing, or walking, or lying down. Then, the second one, mindfulness of feeling, "vedananupassana," so contemplation of sensations; so, there is not so much mood or in terms of emotion but it is more, pain, pleasure, neutral feeling. It's mindfulness of sensation: are you comfortable or are you uncomfortable. Is there a neutral feeling? The sensations of the body.*

Then, the third one, *"cittanupassana,"* is mindfulness of mind states. So, that's are you feeling agitated, or are you feeling peaceful, or are you feeling angry, or are you feeling friendly? Are you excited or are you sleepy? What's the mood of the mind? So, cittanupassana covers a vast range of mental activity and really just knowing what is going on. In the Satipatthana Sutta, the Buddha's discourses about the nature of mindfulness, one of the things that is particularly interesting about cittanupassana is he doesn't make any value judgement with respect to wholesome or unwholesome. He says knowing the angry mind is angry. Knowing the free mind is free of anger. Knowing the peaceful mind is peaceful.[6] Knowing the agitated mind is agitated. So, there is no value judgement in that. It's just in this moment there is this. That very quality there is this-ness, that appreciation. That is the establishment of mindfulness in relationship to that. Then, as an adjunct or as a natural outcome, the more complete that quality of mindfulness is then if it is an unwholesome state then the mind will incline away from it. And work to diminish it and let go of it. Then, the wholesome state like concentration or kindness, peacefulness, then it will incline towards that. And work towards establishing it more completely. Then, the last of the four of the foundations of mindfulness or the establishments, the domains of mindfulness, is what is called *"dhammanupassana."* And so there is different ways of interpreting this but it is seeing things in their fundamental nature, *"dhammanu," "nature"* in this respect. So, *"dhammanupassana,"* so it is seeing the process of experiencing itself. So, the first three, the body, sensations, mind states, are kind of in one category. They are the content of experience. And then, the fourth of the foundations of mindfulness is really stepping out of the content and looking at the *"process of experience itself."* So, in this moment, here I am holding a piece of paper with your questions printed out on them. And my i-Pad is sitting on my lap. And I am speaking and giving you these responses but I am aware in this moment is made up of seeing, hearing, smelling, tasting, touching. I've got a cup of coffee by my right hand and a glass of water to my left to ease my throat as I do all of this talking. And it's a Friday afternoon, it's a beautiful spring day here in Hertfordshire [England], the wisteria is blossoming on my veranda. These are seeing, smelling, touching, thinking. The words arise: wisteria, Friday, coffee, i-Pad, paper, printed words; so the *"dhammanupassana"* is recognizing these are mental events. These are formed of say a *"qualia of experience,"* arising and passing away. They are fabricated and compounded from individual bits of experience. The qualia of feeling and experience and they are woven together. So, this is a mental event. I am sitting in my cottage here in Hertfordshire but my cottage in Hertfordshire are known as a mental event. They are patterns of experience. They are known through the agency of this mind in this moment. So, that in terms of mindfulness, there are those four dimensions of it. And what we call the foundations of mindfulness. And as I was saying there are degrees and depths of mindfulness as well. So that there can be like a superficial level. Whereby there is just a noting of what's going on. At the most a rudimentary or mechanistic level, but even within that there is a recognition of wholesome and unwholesome, a mood may be wholesome or unwholesome, or an action may be wholesome or unwholesome or neutral. So, that is recognized within that. But then the next level of mindfulness I would say is an informed mindfulness, what we would call "sampajanna." Sampajanna means a comprehensive knowing.[7] So, that is being aware of not just of the thing that is being experienced in a surface level but also the time, the place, the situation ... So, that sampajanna is comprehensive inclusivity of the factors of the present moment. And the most profound level is what we call "satipanya," mindfulness and wisdom. So, it is taking that fourth domain of mindfulness "dhammanupassana" to a more complete and let's say fulfilled quality. Taking that quality to its full and complete extent. So that when there is mindfulness and wisdom there is an ongoing moment by moment appreciation that all of this is built up of perceptions, thoughts, feelings, arising and passing away. These are sankara or compounded of experience. They are the qualia of experience that are intrinsically in a state of change. None of them can satisfy permanently or completely. And they are not self. So, we talk about these qualities of the nature of all experience which is that they are "inicha," a state of change, uncertainty. They are "dukkha," incapable of completely satisfying and they "anata," not self, they don't belong to a self. So that when we use the word mindfulness. It is a single word but it encompasses a large range of qualities. So, when the word is used it is also helpful to understand what the presumptions are and the person who is using the word. And they might mean a mechanistic kind of mindfulness or just paying attention to the present in a superficial way. Or it might be all the way to that fully comprehensive, awakened awareness of the flow of experience of the most profound level of wisdom and understanding.

So, the second part, how does a person become more mindful. Firstly, the individual has to see the value of it. If they think it is a waste of time they won't put any effort into it. So, if a person say sees the value of say paying attention to their life and not just pursuing different forms of distraction or numbing. Then, that is the primary condition to support learning. Secondly, they need to make effort. So, it won't just happen on its own. It's like mindfulness is not like putting a sticker on your fridge [refrigerator], or wearing a *t-shirt saying mindfulness is great stuff.* But we need to make effort moment by moment to wake up to be mindful. Thirdly, I would say we need to be ready to fail and be distracted and not to think that I decided to be mindful and I will be mindful all the time. But rather, the intention is one thing and the actuality is another. To quote T.S. Elliot, "Between the idea and the fact there falls the shadow." So, you have the idea of mindfulness but the habits of distraction are many and varied. To be ready to fail, to get distracted, to lose your way, to fall asleep, but then to recognize that is part of the process when the mind has been distracted or lost its way then to be ready to begin again. And the, maybe as an outcome of that or as a part of that, it's important to be ready to learn from everything. There are times of failure when you are completely lost in hopes and fears... So, the way the mind gets lost in its projections. Its fears, its hopes, to be able to see okay I have been rejected... What do I learn from that? Or, they say the opposite, this is great... That readiness to learn from all experiences, pleasant, painful, and neutral is an essential part of becoming more mindful. Because the mind according to our instincts and our conditioning we get pulled by pain and pleasure, gain and loss, praise and criticism, fame and disrepute. Those are the worldly winds that blow the mind around and so the more mindfulness there is then the more those worldly winds do not have a destructive effect.

**Question 8: How may an average person learn from Buddhism to become a person of peace without necessarily renouncing modern life? And how should an average person incorporate Buddhist practices into their lives? (Please explain in detail.)**

I would say that the way that one can be a person of peace regardless if you are an adherent to Buddhist principles consciously, or whether you want to call yourself a Buddhist or not. Whether you are a committed Christian or a Muslim or you are a secular materialist or you are Professor Dawkins [referring to evolutionary biologist, Richard Dawkins] or you are whoever.[8] Primarily, peace comes from right understanding. It comes from seeing life, really appreciating life in its true nature from an unbiased perspective. So, peace I would say is a quality of understanding and vision. It's not a matter of everything calming down around us. So, you can be a person of peace in the midst of great agitation and turbulence. So, primarily, by learning to be unselfish. To establish an attitude of how can I be more important than you? How can my feelings be more important than yours? Not just in relationship to other people but also to the other creatures we share our world with. Like the green fly eating my roses. What makes it my rose and not the rose of the green fly? They are hungry too. So, I cannot say that's my rose. I like to eat as well. I get hungry. Food is appealing so what's to stop this green fly from feasting on this particular succulent rose. So, being unselfish. Living simply and being adaptable. So, one of the things is that the Buddha lived a renunciant lifestyle but also when things were comfortable and luxurious he did not push them away. He saw that what really mattered was the attitude. So that if he was offered say delicious or abundant food. He was invited to one of the royal palaces and the king and queen laid on a large feast to offer the Buddha and his monastic community, the Buddha wouldn't say no take it away, just give me broken boiled rice. No, he was quite open to eating the delicious food. Because he had not sought after it. He had not asked for it. And our rules prohibit that kind of hinting or requesting. So, to be adaptable. So, if there is abundance, you can enjoy abundance. If there is amenity like an i-Pad and a WiFi connection, go ahead and use it. But if it is not there then there is nothing lacking. So, you are basically learning to live simply with a minimum number of requirements and dependencies and establishing a heart that is adaptable. So, I often say adaptability is the key to happiness. So, if things are simple and harsh and sparse. You are out on a hike and you get marooned on a hillside in [Mt.] Snowdonia [Wales] and you twisted your ankle so you can't get back. You have got to bivouac and it is pouring with rain and everything is soaking wet. You find you have to crawl into a sleeping bag under the shelter of a tree. You can actually find you can be quite comfortable with that. There is actually up to the mind whether you complain about it or not. You may be cold, and wet, and uncomfortable but you don't need to create suffering around it. Similarly, you can be enjoying a delightful event with your best friends and with good humor and great bonhomie and good food and beautiful surroundings and you can be enjoying it and not feel guilty that it is there. But also not getting carried away with it. It's delightful, it's sweet, it's enjoyable but you don't have to hang onto it. Or be possessive. Again, quote an English poet, William Blake: "He who binds himself to a joy, does the winged life destroy, he who kisses the joy as it flies, lives in eternity's sunrise." Though in terms of development of qualities, being unselfish, living simply, being adaptable, and those kind of skills or those changes of attitude are built around three qualities. So, we say generosity, "dana," being unselfish, being ready to share what you have in an unselfish way, so generosity. "Sila" being virtuous, so being committed to non-violence, to honesty, to sexual propriety, to being faithful in your relationships, to be honest in your speech, to refrain from lying, to choose honesty and truthfulness, and to refrain from using intoxicants ... The quality of "sila" or virtue is benefiting ourselves and benefiting the people around us ... So, the last of the three trainings, "dana," generosity, and "sila," virtue, are the first two and the third one is meditation or "bhavana." It is a principal tool whereby the mind is understood and is recognized how the mind works. And then the mind can be trained to work skillfully with feelings, with thoughts, with emotions, with the activities of our daily life. Train the attention to be awake and to focus on the present moment. And also to know the very fabric of experience, the self. To know how the mind experiences things. To know the very nature of experiencing. And through understanding that fabric of experience, then to really free the heart from bondage through praise and criticism, through gain and loss, happiness and unhappiness, and comfort and discomfort.[10]

Question 9: How do we make a more peaceful world? What can average people do to make the world more peaceful from a Buddhist perspective? (Please explain in detail.)

Peace begins within the individual. This is a well-worn chestnut as they say, a truism. Not just from the Buddhist tradition but from many spiritual traditions. Peace begins within the individual. And peace within the individual leads to peace within the home, leads to peace within the country, leads to peace within the world. So, the primary thing we can do is to discover how we can peaceful within ourselves and to work from a place from say responsivity rather than reactivity. Also, and in particular to consider the work we do, not just in our relationships and our casual conversations. But what's our livelihood, what do we bring into the world? We put effort into our work. What company do we work for? What institution do we work for? Are we happy? Are we happy with everything that they do? Are we happy with what they represent? What are consequences of putting effort and work into this particular company? Can we be putting our energies into something more helpful? And so I think that is an important area to consider. So, sometimes we are mindfully working in an institution that is causing great harm and destruction, what they call "structural violence," being caused by the very institution we are within. So, I think it is important to be aware of that. We might have skillful intentions and we might be doing say good work within our field but it can be the very field we are a part of that has a very destructive relationship in relation to the world. I also realize that is a bit of a grey area and it is difficult to step out of a situation ... Sometimes if we are part of an organization we can help to change the direction of it within. So, for example a number of years ago I was having a conversation with a major CEO from a major corporation [names omitted for privacy reasons]. I was in America and I was introduced to him and went to visit him and I was invited to visit his home and meet him and his family and he was quite keen to step out of the *whole thing at that time [quit his job] … He was talking to a Buddhist monk. I think he was quite of a mind to say that I would assume to approve of his idea of signing off from the [major corporation] and going off to live in a cabin in Vermont and bringing his kids up with his wife in the countryside, growing their own veggies [vegetables], and living an organic, eco-friendly life in the woods. And I think he was a bit surprised when I said: "Well, you are kind of wedded to the [major corporation] so while you are doing that maybe you can do what you can to help change its values from the inside." And even though he might have been surprised to hear a Buddhist monk encouraging him to carry on or to support that. I felt that you know he is in there. He is the company's name, it's in his name. He is part of it so maybe he can do a bit to change the ethos of the company and the working principles of the company at least for a time while he was CEO. I would not say it was solely based upon what I said to him that day. I would not want to be so presumptuous. But he did stay in the company and he did try to do what he could to try to steer the company toward eco-friendliness. He even at the annual general meeting, "I don't think the [major corporation] is about motor vehicles, which I think surprised many of the shareholders." But he said: "What we are about is helping people to connect." I thought that was extraordinarily insightful. It was a very skillful way of putting it. And so, expanding the vision of what the company is there to do. And similarly, there was a Swiss physiology professor I met. If you have been near a physiology department, there is a lot of animals that get killed along the way through the lab work of physiology departments. And you know he was a tenured professor if I remember correctly. He was having a lot of misgivings about being part of this. And so, I agree, I was a student of physiology as well. I felt a lot of queasy and uncomfortable feelings with the lab work. And the many, many frogs and the cats that were killed along the way just in the undergraduate field. So, I could empathize with that. So, I said while you are committed as a professor in your role in this field perhaps you can do what you can. You can be a good influence by minimizing the use of animals in the work that is done. You can help change the ethos, the kind of principles the department is built around. You can change the way that they teach and the way things are studied. You can perhaps be a good influence from the inside. So, what I feel we can do to make the world more peaceful doesn't mean changing our lifestyle but as long as we are in some situation to do what we can to bring it in more wholesome, skillful, benevolent attitudes, and things that conduce to harmlessness, that conduce to honesty, that conduce to say wholesome behavior. Similarly, you are asked to make directly unethical choices. A friend of ours who is in the* *advertising industry, told us when he was working in New York City on Madison Avenue. His company was taken over by a bigger corporation and after a few months of working under the new management he became puzzled by some of the invoices he was approving. And he went into his boss's office and he said: "I'm a little surprised. There is only three people working on this advertising program but we are billing the client for twelve people that's not accurate. And then, his new boss said there is nothing wrong with lying to the client. And the person in question, turned around and walked out and signed off his job right then and there. He decided I am not going to work for these people if I am required to deceive. That was an ethical choice and did involve leaving the company. So, sometimes I feel that is the appropriate thing to do. He felt he was not going to be able to change the ethics of that particular group so he chose to walk [quit the company]. Again, mindfulness is really helpful to bring those questions to heart and really contemplate about those kind of things in a skillful way. So, is it time to work with the situation and work within or is it time to vote with my feet and leave it. Because also that's a message to the deceitful boss. That was a criminal boss. It's a matter of message. Here is a person who was a long-standing and very competent member of the company just walked out because of what I said to him. So, some may reject that or laugh at that. On the surface level but something is touched I would say. Something gets through. If it's not wanted. That's their opinion they walk. It can have a good effect. Another example of ethics I might tell of someone working in the workplace. Another person from New York City, she is a lawyer for a financial corporation. And they were having a lunch with a prospective client and her boss invited her along to find out about the prospects of this new client, an investor. And at the end of the lunch, it was an outdoor restaurant in New York, this was a few years ago ... the boss said to the potential client what do you say it is an attractive contract for a few million dollars. And she as the lawyer for this particular deal, she would have stood to receive a percentage. And you know for a $500 million contract she would have got like you know half a percent. She was looking at a couple of million dollars coming into her pocket from it. She said we don't want to work with that man. "Why not?" The boss said. "It is an attractive investment. It is a $500 million contract. What's your concern?" The boss said. She said while we were sitting here did you see there was a fly that landed on the rim of his fruit juice. And he said: "Yeah, I guess I did." And did you see how he took his straw and knocked the fly into the dregs of his orange juice? And he said: "Yeah, that was kind of weird wasn't it?" Not only did he knock the fly into the dregs of his orange juice but he took his straw and held the fly down and* watched it squirm and drown at the bottom of his glass. He said: "Yeah, that was really pretty weird, wasn't it?" She said, we don't want to work with a guy who would treat other living beings like that. So, again, that might seem a bit of an extreme walking away from a couple of a million dollars on the life of a fly. But I also feel how "sila," the quality of virtue, informs moral integrity and informs our lives. Because that is a metaphor and that is a message to her bosses. Some people will have values which are profoundly respectful. And are based on a deep and very moral quality and that's more important than money. Someone would walk away from a couple of million dollars going into their account on the life of a fly, that's something that touched that person. I can be pretty sure that even today that that boss of that company won't forget that encounter. That's something that would have touched him and benefited him and thereby influenced his other considerations and encounters. And his own choices into the future.

Question 10: Is there an issue you would like to discuss or elaborate upon, which was not asked in the above questions? Please elaborate on anything else you would like to say about empathy, love, mindfulness, and peace? (Please explain in detail.)

Peace doesn't happen from having the world going quiet around us. Indeed, it doesn't even come without having problems or challenges in our lives. It doesn't come from things being easy or always being comfortable for us. But rather peace comes from the quality of understanding and openheartedness. The sense of the mind, the heart, open and attuned to the way things are and seeing things in their true light, free from the biases of fear, of aversion, of greed, and of delusion, habitual opinions and judgements. And so, for example, things are very calm and quiet in this lockdown situation [2020 pandemic lockdown in the UK and elsewhere], I am not sure where you are at the moment, but people are confined to their homes unless they are in essential work at hospitals or food suppliers, also the construction industry. So, a large, large proportion of the population both within the UK and around the world is in lockdown. It is a quiet situation. But it is also far from peaceful. And in this country alone, instances of domestic violence have escalated by a significant percent, by twenty or thirty percent. And so there is a lot of effort having the emergency services and the police and social services are having to deal with domestic violence because of people being in a quiet situation together. People could be at home. They don't have to go to work. They are with their families. But yet that quiet, contained, would be quiet situation actually is leading to far more conflict and violence and difficulty. So, I would say that when we want to be a person of peace the key thing is the attitude.

*Everything evolves around attitude. And part of that attitude is learning from the challenges that we experience. We are working with the challenges and difficulties of life rather than resenting them or fighting against them or blaming someone else for having produced them. So, "taking arms against a sea of troubles" in Hamlet's soliloquy [Shakespeare]. Or just going numb, just sort of shutting down, again with the lockdown, I understand there is a far greater consumption of alcohol and Netflix and the distractions than is usually the case. People going numb just sort of switching off and disconnecting when challenged when dealing with difficulty or frustration. So again, to quote Hamlet, "we are not just suffering the slings and arrows of outrageous fortune" [Shakespeare]. But rather those challenges there is a readiness to work with the way things are. To work with those challenges. And to learn from them whether we like them or not. So, peace I would say and peace and effective action, not just peace because peace doesn't mean passivity but peace and the capacity to work in an effective and skillful way to the greatest benefit comes from the attitude, having a skillful attitude and a readiness to learn from the challenges we experience. Whether it is what we like, what we don't like, success or failure, praise or criticism, gain or loss, comfort or discomfort. If there is a primary attitude of wanting to learn from way things are. And to work with the way things are, then the outcome is always going to be leading to a maximum benefit. And also, the mind, the heart of the individual, is peaceful along the way. The mind is not creating distress around things that are difficult. Or it is not trying to hang on to things which are pleasant and comfortable as we like them.*

\* \* \*

**Sister Peace, (Sister An Nghiem), Buddhist Nun, Sixty-Three Years Old**
**(African-American), Mahayana Tradition**
**Located in Santa Fe, New Mexico (Memphis, Tennessee) in the United States,**
**Disciple of Zen Master Thich Nhat Hanh**
**Question: How did you get involved with Buddhism and what made you become a nun? What was your journey? (Day 1 Interview)**
*Well, I guess I have to back to my days in politics. I worked for Mayor Anthony Williams in Washington, DC.[11] I worked on his election team and re-election team and I went into government with part of the executive office as mayor. I had spiritual study but I was really gung-ho [working for the*

*mayor]. Bit by bit some of my [spiritual] practices kind of fell off. Because it was really important to do these things. At one point I realized I was spiritually bereft and realized there was a void and I needed to get back into that particular practice. And then I thought of all the practices and things I studied throughout my life to that point, Buddhism was the one that really appealed to me. I had come from a Christian or Catholic background, which I also still embrace. I realized I needed to get back to practice, I needed to get grounded again. And I found a community in Washington, DC, called the "Washington Mindfulness Community" ... Then they asked me we have a committee on mindful politics, would you like to join it? I looked and thought there cannot be such a thing. But in fact there was. The committee was working to bring Thi [Thich Nhat Hanh] and the Plum Village monastics [in France] to come to Capitol Hill to have a retreat for [the U.S.] Congress. That was just fantastic to just be a part of that ... That is when I first met Thi [Thich Nhat Hanh] and it was a profound experience. It was profound to visit some of the Congressman and Senators offices at that time and to see in action what I later described as "altruistic politicians." The Dalai Lama and Thi know politics and they know politics is about the greater good for people ... They know about "ahimsa," which is non-violence and they know about "interbeing" which is another beautiful concept, not a concept it is a practice. It is a law of nature. Just as it is described in Voodoo, African-minded concept, I am here because you are there. You are there because I am here. We're all here because each other is here. No one is individually. So, I learned so much and eventually I started going to retreats and such and realized "wow! you can actually live in a monastery for a while. This is pretty cool." I put everything in storage and I went to one of our monasteries here in America, Deer Park [near San Diego in California; one of Thich Nhat Hanh's monasteries] and parked myself there for about 6 months. Then, one of the sisters there asked me "are you going to become a nun?" I thought, "Well I don't know." I came there to practice. I became attracted for lack of a better word because you live in community and you could practice all the time. You didn't have many of the distractions that we have in life. Which are not bad things, it is just the reality of life. So, I did go to Plum Village and lo and behold a couple of years later I was ordained in 2008 as a novice, in 2012 as a bhikkuni, in 2017 as a dharma teacher ... I was in Plum Village [France, where Thich Nhat Hanh resides] from 2006 to 2017 and came back to America to take care of my father, who eventually died that year.*

Question: What are your views on "gender and Buddhism'? Do you believe that nuns (bhikkuni) are treated the same as the monks (bhikku)?

*Historically not. Buddhism like Christianity and any other religion there are various means of interpretation. There are some who believe despite what the Buddha said, you have to be a monk to be enlightened. Well, our teacher [Thich Nhat Hanh] does not teach that and neither did the Buddha. But culturally things can sometimes come to be in different ways. But there are those traditions like our own where we are equanimous ... Bhikkhus [monks] and bhikkuni [nuns] each have our separate communities because of the vows we take but we also come together two or three times a week in Plum Village [Buddhist monastery in France founded by Thich Nhat Hanh] to practice. And we do many other things together. And Thi [Thich Nhat Hanh] set that as a beautiful example. And I remember monks and nuns from other traditions would come to visit and were surprised that nuns were walking next to Thi with reverence because Thi is a teacher. But it was two lines of monks and nuns. It was different than what others [other traditions] would practice was that oldest Bhikkuni would have to walk behind the youngest novice. And again I don't have a judgement on that. But that was one of the things that attracted me to our tradition. So, in the way we practice and how we embody our practice is always meant to inform others ... It is still hard. It is not to say it isn't hard ... The disparity does exist but it does not deter women to be nuns to be daughters of the Buddha.*

Question 1: What does the concept of "love" mean to you? (Please explain in detail.)

*To me love means, practice, it means to be as self-less as possible. When I think of love and the teachings of my teacher [Thich Nhat Hanh]. He talks about the four elements of love: my true love and kindness, compassion (karuna), joy (mudita), and equanimity (upeksha)*[12] *... How do we incorporate that into our lives. First of all, for us to accept ourselves, all parts of ourselves, so that we can be better able to look to others non-discriminately. For me, I touch it [love] in many different ways. I touch it [love] when I started going to the prisons to see the children [children in juvenile detention centers]. I have to tell you it felt like home. I experienced no fear. Somebody said to me: "Aren't you afraid?" I said: "how can I be afraid? We took the vows to go to the hell realm to help people to relieve suffering. That means also I have to relieve my own suffering. But I certainly could do what I can to help kids 12, 13, you know 17 years old negotiate a jail cell where they had a 6 x 8 cell to live in 24 hours a day. That made the bottom of the well of my compassion* to fall out ... It gives me great joy ... To see people as they are, not as we want them to be but to accept them or to practice, very hard to accept them as they are. Then, if we can see people as they "are" then we can reduce things like discrimination and judgement. Because we are all holding things like compassion, love, and joy.

**Question 3: How may a Buddhist understanding of "love" improve our world and make it a better place? (Please explain in detail.)**

I think you know the discourse on love and the way Thi [Thich Nhat Hanh] translates that. It is very beautiful ... But Thi has something called the four mantras. You know the idea is that we have to take care of ourselves, then our nuclear families, then concentrically the circles go out. In terms of who we can care for and help. The first mantra is you know: "Darling I am here for you." Can you imagine you are saying to someone you know to offer your presence and to know that you are there. When you are in their presence they have your attention ... The second mantra: "Darling I know you are there and I am so happy." To recognize the person in front of you, especially your beloved one, embracing them with mindfulness and presence of mind. To be recognized is an extraordinary thing. The third mantra is: "Darling I know you are suffering and that is why I am here for you." To be able to acknowledge the suffering of another. To know they are hurting even if they are not ready to talk about it. Just someone knows there is another human being that is having a deep empathy ... It enlightens that suffering ... The fourth one is: you know sometimes we believe our suffering is caused by other people and it makes it really hard for us to reach out to help. So, Thi's [Thich Nhat Hanh] fourth mantra is: "Darling I suffer, please help." I think if we can do that. We are expressing, we have trust, we have confidence, we have respect. We don't want to punish them or punish them any more if we walked away and closed the door behind us. But we suffer. And, it is an acknowledgement on our part we need more information. What you said, or did, or did not do, or say, hurt me. What courage or love it takes to be able to say that and ask for more clarification. If we need to have help at that point, then we also have ways of beginning anew and communicating better. I feel if people can practice any one or all of these four mantras. Acknowledging another. Letting the other know you are there. Recognizing their suffering. And sharing and recognizing their suffering with you. Then, I think it can and will grow concentrically. It will help us with many different practices, Buddhist or otherwise. So that, it can make the world a better place. And we can all practice love and peace ... But this is a deep place of commitment. That anchors us, even when things are rough.

Question 4: Do you believe a person can learn to love better? And, how does Buddhism help a person become a person of love and peace and therefore a better person? (Please explain in detail.)

Yes, I think that we can learn to love better. I think that Buddhism teaches us to turn the lens within and to help us to recognize and embrace what is happening within us and building our capacity to do that. To build our self-love, not a selfish love, but a self-compassionate love ultimately is what can help us to understand and to love others. I can just give you an example. This did not happen until I became a nun. I went to the African continent for the first time. What an extraordinary experience that was. Some of the things came up in me that I believed about my own folk because where I lived and the same year ending up in Britain where I could trace my descendent ... uh the slave owner to Britain. There I was I am looking at one of my brothers who is British. You know this is the land of my ancestors too. I am not just one thing. You know the conventional wisdom is that we focus on what is most obvious. And where there has been a lot of recognition of pain. But I went and visited one of the places there. I saw how the nobility treated the serfs. Let me tell you something. They did not look any different than the slave quarters in Winchester, Virginia. I thought my God if you could do this to your own people, no wonder you could do this to so-called someone else [to African-Americans]. I began to understand, not to condone but to have a sense of understanding maybe it was based on greed or selfishness the things that you do to preserve what you want and convince yourself you are only entitled to. But having that understanding you know made me realize the blood of both [African and English] runs through these veins. I had to begin to try to reconcile that in me. That makes love grow. That is really true love to have an understanding. We are taught without understanding there is not true love. Without respect there is not true love. Being able have these things for ourselves and those around us you begin to understand people. You begin to understand, so you have to treat people with respect.

Question 6: How does an average person become more "empathetic" and how does Buddhism help a person become more empathetic? (Please explain in detail.)

Empathy, yeah, when I thought about empathy. It made me think about "interbeing." You know the idea that we are all interconnected. You know how you address things yourself. You begin to see you know we all sort of here together. What we can do to help each other. If all the conditions in the world for us to come into being. What is it 1 in 400 trillion chances for us to be born a human.[13] If we can see that we are not on the one hand islands on the other we take refuge in the island of ourselves so that we can be there for ourselves and for other people. The idea of interbeing and interconnectedness. I think those things can help us to be more empathetic.

**Question 7: What does "mindfulness" mean to you from a Buddhist perspective? And, how does a person learn to become more mindful? (Please explain in detail.)**

*You know any time I go away what I tell anyone who I tell a little kid or I tell a grandfather. You know mindfulness is to have awareness. It is to be conscious in the present moment. You know Thi [Thich Nhat Hanh] will often say we can do our best to be a part-time Buddha. You know Buddha was mindful all the time but if we can be mindful part of the time we are doing pretty good. And it is a simple practice to remember to breath. Remember we are breathing whether we remember it or not. Being conscious and coming back to this moment. Being there for ourselves and for others. It doesn't mean you can't do anything else. You can't plan for the future or you can't examine the past. It just means you do it with awareness. You do it with intention. You know you do it and you are not doing anything else. You know it is what you call it mono-tasking. There is no such thing as multi-tasking right we know that. Multi-tasking is a juggler. A juggler is drawing one ball in the air at a time you know. And you know it is just one thing at a time if we can. We may have two or three things going but we really want to practice. Okay, I am going to walk. Okay, let's just walk. Let's not talk for a minute. Let's just enjoy walking. I'm about to eat. Am I aware of what I am eating. Am I aware of this carrot, this broccoli, am I aware where it came from? How it came here in front of me. Am I aware how I am speaking? Am I speaking as harmlessly as possible? That is my practice. What I am saying to whomever I am saying. Am I speaking clearly? Am I speaking in a tone that is disarming. Am I aware of what I am saying. Am I listening to this person. Being able to have the courage to say. Now is not a good time, I really want to share what you are saying. You know I am not with it right now. How about if we get back together in an hour or tomorrow? When I can be more fully present for you. And this mindfulness is everything you do to cooking, going to the bathroom, brushing our teeth, opening a door, turning on a light, whatever it has to be can we bring our full awareness in that moment to what it is we are doing.*

**Question 9: How do we make a more peaceful world? What can average people do to make the world more peaceful from a Buddhist perspective? (Please explain in detail.)**

*Well, I think it is both individually and collectively. You know Thi [Thich Nhat Hanh] teaches peace in ourselves and peace in the world. So, those are two things. So, how can we bring peace in the world if there is not peace in ourselves? So, when in fact there is peace in ourselves there is peace in the world. So, we can affect others to do the same. So, it is both an individual and a collective arrangement you could say. We have to work on both. During the times of protest. During wars we have so-called angry peace activists. Well, that is a bit of an anomaly. They may be rightfully angry but they want to practice peacefully. And there are some situations where understandable you don't do that and you can't do that. There are situations where you saw here [following death of George Floyd] and the riots were angry at first and then gradually they became peaceful ... So, it is not mutually exclusive. You cannot have one without the other.*

**Question 13: What are your views of "dukkha" (suffering) and how does the Buddhist understanding help us to overcome suffering?**

*I think that sometimes we are afraid of suffering and we think that the purpose of life is not suffer but the Buddha taught us that suffering is a part of life. And it's not that we want to stamp it out and we want to repress it. We want to take a look at it and we want to see how we can transform it. Turn it into a gem or pearl of wisdom that informs us or perhaps as a conveyor that informs other people. You know we feel and this is part of our culture [American] too that things should be good all the time but forgetting the value of suffering. You know the lotus is an iconic, an iconic symbol in the Buddhist cosmology because it grows only in the mud. It is one of the most beautiful and delicate beings on the planet but it only grows in the mud and grows through muddy water before it breaches the surface of the water and becomes this beautiful thing called a lotus. And this is an analogy for us. You know garbage and fertilizer makes the most beautiful gardens and orchards and fruit trees. So, if we look at it non-discriminately in terms of I am suffering and I need to get to the bottom of this and knowing that it is going to turn into a beautiful insight that can be shared with others in addition for us to feel whatever stress or trauma we have gone through.*

**Follow-up Question: What was it like growing up African-American in Washington, DC, anywhere you like to begin? (Day 2 Interview)**

*It was a palpable time even as a young child. I remember the death of King [Dr. Martin Luther King, Jr.] even as the reactions of adults around me ... I come from a family of six and I am in the middle ... So, I was quite sort of independent ... My mother worked teaching nursing and my father spent his life working for the post office. Yet, they managed to get 6 kids through parochial school. If we wanted to go to college, they committed to taking out loans and things like that. So, I feel very fortunate. I went to Georgetown University. I have always had an interest in, back then it was called "New Age," but I have always had an interest in you know meditation, various other subjects. It really put me in good stead. Through my investigations I came across many different things. I got a really broad education in these subjects. Many years passed and eventually working in politics. I left and did some contracting. But then I allowed myself to let go some of my spiritual practices. I look back on and what was the most meaningful. What did I connect with the most? Which was not to cast aside my Christian or Catholic upbringing but I felt that I had to sort of go deeper into spirituality rather than dogma. I think I told you before that a nun said: "God is everywhere." So, mama if God is everywhere why do I have to go to church? My mana said get yourself out of bed and get ready for church. I am so grateful for that. At the moment, of course, at that time I did not have as much latitude as I do now. But that gave me a very strong spiritual background and foundation ... I did find something that worked for me .... I became connected with the "Washington Mindful Committee" ... By the time I get to Plum Village ... There is one in Mississippi called the Magnolia Grove Monastery. They have a gorgeous statue there of Thi [Thich Nhat Hanh] and Dr. King [Dr. Martin Luther King, Jr.] holding a scroll called the "beloved community" ... This statue really appealed to me because it represented two of my teachers Thi [Thich Nhat Hanh] and Dr. King [Dr. Martin Luther King, Jr.]. Part of the reason I was even attracted to Thi was because I knew Dr. King nominated Thi for the Nobel Peace Prize in 1967 because of the [Vietnam] War ... So, I would walk over to the statue and I would do some walking meditation ... I would look up and say [to myself] "how did you all do it?" You know what they were able to accomplish was just extraordinary. The real question I was asking was how did you get over this little pittance stuff that really could impede our progress. Our practice is we have to recognize it and find out our understanding ... I guess the question I was asking was how did you get through all this stuff and you prevailed and did so much for so many.*

**Follow-up Question:** I want to take you back to your childhood and ask you when you first experienced racism in this country? (Day 2 Interview)

*Well, I was born in [19]56 and when I started going to school. It was a parochial school but it was mostly Black. I guess when I became aware of it was when I would hear the adults talk about it. That's when I, my first memories about it, was when I would hear about that ... And of course when Dr. King was assassinated [in 1968] and all the bleeding that was happening all over the world ... Memories of having, just awareness of, and when I was just a little girl, things happened but I did not know what it meant until I was an adult ... I would go shopping with my grandmother and we would go to the department stores in downtown [Washington] DC. Most of those stores now have closed. We would go to the dress department and she would look for dresses and I would always say: "Grammy why don't you try them on." And she would say, "Honey I don't need to try them on, I'll just try them on when we get home." Little did I know she was saving me the possible pain or trauma you know asking for a fitting room and then being turned down because we were Black. And I didn't realize that until I was an adult. She was also careful to take me to places where she knew we could be served ... So, yeah, and when I got older I was so grateful ... You know when I did realize I went "Oh wow!" You know ... As I was an adult ... You know I grew up in a Black neighborhood and I went to predominately Black schools ... I knew racism was out there. I did not have any personal instances. But I did as an adult. I remember for instance ... But I remember working and working downtown and trying to get back and forth for work and a number of times I couldn't catch a cab [taxi cab]. You know I was a Black female and you know I was dressed professionally. But cabs would go by before someone would pull over. So, it just didn't happen to men of course. And then sometimes I would ask a white colleague, "you know I don't have time" and have them catch a cab for me. There was Barack Obama as a Senator experienced this. There wasn't many Black people who didn't experience this ... Then of course walking in a store and if I'm with another friend say with much lighter complexion or Hispanic or White, you know who they would follow right? The security you know ... So, yes, I guess I became more aware of it when I was older ... It wasn't until I became a monastic that I went to Africa for the first time. I actually went three times. It was a profound experience to go to Africa, the motherland of all human beings. It is just extraordinary, especially after I had some training and experience. I remember hearing ... Sometimes you don't know it is trauma until after the fact. I remember hearing an adult they needed a doctor or lawyer about whether you should get a Black one or a White one. You know because the White ones were better educated and could represent you better in a court of law ... I heard this conversation you know when I was younger. But it did not connect with my own thinking until I was in Africa. You know I saw folks who looked like me in charge of everything ... And I realized could this be true and not only was it true but it was wonderful and it was okay. You know with white supremacy or colonization you actually begin to believe what they say about you. As a child I believed what I* heard, of what the adults were saying. As painful as it was to have that realization, I was so grateful for it. It was like pulling out these worms that made me doubt who I was or how good any other person of color might have been because we are always told how less than, half than, gotta work harder than ... I was in Botswana, six or seven years ago ... Of course, I knew those things weren't true but when I was faced with a reality. I did not know those worms had been planted there. So, you know I didn't get angry. I just embraced it. I saw the hospitals in Africa and the nurses run the hospitals and I saw doctors and CEOs. And I met this beautiful activist and human rights attorney and when I was sitting with her was actually when I came up. I was happy to have seen it. I was happy to have seen it.

Follow-up Question: What are your thoughts on the #BlackLivesMatter Movement? (Day 2 Interview)

Well, a lot of people have difficulty with it ... You know all lives matter, this lives matter, and no one is saying that isn't true. What we're saying is the simplest thing I say is the Black lives matter too. Where the emphasis is on "too." And finally, after George Floyd and these string of things happened and after by the way. Some people are realizing, something woke up in them. It's right. They are treated differently. And we do need to do better. And it's a question about us too. Our lives are as important as anybody else's life. That's what we're saying. And we're not treated equally, especially in the eyes of the law and other instances as well. The short answer for me is that Black lives matter too.

Follow-up Question: What are your thoughts on the resolution to #BlackLivesMatter, coming after this in a conflict resolution mode? (Day 2 Interview)

I think in the larger picture which is what had to happen is that people woke up. And not just people of color but everybody. And it is not just people in America but it is everywhere. People have woken up and that's the first thing. What they say in Buddhism is real recognition. You have to recognize and see what the truth is. And then taking action to help transform. And like I said the people who could help with transforming are police, health care, education ... all of these areas. And when those things are addressed to help one segment of the population, it really does lift up the whole population.

Follow-up Question: How does awareness about #BlackLivesMatter play into the idea of "mindfulness" from a Buddhist perspective? (Day 2 Interview)

In "mindfulness" we talk about "interbeing." And we inter-are and the world inter-is. You know just with the planet and of course it's like that with people even though it's not manifested that way yet. Uhm ... There is also the *law of impermanence. That is things change. The only constant in the universe is change. And we are at a precipice of that right now, which is a beautiful thing. It is a painful thing. It's you know it can be a struggle. People have lost their lives. People have risked their lives protesting in a time of a pandemic. You know but sometimes that is part of what it is. You don't have to harken back far to the Civil Rights [Movement]. Back then [during the Civil Rights era], people put their lives on the line and were trained how to be non-violent. So, I don't even want to say concepts, I don't know how to describe them, but Buddhism of interbeing, of being interdependent ... Simply to say we inter-are, we inter-be and the law of impermanence. These things are now coming to the fore. You know things change. Regimes come and go. There is an incline and there is a decline. You know there are paradigm shifts. Right now, the paradigm is not only shifting but it is shattering and that is really good news.*

Photograph of Vietnamese Buddhist monk Thich Nhat Hanh

Photograph of Buddhist monk Geshe Lama Phuntsho

7 EMPATHY, LOVE, AND PEACE 291

Photograph of Buddhist monk Geshe Lobsang Tsultrim

Photograph of Buddhist monk Ajahn Amaro Bikkhu

## 7 EMPATHY, LOVE, AND PEACE 293

Photograph of Buddhist nun Sister Peace (An Nghiem)

## INTRODUCTION

In examining these Buddhist narratives, we see how varied and rich in information they are. Even so, they are not representative of Buddhism, as Buddhism has many traditions, many voices, and because of this there are many Buddhisms. What is depicted here is partial and a metaphor for "some" Buddhist thought. From the narratives though, many questions come to mind which I will touch on here through my analyses of them, namely, what is love? What is peace? How do we create a better world, and so on. Again, my sampling is not all-inclusive, only three Buddhist monks and one Buddhist nun were interviewed. So, the information received is limited, but it is qualitative and, as such, like the other narratives in this book, it is a metaphor for broader issues.

According to the Buddhists I spoke with and interviewed, true love is without attachment. True love is unconditional. This was the message of Geshe Lama Phuntsho. Buddhism also teaches gratitude. We need to be grateful about what we eat, the air we breathe, and so on. It is also gratitude according to Phuntsho that may help us love the world better and make it a better place. In order to make the world a better place you have to help yourself first according to Geshe Phuntsho. One cannot expect to help others without helping oneself first. Also, Phuntsho does not believe in the concept of "empathy" because to him it is too distant. Instead, he believes in what he calls "brave love," because it takes a lot of bravery to love and to love in the right way.

On the other hand, Geshe Lobsang Tsultrim echoes some of what Geshe Phuntsho said by stating we have to love ourselves and how we are dependent on others. If you do not love others, you cannot survive. It is what is called the "compassionate way" in his monk training. Tsultrim also talks about changing one's attitude to be more positive, which then leads to changing the structure of the mind to be positive. Positive thinking is very powerful. In psychological terms, it is known as "cognitive behavior therapy."[14]

Ajahn Amaro Bhikkhu's answers are more lengthy. In terms of love, Amaro Bikkhu discusses two types of love: possessive love and liberative love. The former is attributed with attachments and suffering. The latter, liberative love, is without attachment and includes compassion and empathy according to Buddhist tradition. Specifically, Amaro Bikkhu states that liberative love is about loving kindness, compassion, sympathetic joy and serenity, which are also qualities of mind. Amaro also discusses why possessive love is a problem and can be a problem. The idea all sorts of suffering results from possessing another and not letting go. But possession also extends toward our own identities. I'm from here or there and those attachments of identity also do damage to people because they are possessions of identity. Letting go in the Buddhist tradition allows the individual not to suffer. To be free of attachments according to Amaro Bikkhu is liberating. Likewise, Amaro discusses how to become more empathetic by letting go of the self. Of letting go of I, my, myself, and letting go of I must, I should, and comparing oneself to others in unhelpful ways. Empathy to him means having compassion for oneself and for others.

Similarly, Sister Peace discusses the acceptance of self and promotion of selflessness and she quotes from her teacher, Zen Master Thich Nhat Hanh, on four types of love: my true love and kindness, compassion, joy, and equanimity. She also quotes from him in answering the question about how a Buddhist concept of love may make a better world by stating from Thich Nhat Hanh the four mantras of loving another: "Darling I am here for you'; "darling I know you are there and I am so happy'; "darling I know you are suffering and that is why I am here for you'; "darling I suffer, please help." This is a very compelling perspective about how to better love your beloved.

Another important subject for the interviews was peace, specifically how can Buddhism make the world more peaceful. For example, Geshe Lama Phuntsho remarked you cannot change the whole world at once. However, one may do so gradually and change one person at a time. Geshe Phuntsho also emphasized the reason we have conflict is because of lack of communication. He said: "We don't have time to listen." For Geshe Lobsang Tsultrim peace comes after ethics and morality. Tsultrim also mentioned six virtues for peace: generosity, ethics, patience, effort, concentration, and wisdom. On the other hand, for Ajahn Amaro Bikkhu, peace begins with the individual, and from the individual, there may be a peaceful world. He gave examples of how the individual may create more peace within institutions and thereby to create less structural violence. Sister Peace (An Nghiem) echoes Amaro Bikkhu in that peace begins with the individual and that we have to work both individually and collectively for peace.

Another major theme in the interview was asking the Buddhist monks and Buddhist nun about "mindfulness" as it is so central to Buddhism. Geshe Lama Phuntsho commented: "One thing we always say is that if you want to meditate then motivation is important. If you want to use meditation in your daily life, then mindfulness is important." While Geshe Lobsang Tsultrim talks about real mindfulness by being mindful of where you go, what you eat, how you speak, and what you think are all aspects of mindfulness by paying attention to one's actions, speech-actions, and mind; by contrast, Ajahn Amaro Bikkhu provides the most detailed speech on the subject of mindfulness. Amaro quotes the Buddha by declaring: "mindfulness is the path to the deathless, heedlessness is the path to death." Thus, Amaro Bikkhu examines the subject of mindfulness in extensive specifics. He discusses the four foundations or four domains of mindfulness as: kayanupassana, the contemplation of the body; vedananupassana, the contemplation of sensations; cittanupassana, the mindfulness of mind states; and lastly, dhammanupassana, the process of experiencing itself. All of these different facets encompass mindfulness. On the other hand, An Nghiem, Sister Peace, talks about being aware and having awareness and being conscious in the present moment; she also talks about mono-tasking, doing one thing at a time and doing things with intention.

One of the unique aspects of these Buddhist interviews which came to the fore was the issue of "racism" as discussed by Sister Peace, An Nghiem, especially what it was like for her to grow up African-American and discussing the recent #BlackLivesMatter protests over the death of George Floyd. She mentioned when she was a girl how her grandmother was too embarrassed to ask to use the fitting room on the chance she might be rejected because of her race; and also as a young professional Black woman how difficult it was to get a taxi cab in Washington, DC, because of her race. Another persuasive message brought forward was Sister Peace's recognition about her own identity in being Black and being descendant from Black slaves and White slave owners and how serfs were treated in Medieval England. She expressed how the slave quarters she encountered in Virginia were the same as serf quarters in Medieval England. Then she said: "I thought my God if you could do this to your own people, no wonder you could do this to so-called someone else [to African-Americans]." Additionally, she commented on the #BlackLivesMatter movement following the death of George Floyd and how there had been a general awakening across the United States and why this change was for the good. This also brought forth her opinions about inter-being, how we are all interrelated and why this is consequential in terms of people's self-realization. Sister Peace stated: "Right now, the paradigm is not only shifting but it is shattering and that is really good news" because of the protests from the George Floyd murder and #BlackLivesMatter movement.

\* \* \*

Aside from these narratives what may Buddhism tell us in general about peace and peacebuilding. One of the more significant concepts is "inter-being," which is an idea respecting all people and all life, and which all the Buddhist respondents shared. As Thich Nhat Hanh (1987/2005: 88) observes: "I am, therefore you are. You are, therefore I am. That is the meaning of the word 'interbeing.' We interare." In mindfulness training according to Nhat Hanh they make promises to do no harm: "The first promise is: 'I vow to develop my compassion in order to love and protect the life of people, animals, plants, and minerals.' The second promise is: 'I vow to develop understanding in order to be able to love and to live in harmony with people, animals, plants, and minerals'" (Nhat Hanh 1987/2005: 89). Added on to these, there are the fourteen mindfulness trainings, which begin with training the mind according to the teachings of Buddha (Nhat Hanh 1987/2005: 90). It is essential to understand all fourteen of these trainings in order to create an "inter-being" awareness through "mindfulness," which I am excerpting here. The first is: "Aware of the suffering created by fanaticism and intolerance." The second is: "Aware of the suffering created by attachment to views and wrong perceptions." The third is: "Aware of the suffering brought about when we impose our views on others." The fourth is: "Aware that looking deeply at the nature of suffering can help us develop compassion and find ways out of suffering." The fifth is: "Aware that true happiness is rooted in peace, solidity, freedom, and compassion." The sixth is: "Aware that anger blocks communication and creates suffering." The seventh is: "Aware that life is available only in the present moment and that it is possible to live happily in the here and now." The eighth is: "Aware that the lack of communication always brings separation and suffering." The ninth is: "Aware that words can create suffering or happiness." The tenth is: "Aware that the essence and aim of a Sangha [a Buddhist community of monks, nuns, novices, and laity] is the practice of understanding and compassion." The eleventh is: "Aware that great violence and injustice have been done to our environment and society." The twelfth is: "Aware that much suffering is caused by war and conflict." The thirteenth is: "Aware of the suffering caused by exploitation, social injustice, stealing, and oppression." The fourteenth is: "(For lay members): Aware that sexual relations motivated by craving cannot dissipate the feeling of loneliness but will create more suffering, frustration, and isolation" (Nhat Hanh 2005: 90–103). In other words and according to Thich Nhat Hanh—a Zen Master Buddhist monk, who in many regards is a living saint—how does one become aware of human suffering and what can be done to prevent it.

If anything was learned from the previous chapters, it is that suffering is quite extensive and humans attach themselves to all sorts of identities however wrongly—nationalism and racism, for example, leading to in some cases extremes like terrorism from the former and genocide from the latter. As the Buddhist monks and Buddhist nun alluded to in conversation, one of the most prominent ideas from Buddhism is inter-being. The notion that a flower is not just a flower but it embodies in it "soil, rain, and sunshine. It is also full of clouds, oceans, and minerals. It is even full of space and time. In fact, the whole cosmos is present in this one little flower" (Nhat Hanh 2017: 11). And just as a flower embodies the wider wholes of the cosmos, so do we through our parents and grandparents and through "education, food, and culture" (Nhat Hanh 2017: 12). We are all part of complex wholes. This is why not only protecting ourselves is important, but so too our environments. As Thich Nhat Hanh (2017: 13) opines: "The whole planet is one giant, living, breathing cell, with all its working parts linked in symbiosis." If only we, all of us, could have a greater sense of inter-being and know how we are all interconnected and interlinked might we have a better world with less conflict in it.

\* \* \*

Another lesson to be drawn from Buddhism is what we can learn from it in terms of science and what we may say about religion in general from cognitive and evolutionary perspectives. As Robert Wright (2017: 266), in his book *Why Buddhism Is True*, quips: "There's a lot to dislike about the world we're born into. It's a world in which, as the Buddha noted, our natural way of seeing, and of being, leads us to suffer and to inflict suffering on others. And it's a world that, as we now know, was bound to be that way, given that life on this planet was created by natural selection. Still, it may also be a world in which metaphysical truth, moral truth, and happiness can align, and a world that, as you start to realize that alignment, appears more and more beautiful. If so, this hidden order—an order that seems to lie at a level deeper than natural selection itself—is something to marvel at." If Wright is correct and I think he might be, then there is much to appreciate through Buddhist philosophy as a particular worldview.

Buddhism like Jainism began around the fourth century BC as one of the great religions of renunciation in the Ganges Basin (See Laidlaw 2004b). By the eleventh century it had largely disappeared from the Indic peninsula and survived in Southeast Asia and in Southeast Asian kingdoms (Laidlaw 2004b: 91). Indeed, Buddhism would survive and develop several traditions throughout Asia, and eventually throughout the world, including even in the West. And although it is not my purpose here to describe Buddhism's historicity, I am more interested in analyzing how Buddhism may be complimentary to science and in analyzing it from the perspective of an anthropology of religion (see Laidlaw 2004b for a more in-depth historical analysis).

Thus, Buddhism unlike many religions has both "doctrinal" and "imagistic" modes, which follow particular doctrines in some forms and in others ecstatic rituals, which Laidlaw (2004b: 106) describes as "modes dynamics." In turn, these divergent modes of religiosity according to Harvey Whitehouse (2004: 64–74) may be tied to certain memories with doctrinal religio-modes (texts) more tied to semantic memories and with ecstatic religio-practices (rituals) with episodic memories. Whitehouse (2000: 1) expounds on these differences this way: "The imagistic mode consists of the tendency, within certain small-scale or regionally fragmented ritual traditions and cults, for revelations to be transmitted through sporadic collective action, episodes, and producing highly cohesive and particularistic social ties. By contrast, the doctrinal mode of religiosity consists of the tendency, within many regional and world religions, for revelations to be codified as a body of doctrines, transmitted through routinized forms of worship, memorized as part of one's "general knowledge," and producing large, anonymous communities." The fact that Buddhism in its many forms throughout the world may have both of these different religio-features, "imagistic" and "doctrinal," tells us how complex Buddhism as a religion and philosophy is.

Nonetheless, explaining religion from a cognitive perspective tends to be difficult because religions tend to connect with varying systems in the brain whether by inference or recall or communication or emotion or those underlining sociality. The religions "that do *all* are the religious ones we actually observe in human societies. They are most successful because they combine features relevant to a variety of mental systems" (Boyer 2001: 50). Generally speaking, religions have in common "the presence of minimally counterintuitive beliefs in religious belief sets favors the production, transmission, and cultural survival of those belief sets over time" (Atran 2002: 108). Likewise: "Humans have a metarepresentational ability to form representations of representations. This ability allows people to understand a drawing or picture of someone or something *as a drawing or picture* and not the real thing. It lets us enjoy novels and movies *as fiction* that can emotionally arouse us without actually threatening us." In sum, metarepresentation also allows us to comprehend religious thought, past and future events distinct from the present, and interact with each other's minds in comprehending abstractions (Atran 2002: 108). Regardless, the capacity of metarepresentation is "common to everyday cognition and communication and not particular to religion" (Atran 2002: 108). Suffice it to say there are many other cognitive processes stimulated by religio-experience depending whether or not it is ecstatic ritual or doctrinal memorization. Likewise, Buddhism because of its varying practices across the world may stimulate different cerebral regions dependent on practice, differing from meditation to doctrinal recitation and so on.

Apart from analyzing Buddhism as a religion and what religions in general have in common from cognitive and evolutionary perspectives, what do Buddhism and neuroscience have in common? Or rather, what may neuroscience learn from Buddhism and vice versa? Therefore, as per B. Allan Wallace (2007: 166): "The very categories of mind and matter, space and time, and mass and energy are human, conceptual constructs superimposed on the world of experience, and they have no existence apart from the conceptual frameworks in which they are conceived." In general, scientists have studied medium- and low-level bandwidths of human consciousness, whereas many Buddhists are interested in high-energy states of consciousness (Wallace 2007: 167). Thus, "Buddhist contemplatives have been principally interested in developing "high-energy" states of consciousness, in which *samadhi*, the primary "technology" of contemplative inquiry, plays a crucial role. In contemplative as well as scientific inquiry, truth and measurement technology are inextricably linked. Since the possibility of the higher-frequency range of consciousness has hardly been considered by cognitive scientists, such states have never been factored into the scientific account of the mind."

On the one hand, the separate truths of Buddhism and science are very divergent, yet on the other, they may be complementary as well. "Science has provided multiple conceptual revolutions in our way of viewing reality, but these have had little impact on the cultivation of genuine happiness or virtue. The contemplative traditions of the world [like Buddhism] have provided multiple experiential revolutions in ways of viewing reality, which have directly altered the hearts, minds, and lives of those who have acquired such contemplative insights and indirectly influenced their host societies" (Wallace 2007: 168). Similarly, Matthieu Ricard and Wolf Singer (2017) debate how Buddhism and neuroscience divergently examine the mind through empirical observation and discuss shared topics of interest concerning the mind, self, consciousness, the unconscious, free-will, epistemology, meditation, and neuroplasticity. In other words, science may learn much from Buddhism in terms of understanding mind, consciousness, and the unconscious—ponderings in Buddhism for the last 2500 years and much longer than the tradition of Western science.

\* \* \*

In this chapter, apart from the analyses of the Buddhist narratives, I discuss varying subjects. One subject is why peaceworkers should be more celebrated in our society and by peaceworkers I mean all those who work for the betterment of others such as teachers, psychologists, social workers, emergency physicians, nurses and so on—those who are largely unrecognized but no doubt make our world a better place. Another aspect of this chapter is analyzing the concept of love in-depth from the inspiration of Dr. Martin Luther King, Jr. to the meaning and scientific understanding of romantic love. Lastly, I discuss why a "re-indigenization" of society makes sense. In other words, appreciating our environment and the world we live in before mass-extinction takes place and before climate tragedy happens beyond repair. This last part of the chapter on "re-indigenization" is similar to the analysis of "inter-being'—how we are all interrelated and need each other for the survival of the planet.

## It's Not Batman, or Superman, or Wonder Woman, but Peaceworkers

When I was growing up, DC Comics and comic heroes like "Batman," "Superman," and "Wonder Woman" were ubiquitous at local convenient store stands. I remember eagerly reading about the so-called comic book *Justice League* and how these fictional heroes gathered forces and jointly fought off evil foes.[15] The heroic exploits extended to Saturday morning cartoons in the 1970s to 1980s with the "Super Friends."[16] In grade school, I too had learned about Greek myths and Greek mythological heroes. So, there were overlaps in my readings about fictional heroes.

Today, I look back on these years and wonder how much such readings have shaped my current worldview. I know now the world is a much more complex place than comic books and Greek myths allude to. Even so, these past fictional heroes are still etched in my mind.

Most real heroes we know have feet of clay as indicated in the Book of Daniel in the Bible but so too in Lord Byron's poem "Ode to Napoleon Buonaparte" (1814):

> Those Pagod things of sabre sway
> With fonts of brass, and feet of clay.[17]

The hero, Napoleon Buonaparte, is flawed, as all humans are and whether or not, one's heroes are American presidents, or military leaders, or civil rights leaders, or peace activists, and so on. This is also why the Greek mythological gods were so knowable and relatable because they are so humanlike. It is also how comic book heroes are depicted today, as human and imperfect, in films such as *Iron Man*, also the super-ego of character Tony Stark.[18]

Moreover, Mohandas Gandhi, despite being an icon for peace and political peace movements worldwide, allegedly mistreated women in his life, including his wife.[19] Likewise, Dr. Martin Luther King, Jr. supposedly had several extra-marital affairs with women. On the other hand, more recently, there have been more dubious claims from newly revealed FBI reports about King's behavior as noted by historian David Garrow.[20] Yet, as other historians have rightly pointed out, much of these allegations are based upon rumors.[21]

Regardless, all human heroes, as mentioned, and no matter how famous, are flawed in some way because they are human. More importantly, the historic peaceful actions of both Mohandas Gandhi and Dr. Martin Luther King, Jr. are undeniable and worthy of timeless praise. Their historic influences and legacies in how we view mediation, peace, and peaceful movements have left indelible impressions upon our world and also both men live on today in how we create a more peaceful existence.

It is my contention that we celebrate not only great peace heroes like Gandhi and King but the ones who are everyday peacemakers and peaceworkers. Here, by peacemaker and peaceworker, I mean broadly those who work toward making a better society and through their actions create a more livable and peaceful coexistence. Such monikers for these "everyday people," may seem unusual for those who actually work in peace studies, but I think not.

Most are unsung heroes like teachers working in lower socio-economic public schools; or psychiatrists working in mental health clinics; or nurses in hospitals and different health settings; or medical doctors in emergency rooms; or social workers; or psychologists; or many governmental workers; or firemen; or policemen; or public defenders; or clergy who defend migrants; or clergy working with the poor; or those who work with the homeless; and all those who spend their careers in mediation and working in conflict resolution and peace studies. Some of these unsung heroes may find it strange, I call them peaceworkers, but I think it can be argued they are indeed such people for making our own existence more peaceable.

And while we have made so many notable technological advancements, we hardly think how we have socially advanced toward better living.

There are so many unsung heroes who work behind the scenes in order to make our world a better place but we barely recognize them at all. As a society, we seem to be fixated by the lives of the Kardashians, or The Real Housewives of Beverly Hills, or The Real Housewives of New Jersey, or Hollywood movie stars, or rock stars, or sports stars, and so on, rather than those everyday heroes making our society livable and more peaceable.[22]

We seem to forget how beyond the false glamor and veneer of the Hollywood-ization of America, there are those who work every day to make the world a better place for everyone. So, why are the everyday heroes "not" celebrated as much as they should be? Or, why are those working toward peace and those working in mediation less known and often ignored? It seems many of us would rather aspire to fame and wealth than work toward meaningful change. But there are enough of the latter in society who continue to do good works despite the non-recognition. Undoubtedly, most working toward a better world and those working toward making society better do so out of a sense of duty and a love of their work. Most of these good people do not expect to be recognized, nor want to be.

What is more, we know our world today is a much less violent place than it was in the distant past according to the likes of Steven Pinker in his well-regarded book (2011) *The Better Angels of Our Nature: Why Violence Has Declined*.[23] And even though I believe Pinker's thesis to be generally true, there is still so much work to be done. For example, we cannot deny the numerous genocides of the twentieth century, inclusive of the Holocaust. Nor can we deny the impact of World War II on humanity and its estimation of 70 million worldwide deaths, or even the almost 22 million deaths from World War I.[24] Nor can we also deny the human propensity in general for being peaceable as evident by the work of the likes of anthropologist Douglas Fry (2006, 2007, 2013). It may be that prior to the Agricultural Revolution around 10,000–15,000 human societies as a whole were more peaceable. This would be most of human existence on the planet!

On the other hand, World War II was responsible for more worldwide deaths in the millions than any previous war.[25] And yet, if we compare the millions of deaths in either World War I or World War II to the distant past and more distant wars, we find that in comparison to the general world population these wars in the twentieth century were dwarfed by past major conflicts—an example, the Mongol conquests of the thirteenth and fourteenth centuries, with deaths numbering as much as 40 million out of an estimated global 380 million population, or 10 percent of world deaths.[26] On the other hand, World War II caused approximately 3 percent of worldwide death of the 2.3 billion population at the time.[27]

Moreover, since World War II the major economic world powers have not fought each other and in historical terms this post-war period has been labelled the "Long Peace" by historian John Lewis Gaddis.[28] However, major world powers, such as the United States, have invaded smaller countries and have caused much damage as in conflicts in Vietnam, El Salvador, Nicaragua, Iraq, Afghanistan, and so on. Hence, the label of "peace" may be overstated.

In sum, my point is that because violence is overall decreasing as a trend among humans from the past to present, we should be more mindful of those who actually make our society better from day to day. We should be mindful of those "unsung heroes" who day in and day out work in "helping people." They are not Supermen or Wonder Women per se as comic heroes, but certainly are in their own right, and in a real way they are "the real heroes." They make a difference in people's lives. And these differences have wide reaching consequences and effects—peaceful outcomes.

Additionally, all the major world religions—Hinduism, Buddhism, Judaism, Christianity, and Islam—all promote charity and peace and betterment. As such, the peace project does not have to be limited to practitioners or specialists but something we may share in, even in small ways. As the author and activist Arundhati Roy wrote in her 1997 novel *The God of Small Things*: "And the air was full of Thoughts and Things to say. But at times like these, only the Small Things are ever said. Big Things lurk unsaid inside."[29] May the small actions of helping people become big things and may they be celebrated more often.

## In the Name of "Love"

This section's heading borrows from the rock band U2's song "Pride (In the Name of Love)," commemorating Dr. Martin Luther King, Jr. and the resounding lyrics: "One man come in the name of love … what more in the name of love? In the name of love." Indeed, these words resonate with me in more than one way and echo in my mind. So too, I hear King himself stating the prophetic words: "Darkness cannot drive out darkness; only light can do that."[30]

Perhaps we need some Promethean light for an expansive examination of these very human thoughts on "LOVE." As such, there are two primary directions for this section.

In one direction, I wish to emphasize the necessity for politicians and others to be "love" directed in their thinking in order to adopt policies of "empathy" and "empathic politics" which in turn inform how to overcome some of our worst social problems. Secondly, I wish to explore ideas of "love" from Buddhist and Christian points of view, thereby allowing us to contemplate where we go from here.

Recently, I was heartened by the new Prime Minister of New Zealand Jacinda Ardern's words, who was elected in 2017 at the young age of thirty-seven, and also became a new mother.[31] No doubt "motherhood" has informed her thinking in bringing compassion, empathy, and kindness into the political realm over realpolitik and Machiavellian power games. Truly, I wish we had more un-cynical politicians like her in the United States.

Ardern articulated her view right before being sworn in as the NZ PM in 2017: "I know I need to transcend politics in the way that I govern for this next term of Parliament but I also want this government to feel different, I want people to feel that it's open, that it's listening and that it's going to bring kindness back … I know that will sound curious but to me if people see they have an empathetic government I think they'll truly understand that when we're making hard calls that we're doing it with the right focus in mind." Such a view of humanity, and governance, is enlightening and enlightened and perhaps has its antecedents for her from Christianity?[32]

Regardless of the origins of Ardern's message, it is an important one. Why not expand it to include some Buddhist ideas about compassion and love and kindness and caring aside from Christian ones.

Why not compare how Buddhism and Christianity inform our philosophical thinking on the subject of "love"? This is not to say most other major religions are not equally important on the subject of "love" whether they be Baha'i, or Islam, or Judaism, or Jainism, or Hinduism, or Sikhism, and so on. They are all of course significant.

However, for my purposes here, my views will be informed by those of Thich Nhat Hanh on Buddhism and C.S. Lewis on Christianity and in very limited ways to elucidate this discussion.

In my mind, two very important concepts from Buddhism are: "inter-being" and "mindfulness." For this exposition, I turn to the writings of Thich Nhat Hanh, because for many reasons he is likely a living saint, if there is such a possibility. The idea of "inter-being" is according to him that everyone and everything in the known universe is interconnected. As he explains in his book *Living Buddha, Living Christ* (1995/2007: 11): "When we look into the heart of a flower, we see clouds, sunshine, minerals, time, the earth, and everything else in the cosmos in it."

A biologist might say, well these are symbiotic relationships. Hanh's Buddhist view likewise would seem to support the controversial "Gaia hypothesis," whereby the Earth is a self-maintaining and complex interrelated system between inorganic matter and organic matter.

The lesson here is that we are all inter-beings on this planet Earth and have the responsibilities of taking care of it and saving the environment as we are interrelated to it. As an example, most indigenous people did not devolve away from such an interconnected relationship of being and nature; whereas we in the West have done so and have for millennia, in Cartesian separation, unfortunately and to our detriment.

Mindfulness is the Buddhist concept of "hyper awareness in the moment" or *smrti* in Sanskrit. We are all witnesses in the present moment and we all need to elevate this awareness to solving social problems through the emphasis of kindness and wellness and caring and empathy and love.

As Thich Nhat Hanh (1995/2007: 14) clarifies: "When we are mindful, touching deeply the present moment, we can see and listen deeply, and the fruits are always understanding, acceptance, love, and the desire to relieve suffering and bring joy." Further, Hanh goes on to explain all of us have the potential for these "awakened qualities" through practicing mindfulness and by being aware in the moment not only of ourselves but also of our world in which we live. In so doing we will be able to touch upon the living Buddha and the living Christ.

In regard to understanding the greater love of God, I turn to the works of C. S. Lewis, who was an Oxford scholar, a Christian, friends with J.R.R. Tolkien, and famously known for his children's novel series *The Lion, the Witch, and the Wardrobe*.

Like Lewis, I have waivered in my own beliefs as have other writers. Those similarly struggling with belief and faith were such literary luminaries as Miguel de Unamuno, his personal views about faith exemplified by his famous novella *Saint Emmanuel the Good, Martyr*, and Nikos

Kazantzakis, his personal opinions about Christ exemplified by his novel *The Last Temptation of Christ*. Interestingly, both Unamuno and Kazantzakis were good friends, the former Spanish-Basque, and the latter Cretan-Greek—both men sharing a certain outlook on life and both questioning how best to interpret belief, faith, and Christianity.

As an intellectual, C.S. Lewis also struggled in defending Christianity and its finer philosophical points of view. In the Gospel of Matthew 22: 39 Jesus is quoted as saying: "Thou shalt love thy neighbour as thyself"—in other words, the "Golden Rule," treat others as you yourself would like to be treated. And in the Christian sense, it includes your enemy—treat your enemy too with love and understanding and turn the other cheek in the face of violence (Matthew 5: 39).

In his book *Mere Christianity* (1977), Lewis elaborates on the idea of "forgiveness." "God intends us to love all selves in the same way and for the same reason … Perhaps it makes it easier if we remember that that is how He loves us. Not for any nice, attractive qualities we think we have, but just because we are the things called selves. For really there is nothing else in us to love: creatures like us who actually find hatred such a pleasure that to give it up is like giving up beer or tobacco."

In other words, we need to overlook each other's personal shortcomings, and begin to see the good in everyone. We also need our politicians to create policies of "wellbeing" for society—for those suffering from mental health issues, for the homeless, for the impoverished, for the undereducated, for the uninsured—and therefore, completely rethink our domestic policies.

And so, I return to the hopeful messages of the New Zealand Prime Minister Jacinda Ardern and her remarks at the World Economic Forum in Davos, Switzerland, in 2019: "I don't think it's the end of GDP, I think it's the beginning of doing things differently … It's about bringing kindness and empathy to governance … Our people are telling us that politics are not delivering and meeting their expectations. This is not woolly, it's critical."

And once more returning to Dr. Martin Luther King, Jr., whose words should echo for everyone for all time: "Hate cannot drive out hate; only love can do that."

May we all learn to love better and drive out all the hatred.[33]

## What Is Love?

This discussion will explore notions of love and its meanings from varying studies. In writing about "love" is a call of hope, whereby we may find ways toward peace, not only within ourselves, but among all peoples everywhere.

Part of this discussion will analyze "higher love," or the love of the muse, and its significance for understanding "our creative output," some of our best human qualities. This is known to artists, sculptors, musicians, theoretical physicists, mathematicians, philosophers, and everyone following a higher calling who also contribute something marvelous for humanity.

While many theorists have discussed cognitive functionality associated with artistic processes as Bayesian, or computational, or situated, or structural, and so on, it has also been well established how many neural chemicals are utilized for artistic creation, many of which are shared by "being in love."

According to Katherine J. Wu, PhD, Harvard University, we go through stages in the "love process" from "lust," releasing testosterone or estrogen; and if "attraction" persists, releasing dopamine, norepinephrine, and serotonin; and through "long-term attachment," releasing oxytocin and vasopressin.[34]

Certainly, the brain is situated in cognitive action and function, and with the extended mind, and even categorical and computational, but in works of genius there is likely much more going on. Ponder for a moment: Mozart's *Requiem*, or Beethoven's *9th Symphony*, or Michelangelo's *Sistine Chapel*, or Rodin's *The Thinker*, or Einstein's $e = mc^2$, or Plato's *The Republic*, or Darwin's *On the Origin of Species*, or Tolstoy's *War and Peace*, or Shakespeare's *Hamlet*, and so on. Therefore, what is "artistic inspiration" or mental inspiration in these great works of complexity?

In the brain and during the artistic process, according to neuropsychologist, Dahlia Zaidel of UCLA, the amygdala, hypothalamus, ventral tegmental, limbic system, subcortical regions, motor cortex, and orbitofrontal cortex are activated, regions associated with emotions, reward, vision, and movement, while dopamine and oxytocin levels also increase.[35]

In the visual realm, the caudate nucleus, bilateral occipital gyri, bilateral fusiform gyri, and the cingulate sulcus are activated through pictorial artwork. On the other hand, language is mostly limited to the "left brain hemisphere" in contrast to the musical and visual as part of the "right hemisphere." In other words, art and creation are dependent upon multiple cerebral capacities. This has been called "neuro-aesthetics."[36] Furthermore, according to neuro-psychologist Robert Bilder of UCLA, those with enlarged amygdala may have exceptional artistic abilities.[37]

Of course, we may simply relegate answers to these questions to the chemical and material without acknowledging, or even encompassing, true accomplishments at the highest cognitive levels. Beyond the biological, how do we understand such tremendous accomplishments from geniuses in the arts, mathematics, physics, and so on?

Artistic endeavors are likewise situated in memory and are formulated distinctly in cognitive action utilizing different "neuroimaging" processes, depending on the skills employed. Many also believe in "Divine Love," like C.S. Lewis in his book *The Problem of Pain*, "God is Goodness. He can give good, but cannot need or get it. In that sense all His love is, as it were, bottomlessly selfless by very definition, it has everything to give and nothing to receive."[38]

The cognitive anthropologist, Harvey Whitehouse, explains religio-experiences may be what he calls "divergent" as consigned to different memory forms, long-term through texts as the Bible, or imagistic through shocking rituals such as some Filipinos carrying the cross for penance during Easter.[39]

The novelist and survivor of Auschwitz Elie Wiesel once remarked: "The opposite of love is not hate, it's indifference."[40] Indeed, humans need other humans for survival. We are social beings and we are constrained biologically, emotionally, and psychologically needing mammalian care. Indeed, we are born in neonatal states because of our large brains. Such a state of helplessness necessitates care much more than our closest non-human-primate relatives, Chimpanzees. Certainly, the lack of human affection through indifference and neglect certainly negates love. By not having been loved, we cannot in turn love in healthy ways.[41]

Hence, in understanding "what is love," we need to understand "what is emotion," and thus, we need to analyze what we mean by "emotions." As such, human emotions are quite complex, as are most things humans do. In some way, they are biologically and neurologically driven, and in other ways, they are socio-culturally derived. As anthropologist, Andrew Beatty has pointed out, we narrate our emotions, and emotional experiences through linguistic expressions. Other species never reach the complexities of such communication, whether personally, or musically, or dramatically, or fictionally, and so on.

As Beatty declares about emotions: "Whatever their ontological status as cultural inventions, biological states, or constructed social roles—emotions are unified experiences; and this subjective unity, which bears heavily on social processes, is due to their conceptual or narrative structure as construals of personal situations."[42]

The biological anthropologist Helen Fisher, in her book *Why We Love*, has demonstrated how neurochemicals influence how people love, or which brain chemicals are released for those in love.[43] Fisher conducted a cross-cultural survey and found 88 percent of 166 examined cultures experienced euphoric-romantic love. She later tested some 2500 individuals with fMRI brain scans to ascertain which parts of the brain lit up and utilized comparative neural-chemical analyses. She and her colleagues showed how the brain regions of the amygdala, hippocampus, prefrontal cortex, and ventral tegmental activated their reward systems from "being in love," as well as increasing cortisol and dopamine, and for those "remaining in love," releasing oxytocin and vasopressin.[44]

Non-human primates engage in communal grooming when empathizing with another's suffering. For example, when a lower-ranking male is beaten up by a higher-ranking male for no apparent reason, the victim is then communally groomed according to primatologist and neurologist Robert Sapolsky.[45]

Thus, whether we think of love as expressing our muse, or being in love with others, or the greater love of God, we are describing or narrating our emotions as humans. Such emotional states, and their origins, may have biological and neurological underpinnings, and may have evolved with us as mammals, helping us care for one another.

We as humans, the most intelligent species on this planet, must continue to strive to care for one another better, to love each other more, to empathize with those who suffer, to love ourselves, to love our planet, to love others in healthy ways. We need to find ways to make a better world with love and for love and for the love of a future for our loved ones and for all of us—for a love of humanity.

## Why a "Re-indigenization" of Society Makes Sense

It may sound patently absurd to discuss a "re-Indigenization" of society. Yet, I argue not only is it practical but necessary if humanity is to survive into this century and beyond. Humans, for most of their history, lived as hunter-gatherers, for about the first 290,000 years or so.[46] It is only in the last ten to fifteen thousand years from the "Agricultural Revolution or Neolithic Revolution," did we begin domesticating animals and plants, and thus began so-called civilization with writing, hierarchies, state systems, endemic warfare, and worst of all, slavery.[47] In fact, most of us do not even think about this pre-history. We simply "are" in the world today—a globe we inherited from our collective human shift of moving away from hunting and gathering to a world of domesticating the natural environment.

If we are to legitimately address a history of these inequalities and their historical consequences, "environmental destruction," "genocide," "racism," "systemic warfare," "human exploitation," and "state system oppression," we must begin by examining if progress means a continuation on our present path toward self-destruction. In part, I address some of the effects of these colossal man-made calamities in my new book *Epochal Reckonings* (2020; co-winner of the Proverse Prize)—a poetic guide to some of our twenty-first-century crises.[48]

What I wish to examine here is a re-thinking of ourselves on our planet earth, in relation to an indigenous understanding of "Mother Earth." Moreover, I will argue that while we have moved well beyond the likes of French philosopher René Descartes, for many reasons, his intellectual legacy still remains as we struggle to come to terms with our environment and our heritage from the Agricultural Revolution.

Descartes is well known for his "*Cogito, ergo sum*," "I think, therefore I am," which in many ways, makes Descartes the father of "philosophy of mind" and "consciousness" from a Western perspective.[49] He thinks and therefore he knows he exists. But what does existence mean though in terms of our own present day understanding in relation to the world and the environment? In biology, cognition, and neurology alone, our knowledge of brain, mind, and body are indeed profound. With basic evolutionary knowledge, we know biologically we are animals, although perhaps a special kind, and why it is a false narrative to separate humankind from nature. When René Descartes wrote, for example: "For as to reason or sense, inasmuch as it alone makes us men and distinguishes us from the beasts, I prefer to believe it exists whole and entire in each of us" (*Discourse on Method and Meditations on First Philosophy*, 1637 & 1641, 1998, trans. Donald Cress, p. 2), Descartes had no way of knowing the future of human epistemology.[50] Perhaps he might even have been amused by the contemporary subdiscipline of primatology as aiding our comprehension of human behavior. Who is to know?

What is extremely dangerous, however, is holding on to a kind of Medieval thinking that somehow our world is centered around us, humans and humans alone, and God made man (humans) for the world and for him (them) alone. In the Old Testament, Isaias (45: 18) in the Bible (1899 edn.) it states: "For thus sayith the Lord that created the heavens, God himself that formed the earth, and made it, the very maker thereof: he did not create it in vain: he formed it to be inhabited. I *am* the Lord, and there is no other." Yet, it is in Descartes' *Meditation 6* where he explicitly outlines why he separates "Mind from Body" as if the mind itself in all its abstractive capabilities can somehow be divorced from our corporeal selves.[51] And thus, if men's (human's) minds may be divided from our bodies then humans may be divided from nature. Here is what he asserts: "Thus it seems to follow that the power of imagining depends upon something distinct from me. And I readily understand that, were a body to exist to which a mind is so joined that it may apply itself in order, as it were, to look at it any time it wishes, it could happen that it is by means of this very body that I imagine corporeal things" (p. 93). Of course, and to be fair, René Descartes was well ahead of his time on his discourse about the mind, human perception, and the brain. Even so, there are remnants from what he contended which have remained with us, namely, "Cartesian Dualism," or our complete divorce from nature.[52]

In Maurice Bloch's (2013) seminal work *In and Out of Each Other's Bodies: Theory of Mind, Evolution, Truth, and the Nature of the Social*, he explains rather than thinking of the separation of mind and body, or culture and nature: "The social is understood as the flow of interaction between people: I call this the transactional. On the other hand, the transactional social is contrasted with conscious, explicit representation of the social: these I call the transcendental social. I argue that the transcendental social consists of second-order phenomena created and maintained by rituals. The transactional social is governed by norms and ways of doing things that are largely subconscious. It involves the continual mutual monitoring of each other by the members of a social group" (p. vii).[53] In other words, there is no separation between mind and body, nor nature and humankind, nor between culture and nature, the biological is intertwined with the social and vice versa.

In addressing the human issue of our separation from nature may have its Western roots in the so-called Scientific Revolution of the 1500s–1600s and the Age of Enlightenment of the 1700s, but today, we may re-examine some of the erroneous philosophical carryovers and create a future of cohabitation and inter-being akin to an indigenous understanding of our world.[54] A skeptic may declare, "Well that's all fine and good but what about poverty, starvation, over-population, and the like?" A re-indigenization of society means a re-orientation of human thought. It does not mean becoming Native or indigenous. It means re-imagining our humanity.

As a society we need to think beyond technological progress and using the planet as an unending natural resource. Here is how in my humble opinion. (1) Accept human beings as part of Earth, and not apart from it, and by this acceptance, accept our dependence upon it. (2) Accept Earth as a living being, the Gaia theory.[55] And if we are to take care of ourselves, we need to take care of the Earth too and become its guardians. We need to love the Earth and respect it as much as indigenous peoples everywhere do. (3) Being grateful for our being on this planet and not endlessly destroying it and polluting it is a good beginning which has been around for a while in ecological consciousness circles. (4) Instead of putting resources into warfare, put resources into renewable energies and into solving malnutrition and poverty in sustainable ways.[56] Make farming more sustainable too instead of a form of factory production and endless soil depletion. (5) Allow indigenous peoples to have "more voice" with first-world nations (Europe, the United States, Japan, Canada, Australia, New Zealand, and other powerful states as China and Russia) in United Nations forums and such environmental decision-making as the Paris Agreement of 2015.[57] (6) Protect indigenous peoples and their rights and allow for indigenous parks and reserves to remain and to be expanded upon by protecting larger tracts of land, instead of developing and exploiting natural resources on indigenous lands for industrial farming, mining interests, oil extraction, electric dams, lumbering, and ranching. (7) Make the "re-indigenization" project official in international law and international treaties, and along with other international laws concerning indigenous peoples (e.g., ILO Convention Number 169 of 1989 and the 2007 UNDRIP, United Nations Declaration on the Rights of Indigenous Peoples).[58] Make all nation-states adhere to such a project if possible. (8)

Create more public awareness through more education programs through universities, and above all, create an ecological consciousness understood from indigenous perspectives and in their own voices. (9) Remember scientists believe we are entering the Sixth Extinction phase on the planet and we must prevent this by all productive means necessary.[59] (10) And finally, allow more indigenous peoples to be spokespeople and to become planetary ambassadors for realizing such a re-indigenization project before it is too late.

One indigenous leader in Ecuador, Nemonte Nenquimo, First Female President of the Waorani Organization of the Pastaza Province and Co-founder of the Ceibo Alliance, declared in an open letter to world leaders: "My name is Nemonte Nenquimo. I am a Waorani woman, a mother, and a leader of my people.[60] The Amazon rainforest is my home. I am writing you this letter because the fires are raging still. Because the corporations are spilling oil in our rivers. Because the miners are stealing gold (as they have been for 500 years), and leaving behind open pits and toxins. Because the land grabbers are cutting down primary forest so that the cattle can graze, plantations can be grown and the white man can eat. Because our elders are dying from Coronavirus while you are planning your next moves to cut up our lands to stimulate an economy that has never benefited us. Because, as Indigenous peoples, we are fighting to protect what we love—our way of life, our rivers, the animals, our forests, life on Earth—and it's time that you listened to us. In each of our many hundreds of different languages across the Amazon, we have a word for you—the outsider, the stranger. In my language, *WaoTededo*, that word is "*cowori*". And it doesn't need to be a bad word. But you have made it so. For us, the word has come to mean (and in a terrible way, your society has come to represent): the white man that knows too little for the power that he wields, and the damage that he causes. You are probably not used to an Indigenous woman calling you ignorant and, less so, on a platform such as this. But for Indigenous peoples it is clear: the less you know about something, the less value it has to you, and the easier it is to destroy. And by easy, I mean: guiltlessly, remorselessly, foolishly, even righteously. And this is exactly what you are doing to us as Indigenous peoples, to our rainforest territories, and ultimately to our planet's climate" (*The Guardian*, October 12, 2020).[61]

## Conclusion

In contemplating this last chapter, it occurs to me how much the Buddhist narratives pointed to life lessons. Although not specific to the conclusions I would like to make here, each of the participating Buddhist monks and Buddhist nun elaborated upon the following wisdom in their understandings about love, peace, empathy, mindfulness, and generally, in making the world a better place. Here is some of the wisdom I gained from these exemplars of human compassion:

- Peace through acceptance
- Peace through knowledge
- Peace through understanding
- Peace through love
- Peace through communication and dialogue
- Peace through listening
- Peace through compassion
- Peace through empathy
- Peace through brave love (instead of empathy)
- Love is love

Through the Buddhist philosophy of "inter-being" we must learn to accept others who they are. This includes accepting of ourselves how we are. Further, peace may happen through a knowledge about training the mind, and for example, the fourteen-point mindfulness training portrayed by Thich Nhat Hanh. Understanding is part of acceptance. Understanding is likewise knowing life is impermanent and understanding how we are all interrelated and therefore co-dependent on each other. This includes all life forms.

Peace also happens through love but not just any kind of love but "unconditional love," an unselfish love, an unpossessive love, which is in turn a "liberative" kind of love. Love in the Buddhist sense is about compassion, that is a compassion for self and others. It is to be selfless. It also encompasses empathy for the suffering of others.

Moreover, peace may only be achieved through true communication and dialogue and active listening. Peace through listening happens when we try to listen to another's point of view, which may be divergent from our own. This means also knowing there are two sides of a conflict. Compassion and empathy follow a way of seeing the world, which means appreciating the suffering of oneself, but equally important, appreciating the suffering of others. This is also knowing all beings in the world, inclusive of animals and plants have the right to be as much as humans do.

While two of the monks disagreed over the term "empathy" because, for one, it was too distant a term while, for another, it was a more accurate translation of compassion, both would agree that the world needs "brave love" and compassion to overcome conflict, divisiveness, and ignorance.

And finally, "love is love," which means that the concept and idea of love are in essence the highest form of human emotional understanding. Love in this sense conquers all because it is the basis of caring for oneself and others. Such a worldview encompasses inter-being as respect for all others and all living things. It is a mindfulness which ultimately rests upon compassion, empathy, and the celebration of life, inclusive of overcoming suffering through love. It is also not any kind of love but "unconditional love," which exemplifies the highest order of human compassion.

If we manage to pay attention to the lessons taught by the three Buddhist monks and Buddhist nun, not only because of the beauty of Buddhism and Buddhist philosophy, but because their interpretations of love, peace, mindfulness, and empathy are life lessons for all time. Their words are significant for overcoming conflicts in general.

\* \* \*

Aside from the Buddhist narratives in this chapter, the analysis elaborated on how important peaceworkers are to society. These are unsung heroes like teachers working in lower socio-economic public schools; or psychiatrists working in mental health institutions; nurses in hospitals and other care facilities; medical doctors in emergency rooms; social workers; psychologists; firemen; policemen; public defenders; clergy who defend migrants and who work with the poor; volunteers who help the homeless; all those who work in conflict resolution and peace studies—are just some of those not often celebrated in society for the very difficult work they do for the betterment of us all.

In the section "In the Name of Love," I reiterate some of the examination of "inter-being" by Thich Nhat Hanh, but also expand the explanation to include C.S. Lewis and his notions of love and Christianity. This section of the chapter was inspired by Dr. Martin Luther King, Jr., but also the New Zealand Prime Minister Jacinda Ardern and her words of compassion. From my perspective, other politicians should look to her example as well as these luminaries who promote a more loving world.

Another section—"What Is Love?"—of this chapter analyzes the meaning of love from a scientific perspective. It draws on anthropological analyses of love and emotions with the hope of finding ways toward peace, not only within ourselves, but among peoples everywhere.

The final section of this chapter imagines why a "re-indigenization" of society makes sense. As Douglas Fry (2013: 5) argues: "In the ever-more interdependent world community, global cooperation to successfully address climate change and other shared challenges to human survival is critically needed, and holding an erroneous warlike image of human nature only hinders the process of working together on the scale that is necessary." Indeed, a whole new conceptualization of society is needed and called for in order to prevent impending disaster from climate change, mass extinction, and nuclear warfare. For most of human existence, we lived as hunter-gatherers and depended on nature. We need to return to such a conceptualization in order to prevent the doom of the human species. As one indigenous leader, Nemonte Nenquimo of the Waorani of Ecuador states in her open letter to world leaders, whites and Western society are ignorant about the damage they are causing the environment. We must embrace new ways if we are to survive on this planet.

In general, I agree with Douglas Fry (2007: 233) when he argues: "At a specific level, anthropology suggests a full palette of often complementary approaches that could be implemented to move humanity beyond war: enhancing crosscutting ties, recognizing the new reality of global interdependence and the necessity of working together to effectively address common challenges, adopting new attitudes, values, and beliefs that are appropriate to an interdependent world and promote non-violent conflict resolution, creating overarching authority structures for effective governance, and utilizing conflict management processes in place of war." As such, if humans are to survive, we need to look beyond hate and unnecessary attachments and toward a reconciled world with ourselves and our environment. Only then can we hope to move beyond racism, nationalism, terrorism, genocide, trauma, and hate.

## Notes

1. http://www.goldcoastyogacentre.com/articles/meditation/the-51-mental-factors-of-your-mind/.
2. https://kamaltouhid.medium.com/the-ten-non-virtues-from-buddhist-doctrine-e96dd82d1f3f.

3. https://en.wikipedia.org/wiki/Brahmavihara.
4. https://www.wisdomlib.org/definition/anukampa.
5. https://www.wisdomlib.org/definition/sakkaya-ditthi.
6. https://www.wisdomlib.org/buddhism/book/vipassana-meditation/d/doc1344.html; https://en.wikipedia.org/wiki/Satipatthana_Sutta; https://en.wikipedia.org/wiki/Satipatthana.
7. https://en.wikipedia.org/wiki/Sampajañña.
8. https://en.wikipedia.org/wiki/Richard_Dawkins.
9. https://poets.org/poem/eternity.
10. https://tricycle.org/trikedaily/dana-sila-bhavana/.
11. https://www.dcpolicycenter.org/people/anthony-a-williams/.
12. https://creativesystemsthinking.wordpress.com/2015/02/15/the-four-qualities-of-love-by-thich-nhat-hanh/.
13. https://www.huffpost.com/entry/probability-being-born_b_877853.
14. https://www.mayoclinic.org/tests-procedures/cognitive-behavioral-therapy/about/pac-20384610.
15. https://en.wikipedia.org/wiki/Justice_League.
16. https://en.wikipedia.org/wiki/Super_Friends.
17. https://www.bartleby.com/205/31.html.
18. https://www.imdb.com/title/tt0371746/.
19. https://www.pri.org/stories/2016-01-30/gandhi-s-death-anniversary-not-everyone-grieving.
20. https://www.washingtonpost.com/history/2019/05/30/irresponsible-historians-attack-david-garrows-mlk-allegations/.
21. https://www.nytimes.com/2019/06/03/opinion/martin-luther-king-fbi.html.
22. https://www.nbc.com/keeping-up-with-the-kardashians; https://www.bravotv.com/the-real-housewives-of-beverly-hills; https://www.bravotv.com/the-real-housewives-of-new-jersey.
23. https://www.amazon.com/Better-Angels-Our-Nature-Violence/dp/0143122010/ref=sr_1_1?keywords=pinker+the+better+angels+of+our+nature&qid=1575010466&s=books&sr=1-1.
24. https://www.secondworldwarhistory.com/world-war-2-statistics.php; https://en.wikipedia.org/wiki/World_War_I_casualties.
25. https://waitbutwhy.com/2015/06/spectacular-video-putting-wwii-deaths-perspective.html.
26. https://en.wikipedia.org/wiki/List_of_wars_by_death_toll; https://www.zmescience.com/ecology/genghis-khan-environment-26052014/.
27. https://www.google.com/search?safe=strict&client=safari&channel=mac_bm&source=hp&ei=crjgXY2wB8KusAX35pOADQ&q=percentage+of+deaths+of+world+population+caused+by+world+war+2&oq=percentage+of+deaths+of+world+population+caused+by+world+war+2&gs_l=psy.

28. https://www.amazon.com/Long-Peace-Inquiries-Into-History/dp/0195043359.
29. https://www.amazon.com/God-Small-Things-Novel/dp/0812979656/ref=sr_1_1?keywords=the+god+of+small+things&qid=1575011769&sr=8-1.
30. https://www.nps.gov/mlkm/learn/quotations.htm.
31. https://en.wikipedia.org/wiki/Jacinda_Ardern.
32. https://www.nzherald.co.nz/nz/graham-adams-is-jacinda-ardern-the-messiah-or-just-a-very-crafty-politician/OX6JWIDJE2TA2RSCXVGMJVH77Q/.
33. https://www.nps.gov/mlkm/learn/quotations.htm.
34. https://sitn.hms.harvard.edu/flash/2017/love-actually-science-behind-lust-attraction-companionship/.
35. https://www.ncbi.nlm.nih.gov/pmc/articles/PMC2815940/.
    https://www.semanticscholar.org/paper/The-brain%2C-biology-and-evolution-in-art-and-its-Zaidel/e824532b02cd5530d31b6432b1b58d5a85c82227?p2df.
36. https://www.frontiersin.org/articles/10.3389/fnhum.2015.00080/full.
37. https://www.fastcompany.com/3052659/what-happens-inside-an-exceptionally-creative-brain.
38. C. S. Lewis (1940). *The Problem of Pain*. New York: Harper Collins, 2001 edn, p. 43.
39. Harvey Whitehouse (2000). *Arguments and Icons: Divergent Modes of Religiosity*. Oxford: Oxford University Press.
40. https://www.entrepreneur.com/article/278587.
41. Frans de Waal (2009). *The Age of Empathy: Nature's Lessons for a Kinder Society*. New York: Harmony Books, pp. 13–14.
42. https://bura.brunel.ac.uk/bitstream/2438/11699/2/Fulltext.pdf.
43. Helen Fisher (2004). *Why We Love: The Nature and Chemistry of Romantic Love*. New York: Henry Holt and Company, LLC.
44. http://www.helenfisher.com/downloads/articles/17brokeheart.pdf; http://www.helenfisher.com/downloads/love-addiction.pdf.
45. https://www.latimes.com/opinion/op-ed/la-oe-sapolsky-empathy-animals-aung-san-suu-kyi-20170924-story.html.
46. https://www.sciencemag.org/news/2017/06/world-s-oldest-homo-sapiens-fossils-found-morocco.
47. https://www.history.com/topics/pre-history/neolithic-revolution.
48. https://www.amazon.com/Epochal-Reckonings-Winners-Proverse-Prize/dp/9888491946/ref=tmm_pap_swatch_0?_encoding=UTF8&qid=&sr=.
49. https://www.britannica.com/topic/cogito-ergo-sum.

50. https://www.amazon.com/Discourse-Method-Meditations-First-Philosophy/dp/0872204200/ref=sr_1_3?dchild=1&keywords=Discourse+on+Method+and+Meditations+on+First+Philosophy&qid=1607614658&s=books&sr=1-3.
51. https://www.amazon.com/Discourse-Method-Meditations-First-Philosophy/dp/0872204200/ref=sr_1_3?dchild=1&keywords=Discourse+on+Method+and+Meditations+on+First+Philosophy&qid=1607614658&s=books&sr=1-3.
52. https://en.wikipedia.org/wiki/Mind–body_dualism.
53. https://www.amazon.com/Out-Each-Others-Bodies-Evolution/dp/1612051022/ref=sr_1_1?dchild=1&keywords=bloch+In+and+Out+of+Each+Other's+Bodies&qid=1607615135&s=books&sr=1-1.
54. https://www.britannica.com/science/Scientific-Revolution.
    https://www.history.com/topics/british-history/mankind-the-story-of-all-of-us-videos-enlightenment-video.
55. https://courses.seas.harvard.edu/climate/eli/Courses/EPS281r/Sources/Gaia/Gaia-hypothesis-wikipedia.pdf.
56. https://www.researchgate.net/publication/273852768_Ecological_Thinking_Consciousness_Responsibility; https://www.concernusa.org/story/solutions-to-poverty/.
57. https://unfccc.int/process-and-meetings/the-paris-agreement/the-paris-agreement.
58. https://www.ilo.org/global/topics/indigenous-tribal/lang%2D%2Den/index.htm.
    https://www.un.org/development/desa/indigenouspeoples/declaration-on-the-rights-of-indigenous-peoples.html.
59. https://www.euroscientist.com/mother-of-us-all/.
60. https://www.theguardian.com/commentisfree/2020/oct/12/western-worldyour-civilisation-killing-life-on-earth-indigenous-amazon-planet.
    https://time.com/collection/100-most-influential-people-2020/5888337/nemonte-nenquimo/.
61. https://www.theguardian.com/commentisfree/2020/oct/12/western-worldyour-civilisation-killing-life-on-earth-indigenous-amazon-planet.

## Bibliography

Atran, S. 2002. *In Gods We Trust: The Evolutionary Landscape of Religion.* New York and Oxford: Oxford University Press.

Bloch, M. 2013. *In and Out of Each Other's Bodies: Theory of Mind, Evolution, Truth, and the Nature of the Social.* London: Paradigm Publishers.

Boyer, P. 2001. *Religion Explained: The Evolutionary Origins of Religious Thought.* New York: Basic Books.
Fry, D.P. 2006. *The Human Potential for Peace: An Anthropological Challenge to Assumptions About War and Violence.* Oxford: Oxford University Press.
———. 2007. *Beyond War: the Human Potential for Peace.* Oxford: Oxford University Press.
———., ed. 2013. *War, Peace, and Human Nature: The Convergence of Evolutionary and Cultural Views.* Oxford: Oxford University Press.
Laidlaw, J. 2004a. Introduction. In *Ritual and Memory: Toward a Comparative Anthropology of Religion,* ed. H. Whitehouse and J. Laidlaw, 1–9. Oxford: Altamira Press.
———. 2004b. Embedded Modes of Religiosity in Indic Renouncer Religions. In *Ritual and Memory: Toward a Comparative Anthropology of Religion,* ed. H. Whitehouse and J. Laidlaw, 89–109. Oxford: Altamira Press.
Nhat Hanh, T. 1987, 2005 edn. *Being Peace.* Berkeley, CA: Parallax Press.
Nhat Hanh, T. 1995, 2007 new edn. *Living Buddha, Living Christ.* New York: Riverhead Books, The Penguin Group.
Nhat Hanh, T. 2017. *The Art of Living: Peace and Freedom in the Here and Now.* New York: Harper One, Harper Collins Publishers.
Pinker, S. 2011. *The Better Angels of Our Nature: Why Violence Has Declined.* New York: Viking, the Penguin Group.
Ricard, M., and W. Singer. 2017. *Beyond the Self: Conversations Between Buddhism and Neuroscience.* Cambridge, MA: The MIT Press.
de Waal, F. 2009. *The Age of Empathy: Nature's Lessons for a Kinder Society.* New York: Harmony Books.
Wallace, B.A. 2007. *Contemplative Science: Where Buddhism and Neuroscience Converge.* New York: Columbia University Press.
Whitehouse, H. 2000. *Arguments and Icons: Divergent Modes of Religiosity.* Oxford: Oxford University Press.
———. 2004. *Modes of Religiosity: A Cognitive Theory of Religious Transmission.* Walnut Creek, CA: AltaMira Press.
Wright, R. 2017. *Why Buddhism Is True: The Science and Philosophy of Meditation and Enlightenment.* New York: Simon & Schuster Paperbacks.

CHAPTER 8

# Concluding Remarks

At the outset of the book, I alluded to "critical race theory" (CRT) as being relevant in the hope that this writing will help change minds about race, racism, and power, and align with an educational opportunity for the betterment of the world. Yet, as I stated in the introduction, this book humbly aspires to be much more than CRT, as it is broader in scope by analyzing not only racism but nationalism, terrorism, genocide, trauma, and love and peace. Specifically, the topics covered are "immigration and racism"; "nationalism and terrorism"; "cultural genocide, genocide, and Amerindian genocide"; "racism and racial trauma"; "environment, humanism, science, and tolerance"; and "empathy, love, and peace."

Moreover, this book discussed the complexities of racism against new immigrants in the United States, especially against Latinos from El Salvador, Guatemala, Honduras, and Mexico, and the racist rhetoric of the last Trump presidency. Important in this analysis was understanding the epistemological possibilities of ethnicity and populism. To this end, I defined ethnicity as those actions, categories, identities, and norms, which are often carried out at the subconscious level and whereby differences are maintained through cognitive underpinnings, social networks, and boundaries. Ethnicity explains not only how people define themselves but how others define particular groups. In recent years, the former Trump administration and former President Donald Trump targeted immigrants as scapegoats to promote a white nationalist agenda by emphasizing that Latino immigrants were supposedly dangerous and not to be trusted.

© The Author(s), under exclusive license to Springer Nature Switzerland AG 2022
J. P. Linstroth, *Politics and Racism Beyond Nations*,
https://doi.org/10.1007/978-3-030-91720-3_8

Such racist rhetoric surrounding these views is also known as "populism." Generally, populist ideology underscores those who allegedly threaten the homogeneity of the people. Intrinsically, populists like Donald Trump argued that the so-called liberal elite led by the Democrats favored the interests of immigrants over average people, particularly Nativist people. By contrast, the discussion also concerned the policy of neglect by Indian Prime Minister Narendra Modi and his BJP party locking down India for COVID-19 in 2020, which left thousands of rural migrant laborers stranded in major Indian cities. Both Trump and Modi promote their own style of populism. For Trump, his poll numbers increased with each egregious statement against the handicapped, immigrants, women, minorities, and/or political rivals. On the other hand, Modi's politics in India exposed a standpoint against the socio-economic destitute and an unwillingness to aid migrant laborers in large Indian metropolises during India's Coronavirus lockdown.

Likewise, the book examined how some ethno-nationalists maintain terrorist-minded values well after peace processes. This was demonstrated by some in the Spanish-Basque Country celebrating the return of ETA (*Euskadi Ta Askatasuna*, Basque Homeland and Freedom) political prisoners in 2019 well after ETA's permanent ceasefire in 2011. Furthermore, there was the murder of Irish journalist, Lyra McKee, by the so-called New IRA (Irish Republican Army) in 2019 well after the Good Friday Agreement in 1998. It was shown that some ethnic minorities like some Basques, some Catalans, and some Northern Irish Catholics uphold their viewpoints of ethno-subordination and respectively imagine independence for the Basque Country and Catalonia and unification for Ireland (Northern Ireland with the rest of Ireland). A subordinate group's critique of power is what James Scott (1990) called "hidden transcripts," which may be spoken behind the back of the dominant power but also may include the representation of the dominant's rule, which may not be openly acknowledged. Certainly, however, some Basques, Catalans, and Northern Irish Catholics overtly express their open insubordination as well through parades, symbols, protests, and material forms of resistance (i.e., t-shirts, graffiti, jewelry, etc.) (see Linstroth 2002).

What is more, the idea of a "nation" is in and of itself debatable. It may, on the one hand, encompass an "imagined community" after Benedict Anderson (1983), such as the nation-state of Spain but on the other it may include ethno-nationalist minorities within it, like Basques and Catalans, who vie for power and recognition for their own ethno-nationalist identities and aspirations. Then, there are the factionalized politics between nationalist secessionists who have differing visions for the Basque nation or the Catalan nation. Some of these nationalists are radical and some are moderate. But this of course all depends on one's perspective on secessionism and such non-nation-state independence movements. To some (e.g., some Spaniards), for example, all secessionist aspirations are radical and not moderate. Regardless, what I attempted to elaborate upon was how some minorities like Basques and Catalans question the legal basis of a nation-state because of their own ethno-nationalist and ethno-cultural values. And while the nation-state remains viable for the foreseeable future, questions remain how to incorporate non-nation ethno-nationalist minorities like Basques, Catalans, Scots, Welsh, British Southern Cameroonians, Quebecois, Kurds, and Puerto Ricans, among many others, into the current league of nations. Do such ethno-nationalists have reasonable claims to statehood, and if not, why not?

In addition, this book, *Politics and Racism Beyond Nations*, examined the genocide in Guatemala against Mayan Indians and the ongoing genocides against Sentinelese-Jarawa Islanders, Chinese Uighurs, and Brazilian Amerindians. It attempted to make sense of the discourses of violence in the present and in the past (Sanford 2008) by addressing how extreme forms of racism lead to genocide, and in this book, mostly against indigenous peoples. In my view, such present-day practices against the Sentinelese Jarawa Islanders, Chinese Uighurs, and Brazilian Amerindians are more than so-called ethnocide, a concerted effort to wipe out their respective cultures, because what has been and what is being done against these peoples amounts to genocide. Adding to this point of view, I have seen anthropologists reluctant to use the term genocide, when in my view, it is altogether appropriate because of the extreme vulnerabilities of these minorities. The Sentinelese are threatened by those who want to proselytize and convert them to Christianity; the Chinese Uighurs are put in mass concentration camps in Western China; and the Brazilian Amerindians, by the negligence of the current Bolsonaro government, have allowed illegal mining and illegal logging activities to continue on indigenous lands. Genocide in these areas of the world is happening now and there needs to be more resolute determination to stop it. There needs to be a realization that these ongoing genocides do not have to be limited to massacres and actual violence but may be carried onward through structural violence as well. What are the results of structural violence of oppression amounting to genocide? Alcoholism, domestic abuse, sexual abuse, depression, suicide, and endemic health issues in indigenous populations are the consequences of covert genocide, indirect forms of oppression amounting to the same as massacres through forms of assimilation and acculturation. In sum, we need to hold governments accountable for their treatment of their Native populations before it is too late.

Furthermore, in the book, I examined the narratives of Guatemalan-Mayas and Brazilian urban Amerindians and their experiences with racism. I established racism is a kind of trauma and trauma itself may be analyzed through memories of such incidents of racism. In my analyses, I explained that memories of racism are semantic in character because such memories are ways of knowing about discrimination and oppression. Forms of discrimination and racism may be linked to structural violence which may be suffered in routine ways of humiliation. Memories of these happenings may likewise be tied to notions of time whereby specific episodes of racism form into what I consider to be "synchronic trauma" and if episodes of racism have long-lasting qualities these may in turn form into what I consider to be "diachronic trauma" (see Linstroth 2009). In many cases, such trauma forms do not have to be separable. Since they are memories about time, specific episodes, and long-term episodes, which may be part of an individual's repertoire of memories about racism in general.

Besides memories of trauma, I likewise expounded upon the "politics of racism," not only that race is a social construct but how racism forms part of the political landscape, especially from the populist rhetoric of political leaders like former President Donald Trump of the United States and current President Jair Bolsonaro of Brazil. Both men in their own way represent a kind of populist bigotry. Trump targeted Latin American immigrants, Congresswomen of color, the handicapped, women in general, minorities and his political enemies, while Bolsonaro targeted indigenous peoples, homosexuals, women, and his own political enemies. Making matters worse in Brazil, Bolsonaro neglected the severity of Coronavirus, which has led to a Brazilian Congressional investigation.

In *Politics and Racism Beyond Nations*, the book established how COVID-19 may be linked to structural violence in that the so-called developing world across Africa, Asia, and Latin America may not be able to lessen the curve of the pandemic because of a lack of resources in comparison with first world nations like the United States, Canada, Australia, New Zealand, Japan, and throughout Europe. Other injustices were also highlighted by the book such as how racism persists in policing in the United States. This was evident by the murder of George Floyd as well as the many other instances of racist violence by the police against African-Americans throughout the United States.

Of course, race not only "matters" within the United States but across the globe as well. Racism is played out in different contexts, whether in the United States, Brazil, or elsewhere across Europe, or throughout the developing world. Different peoples also experience racism differently but their experiences may also be shared as those of African-Americans and Native Americans in the United States. In general, minorities have been adversely affected by COVID-19. This is evident from income inequalities of African-Americans and Hispanic-Americans, whereby many African-Americans could not afford not to work during the pandemic and whereby many Latinos had no healthcare insurance in comparison to Whites. So too, the Brazilian indigenous populations have been more adversely affected by Coronavirus than the Brazilian population in general.

In part, this book is meant to address the inequities of racism and their results, not only by pointing out the populist and bigoted rhetoric of former President Donald Trump and current President Jair Bolsonaro of Brazil but how minorities are treated by varying societies leading to ethno-nationalist aspirations for some as among Basques and Catalans; leading to genocide in some cases as against Sentinelese-Jarawa Islanders, Chinese Uighurs, and Brazilian Amerindians; and also resulting in the trauma of minorities like Guatemalan-Mayas and Brazilian urban Amerindians from persistent oppression and racist discourses. As Ibram Kendi (2019: 238) articulates: "Racist power is not godly. Racist policies are not indestructible. Racial inequities are not inevitable. Racist ideas are not natural to the human mind. Race and racism are power constructs of the modern world. For roughly two hundred thousand years, before race and racism were constructed in the fifteenth century, humans saw color but did not group the colors into continental races, did not commonly attach negative and positive characteristics to those colors and rank the races to justify racial inequity, to reinforce racist power and policy." As such, race is a social construct and has no basis in biology. Mostly, it is based on phenotypes, the physical characteristics of individuals; whereas genotypes, one's genetic characteristics, among individuals are more similar than different. As Kendi (2019) iterates, race is a modern power construct which began in the fifteenth century and has wrongly placed groups into categories based on phenotypes and in juxtaposition to Eurocentric views of the world.

*Politics and Racism Beyond Nations* also assessed the narratives from three gay men and what such narratives tell us about the ways the LBGTQ community are discriminated against by society. The biographical lives of these three gay men proved that religion for two of the respondents was oppressive and adversely affected how they grew up. The book showed that while gender and sexuality are culturally and socially constructed, one cannot dismiss biological factors in determining one's sexuality. This was evident from the biological analyses confirming that over 300 species of birds and mammals exhibit some forms of homosexual and transsexual behaviors. Moreover, one's sexual orientation is established at the embryonic stage of life and how different hormones act upon the hypothalamus, for example. Homosexuality is "accompanied by complex physical, functional, and behavioral changes," affecting not only sexual behavior but also a multitude of other traits unrelated to one's sexuality (Balthazart 2012: 155–156). By examining some homosexuals through qualitative analysis was meant to illuminate how science and scientific analyses may overcome intolerance such as religious intolerance. Therefore, in the book I promoted a kind of tolerance through comprehending some aspects of biology, neuro-biology, and primatology.

Specifically, I explored how some neuro-chemicals and some structures of the brain influence human behavior. For example, the neurochemical oxytocin is noteworthy for enhancing in-group and out-group behaviors, and as such partly explains "otherness" and "othering" in human minds. On the other hand, amygdala is part of the fear and anger center, promoting certain other behaviors. Likewise, there is the insular cortex (insula), which evolved in part to avoid disgusting smells and tastes but in humans may be stimulated to show moral disgust as well, such as negative attitudes toward Latino immigrants, or other so-called maligned minorities (Sapolsky 2017: 398). On the other hand, the anterior cingulate cortex (ACC) is another area of the brain which enhances empathy, particularly by empathizing with other people's agony and distress (Sapolsky 2017: 528). Further, I investigated what some non-human primate behaviors tells us about being human (e.g., aggression toward subordinates) but also the conspicuous altruistic behavior of non-human primates. In other words, following Maurice Bloch (2013: 19): "The source of the social is to be found in the cognitive capacities of humans, though, of course, the evolutionary line of causation between the social and the cognitive is not unidirectional but rather ... a single process." What does this mean? "This socio/cognitive means that, even more than is the case for nonsocial animals and differently from the case for other social animals, the boundaries between human individuals are partial at best. This fact and our consequent bodily connectedness, which supplements and sometimes competes with the connectedness of kinship, are fuzzily available to our consciousness. It is this awareness that becomes a recurrent element in a great variety of representations in different cultures, representations that we must not forget are different kinds of phenomena from the simply psychological" (Bloch 2013: 19). To put it another way, we are not simply social animals but biological animals as well and we must consider the cognitive and the social together. Only then will we have a true understanding of what it means to be human.

Another significant aspect of this book was to analyze how the massive fires throughout Amazonia are in part due the Brazilian Bolsonaro administration's negligence in not punishing and/or regulating ranchers and their clearing of land with fire. As of this writing in July 2021, according to several scientists, carbon release from the Amazon is greater than carbon capture because of the mass conflagrations there. Not only is the Amazon rainforest endangered by the inaction of the Bolsonaro administration but likewise the lives and livelihoods of many Brazilian indigenous peoples.

An additional issue pointed out in the book was the negative effects of associating the COVID-19 pandemic with the Asian population and made worse by rhetoric from the likes of former President Donald Trump who called Coronavirus the "China Virus." Race should never be associated with diseases as this harkens back to the pogroms in the Middle Ages against Jews when Jewish people were said to be responsible for the Plague or "Black Death."

Furthermore, it was established that history and science should be candles in the dark to avoid superstitions and avoid the spread of so-called fake news. During the sixteenth and seventeenth centuries, Puritans engaged in harmful witch hunts by spreading unjustified propaganda about alleged witches and supposed witch behavior, especially in Cambridgeshire. The same may be said about former President Donald Trump's attempt at circulating news that presidential race of 2020 was rigged. Only through rational discourse and rational analyses can we hope to avoid the pitfalls of such nonsensical propaganda.

Lastly, from the narratives of three Buddhist monks and one Buddhist nun, I analyzed concepts such as love, peace, and bettering the world. Their notions of love helped us to understand how to love better. True love according to them is without attachment and/or attachments. True love is "unconditional love," which is pure love without attachments or expectations placed on the individual. It is loving ourselves as we are and loving everyone and everything around us without any conditions. True love is also "unpossessive," and as Ajahn Amaro Bikkhu put it, it is "liberative" or liberating. Thus, liberative love is about letting go of the "I, my, myself" and the "I must," the "I should," and the "I have to," and so on. According to Geshe Lama Phuntsho, true love is also to be grateful for everything—what we eat, the air we breathe, and being in the moment. It is practicing gratitude. For Geshe Lobsang Tsultrim, love is following the compassionate way and being compassionate toward oneself and toward others. For Sister Peace (An Nghiem), her understanding of love follows her teacher, Zen Master Thich Nhat Hanh. When Nhat Hanh in recognizing the love of another and one's true love, he states four mantras: "Darling I am here for you"; "darling I know you are there and I am so happy"; "darling I know you are suffering and that is why I am here for you"; "darling I suffer, please help." This is a very powerful perspective about how to better love your beloved (partner, husband, or wife).

It was also significant to find out from the Buddhist monastics how to make the world more peaceful from their perspectives. For Geshe Lama Phuntsho one cannot change the world all at once. However, according to him, one may do so one person at a time. He also emphasized the reason why there is so much conflict in the world is because of lack of communication and nobody takes the time to listen to one another. On the other hand, for Geshe Lobsang Tsultrim, peace follows ethics and morality. For Tsultrim, there are six virtues for peace: generosity, ethics, patience, effort, concentration, and wisdom. By contrast, for Ajahn Amaro Bikkhu, peace begins with the individual and from there he or she may influence the collective. Sister Peace (An Nghiem) has a similar perspective to Amaro Bikkhu in that peace begins with the individual and that one must work both individually and collectively toward peace.

Another important topic from discussions with the Buddhists was "mindfulness." As Geshe Lama Phuntsho remarked: "One thing we always say is that if you want to meditate then motivation is important. If you want to use meditation in your daily life, then mindfulness is important." On the other hand, for Geshe Lobsang Tsultrim, real mindfulness means being mindful about where you go, what you eat, how you speak, and what you think. It is paying attention to one's actions, speech-actions, and mind. By comparison, Ajahn Amaro Bikkhu declared from the Buddha: "mindfulness is the path to the deathless, heedlessness is the path to death." And as such, he discussed the four foundations or four domains of mindfulness, which are "the contemplation of the body"; "the contemplation of sensations"; "the mindfulness of mind states"; "the process of experiencing itself." On the other hand, for An Nghiem, Sister Peace, her views of mindfulness encompassed having awareness and being conscious in the present moment. She also emphasized doing things, one at a time, or mono-tasking and doing them with intention.

Another key aspect of the Buddhist interviews was the issue of racism as experienced by Sister Peace, An Nghiem, as an African-American woman growing up in the Washington, DC, area. She related several stories, which highlighted experiences of racism. For example, she mentioned when she was a girl her grandmother never asked to use the fitting room when buying clothes because of the possibility of being rejected for trying clothes on because of her race. Sister Peace also expressed how as an African-American how difficult it was to try to hail down a taxi cab in Washington, DC, because of her race, at least this was true years ago before she was ordained a nun. Likewise, she related how she visited England and examined the serf quarters. She observed how similar the serf quarters were to the slave quarters she had visited and seen in Virginia. She commented: "I thought my God if you could do this to your own people [in Medieval England], no wonder you could do this to so-called someone else [to African-Americans]." Furthermore, Sister Peace believed there was a paradigm shift for the better happening in the United States following the murder of George Floyd and because of the #BlackLivesMatter protests.

Finally, what is important in this book, *Politics and Racism Beyond Nations*, is the idea of "inter-being," both from a Buddhist perspective and an indigenous perspective. From Buddhism, I derived my understanding of inter-being from the Zen Master, living saint, and Buddhist monk Thich Nhat Hanh. In my view, the compelling notion of "inter-being" from Buddhist philosophy and indigenous philosophy has great potential for inspiring change in peacebuilding in general. As Thich Nhat Hanh (2005: 88) declared: "I am, therefore you are. You are, therefore I am. That is the meaning of the word 'interbeing.' We interare." The view promises to do no undue harm to people, animals, and all living things. From mindfulness training, Buddhist monks make two vows: "The first promise is: 'I vow to develop my compassion in order to love and protect the life of people, animals, plants, and minerals.' The second promise is: 'I vow to develop understanding in order to be able to love and to live in harmony with people, animals, plants, and minerals'" (Nhat Hanh 2005: 89). Similarly, Amerindian notions of "inter-being" may be understood from what Eduardo Viveiros de Castro termed "Amerindian Perspectivism" (1998), the idea of interrelatedness among animals and humans and all life.

In terms of Buddhism, and more specifically, there are fourteen mindfulness trainings, which express compassion, understanding, and living mindfully and in peace. It is critical to understand all fourteen of these trainings in order to generate "inter-being" awareness through "mindfulness," which I am excerpting here again from the last chapter. The first is: "Aware of the suffering created by fanaticism and intolerance." The second is: "Aware of the suffering created by attachment to views and wrong perceptions." The third is: "Aware of the suffering brought about when we impose our views on others." The fourth is: "Aware that looking deeply at the nature of suffering can help us develop compassion and find ways out of suffering." The fifth is: "Aware that true happiness is rooted in peace, solidity, freedom, and compassion." The sixth is: "Aware that anger blocks communication and creates suffering." The seventh is: "Aware that life is available only in the present moment and that it is possible to live happily in the here and now." The eighth is: "Aware that the lack of communication always brings separation and suffering." The ninth is: "Aware that words can create suffering or happiness." The tenth is: "Aware that the essence and aim of a Sangha [a Buddhist community of monks, nuns, novices, and laity] is the practice of understanding and compassion." The eleventh is: "Aware that great violence and injustice have been done to our environment and society." The twelfth is: "Aware that much suffering is caused by war and conflict." The thirteenth is: "Aware of the suffering caused by exploitation, social injustice, stealing, and oppression." and The fourteenth is: "(For lay members): Aware that sexual relations motivated by craving cannot dissipate the feeling of loneliness but will create more suffering, frustration, and isolation" (Nhat Hanh 2005: 90–103).

Philosophically, Buddhism promotes inter-being through analogies. For example, take the idea of a flower. It is not just a flower but it embodies the whole cosmos in just one flower because within it there is sunshine, nutrients from the soil, and nourishment from the rain (Nhat Hanh 2017: 11). We too are like flowers as there is in us our parents and grandparents and our education, our food, and our culture. In other words, we are all of many things and many people. We inter-are (Nhat Hanh 2017: 12). We are all connected on this planet to each other and each living thing.

In this regard, Buddhism is similar to Amerindian and indigenous views of the cosmos (see Viveiros de Castro 1998). To most Native American peoples, everything has a spirit and are part of the Great Spirit, however, defined by the particular indigenous people of interest. Thus, in my view we need to think beyond technological progress and using the planet as an unending natural resource. In the last chapter, I spoke about a "re-indigenization" mentality by respecting all living things on this planet in order to ensure our future survival.

It may be wishful thinking but we need to re-establish our relationship with the Earth in my opinion if we are to survive. Indeed, in recent years, the economic crisis of 2008 and the COVID-19 crisis (2020–present) have shown how fragile the entire system is. While we live in an interconnected planet due to cell phone communication, the Internet, television, radio, air-travel, and so on, it would be difficult to imagine a mass transition whereby the world becomes more empathic and mindful. Yet, it is worth mentioning and promoting. As Buddhist monk Geshe Lama Phuntsho remarked in our interview, you may not be able to transform the whole world at once. It may begin with one person at a time.

While at the same time, it is difficult not to be listened to like the proverbial canary in the coal mine, but it is worth singing out and striving for change, even if such change for peace at the moment appears to be entirely remote. Here it is worth repeating and reiterating from the last chapter why a so-called re-indigenization of society is important and beyond wishful thinking, what about such a proposal is practical, if at all. Some of the re-indigenization project may be more practicable than other parts for possible consideration and possible implementation.

Let me now elaborate from the discussion of the last chapter about "re-indigenization" and why some parts of it are more practicable than others. Such a set of views may be overly hopeful but they do point to some directions in which to consider how to address climate change and overall our current existential crisis. Let's begin with the first point:

1. Accept human beings as part of Earth, and not apart from it, and by this acceptance, accept our dependence upon it. In doing so, this may take a mindset shift. How do we become ecologically aware? Is there a reason to care? In my view, if we are to believe the science behind Anthropocene climate change then all of us should take this seriously. Human beings are not above nature, even though the

history of Western thought has allowed for such a perspective to our detriment.
2. Accept Earth as a living being, the Gaia theory. And if we are to take care of ourselves, we need to take care of the Earth too and become its guardians. We need to love the Earth and respect it as much as indigenous peoples everywhere do.

Again, similar to the first point, this would require a massive shift in recognizing that mass extinction of millions of animal species because of the Anthropocene are possible. But let us hope not inevitable. Scientists and ecologists are making concerted efforts to make people aware of the possibility for mass extinction. I am just repeating what many in the scientific community believe to be true. Yet, having people care for the Earth and change their perspectives to match indigenous knowledge of the environment and nature may be unrealistic but it should nevertheless be a goal.

3. Being grateful for our being on this planet and not endlessly destroying it and polluting it is a good beginning which has been around for a while in ecological consciousness circles. In this book, I have tried to demonstrate from the Buddhist example that "mindfulness" is a central idea if we are to better take care of this planet. Indeed, mindfulness training in education is quite popular today.[1] Perhaps, one idea would be to extend mindfulness training to include ecological consciousness and to make this part of educational curricula as well.
4. Instead of putting resources into warfare, put resources into renewable energies and into solving malnutrition and poverty in sustainable ways. Make farming more sustainable too instead of a form of factory production and endless soil depletion.

Of course, many would argue why should we lessen our military spending. How does this make sense, given the threats of countries like China, Iran, and Russia or asymmetric combatants like ISIS and the remnants of Al-Qaeda? Even so, it is clear we put far too many resources into defense budgets. Furthermore, I am not the first to warn against the military-industrial complex. Notably, former President Dwight D. Eisenhower in his farewell address warned against it way back in 1961.[2]

Eisenhower stated in this speech: "Disarmament, with mutual honor and confidence, is a continuing imperative. Together we must learn how to compose differences, not with arms, but with intellect and decent purpose." Even so, many would deride the argument for less military spending as foolhardy and too peace-nicky. Yet, according to the Bulletin of Atomic Scientists and their 2021 Doomsday Clock Statement, we are now 100 seconds to midnight or nuclear annihilation.[3] In other words, the world is less stable by continued nuclear armament buildup across the world. So, while to some, lessening armaments may be a fairy tale; nonetheless, we risk our own destruction by not listening to alternative solutions to warfare.

5. Allow indigenous peoples to have "more voice" with first-world nations (Europe, the United States, Japan, Canada, Australia, New Zealand, and other powerful states as China and Russia) in United Nations forums and such environmental decision-making as the Paris Agreement of 2015.

While to major powerbrokers such as the United States and Europe such relinquishment of power may be untenable; nevertheless, indigenous peoples have powerful voices in regard to the environment. We should be actively listening to their messages and allow them more voice. This is not as unrealistic as perhaps other proposals for re-indigenization here. If we are to learn the lessons from historical colonialism, certainly we may acknowledge how much we have wronged Native peoples. Allowing them more voice about the environment and preventing environmental destruction seems practicable, especially since their warnings come from voices who in many cases maintain their livelihoods from the ecologies they protect.

6. Protect indigenous peoples and their rights and allow for indigenous parks and reserves to remain and to be expanded upon by protecting larger tracts of land, instead of developing and exploiting natural resources on indigenous lands for industrial farming, mining interests, oil extraction, electric dams, lumbering, and ranching.

Earlier in the book, it was proposed that the Amazon River itself and thousands of hectares of adjacent land be preserved as ecological patrimony for the world. Of course, the nations which encompass Amazonia (Bolivia, Brazil, Colombia, Ecuador, Peru, Venezuela, Guyana, French Guiana, and Suriname) would have to approve such a massive and ambitious endeavor. But it is worth thinking about for the long-term future, however unrealistic in the short term such a possibility appears to be. Certainly, Europe and the United States could give incentives for making such a grand reserve. Moreover, as the book pointed out, the Amazon's destruction is happening at an exponential rate and even though such proposals for large-scale ecological protections seem to be fantasies, maybe one day they will be taken seriously.

> 7. Make the "re-indigenization" project official in international law and international treaties, and along with other international laws concerning indigenous peoples (e.g., ILO Convention Number 169 of 1989 and the 2007 UNDRIP, United Nations Declaration on the Rights of Indigenous Peoples). Make all nation-states adhere to such a project if possible.

Again, to many "re-indigenization" is just impractical and unrealistic make-believe. But there are some aspects of it which may be implemented. It may take a herculean effort to get various parties to agree on some of these points but the United Nations has passed the Declaration on the Rights of Indigenous People and the ILO Convention Number 169 are exemplars of such possibilities, however, seemingly remote today. It may take a true disaster for any world leader to think about re-indigenization. For example, the further decimation of the Amazon or the melting of the polar ice caps which might then lead to a tipping point in our climactic and ecological future. In turn, such environmental disasters may thereby inspire future leaders to act rather than wait for further environmental devastation.

> 8. Create more public awareness through more education programs through universities, and above all, create an ecological consciousness understood from indigenous perspectives and in their own voices.

Many universities already have Indigenous Studies departments and thus creating multi-disciplinary programs in ecological consciousness is not as unrealistic as it first may seem. Environmental Science should join with Indigenous Studies departments in multidisciplinary endeavors of the re-indigenization sort if they do not already do so. Certainly, many university aims are to create interdisciplinary and multidisciplinary curricula which enhance student learning and broaden university degrees.

9. Remember scientists believe we are entering the Sixth Extinction phase on the planet and we must prevent this by all productive means necessary.

I suppose the question for this is, when will there be a tipping point for nations and world leaders to act in concert? Will it be another world war? Will it be an impending environmental disaster, the melting of the polar ice caps or the almost complete destruction of the Amazon or the complete decimation of the Great Barrier Reef? Again, it is difficult to know. What is clear is that nations and world leaders are not acting with as much urgency as they should. Even so, there are recent efforts. In October and November 2021, the United Nations will held a Climate Change Conference (UNCC, also known as COP26) in Glasgow, Scotland. Hence, will the UNCC aid in preventing future climate disasters or will much more effort be necessary? I am guessing the latter.

10. And finally, allow more indigenous peoplesf to be spokespeople and to become planetary ambassadors for realizing such a re-indigenization project before it is too late.

Again, this is not as unrealistic as it may seem. Increasingly, those in power are acknowledging and recognizing indigenous knowledge about the environment and how to protect the environment. Yet, such recognition appears to be piecemeal and slow. What effort will it take for world leaders to realize that many Native peoples base their livelihoods with their environments and thereby would be good stewards as ambassadors for protecting varying ecological systems, and perhaps protect against an impending climatic disaster.

In sum, the "re-indigenization" project may just be wishful thinking. However, in my view, such a project is worth contemplating, especially since the stakes are so high for the global environment and global climate and for the future of the human species. In other words, if human beings are to avoid nuclear destruction, environmental nihilism, and an impending Sixth Extinction of millions of animals on our planet (including ourselves), and elude climatic catastrophe, we must think in terms of "inter-being" before it is truly too late. Only then can we create a harmonious planet in which to live and which would eschew attachment to nationalisms, terrorism, racism, and thereby eliminate unnecessary trauma.

## Notes

1. https://news.harvard.edu/gazette/story/2018/04/harvard-researchers-study-how-mindfulness-may-change-the-brain-in-depressed-patients/.
2. https://avalon.law.yale.edu/20th_century/eisenhower001.asp.
3. https://thebulletin.org/doomsday-clock/current-time/.

## Bibliography

Anderson, B. 1991, orig. 1983. *Imagined Communities: Reflections on the Origin and Spread of Nationalism*. London: Verso.

Balthazart, J. 2012. *The Biology of Homosexuality*. Oxford: Oxford University Press.

Bloch, M. 2013. *In and Out of Each Other's Bodies: Theory of Mind, Evolution, Truth, and the Nature of the Social*. London: Paradigm Publishers.

Kendi, I.X. 2019. *How to Be an Antiracist*. New York: One World.

Linstroth, J.P. 2002. The Basque Conflict Globally Speaking: Material Culture, Media and Basque Identity in the Wider World. *Journal of Oxford Development Studies* 30 (2): 205–222.

———. 2009. Mayan Cognition, Memory, and Trauma. *History and Anthropology* 20 (2): 139–182.

Nhat Hanh, T. 2005. *Being Peace*. Berkeley, CA: Parallax Press.

———. 2017. *The Art of Living: Peace and Freedom in the Here and Now*. New York: Harper One, Harper Collins Publishers.

Sanford, V. 2008. ¡Si Hubo Genocidio en Guatemala! Yes! There Was Genocide in Guatemala. In *The Historiography of Genocide*, ed. D. Stone, 543–576. New York: Palgrave Macmillan.

Sapolsky, R. 2017. *Behave: The Biology of Humans at Our Best and Worst*. New York: Penguin Books.

Scott, J.C. 1990. *Domination and the Arts of Resistance: Hidden Transcripts*. New Haven, CT: Yale University Press.

Viveiros de Castro, E. 1998. Cosmological Deixis and Amerindian Perspectivism. *The Journal of the Royal Anthropological Institute* 4 (3): 469–488.

# Bibliography

Anderson, B. 1991, orig. 1983. *Imagined Communities: Reflections on the Origin and Spread of Nationalism*. London: Verso.

Anderson, J. 1995. *Learning and Memory: An Integrated Approach*. New York: John Wiley & Sons, Inc.

Anderson, S., and M. Conway. 1997. Representations of Autobiographical Memories. In *Cognitive Models of Memory*, ed. M. Conway, 217–248. Cambridge, MA: The MIT Press.

Asad, T. 2004. Where Are the Margins of the State? In *Anthropology in the Margins of the State*, ed. Veena Das and Deborah Poole, 279–288. Oxford: James Currey Ltd.

Atran, S. 1990. *Cognitive Foundations of Natural History: Towards an Anthropology of Science*. Cambridge: Cambridge University Press.

———. 2002. *In Gods We Trust: The Evolutionary Landscape of Religion*. New York and Oxford: Oxford University Press.

Augsburger, D.W. 1992. *Conflict Mediation Across Cultures: Pathways and Patterns*. London: Westminster John Knox Press.

Avruch, K. 1998, new edn. 2004. *Culture & Conflict Resolution*. Washington, DC: United States Institute of Peace.

Avruch, K., and P.W. Black. 2001. Conflict Resolution in Intercultural Settings: Problems and Prospects. In *The Conflict and Culture Reader*, ed. Pat K. Chew, 7–14. New York: New York University Press.

Axel, B.K. 2001. *The Nation's Tortured Body: Violence, Representation, and the Formation of a Sikh "Diaspora"*. Durham: Duke University Press.

Azar, E.E. 1990. *The Management of Protracted Social Conflict: Theory and Cases*. Aldershot, UK: Dartmouth Publishing Co. Ltd.

Baddeley, A., M. Conway, and J. Aggleton, eds. 2001. *Episodic Memory: New Directions in Research.* Oxford: Oxford University Press.
Bagemihl, B. 1999. *Biological Exuberance: Animal Homosexuality and Natural Diversity.* New York: St. Martin's Press.
Bakunin, M. 1990, orig. 1873. *Statism and Anarchy,* Trans. M. Shatz. Cambridge: Cambridge University Press.
Balthazart, J. 2012. *The Biology of Homosexuality.* Oxford: Oxford University Press.
Banks, M. 1996. *Ethnicity: Anthropological Constructions.* London: Routledge.
Barnier, A.J., et al. 2008. A Conceptual and Empirical Framework for the Social Distribution of Cognition: The Case of Memory. *Cognitive Systems Research* 9 (1): 33–51.
Bar-On, D., and J. Chaitin. 2001. *Parenthood and the Holocaust.* Jerusalem: Yad Vashem Publications, Search and Research, Lectures and Papers 1.
Barth, F., ed. 1969. *Ethnic Groups and Boundaries: The Social Organisation of Culture Differences.* London: George Allen and Unwin.
Bartlett, F. Sir 1932; 1961 edn. *Remembering: A Study in Experimental and Social Psychology.* Cambridge: Cambridge University Press.
Bartrop, P.R., ed. 2018. *Modern Genocide: Analyzing the Controversies and Issues.* Santa Barbara, CA: ABC-CLIO, LLC.
Bayor, R.H., ed. 2003. *Race and Ethnicity in America: A Concise History.* New York: Columbia University Press.
Beatty, A. 2019. *Emotional Worlds: Beyond an Anthropology of Emotion.* Cambridge, UK: Cambridge University Press.
Berlin, I. 1991. *The Crooked Timber of Humanity: Chapters in the History of Ideas* (Ed. H. Hardy). New York: Alfred A. Knopf.
———. 2006. *Political Ideas in the Romantic Age: Their Rise and Influence on Modern Thought.* Princeton: Princeton University Press. [Based Upon His Unpublished Manuscript of 1952].
Berliner, D. 2005. The Abuses of Memory: Reflections on the Memory Boom in Anthropology. *Anthropological Quarterly* 78 (1): 197–211.
Bernasconi, R., and T.L. Lott, eds. 2000. *The Idea of Race.* Indianapolis, IN: Hackett Publishing Company, Inc.
Biehl, J., and P. Locke, eds. 2017. *Unfinished: The Anthropology of Becoming.* Durham, NC: Duke University Press.
Bloch, M. 1986. *From Blessing to Violence: History and Ideology in the Circumcision Ritual of the Merina.* Cambridge: Cambridge University Press.
———. 1989. *Ritual, History and Power: Selected Papers in Anthropology.* London: The Athlone Press.
———. 1998. *How We Think They Think: Anthropological Approaches to Cognition, Memory, and Literacy.* Oxford: Westview Press.

———. 2004. Ritual and Deference. In *Ritual and Memory: Toward a Comparative Anthropology of Religion*, ed. H. Whitehouse and J. Laidlaw, 65–78. Oxford: AltaMira Press.

———. 2012. *Anthropology and the Cognitive Challenge*. Cambridge: Cambridge University Press.

———. 2013. *In and Out of Each Other's Bodies: Theory of Mind, Evolution, Truth, and the Nature of the Social*. London: Paradigm Publishers.

Bonilla-Silva, E. 2014. *Racism Without Racists: Color-Blind Racism and the Persistence of Racial Inequality in America*. 4th ed. Lanham, MD: Rowman & Littlefield Publishers, Inc.

Boulding, E. 1988, new edn. 1990. *Building a Global Civic Culture: Education for an Interdependent World*. Syracuse: Syracuse University Press.

Bourdieu, P. 1977. *Outline of a Theory of Practice*. Cambridge: Cambridge University Press.

Boyer, P. 2001. *Religion Explained: The Evolutionary Origins of Religious Thought*. New York: Basic Books.

Brown, R., and J. Kulik. 1977. Flashbulb Memories. *Cognition* 5: 73–99.

Brown, M.E., O.R. Coté Jr., S.M. Lynn-Jones, and S.E. Miller, eds. 2001. *Nationalism and Ethnic Conflict: An International Security Reader*. Cambridge: MIT Press.

Bryceson, D., and U. Vuorela, eds. 2002. *The Transnational Family: New European Frontiers and Global Networks*. Oxford: Berg.

Burton, J.W. 1987. *Resolving Deep-Rooted Conflict: A Handbook*. Lanham, MD: University Press of America.

Butler, J. 1990. *Gender Trouble: Feminism and Subversion of Identity*. London: Routledge.

———. 1993. *Bodies That Matter: On the Discursive Limits of 'Sex'*. London: Routledge.

———. 2004. *Undoing Gender*. London: Routledge.

Carter, R. 2002. *Exploring Consciousness*. Berkeley, CA: University of California Press.

Cave, A.A. 2008. Genocide in the Americas. In *The Historiography of Genocide*, ed. D. Stone, 273–295. New York: Palgrave Macmillan.

Chew, P.K., ed. 2001. *The Conflict and Culture Reader*. New York: New York University Press.

Chomsky, N. 2001. *9-11*. New York: Seven Stories Press.

———. 2002. Terror and Just Response. In *War Plan Iraq: Ten Reasons Against War on Iraq*, ed. M. Rai. London: Verso.

———. 2004. The New War Against Terror: Responding to 9/11. In *Violence in War and Peace: An Anthology*, ed. N. Scheper-Hughes and P. Bourois. Oxford: Blackwell Publishing.

Clark, R.P. 1990. *Negotiating with ETA: Obstacles to Peace in the Basque Country, 1975–1988.* Reno, NV: University of Nevada Press.
Clark, A., and D. Chalmers. 1998. The Extended Mind. *Analysis* 58 (1): 7–19.
Clifford, J. 1988. *The Predicament of Culture: Twentieth-Century Ethnography, Literature, and Art.* Cambridge, MA: Harvard University Press.
Collingwood, R.G. 1946. *The Idea of History.* Oxford: Oxford University Press.
Comaroff, J., and J. Comaroff. 1992. *Ethnography and the Historical Imagination.* Oxford: Westview Press.
———. 2009. *Ethnicity, Inc.* Chicago: The University of Chicago Press.
Connerton, P. 1989. *How Societies Remember.* Cambridge: Cambridge University Press.
Conway, M., ed. 1997. *Cognitive Models of Memory.* Cambridge, MA: The MIT Press.
Coogan, T.P. 1996. *The Troubles: Ireland's Ordeal 1966–1996 and the Search for Peace.* Boulder, CO: Roberts Rinehart Publishers.
Cornwall, A., and N. Lindisfarne, eds. 1994. *Dislocating Masculinity: Comparative Ethnographies.* London: Routledge.
Cowan, J.K., Marie-Bénédicte Dembour, and R.A. Wilson, eds. 2001. *Culture and Rights: Anthropological Perspectives.* Cambridge: Cambridge University Press.
Crocker, C.A., ed. 2005. *Grasping the Nettle: Analyzing Cases of Intractable Conflict.* Washington, DC: United States Institute of Peace Press.
Crocker, C.A., et al. 2004. *Taming Intractable Conflicts: Mediation in the Hardest Cases.* Washington, DC: United States Institute of Peace Press.
D'Andrade, R. 1995. *The Development of Cognitive Anthropology.* Cambridge: Cambridge University Press.
D'Andrade, R., and C. Strauss, eds. 1992. *Human Motives and Cultural Models.* Cambridge: Cambridge University Press.
Daniel, E.V. 1996. *Charred Lullabies: Chapters in an Anthropology of Violence.* Princeton: Princeton University Press.
Das, V., and D. Poole. 2004. State and Its Margins: Comparative Ethnographies. In *Anthropology in the Margins of the State*, ed. V. Das and D. Poole, 3–33. Oxford: James Currey Ltd.
Davis, S. 1977. *Victims of the Miracle: Development and the Indians of Brazil.* Cambridge: Cambridge University Press.
De Las Casas, B. 1974 edn., 1474–1566. *The Devastation of the Indies: A Brief Account,* Trans. H. Briffault. Baltimore, MD: The Johns Hopkins University Press.
Delgado, R., and J. Stefancic. 2017. *Critical Race Theory: An Introduction.* 3rd ed. New York: New York University Press.
Derrida, J. (trans. M. Quaintance). 1990. Force of Law: The "mystical foundation of authority". *Cardozo Law Review* 11: 919–1045.

Diamond, L., and J. McDonald. 1996. *Multi-Track Diplomacy: A Systems Approach to Peace*. 3rd ed. West Hartford, CT: Kumarian Press.

Diangelo, R. 2018. *White Fragility: Why It's So Hard for White People to Talk About Racism*. Boston: Beacon Press.

Douglas, M. 1950. Introduction: Maurice Halbwachs (1877–1945). *The Collective Memory*, M. Halbwachs, Trans. F. Ditter and V. Y. Ditter. New York: Harper & Row, Publishers, pp. 1–21.

———. 2000. Memory and Selective Attention: Bartlett and Evans-Pritchard. In *Bartlett, Culture and Cognition*, ed. A. Saito, 179–193. London: Psychology Press (Taylor & Francis Group).

Dyson, M.E. 2007. *Debating Race with Michael Eric Dyson*. New York: Basic Civitas Books.

Eller, J., and R. Coughlan. 1996. The Poverty of Primordialism. In *Ethnicity*, ed. J. Hutchinson and A.D. Smith. Oxford: Oxford University Press. [Orig. 1993].

Eriksen, T.H. 1993. *Ethnicity and Nationalism*. 2nd ed. London: Pluto Press. [2002 revised edn].

Espiau Idoiaga, G. 2006. The Basque Conflict: New Ideas and Prospects for Peace. In *Special Report: United States Institute of Peace (USIP)*, no. 161, 1–12. Washington, DC: United Institute of Peace Press.

Fabian, J. 2001. *Anthropology with an Attitude: Critical Essays*. Stanford: Stanford University Press.

Farmer, P. 1999. *Infections and Inequalities: The Modern Plagues*. Berkeley: University of California Press.

———. 2005. *Pathologies of Power: Health, Human Rights, and the New War on the Poor*. Berkeley: University of California Press.

Fassin, D., and R. Rechtman. 2009. *The Empire of Trauma: An Inquiry into the Condition of Victimhood*. Princeton: Princeton University Press.

Feldman, A. 1991. *Formations of Violence: The Narrative of the Body and Political Terror in Northern Ireland*. Chicago: The University of Chicago Press.

Fentress, J., and C. Wickham. 1992. *Social Memory*. Oxford: Blackwell.

Fisher, R., and W. Ury 1991, orig. 1981. *Getting to Yes: Negotiating Agreement Without Giving in*. New York: Penguin Books.

Fonkem Achankeng, M., ed. 2015. *Nationalism and Intra-State Conflicts in the Postcolonial World*. Lanham, MD: Lexington Books.

Font-Guzman, J. 2015. *Experiencing Puerto Rican Citizenship and Cultural Nationalism*. New York: Palgrave Macmillan.

Foster, R.J. 2002. *Materializing the Nation: Commodities, Consumption, and Media in Papua New Guinea*. Bloomington: Indiana University Press.

Foucault, M. 1969. *The Archaeology of Knowledge*, Trans. A. M. Sheridan Smith, 1994 edn. London: Routledge.

Fry, D.P. 2006. *The Human Potential for Peace: An Anthropological Challenge to Assumptions About War and Violence*. Oxford: Oxford University Press.

———. 2007. *Beyond War: the Human Potential for Peace*. Oxford: Oxford University Press.

———., ed. 2013. *War, Peace, and Human Nature: The Convergence of Evolutionary and Cultural Views*. Oxford: Oxford University Press.

Fry, D., and G. Souillac 2021. Peaceful Societies Are Not Utopian Fantasy. They Exist. *Bulletin of the Atomic Scientists*, pp. 1–7.

Fry, D., et al. 2021. Societies Within Peace Systems Avoid War and Build Positive Intergroup Relationships. *Humanities and Social Sciences Communications* 8 (17): 1–9.

Fukuyama, F. 2004. *State-Building: Governance and World Order in the 21st Century*. Ithaca, NY: Cornell University Press.

Galtung, J. 2000. Conflict, War and Peace: A Bird's Eye View. In *Searching for Peace: The Road to TRANSCEND*, ed. Johan Galtung, Carl G. Jacobsen, and Kai Frithjof Brand-Jacobsen. London: Pluto Press.

Galtung, J., et al., eds. 2000. *Searching for Peace: The Road to TRANSCEND*. London: Pluto Press.

Geertz, C. 1973. The Integrative Revolution: Primordial Sentiments and Civil Politics in the New States. In *The Interpretation of Cultures: Selected Essays*. New York: Basic Books.

———. 1996. Primordial Ties. In *Ethnicity*, ed. J. Hutchinson and A.D. Smith. Oxford: Oxford University Press. [orig. 1963].

Gell, A. 1975. *Metamorphosis of the Cassowaries: Umeda Society, Language and Ritual*. London: The Athlone Press.

———. 1992. *The Anthropology of Time: Cultural Constructions of Temporal Maps and Images*. Oxford: Berg.

———. 1998. *Art and Agency: An Anthropological Theory*, 1998. Oxford: Clarendon Press.

———. 1999a. Strathernograms, Or, the Semiotics of Mixed Metaphors. In *The Art of Anthropology: Essays and Diagrams*. London: The Athlone Press.

———. 1999b, new edn. 2006. Vogel's Net: Traps as Artworks and Artworks as Traps. In *The Art of Anthropology: Essays and Diagrams*, Alfred Gell, ed. Eric Hirsch, pp. 187–214. Oxford: Berg.

Gellner, E. 1983. *Nations and Nationalism*. Oxford: Basil Blackwell.

———. 1994. *Encounters with Nationalism*. Oxford: Blackwell Publishers Ltd.

———. 1997. *Nationalism*. New York: New York University Press.

Gingerich, A., and M. Banks. 2006. *Neo-Nationalism in Europe and Beyond: Perspectives from Social Anthropology*. Oxford: Berghahn Books.

Gladney, D., ed. 1998. *Making Majorities: Constituting the Nation in Japan, Korea, China, Malaysia, Fiji, Turkey, and the United States*. Stanford, CA: Stanford University Press.

Goddard, V.A., J.R. Llobera, and C. Shore. 1994. *The Anthropology of Europe: Identity and Boundaries in Conflict*. Oxford: Berg.

Goodall, J. 1971, 2010 new edn. *In Shadow of Man*. Boston: Mariner Books, Houghton Mifflin Harcourt.
Gordon, C., ed. 1980. *Power/Knowledge: Selected Interviews & Other Writings, 1972–1977 by Michel Foucault*. New York: Pantheon Books.
Graeber, D. 2001. *Toward an Anthropological Theory of Value: The False Coin of Our Own Dreams*. New York: Palgrave.
Gramsci, A. 1971. *Selections from the Prison Notebooks*, ed. and Trans. Q. Hoare and G. N. Smith. New York: International Publishers.
Griffin, J.H. 1962. *Black Like Me*. New York: A Signet Book, Penguin Group.
Grosby, S. 1996. The Inexpungeable Tie of Primordiality. In *Ethnicity*, ed. J. Hutchinson and A.D. Smith. Oxford: Oxford University Press. [orig. 1994].
Gupta, A., and J. Ferguson. 1997. Culture, Power, Place: Ethnography at the End of an Era. In *Culture, Power, Place: Explorations in Critical Anthropology*, ed. A. Gupta and J. Ferguson, 1–29. Durham, NC and London: Duke University Press.
Guss, D.M. 2000. *The Festive State: Race, Ethnicity, and Nationalism as Cultural Performance*. Berkeley: University of California Press.
Habermas, J. 1996. *Between Facts and Norms: Contributions to a Discourse Theory of Law and Democracy*. Cambridge, MA: The MIT Press.
Halbwachs, M. 1950; 1980 edn. *La Mémoire Collective (The Collective Memory)*, Trans. F. Ditter and V. Y. Ditter. New York: Harper & Row Publishers.
Halpern, D. 2000. *Sex Differences in Cognitive Abilities*. 3rd ed. London: Lawrence Erlbaum Associates, Publishers.
Hamilton, C. 2007. *Women and ETA: The Gender Politics of Radical Basque Nationalism*. Manchester: Manchester University Press.
Hanchard, M. 2000. Black Cinderella? Race and the Public Sphere in Brazil. In *The Idea of Race*, ed. R. Bernasconi and T.L. Lott, 161–180. Indianapolis, IN: Hackett Publishing Company, Inc.
Heiberg, M. 1989. *The Making of the Basque Nation*. Cambridge: Cambridge University Press.
———. 2007. ETA: Euskadi 'ta Askatasuna. In *Terror, Insurgency, and the State: Ending Protracted Conflicts*, ed. M. Heiberg, B. O'Leary, and J. Tirman, 19–49. Philadelphia: University of Pennsylvania Press.
Hemming, J. 1978. *Red Gold: The Conquest of the Brazilian Indians*. Cambridge, MA: Harvard University Press.
———. 2008. *Tree of Rivers: The Story of the Amazon*. New York: Thames & Hudson, Inc.
Herdt, G. 1981, new edn. 1994. *Guardians of the Flute: Idioms of Masculinity*. New York: McGraw-Hill.
Hinton, A.L., ed. 2002. *Annihilating Difference: the Anthropology of Genocide*. Berkeley: University of California Press.

Hitchcock, R.K., and T.E. Koperski. 2008. Genocides of Indigenous Peoples. In *The Historiography of Genocide*, ed. D. Stone, 577–617. New York: Palgrave Macmillan.

Hobsbawm, E., and T. Ranger, eds. 1983. *The Invention of Tradition*. Cambridge: Cambridge University Press.

Huntington, S.P. 1996. *The Clash of Civilizations: Remaking of World Order*. New York: Simon & Schuster.

Hutchinson, J., and A.D. Smith, eds. 1996. *Ethnicity*. Oxford: Oxford University Press.

Irvin, C. 1999. *Militant Nationalism: Between Movement and Party in Ireland and the Basque Country*. Minneapolis: University of Minnesota Press.

Irvin Painter, N. 2010. *The History of White People*. New York: W. W. Norton & Company.

Iverson, P. 2002. *Diné: A History of the Navajos*. Albuquerque, NM: The University of New Mexico Press.

Jackson, R., et al. 2011. *Terrorism: A Critical Introduction*. New York: Palgrave Macmillan.

Jaffrelot, C., and L. Tillin. 2017. Populism in India. In *The Oxford Handbook of Populism*, ed. C. Rovira Kaltwasser et al., 179–194. Oxford: Oxford University Press.

James, W. 2003. From Local to Global Peace and War. In *The Ceremonial Animal: A New Portrait of Anthropology*. Oxford: Oxford University Press.

Jarman, Neil. 1997. *Material Conflicts: Parades and Visual Displays in Northern Ireland*. Oxford: Berg.

Jenkins, Richard. 1997. *Rethinking Ethnicity: Arguments and Explorations*. London: SAGE Publications Ltd.

Jonas, S. 2013. Guatemala: Acts of Genocide and Scorched-earth Counterinsurgency War. In *Centuries of Genocide: Essays and Eyewitness Accounts*, ed. S. Totten and W.S. Parsons, 355–393. London: Routledge.

Kadushin, C. 2012. *Understanding Social Networks: Theories, Concepts, and Findings*. Oxford: Oxford University Press.

Kapferer, B., and B.E. Bertelsen, eds. 2009. *Crisis of the State: War and Social Upheaval*. Oxford: Berghahn Books.

Keating, Michael. 1993. Spain: Peripheral Nationalism and State Response. In *The Politics of Ethnic Conflict Regulation*, ed. J. McGarry and B. O'Leary, 204–225. New York: Routledge.

Kelly, T. 2006. *Law, Violence, and Sovereignty Among West Bank Palestinians*. Cambridge: Cambridge University Press.

Kelly, J.D., et al., eds. 2010. *Anthropology and Global Counterinsurgency*. Chicago: The University of Chicago Press.

Kemp, Graham, and Douglas P. Fry, eds. 2004. *Keeping the Peace: Conflict Resolution and Peaceful Societies Around the World*. London: Routledge.

Kendi, I.X. 2016. *Stamped from the Beginning: The Definitive History of Racist Ideas in America*. New York: Bold Type Books.
———. 2019. *How to Be an Antiracist*. New York: One World.
Kiernan, B. 2007. *Blood and Soil: A World History of Genocide and Extermination from Sparta to Darfur*. New Haven, CT: Yale University Press.
Kolbert, E. 2015. *The Sixth Extinction: An Unnatural History*. New York: Picador, Henry Holt and Company.
Kriesberg, Louis, Terrel A. Northrup, and Stuart J. Thompson, eds. 1989. *In-tractable Conflicts and Their Transformation*. Syracuse: Syracuse University Press.
Kurlansky, M. 1999. *The Basque History of the World*. London: Jonathan Cape.
Laidlaw, J. 2004a. Introduction. In *Ritual and Memory: Toward a Comparative Anthropology of Religion*, ed. H. Whitehouse and J. Laidlaw, 1–9. Oxford: Altamira Press.
———. 2004b. Embedded Modes of Religiosity in Indic Renouncer Religions. In *Ritual and Memory: Toward a Comparative Anthropology of Religion*, ed. H. Whitehouse and J. Laidlaw, 89–109. Oxford: Altamira Press.
———. 2007. A Well Disposed Social Anthropologist's Problems with the 'Cognitive Science of Religion'. In *Religion, Anthropology, and Cognitive Science*, ed. H. Whitehouse and J. Laidlaw, 211–246. Durham, NC: Carolina Academic Press.
Lan, D. 1985. *Guns & Rain: Guerrillas & Spirit Mediums in Zimbabwe*. London: James Currey Ltd.
Lang, B. 2017. *Genocide: The Act as Idea*. Philadelphia: University of Pennsylvania Press.
Le Goff, J. 1992. *History and Memory*. New York: Columbia University Press.
Lederach, John Paul. 1995. *Preparing for Peace: Conflict Transformation Across Cultures*. Syracuse: Syracuse University Press.
Linstroth, J.P. 1998. Arrani, Arrain, Arrai: en torno al protovasco 'Arrani' y sus derivaciones lingüísticas'. *Fontes Linguae Vasconum: studia et documenta, Año XXX, Número* 79: 397–406.
———. 2002a. The Basque Conflict Globally Speaking: Material Culture, Media and Basque Identity in the Wider World. *Journal of Oxford Development Studies* 30 (2): 205–222.
———. 2002b. History, Tradition, and Memory Among the Basques. *History and Anthropology* 13 (3): 159–189.
———. 2002c. Basque Imagination and Commemorative Identity: local history and everyday life in relation to the Hondarribian 'Alarde' (1638–2000). D. Phil. dissertation, Institute of Social and Cultural Anthropology, Oxford University (unpublished manuscript).
———. 2005. An Introductory Essay: 'The Age of Resistance' in a Post-9/11 World? *Peace and Conflict Studies, Special Issue*. (ed.) J. P. Linstroth, Vol. 12, no. 2: 1–54.

———. 2009. Mayan Cognition, Memory, and Trauma. *History and Anthropology* 20 (2): 139–182.

———. 2010. Gender as a Category for Analysis of Conflict. In *The Oxford International Encyclopedia of Peace: Volume 2 – Early Christianity and Antimilitarism – Mass Violence and Trends*, ed. Nigel Young, 226–234. Oxford: Oxford University Press.

———. 2015a. *Marching Against Gender Practice: Political Imaginings in the Basqueland*. Lanham, MD: Lexington Books.

———. 2015b. Urban Amerindians and Advocacy: Toward a Politically Engaged Anthropology Representing Urban Amerindigeneities. In *Indigenous Studies and Engaged Anthropology: The Collaborative Moment*, ed. Paul Sillitoe, 116–145. Surrey, UK and Burlington, VT: Ashgate Publishers Limited.

———. 2015c. Brazilian Nationalism and Urban Amerindians: Twenty-First Century Dilemmas for Indigenous Peoples Living in the Urban Amazon and Beyond. In *Nationalism and Intra-State Conflicts in the Postcolonial World*, ed. Fonkem Achankeng, 405–451. Lanham, MD: Lexington Books.

———. 2016. Conflict Avoidance among the Sateré-Mawé of Manaus, Brazil, and Peacemaking Behaviours Among Amazonian Amerindians. In *Creating the Third Force: Indigenous Processes of Peacemaking*, ed. Hamdesa Tuso, Maureen Flaherty, and M.D. Lanham, 249–275. Lexington Books.

Llera, F.J., J.M. Mata, and C.L. Irvin. 1993. ETA: From Secret Army to Social Movement – The Post-Franco Schism of the Basque Nationalist Movement. *Terrorism and Political Violence* 5 (3): 106–134.

Llobera, J.R. 1994. *The God of Modernity: The Development of Nationalism in Western Europe*. Oxford: Berg.

Locke, J. 1689, new edn. 1994. *Two Treatises of Government* (ed. P. Laslett). Cambridge: Cambridge University Press.

Lovell, N., ed. 1998. *Locality and Belonging*. London: Routledge.

Lowndes, J. 2017. Populism in the United States. In *The Oxford Handbook of Populism*, ed. C. Rovira Kaltwasser et al., 232–247. Oxford: Oxford University Press.

MacClancy, J. 1993. At Play with Identity in the Basque Arena. In *Inside European Identities: Ethnography in Western Europe*, ed. S. Macdonald, 84–97. Oxford: Berg.

———. 2007. *Expressing Identities in the Basque Arena*. Oxford: James Currey Publishers.

Macdonald, S., ed. 1993. *Inside European Identities: Ethnography in Western Europe*. Oxford: Berg.

Mandler, J., and L. McDonough. 1997. Nonverbal Recall. In *Memory for Everyday and Emotional Events*, ed. N. Stein et al., 141–164. Mahwah, NJ: Lawrence Erlbaum Associates, Publishers.

Manz, B. 2002. Terror, Grief, and Recovery: Genocidal Trauma in a Mayan Village in Guatemala. In *Annihilating Difference: The Anthropology of Genocide*, ed. A.L. Hintion, 292–309. Berkeley: University of California Press.

Maybury-Lewis, D. 2002. Genocide Against Indigenous Peoples. In *Annihilating Difference: The Anthropology of Genocide*, ed. A.L. Hinton, 43–53. Berkeley: University of California Press.

McClelland, J. 1995. Constructive Memory and Memory Distortions: A Parallel-Distributed Processing Approach. In *Memory Distortion: How Minds, Brains, and Societies Reconstruct the Past*, ed. D. Schacter, 69–90. Cambridge, MA: Harvard University Press.

McClelland, J., B. McNaughton, and R. O'Reilly. 2002. Why There Are Complementary Learning Systems in the Hippocampus Neocortex: Insights from the Successes and Failures of Connectionist Models of Learning and Memory. In *Cognitive Modeling*, ed. T. Polk and C. Seifert, 499–534. Cambridge, MA: The MIT Press.

McCloskey, M. 2002. Networks and Theories: The Place of Connectionism in Cognitive Science. In *Cognitive Modeling*, ed. T. Polk and C. Seifert, 1131–1146. Cambridge, MA: The MIT Press.

McKittrick, D., and D. McVea. 2002. *Making Sense of the Troubles: The Story of the Conflict in Northern Ireland*. Chicago: New Amsterdam Books.

Menary, R. 2007. *Cognitive Integration: Mind and Cognition Unbounded*. New York: Palgrave Macmillan.

———. 2010. Cognitive Integration and the Extended Mind. In *The Extended Mind*, ed. R. Menary, 227–243. Cambridge, MA: The MIT Press.

Messer, Ellen. 2002. Anthropologists in a Wider World with and Without Human Rights. In *Exotic No More: Anthropology on the Front Lines*, ed. Jeremy MacClancy, 319–337. Chicago: University of Chicago Press.

Mitchell, Christopher R. 1997. Intractable Conflicts: Keys to Treatment. Gernika Gogoratuz, Work Paper no. 10, pp. 1–17.

Montagu, A. 1997. *Man's Most Dangerous Myth: The Fallacy of Race*. 6th ed. London: Altamira Press.

Moore, H.L. 1988. *Feminism and Anthropology*. Cambridge: Polity Press.

———. 1994. *A Passion for Difference: Essays in Anthropology and Gender*. Cambridge: Polity Press.

———. 2007. *The Subject of Anthropology: Gender, Symbolism and Psychoanalysis*. Cambridge: Polity Press.

Morrock, R. 2010. *The Psychology of Genocide and Violent Oppression: A Study of Mass Cruelty from Nazi Germany to Rwanda*. London: McFarland & Company, Inc. Publishers.

Mudde, C., and C. Rovira Kaltwasser. 2017. *Populism: A Very Short Introduction*. Oxford: Oxford University Press.

Mukhopadhyay, C. 2004. A Feminist Cognitive Anthropology: The Case of Women and Mathematics. *Ethos* 32 (4): 458–492.
———. 2011. Cognitive Anthropology Through a Gendered Lens. In *A Companion to Cognitive Anthropology*, ed. D. Kronenfeld et al., 393–412. Oxford: Blackwell Publishing, Ltd.
Muro, D. 2005. Nationalism and Nostalgia: The Case of Radical Basque Nationalism. *Nations and Nationalism* 11 (4): 571–589.
———. 2008. *Ethnicity and Nationalism: The Case of Radical Basque Nationalism*. London: Routledge.
Naimark, N.M. 2017. *Genocide: A World History*. Oxford: Oxford University Press.
Neiwert, D. 2017. *Alt-America: The Rise of the Radical Right in the Age of Trump*. London: Verso.
Nhat Hanh, T. 1987, 2005 edn. *Being Peace*. Berkeley, CA: Parallax Press.
———. 1995, 2007 new edn. *Living Buddha, Living Christ*. New York: Riverhead Books, The Penguin Group.
———. 2015. *How to Love*. Berkeley, CA: Parallax Press.
———. 2017. *The Art of Living: Peace and Freedom in the Here and Now*. New York: Harper One, Harper Collins Publishers.
Nordstrom, C. 1997. *A Different Kind of War Story*. Philadelphia: University of Pennsylvania Press.
———. 2004. *Shadows of War: Violence, Power, and International Profiteering in the Twenty-First Century*. Berkeley: University of California Press.
Nordstrom, C., and A.C.G.M. Robben, eds. 1995. *Fieldwork Under Fire: Contemporary Studies of Violence and Survival*. Berkeley: University of California Press.
Passerini, L. 1987. *Fascism in Popular Memory: The Cultural Experience of the Turin Working Class*. Cambridge: Cambridge University Press.
Pérez-Agote, A. 2006. *The Social Roots of Basque Nationalism*, Trans. C. Watson and W. A. Douglass. Reno, NV: University of Nevada Press.
Pinker, S. 2011. *The Better Angels of Our Nature: Why Violence Has Declined*. New York: Viking, the Penguin Group.
Popular Memory Group. 1982. *Popular Memory: Theory, Politics, Method*; *Making History: Studies in History-Writing and Politics*, ed. R. Johnson et al. London: Hutchinson & Co. Ltd.
Portelli, A. 1991. *The Death of Luigi Trastulli and Other Stories: Form and Meaning in Oral History*. Albany, NY: State University Press of New York.
Rabben, L. 1998. *Unnatural Selection: The Yanomami, the Kayapó, and the Onslaught of Civilization*. Seattle: University of Washington Press.
Ranger, T. 1993. In *The Invention of Tradition Revisited: The Case of Colonial Africa; Legitimacy and the State in Twentieth Century Africa*, ed. T. Ranger and O. Vaughan. London: Macmillan.

Ricard, M., and W. Singer. 2017. *Beyond the Self: Conversations Between Buddhism and Neuroscience*. Cambridge, MA: The MIT Press.
Richardson, J.T. 1997a. Introduction to the Study of Gender Differences in Cognition. In *Gender Differences in Human Cognition*, ed. J.T. Richardson, 3–29. New York: Oxford University Press.
———., ed. 1997b. *Gender Differences in Human Cognition*. Oxford: Oxford University Press.
Robben, A.C.G.M., and M.M. Suárez-Orozco, eds. 2000. *Cultures Under Siege: Collective Violence and Trauma*. Cambridge: Cambridge University Press.
Robbins, P., ed. 2009. *The Cambridge Handbook of Situated Cognition*. Cambridge: Cambridge University Press.
Robbins, P., and M. Aydede. 2009. A Short Primer on Situated Cognition. In *The Cambridge Handbook of Situated Cognition*, ed. P. Robbins and M. Aydede, 3–10. Cambridge: Cambridge University Press.
Rosa, A. 2000. Bartlett's Psycho-Anthropological Project. In *Bartlett, Culture and Cognition*, ed. A. Saito, 46–66. London: Psychology Press (Taylor & Francis Group).
Rovira Kaltwasser, C., et al., eds. 2017. *The Oxford Handbook of Populism*. Oxford: Oxford University Press.
Rubin, Jeffrey Z., and Frank E.A. Sander. 2001. Culture, Negotiation, and the Eye of the Beholder. In *The Conflict and Culture Reader*, ed. Pat K. Chew, 15–16. New York: New York University Press.
Sagan, C. 1996. *The Demon-Haunted World: Science as a Candle in the Dark*. New York: Ballantine Books.
Sahlins, M. 1985. *Islands of History*. Chicago: The University of Chicago Press.
———. 2004. *Apologies to Thucydides: Understanding History as Culture and Vice Versa*. Chicago: The University of Chicago Press.
Sanford, V. 2008. ¡Si Hubo Genocidio en Guatemala! Yes! There Was Genocide in Guatemala. In *The Historiography of Genocide*, ed. D. Stone, 543–576. New York: Palgrave Macmillan.
Sansone, Livio. 2003. *Blackness Without Ethnicity: Constructing Race in Brazil*. New York: Palgrave Macmillan.
Sapolsky, R. 2004. *Why Zebras Don't Get Ulcers*. 3rd ed. New York: Henry Holt and Company, LLC.
———. 2017. *Behave: The Biology of Humans at Our Best and Worst*. New York: Penguin Books.
Schacter, D. 1987. Implicit Memory: History and Current Status. *Journal of Experimental Psychology: Learnin, Memory, and Cognition* 13 (3): 501–518.
———. 1996. *Searching for Memory: The Brain, the Mind, and the Past*. New York: Basic Books.

Schank, R., and R. Abelson. 1977. *Scripts, Plans, Goals and Understanding: An Inquiry into Human Knowledge Structures*. Hillsdale, NJ: Lawrence Erlbaum Associates, Inc.

Scheper-Hughes, N. 1992. *Death Without Weeping: The Violence of Everyday Life in Brazil*. Berkeley: University of California Press.

Scheper-Hughes, N., and P. Bourgois, eds. 2004. *Violence in War and Peace: An Anthology*. Oxford: Blackwell Publishing.

Schulz, A., and L. Mullings. 2006. *Gender, Race, Class, & Health: Intersectional Approaches*. San Francisco, CA: Jossey-Bass, A Wiley Imprint.

Scott, J.C. 1990. *Domination and the Arts of Resistance: Hidden Transcripts*. New Haven, CT: Yale University Press.

———. 1998. *Seeing Like a State: How Certain Schemes to Improve the Human Condition Have Failed*. New Haven, CT: Yale University Press.

Shaw, M. 2003. *War and Genocide: Organized Killing in Modern Society*. Cambridge, UK: Polity Press.

Sinclair, U. 1906, new edn. 2001. *The Jungle*. New York: Dover Publications, Inc.

Sluka, J.A., ed. 2000. *Death Squad: The Anthropology of State Terror*. Philadelphia: University of Pennsylvania Press.

Smith, A.D. 1971. *Theories of Nationalism*. New York: Harper Torchbooks.

———. 1979. *Nationalism in the Twentieth Century*. Oxford: Martin Robertson & Co. Ltd.

———. 1981. *The Ethnic Revival*. Cambridge: Cambridge University Press.

———. 1983. *Theories of Nationalism*. 2nd ed. New York: Holmes & Meier Publishers.

———. 1986. *The Ethnic Origins of Nations*. Oxford: Basil Blackwell.

———. 1991. *National Identity*. Reno: University of Nevada Press.

———. 1998. *Nationalism and Modernism: A Critical Survey of Recent Theories of Nations and Nationalism*. London: Routledge.

———. 1999. *Myths and Memories of the Nation*. Oxford: Oxford University Press.

———. 2000. *The Nation in History: Historiographical Debates About Ethnicity and Nationalism*. Hanover: University Press of New England.

———. 2001. *Nationalism: Theory, Ideology, History*. Cambridge: Polity Press.

Sperber, D. 2000. Introduction. In *Metarepresentations: A Multidisciplinary Perspective*, ed. D. Sperber, 3–13. Oxford: Oxford University Press.

Stone, D., ed. 2008. *The Historiography of Genocide*. New York: Palgrave Macmillan.

Strathern, M. 1988. *The Gender of the Gift: Problems with Women and Problems with Society in Melanesia*. Berkeley: University of California Press.

Strathern, A., P.J. Stewart, and N.L. Whitehead, eds. 2006. *Terror & Violence: Imagination and the Unimaginable*. London: Pluto Press.

Strauss, C. 1992. Models and Motives. In *Human Motives and Cultural Models*, ed. R. D'Andrade and C. Strauss. Cambridge: Cambridge University Press.

Strauss, C., and N. Quinn. 1997. *A Cognitive Theory of Cultural Meaning.* Cambridge: Cambridge University Press.
Sullivan, J. 1988. *ETA and Basque Nationalism: the Fight for Euskadi, 1890–1986.* London: Routledge.
Sutton, D. 1998. *Memories Cast in Stone: The Relevance of the Past in Everyday Life.* Oxford: Berg.
Sutton, J. 2005. Memory and the Extended Mind: Embodiment, Cognition, and the Extended Mind. *Cognitive Processing* 6 (4): 223–226.
———. 2008. Between Individual and Collective Memory: Coordination, Interaction, Distribution. *Social Research: An International Quarterly of the Social Sciences* 75 (1): 23–48.
———. 2009. Remembering. In *The Cambridge Handbook of Situated Cognition*, ed. P. Robbins and M. Aydede, 217–235. Cambridge: Cambridge University Press.
———. 2010. Exograms and Interdisciplinarity: History, the Extended Mind, and the Civilizing Process. In *The Extended Mind*, ed. R. Menary, 189–225. Cambridge, MA: The MIT Press.
Tamir, Y. 2019. *Why Nationalism.* Princeton: Princeton University Press.
Taussig, M. 1987. *Shamanism, Colonialism, and the Wild Man: A Study in Terror and Healing.* Chicago: The University of Chicago Press.
———. 1993. *Mimesis and Alterity: A Particular History of the Senses.* London: Routledge.
Telles, E.E. 2004. *Race in Another America: The Significance of Skin Color in Brazil.* Princeton: Princeton University Press.
Theiner, G., C. Allen, and R. Goldstone. 2010. Recognizing Group Cognition. *Cognitive Systems Research* 11: 378–395.
Thomas, N. 1994. *Colonialism's Culture: Anthropology, Travel and Government.* Cambridge: Polity Press.
Tonkin, E. 1992. *Narrating Our Pasts: The Social Construction of Oral History.* Cambridge: Cambridge University Press.
Toren, C. 1988. *Making the Present, Revealing the Past: The Mutability and Continuity of Tradition as Process*, Man (NS) 23, 696–717.
———. 1999. *Mind, Materiality, and History: Explorations in Fijian Ethnography.* London: Routledge.
———. 2001. The Child in Mind. In *The Debated Mind: Evolutionary Psychology Versus Ethnography*, ed. H. Whitehouse, 155–179. Oxford: Berg.
Totten, S., and W.S. Parsons, eds. 2013. *Centuries of Genocide: Essays and Eyewitness Accounts.* 4th ed. London: Routledge.
Totten, S., W.S. Parsons, and R.K. Hitchcock. 2002. Confronting Genocide and Ethnocide of Indigenous Peoples: An Interdisciplinary Approach to Definition, Intervention, Prevention, and Advocacy. In *Annihilating Difference: The*

*Anthropology of Genocide*, ed. A.L. Hinton, 54–91. Berkeley: University of California Press.

Tulving, E. 1972. Episodic and Semantic Memory. In *Organization of Memory*, ed. E. Tulving and W. Donaldson, 381–403. New York: Academic Press.

———. 2001. Episodic Memory and Common Sense: How Far Apart? In *Episodic Memory: New Directions in Research*, ed. A. Baddeley, M. Conway, and J. Aggleton, 269–287. Oxford: Oxford University Press.

Tuso, H. n.d. The Social Construction of the Oromo *Galtuus* in the Ethiopian Empire: Past and Present. [Unpublished Paper].

Urla, J. 1995. Outlaw Language: Creating Alternative Public Spheres in Basque Free Radio. *Pragmatics, Special Issue: Constructing Languages and Publics*, eds. S. Gal and K. Woolard, Vol. 5, no. 2, pp. 245–261.

———. 2001. We Are All Malcolm X!': Negu Goriak, Hip Hop, and the Basque Political Imaginary. In *Global Noise: Rap and Hip-Hop Outside the U.S.A*, ed. T. Mitchell, 171–193. Middletown, CT: Weslyan University Press.

———. 2003. Euskara: The 'terror' of a European Minority Language. *Anthropology Today* 19 (4): 1–3.

Vansina, J. 1961. *Oral Tradition: A Study in Historical Methodology*, Trans. H. M. Wright, 1965. London: Routledge & Kegan Paul.

Viswanathan, G. 2001. *Powers, Politics, and Culture: Interviews with Edward W. Said*. New York: Pantheon Books.

Viveiros de Castro, E. 1998. Cosmological Deixis and Amerindian Perspectivism. *The Journal of the Royal Anthropological Institute* 4 (3): 469–488.

Volkan, V. 2006. *Killing in the Name of Identity: A Study of Bloody Conflicts*. Charlottesville, VA: Pitchstone Publishing.

de Waal, F. 2005. *Our Inner Ape: A Leading Primatologist Explains Why We Are Who We Are*. New York: Riverhead Books, Penguin Group, Inc.

———. 2009. *The Age of Empathy: Nature's Lessons for a Kinder Society*. New York: Harmony Books.

———. 2013. *The Bonobo and the Atheist: In Search of Humanism among the Primates*. New York: W. W. Norton & Company.

Wallace, B.A. 2007. *Contemplative Science: Where Buddhism and Neuroscience Converge*. New York: Columbia University Press.

Wallace, S. 2011. *The Unconquered: In Search of the Amazon's Last Uncontacted Tribes*. New York: Crown Publishers.

Waller, J. 2007. *Becoming Evil: How Ordinary People Commit Genocide and Mass Killing*. 2nd ed. Oxford: Oxford University Press.

Warfield Rawls, A., and W. Duck. 2020. *Tacit Racism*. Chicago: The University of Chicago Press.

Warren, J.W. 2001. *Racial Revolutions: Antiracism and Indian Resurgence in Brazil*. Durham, NC: Duke University Press.

West, C. 1993. *Race Matters*. New York: Vintage Books.

Whitehouse, H. 2000. *Arguments and Icons: Divergent Modes of Religiosity.* Oxford: Oxford University Press.
———. 2004. *Modes of Religiosity: A Cognitive Theory of Religious Transmission.* Walnut Creek, CA: AltaMira Press.
———., ed. 2007. *Religion, Anthropology, and Cognitive Science.* Durham, NC: Carolina Academic Press.
Whitehouse, H., and J. Laidlaw, eds. 2004. *Ritual and Memory: Toward a Comparative Anthropology of Religion.* Oxford: Altamira Press.
Whitfield, T. 2014. *Endgame for ETA: Elusive Peace in the Basque Country.* Oxford: Oxford University Press.
Wilson, R.A. 2004. *Boundaries of the Mind: The Individual in the Fragile Sciences.* Cambridge: Cambridge University Press.
———. 2010. Meaning Making and the Mind of the Externalist. In *The Extended Mind*, ed. R. Menary, 167–188. Cambridge, MA: The MIT Press.
Wilson, Richard Ashby, and Jon P. Mitchell, eds. 2003. *Human Rights in Global Perspective: Anthropological Studies of Rights, Claims and Entitlements.* London: Routledge.
Wimmer, A. 2002. *Nationalist Exclusion and Ethnic Conflict: Shadows of Modernity.* Cambridge: Cambridge University Press.
———. 2013. *Ethnic Boundary Making: Institutions, Power, Networks.* Oxford: Oxford University Press.
———. 2018. *Nation Building: Why Some Countries Come Together While Others Fall Apart.* Princeton: Princeton University Press.
Winddance Twine, F. 2005. *Racism in a Racial Democracy: The Maintenance of White Supremacy in Brazil.* New Brunswick, NJ: Rutgers University Press.
Winkler, C., and P.J. Hanke. 1995. Ethnography of the Ethnographer. In *Fieldwork Under Fire: Contemporary Studies of Violence and Survival*, ed. C. Nordstrom and A.C. Robben. Berkeley: University of California Press.
Woodworth, P. 2001. *Dirty War, Clean Hands: ETA, the GAL and Spanish Democracy.* Cork, Ireland: Cork University Press.
Wright, R. 2017. *Why Buddhism Is True: The Science and Philosophy of Meditation and Enlightenment.* New York: Simon & Schuster Paperbacks.
Young, A. 2000. *Women Who Become Men: Albanian Sworn Virgins.* Oxford: Berg.
Zartman, I. William. 2001. The Timing of Peace Initiatives: Hurting Stalemates and Ripe Moments. *The Global Review of Ethnopolitics* 1 (1): 8–18.
———. 2005. Analyzing Intractability. In *Grasping the Nettle: Analyzing Cases of Intractable Conflict*, ed. Chester A. Crocker, Fen Osler Hampson, and Pamela Aall, 47–64. Washington, DC: United States Institute of Peace.
Zulaika, J. 1988. *Basque Violence: Metaphor and Sacrament.* Reno: University of Nevada Press.
———. 2004. Nourishment by the Negative: National Subalternity, Antagonism, and Radical Democracy. In *Empire & Terror: Nationalism/Postnationalism in*

*the New Millennium*, ed. B. Aretxaga et al., 115–136. Reno: University of Nevada Press.
———. 2009. *Terrorism: The Self-Fulfilling Prophecy*. Chicago: The University of Chicago Press.
Zulaika, J., and W.A. Douglass. 1996. *Terror and Taboo: The Follies, Fables, and Faces of Terrorism*. London: Routledge.

# Index[1]

**NUMBERS AND SYMBOLS**
#Black Lives Matter Movement (BLM), 78, 175–179, 288, 296, 331
6th Extinction, 337
13th Amendment, 171
14th Amendment, 171
15th Amendment, 171

**A**
Aborigines, 103
Acculturation, 326
Afghanistan, 304
Africa, 326
African-Americans, 6, 13, 38, 78, 141, 151–156, 162–167, 170–178, 182, 184, 279, 283, 285–288, 296, 327, 331
Age of Enlightenment, 313
Agribusinesses, 224, 225
Agricultural Revolution, 220, 303, 311
Agro-businesses, 103
Alarde parade, 53, 56
Albania, 209
Albanian women, 10
Albert, Bruce, 105, 116, 126
Alcoholism, 98, 102, 103, 128
Alliance for Prosperity, 31
Altruistic behavior, 328
Amazon, 224–228, 245
Amazonia, 103, 107, 109–117, 119, 120, 124–127, 211, 216, 222, 225, 245, 329, 335
Amazonian deforestation, 224, 226, 228
Amazonian rainforest, 222, 223
Amazon region, 222, 226, 227
American Indian Movement (AIM), 102, 177, 178
Amerindian genocide, 87–129
Amerindian/s, 2, 4–6, 11, 13, 323, 331, 333

---

[1] Note: Page numbers followed by 'n' refer to notes.

© The Author(s), under exclusive license to Springer Nature Switzerland AG 2022
J. P. Linstroth, *Politics and Racism Beyond Nations*,
https://doi.org/10.1007/978-3-030-91720-3

## 358  INDEX

Amygdala, 211, 213, 215, 218, 236, 243, 308–310, 328
Andaman and Nicobar Islands, 96, 127
Anderson, Benedict, 3, 6, 26, 62, 78, 83, 324
Anterior cingulate cortex (ACC), 217, 243, 328
Anthropocene, 220, 244
Anthropology, 53
Apurinã, Kambeba, Kokama, Munduruku, Mura, Sateré-Mawé, Tikuna, and Tukano peoples (Brazil), 113
Apurinã people (Brazil), 142, 144, 145, 160
Arbery, Ahmaud, 152, 172
Ardern, Jacinda (PM of New Zealand), 305, 307, 316
Armenians, 101
Asia, 326
Asian-Americans, 6, 232–235, 245, 246
Assimilation, 326
Association of Victims from Terrorism (*Asscociación de Víctimas del Terrorismo*, AVT), 68
Atran, Scott, 299
Attachment/s, 255, 256, 267, 294, 297, 308, 317, 329, 332, 337
Australia, 96, 102, 103, 128, 326, 335
Australian Strategic Policy Institute (ASPI), 100
Auto-ethnographic narrative, 2

### B

Bagemihl, Bruce, 210, 215
Balthazart, Jacques, 210, 211, 328
Banks, Dennis, 178
Banks, Marcus, 27
Barth, Frederick, 27
Basque Country (*Euskadi or Euskal Herria*), 54, 56, 57, 62–66, 69, 74, 75, 80, 81
Basque patriotic left (*Izquierda Abertzaleak*), 65
Basque Regional Government (*Eusko Jaurlaritza, Gobierno Vasco*), 65
Basques, 2–4, 6, 7, 12, 13, 56–58, 60, 62–64, 66, 67, 76, 79–83, 83n1, 324, 325, 327
Basque terrorism, 54, 58, 66, 80
Basque terrorists, 54, 64, 65
Basualdo, Maria, 22, 24
Beatty, Andrew, 309, 310
Berenguer, Erika, 224
Bharatiya Janata Party (BJP) (Indian People's Party), 28, 41, 45
Bible, 10, 200, 205, 242, 301, 309, 312
Biden, Joe (President of United States), 231, 235, 236, 239, 240, 242
Biden administration, 32, 33
Bikkhu, Ajahn Amaro, 265, 292, 294, 295, 330
Bin Salman, Mohammed (Saudi Crown Prince), 101
Biology, 2, 4, 10, 214, 327, 328
Biome, 222, 245
Bisexual, 196
BJP Party, 324
Black Death, 329
Black Fever, 229–231
Black people, 166, 173–175, 177
Black, *see* African-Americans
Blanco, Miguel Angel, 55, 67, 69, 74
Bloch, Maurice, 8, 27, 151, 209, 216, 312, 328, 329
Boarding school system, 102
Body, 260, 261, 269–271, 295, 299, 311, 312
Bolsonaro, Jair (President of Brazil), 2, 13, 14, 94, 96, 99, 104–107, 109, 111, 112, 114, 115, 117–129, 151, 152, 158, 160, 161, 181, 182, 211, 222–228, 245, 325–327, 329

INDEX 359

Bonilla-Silva, Eduardo, 181
Bourdieu, Pierre, 149, 162
Boyer, Pascal, 299
Brands, H. W., 240
Brazil, 2, 3, 6, 11, 13, 27, 92–94, 96–99, 102, 104–117, 119–124, 126–129, 138n135, 139, 146, 151–153, 157–161, 181, 182, 326, 327, 335
Brazilian Amazon, 98, 105, 106, 108, 110, 115, 117, 120, 125, 211, 222–225, 227, 245
Brazilian Amazonia, 111, 114, 118
Brazilian Amerindians, 2, 9, 11, 13, 223, 226, 325, 327
Brazilian Catholic Indigenist Missionary Council (*Conselho Indigenista Missionario*, CIMI), 223
Brazilian government, 96, 108, 111, 116–119, 122, 124
Brazilian Indians, 159, 160
Brazilian military dictatorship (1964-1985), 226
Brazilian National Institute for Space Research (*Instituto Nacional de Pesquisas Espaciais*, INPE), 222, 227
Brazilian urban Amerindians, 139, 140, 142–145, 149–151, 179, 180, 326, 327
BREXIT, 72, 79
British Southern Cameroonians, 325
Brooks, Rayshard, 171
Brown, Michael, 165
*Brumadinho* Dam disaster, 110
Buddha (Siddhartha Gautama), 255, 260, 266, 270, 271, 274, 281, 284, 285, 295, 297, 298, 306
Buddhism, 2, 11, 255–259, 261–264, 266, 268, 273, 279–281, 283, 288, 289, 293–300, 304–306, 316, 331–333

Buddhist, 255–257, 259, 260, 262–270, 273, 275, 276, 281, 282, 284, 285, 288–298, 300, 301, 305, 306, 315, 316, 329–334
Buddhist monastics, 2, 11, 14
Buddhist monks, 329, 331–333
Buddhist nun, 329, 332
Bush, George W. (President of United States), 28
Byron, Lord, 301

C
*Caboclo* (Mixed white and indigenous heritage; ethnic term Brazil), 113
Caminha, Pêro Vaz de, 98
Canada, 96, 102, 104, 128, 326, 335
Carbon release ($CO_2$), 224, 245
CARES Act, 176
Caribbean, 31, 32
Carlson, Tucker, 240
Carmichael, Stokely (Kwame Ture), 176
Castile, Philando, 165, 166
Castro, Marcia, 114, 115
Catalans, 4, 6, 7, 12, 55, 57, 62, 63, 65, 67, 75–78, 80–83, 324, 325, 327
Catalonia (Catalunya), 3, 13, 62, 75, 77, 78, 80, 81
Catholic, 200, 210
Catholic Indigenist Missionary Council (*Conselho Indigenista Missionario*, CIMI), 109
Catholicism, 200, 237
Cattle-ranchers (*rancheiros*), 222
Cattle ranching, 103, 107
Ceaușescu regime, 217
Center for Economic and Policy Research (CEPR), 163
The Center for Migration Studies (CMS), 39

Center for Strategic & International Studies (CSIS), 213
Central America, 30–32, 38, 39, 140
The Centre for 21st Century Humanities at Newcastle University, Australia, 103
Chain gangs, 171
Charlottesville, Virginia incident, 153
Chau, John Allen, 96–98
Chauvin, Derek, 165, 170
Chicago Haymarket Riot (1886), 30
Chickenpox, 113
Child neglect, 103
Children, 17–25, 29, 30, 32–35, 37–40, 42, 44, 45
Children separation, 20–24, 32, 34, 35, 39, 40, 45
Chimpanzees, 309
China, 6, 99–101, 107, 128, 130n12, 232, 234, 240, 245
Chinatown, 232, 233
China Virus, 329
Chinese, 204, 232, 233
Chinese Exclusion Act (1882), 29, 38
Chinese Uighurs, 325, 327
Chinese Virus (pejorative used by Donald Trump), 232, 234
Cholera, 229
Chomsky, Noam, 236
Christian, 196, 197, 199, 214
Christmas, 215
Civilization, 311
Civilized (*civilizados*), 113
Civil Rights Act, 165, 171
Civil Rights Movement (1954–1968), 161, 171, 178, 289
Civil War (1861-1865 in U.S.), 170, 171
Clark, Jamar, 165, 166
Clark, Stephon, 165, 166
Class, 162, 173
Climatic catastrophe, 337
Cognition, 151, 180, 216, 217

Cognitive, 294, 298–300, 308, 309
Cognitive behavior therapy, 294
COICA (Coordinator of Indigenous Organizations of the Amazon River Basin, *Coordinadora de las Organizaciones Indígenas de la Cuenca Amazónica*), 107, 108
Collective, 285, 299, 311
Colombia, 118
Colonialism, 3
Comics, 301, 302, 304
Communication, 259, 261, 295, 297, 299, 310, 315, 330, 332, 333
Compassion, 262, 265, 266, 268, 269, 281, 282, 294, 296, 297, 305, 315, 316, 331, 332
Coronavirus (COVID-19), 6, 13, 28, 41–45, 49n73, 96, 112–126, 129, 138n135, 151, 152, 157–164, 167, 175–177, 182, 212, 229–234, 238, 240, 245, 324, 326, 327, 329, 333
Counter-reformation (1545-1648), 237
Critical race theory (CRT), 1, 14n1, 323
Cultural genocide, 87–129

D

Day laborers, 41, 43
De las Casas, Bartolomé, 98
Delgado, R., 1
Democrats, 32, 37, 235
Deposition, 87–91, 95
Descartes, René, 311, 312
Developing world, 212, 213, 229–231, 245, 326, 327
De Waal, Frans, 11, 216, 217, 244
Diachronic trauma, 7, 8, 13, 150, 156, 326
Discrimination, 1, 9, 326
Domestic abuse, 128
Domestic violence, 98, 103, 112

DSM-V, 18
Du Bois, W.E.B., 168
Duck, Waverly, 183
Dukkha (suffering), 255, 260, 285

E
Earth, 10, 196, 218–220, 244, 260, 306, 311–314, 333, 334
Economic Opportunity Act, 161
Ecosystems, 220, 221, 224, 227
*EH Bildu* (Euskal Herria Bildu, Basque Country Unite), 80
Electoral vote, 235
Elementary and Secondary Education Act, 161
El Salvador, 20, 30–32, 37–39, 140, 304, 323
Embryonic hormones, 210
Empathetic, 258, 263, 268–270, 283, 284, 294, 305
Empathy, 215, 217, 218, 243, 244, 255–317, 323, 328
Enlightenment, 260, 313
Environment, 2, 5, 11, 12, 195–246
Environmental nihilism, 337
Episodic memories, 139, 140, 151
Ethics, 264, 277, 295, 330
Ethnic groups, 223, 226, 232–234
Ethnicity, 6, 10, 26, 27, 195, 234, 323
Ethnic minorities, 140, 162, 163
Ethnocide, 325
Ethno-nationalism, 1, 3, 6, 12
Ethno-nationalists, 324, 325, 327
Europe, 326, 327, 335, 336
European Union (EU), 68, 75, 76, 80
*Euskadi Ta Askatasuna* (ETA, Basque Homeland and Freedom), 54–60, 62, 64–69, 74, 80, 82, 83, 324
Extinctions, 218–222
EZLN (Zapatista Army of National Liberation, *Ejército Zapatista de Liberación Nacional*), 67

F
Fake media/fake news, 111, 205, 212, 228, 235, 237, 238, 246, 329
Farmer, Paul, 229, 231
Farmers (*fazendeiros*), 106, 109, 111, 223, 225, 226
Fassin, Didier, 179, 180
Fauci, Anthony, 240
Fausto, Carlos, 116
Fearnside, Philip, 224, 228
Federal Bureau of Investigation (FBI), 170, 177
Federal Deposit Insurance Corporation (FDIC), 240
Ferguson, Niall, 237
First World, 229–231, 245
Fisher, Helen, 310
Flattening the curve, 231
Floyd, George, 151, 152, 165–167, 170, 172, 175, 178, 182, 285, 288, 296, 326, 331
Font-Guzman, Jacqueline, 79
"Food Stamp Act," 161
Forced migration, 213
FOX News, 212, 235, 236, 240
Franco, Francisco (Spanish dictator), 55, 58, 66, 67, 80
Fricke, Ron, 221
Fry, Douglas, 4, 11, 303, 317
FUNAI (*Fundação Nacional do Índio*, National Indian Foundation), 106, 112, 120, 122, 125
Fundamentalist Christian, 197

G
Gaia Theory, 334
Gandhi, Mahatma, 75
Gandhi, Mohandas, 302
Garner, Eric, 165
Garrow, David, 302
Gay, 195–205, 207–210, 242, 243

Gell, Alfred, 150
Gender, 140, 162, 195, 196, 207–210, 243, 266, 268, 281, 328
Genocide of Native Americans, 156
Genocide/s, 1–4, 6–8, 13, 87–129, 255, 297, 303, 311, 317, 323, 325–327
Gentleman's Agreement (1907), 29, 38
Gilded Age, 29, 38
Gingrich and Banks, 2
Gini Index, 230
Gladney, Dru, 4, 26
Global South, 231
Gold miners (*garimpeiros*), 97, 108–110, 120, 124–126
Goodall, Jane, 212
Good Friday Agreement, 56, 59, 62, 66, 69, 71, 72, 74, 79, 82, 324
Gramsci, Antonio, 6
Grateful, 286–288, 294, 313
Gratitude, 294, 330
Gray, Freddie, 165, 166
Great Irish Famine (1845-1849), 29
Great Plague, 233
Greek myths, 301
Guajajara, Sônia, 107–109, 112
Guajajara people (Brazil), 108, 160
Guarani-Kaiowá (Brazil), 99
Guardians of the Forest, 109
Guatemala, 3, 6, 17–22, 30–32, 37–40, 87, 140, 141, 149, 323, 325
Guatemala Civil War, 17
Guatemalan genocide, 95
Guatemalan guerrillas, 87
Guatemalan-Mayan immigrants, 139–142, 149–151, 179, 180
Guatemalan-Mayan refugees, 17
Guatemalan-Mayas, 2, 9, 13, 18–20, 140, 142, 149, 326, 327

Guatemalan military, 87, 88
Gypsies, 101

# H

Hamilton, William, 217
Hanchard, Michael, 181
Hanukkah, 215, 216
Harris, Kamala (Vice President of United States), 235, 236, 239, 242
Harris, Nancy, 228
Haximu massacre (Brazil), 125
Hegemony, 6
Herdt, Gilbert, 209
Herri Batasuna (HB), 54, 56–60, 83n1
Higher love, 308
Hindu nationalism, 2, 3
Hindu Tamils, 259
Hippocampus, 310
Hispanic-Americans, 140, 162, 163, 167, 176, 180, 182, 327
HIV-AIDS, 229, 231
Hobsbawm, Eric, 7, 216
Hodt, Captain Nicholas, 98
Holocaust, 3, 303
Homosexuality, 197–211
Homosexual/s, 2, 10, 14, 197, 206, 207, 210, 211, 326, 328
Honduras, 6, 20, 30–32, 37–39, 140, 323
Hong Kong, 203, 204
Hoover, Herbert (President of United States), 240, 241
Housing and Urban Development (HUD), 163
Human Rights Watch, 34, 35, 100, 112, 128
Hutus, 101
Hydro-electric dams, 103, 107, 108, 110
Hypothalamus, 210, 214

INDEX 363

**I**
Illegal-land-grabbers, 224
Illegal loggers, 97, 109, 114, 115, 117, 119, 120, 129, 223, 245
Illegal miners, 223, 245
ILO Convention 169, 336
Imagined community, 6, 62, 75–77, 81, 324
Immigrant caravan, 29, 31
Immigrants, 1–3, 6, 7, 9, 12, 13, 19, 20, 26–31, 33–35, 37, 38, 40, 45, 214, 323, 324, 326, 328
Immigration, 1, 2, 5, 6, 17–45
Immigration Act (1924), 29
Independence, 57, 58, 63, 65, 66, 68, 70, 73, 75–80, 83
India, 27, 28, 41–45, 49n73
Indian Removal Act (1830), 175
Indians (Native Americans), 102
Indians (Natives), 139, 140, 142–145, 149, 158–160, 180
Indigenous, 95–97, 99, 102–129
Indigenous land, 223, 224
Indigenous peoples, 139, 140, 142, 144, 152, 158–161, 176, 180, 181, 306, 313, 314, 325, 326, 329, 333–337
Indigenous reserves, 224, 226
Indigenous views, 333
Individual, 256, 266, 271, 272, 275, 279, 285, 294, 295, 310
Inequalities, 152, 162, 166, 167, 181, 182
Inequities, 327
Influenza, 113
In-group and out-group, 328
*Instituto Brasileiro de Geografia e Estatística* (IBGE), Brazilian Institute of Geography and Statistics, 223, 226
Insular cortex (Insula), 211, 217, 236, 243, 328

Inter-being, 5, 11, 14, 280, 283, 284, 288, 289, 296, 331
Intergovernmental Science-Policy Platform on Biodiversity and Ecosystem Services (IPBES), 218, 220, 222, 244
Internally displaced persons (IDPs), 213
International Criminal Court (ICC), 121
Invented traditions, 216
Iraq, 304
Irish Republican Army (IRA), 54, 56, 57, 69–72, 79

**J**
Japan, 101, 326, 335
Japanese-American internment camps (1942-1945), 30
Jean, Botham, 165, 166
Jefferson, Thomas, 239, 241
Jews, 4, 6, 7, 101, 107, 212, 233, 329
Jim Crow Laws (1877–1964), 171
Jim Crow South, 156, 172
Johnson, Lyndon B. (President of United States), 161, 164, 174
Jones, Van, 170, 171

**K**
Kadushin, Charles, 212, 237
Kaepernick, Colin, 77–79
Kaltwasser, Cristóbal Rovira, 27, 28
Kanari, Kuikuro, 116
Kayapó people (Brazil), 105, 108, 110, 117, 118
Kazakhs, 99, 100, 127
Kazantzakis, Nikos, 306–307
Kendi, Ibram, 152, 183, 184, 327
King, Dr. Martin Luther, 69, 147, 157, 161, 168, 169, 171, 174, 175, 182, 285, 286, 302, 304

## K

Kipling, Rudyard, 101
Kokama people (Brazil), 142, 145, 160
Kolbert, Elizabeth, 221
Kopenawa, Davi, 105, 107, 108, 116
Krenak, Ailton, 160, 225
Krenaki people (Brazil), 160
Kurds, 325

## L

Laban Hinton, Alexander, 95, 96
Ladinos, 140, 141
Laidlaw, James, 298, 299
Land-grabbers, 109, 111
Latin America, 32, 141, 152, 157–159, 180, 326
Latin American immigrants, 28, 40, 45, 151, 326
Latino immigrants, 211, 243
Latinos, 141, 152, 163, 181, 182, 323, 327, 328
Lazarus, Emma, 31
Lesbian, 196
Lesbian Bisexual Gay and Transgender (LBGT), 10, 14, 160, 195, 196, 209
Lesbian, Bisexual, Gay, Transgender, Queer (LBGTQ), 210, 211, 242, 243
Lesbian Gay Bisexual Transgender Queer Intersex Asexual (LGBTQIA), 201, 202
Lesbian Gay Bisexual Transgender Queer (LGBTQ), 167, 196, 201, 203, 208, 214, 327
Lewis, C. S., 305–307, 309, 316
Lewis Gaddis, John, 304
LGBT, 72, 140
Liberative Love, 265, 294, 330
Linstroth, J. P., 8, 9, 150, 151, 180, 208, 209, 226, 324, 326
Locke, John, 239
*Londonderry Sentinel*, 73, 74, 82
Looking Horse, Chief Arvol, 179
Love, 1, 2, 5, 12, 14, 255–317, 323, 329–331, 334
Lowndes, Joseph, 28
Lynching, 156, 165, 170–172, 174

## M

Macuxi people (Brazil), 118
MAGA (make America great again – motto Donald Trump presidential campaign), 153, 156, 236, 238
Majorities, 20, 26, 27
Malcolm X, 148, 165–169, 171, 182
Manaus (Brazil), 92–94, 112–116, 120, 129, 142–144, 146, 149, 158, 160
Manifest Destiny, 99, 102
Manufacturing consent, 236
Manz, Beatriz, 95
*Mariana* Dam disaster, 110
Mashco-Piro (Brazil), 99
Mass-fires, 222–225
Massive fires, 329
Matis people (Brazil), 119
Mayan Indians, 325
Maybury-Lewis, David, 128
McCain, John (U.S. Senator), 154
McCarthy, Joseph (U.S. Senator), 239
McDonald, Laquan, 165, 166
McKee, Lyra, 61, 69–73, 81, 324
Mead, Margaret, 228
Measles, 111, 113, 116
Media, 202, 212, 228, 231, 233, 236–238, 241
Memory/memories, 8, 9, 13, 95, 97, 126, 139, 140, 149–151, 155, 156, 168, 286, 287, 299, 326
Metuktire, Raoni, 107, 108, 118
Mexico, 6, 21, 22, 30, 31, 33, 36, 37, 39–41, 140, 158, 323
Middle Ages, 212, 233, 329

Migrant laborers, 28, 43–45
Mindful, 261, 270, 273, 280, 284, 295, 304
Mindfulness, 261, 263, 264, 270–273, 277, 278, 282, 284, 288, 295–297, 306, 315, 316, 330–332, 334
Mind/s, 261, 263, 265, 266, 268–276, 279, 293–295, 297, 300, 312, 323, 327, 328, 330, 331
Mining, 96, 103–105, 107, 111, 124–126, 129
Minorities, 1, 3, 4, 7, 9, 12, 26–28, 45, 95, 99, 101, 127, 130n12, 140, 152, 160, 162, 166, 167, 176, 181, 182, 184, 324–328
Modi, Narendra(PM of India), 3, 28, 41, 42, 44, 45, 324
Mohawk, Cayuga, Onondaga, Oneida, Seneca, and Tuscarora people (Canada), 104
Monastics, 274, 280, 287
Mongol conquests, 304
Monks, 255, 256, 259, 262, 263, 265, 276, 281, 289–295, 297, 315, 316
Monroe Doctrine, 31
Morality, 264, 295, 330
MSNBC, 212, 236
Mudde, Cas, 27, 28
Munduruku people (Brazil), 113, 126, 127, 142, 143, 160
Mura people (Brazil), 142, 145, 160
Muslims, 99, 127
Myanmar, 259, 262

# N
*NAIZ*, 74, 82
Narratives, 139, 149, 151, 177, 208–211, 242, 293, 296, 301, 310, 311, 315, 316, 326, 327, 329

Nation, 324–326, 335, 337
National Association for the Advancement of Colored People (NAACP), 163
National Football League (NFL), 77–79
Nationalism, 3–5, 7, 53–83
National Partnership for Women and Families (NPWF), 163
Native Americans, 38, 99, 102, 141, 151, 153, 175–178, 184, 327, 333
Native populations, 326
Natives, 6, 11, 13
Nativism, 29
Nativist, 27, 38
 *See also* Racism; Racist
Nativists (as in only whites), 2, 3, 6
Nature, 196, 198, 216, 220, 221, 225, 239
Navajos (United States), 98
Nenquimo, Nemonte, 314, 317
Neolithic Revolution, 311
Neo-nationalism, 2
Neo-nationalists, 3
Nestlé Corporation, 104
Neuro-biology, 211, 243, 328
Neurology, 216, 243, 244
Neuroscience, 300
New' Irish Republican Army (IRA), 3, 12, 13, 61, 62, 69, 73, 81, 82, 324
New Zealand, 326, 335
Nhat Hanh, Thich, 11, 14, 279–282, 284, 286, 289, 294–298, 305, 306, 315, 316, 330–332
Nicaragua, 30, 304
Nixon administration, 177
Non-nation state nationalism, 4, 6, 7
Non-violence, 259, 274, 280
North American Free Trade Agreement (NAFTA), 30, 38

Northern Ireland, 3, 13, 59, 61–63, 66, 69–72, 74, 79, 81–83
Northern Irish Catholics, 62, 82, 324
Northern Triangle (Central America – El Salvador, Guatemala, Honduras), 37, 38
Nuclear destruction, 337
Nuclear warfare, 11
Nun, 255, 279–281, 283, 286, 293, 295, 297, 315, 316

## O

Obama, Barack (President of United States), 152, 154, 155
O'Brien, Robert, 167
Ocaina people (Colombia), 118
Ocasio-Cortez, Alexandria (U.S. Congresswoman), 155
Office of Minority Health (OMH), 164
Oil exploration, 107
Omar, Ilhan (U.S. Congresswoman), 155, 156
Oombulgurri people (Australia), 103
Oppression, 1, 5, 7, 9
O'Sullivan, John, 99
Otegi, Arnoldo, 80
Othering, 2, 3, 5, 7, 328
Otherness, 328
Other/s, 2, 4, 139, 140, 142–144, 149–153, 156, 157, 159, 160, 162–167, 169–173, 176, 178, 181, 182, 184
Overstayers, 37
Oxytocin, 211, 213, 237, 243, 308, 310, 328

## P

Palmer Raids, 239
Pandemic, 229, 230, 232, 234, 245
Papua New Guinea, 209
Paraguay, 223, 226, 227
Paris Agreement, 335
Parque Tarumã Cemetery (Manaus), 113
*Patanal* (wetlands in Brazil), 110, 111, 224
Patriotic Left (Abertzaleak), 58
Peace, Sister (An Nghiem), 279, 293–296, 330, 331
Peace, 1, 2, 5, 11–14, 255–317, 323, 324, 329, 330, 332, 333
Peacebuilding, 255, 296
Peace processes, 57, 59, 60, 62–64, 66–68, 71, 72, 74, 81–83
Peace studies, 255, 302, 316
Peaceworkers, 301–304, 316
Pelosi, Nancy (House Speaker, U.S. Congress), 153, 155
Permanent ceasefire (ETA 2011), 55–58, 60, 62, 68
Peru, 97–99, 120, 127
Phuntsho, Geshe Lama, 256, 259, 290, 294, 295, 330, 333
Pinker, Steven, 303
Plague, 329
Poachers, 109, 111, 119, 223, 224, 245
Pogroms, 212, 233, 329
Police abuse, 176
Police reform, 171
Policing, 152, 165, 167, 171, 174
Political prisoners, 324
Politics of racism, 151, 180, 326
Populism, 2, 12, 26–28, 45, 323, 324
Populist, 1–3, 12, 27, 28, 38, 45, 324, 326, 327
Positive thinking, 294
Possessive love, 265–267, 294
Post-traumatic stress disorder (PTSD), 18, 21, 23
Poverty, 152, 161–164, 182

## INDEX 367

Power, 323, 324, 327, 335, 337
Prefrontal cortex, 310
Presidents of the United States, 235
*Presoak Etxera* (Prisoners Return Home), 65
Pressley, Ayanna (U.S. Congresswoman), 155
Primates, 211, 215–218, 237, 243, 328
Primatology, 211, 244, 328
Printing press, 237
Progressive Era, 29
Propaganda, 329
Psychology, 18
Puerto Ricans, 325

## Q
Quebecois, 325
Queer, 201, 203
*Quilombos* (isolated Brazilian Afro-communities), 225

## R
Race, 1, 6, 13, 14, 142, 151–153, 162, 170–175, 181, 183, 208, 212, 232–234, 243, 323, 326, 327, 329, 331
Racial trauma, 139–184
Racism, 1–5, 7–9, 13, 17–45, 139–184, 212, 214, 232–234, 245, 246, 255, 286, 287, 296, 297, 311, 317, 323, 325–327, 331, 337
Racist, 107, 111, 113, 120, 233
Racist discourse, 28
Racist rhetoric, 5, 6, 13, 151, 153, 155, 156, 181, 182
Rajoy, Mariano (PM of Spain), 75
Ranger, Terrence, 7, 216
Reagan administration, 140

Rechtman, Richard, 179, 180
Reconstruction (1863–1877 in U.S.), 171
Re-education camps, 100, 128
Re-indigenization, 333, 335–337
Religion, 2, 6, 7, 10, 195–202, 204–205, 210, 216, 221
Republicans, 31, 32, 37, 238, 241, 242
Rhetoric, 101, 107, 109, 111, 117, 126, 129
  as in racist rhetoric, 111
Ricard, Matthieu, 300
Rice, Tamir, 165, 166
Rio de Janeiro, Brazil, 158
Rituals, 215, 216
Rocha, Bruna, 118
Rohingya people (Myanmar), 259
Romanian orphanages, 216, 217
Roosevelt, Franklin D. (President of United States), 161, 240
Roosevelt Corollary, 31
Ross, Gyasi, 177
Roy, Arundhati, 41–45, 304

## S
Sagan, Carl, 236, 238, 242
Salles, Ricardo (Brazilian Environmental Minister), 227
Sambia (Papua New Guinea), 10
Sánchez, Pedro (PM of Spain), 81
Sand Creek Massacre (1864), 175
Sanford, Victoria, 95, 325
São Gabriel de Cachoeira, Brazil, 158, 159
São Paulo, Brazil, 158, 227, 228
Saoradh (Liberation), 71, 72
Sapolsky, Robert, 162, 211, 213, 216–218, 236, 243, 310, 328
Sateré-Mawé people (Brazil), 142, 143, 146, 160, 161

Scheper-Hughes, Nancy, 149, 162
School of the Americas, 30
Science, 195–246
Scientific Revolution, 313
Scientific-tolerance, 2
Scots, 7, 325
Scott, James, 4, 62, 82, 324
Scott, Walter, 165, 166
Secessionism, 77
Secessionists, 325
Second-Industrial Revolution, 29
Securities and Exchange Commission (SEC), 240
Semantic memories, 150, 151
Senses, 265–267, 269, 278, 283, 298, 301, 303, 307, 309, 311–317
Sentinelese-Jarawa Islanders, 325, 327
Sentinelese Jarawa people (Andaman Islands), 96, 97, 99
Separation of children, 20
Sex, 199, 204, 205, 207, 210, 215
Sexual abuse, 103, 128
Sexuality, 195, 196, 203–206, 208, 209, 211, 215, 243, 328
Seymour, Frances, 228
Sharecropping, 171
Sinclair, Upton, 30
Singer, Wolf, 300
Sinhala Buddhists, 259, 262
Sinn Fein, 54, 56, 57
Sioux (United States), 98, 102
Sixth Extinction, 5, 11, 218, 220, 244
Slavery, 156, 171, 175, 176, 178, 182, 311
Smallpox, 113
Socialism, 239, 240
Social Security Administration (SSA), 240
Society for the Anthropology of Lowland South America (SALSA), 111, 123, 160, 224
South Florida, 139

Spain, 54–58, 60, 62–67, 69, 74–82, 324
Spaniards, 325
Spanish Basque Country (El País Vasco), 53, 60, 62–64, 67, 324
Spanish Flu, 233
Spanish state, 57, 58
Sri Lanka, 262, 264
Stanner, William, 103
States, 3–5, 7, 9, 11, 14n1
Stefancic, J., 1
Sterling, Alton, 165, 166
Strathern, Marilyn, 33
Structural violence, 1, 9, 140, 149, 150, 152, 156, 161–164, 170, 174, 180, 182, 231, 325, 326
Subcomandante Marcos, 67
Suffering, 255, 260, 261, 266, 268, 274, 279, 281, 282, 285, 294, 295, 297, 298, 306, 307, 310, 315, 316
Symbolic violence, 149, 162
Synchronic trauma, 8, 9, 13, 150, 156, 326

T
Tamir, Yael, 62, 82
Taylor, Breonna, 165, 166, 171
Terrorism, 1–3, 53–83, 323, 337
Terrorist, 54–56, 58–60, 62–67, 74, 80
Terrorist violence, 58, 59, 80
Thailand, 259, 262
Thankful, 257
Thunberg, Greta, 224
Timber extraction, 103, 104, 107
Time, 326, 330, 331, 333
Tinker, Tink, 178
Tlaib, Rashida (U.S. Congresswoman), 155
Tolerance, 195–246

INDEX 369

Torture, 57, 58, 67, 83n1
Trail of Tears (1838-1850), 175
Transsexual, 328
Trauma, 1, 2, 4, 5, 7–10, 13, 22–25, 40, 43, 45, 102, 103, 128, 139, 140, 149–151, 153–157, 175, 179, 180, 196, 201, 210, 214, 215
Trevor-Roper, Hugh, 237
Trophic cascade, 221
The Troubles, 62, 70
Trump, Donald J.(President of United States), 1, 6, 12, 13, 26–29, 31–34, 36, 45, 78, 151–156, 167, 175, 181, 198, 201, 206, 212, 228, 229, 232, 234–236, 238–241, 245, 246, 323, 324, 326, 327, 329
Trump administration, 20, 21, 27, 28, 31, 32, 34–36, 38, 39, 45, 47n27, 140, 161, 175, 176
Tsultrim, Geshe Lobsang, 256, 262, 291, 294, 295, 330
Tuberculosis, 229
Tukano people (Brazil and Colombia), 113, 123, 142, 145, 160
Turkey, 101
Tuskegee Institute, 171
Tutsis, 101
Twitter, 236, 241

U
U2, 304
Uighurs or Uyghurs (China), 4, 6, 13, 96, 99, 100, 127
Unamuno, Miguel de, 306, 307
Unconditional love, 257, 315, 316, 329
Uncontacted Amerindian groups, 223, 226
Uncontacted indigenous people, 97, 127

UN International Organization for Migration (IOM), 213
United Nations Declaration on the Rights of Indigenous Peoples (UNDRIP), 336
United Nations Educational, Scientific, and Cultural Organization (UNESCO), 218
United Nations (UN), 76, 80, 99, 122, 221
United States (US), 18–22, 26, 27, 29–31, 33, 34, 36–40, 45, 96, 99, 101, 102, 119, 128, 140, 149, 151–155, 158, 161–167, 170–184, 195, 196, 198, 199, 205–207, 212–214, 223, 229–235, 239–242, 245, 246, 323, 326, 327, 331, 335, 336
Upper Xingu Region (Brazil), 117
Urban Amerindians, 139, 142, 146, 158, 160, 161
Uru-Eu-Wau-Wau people (Brazil), 104, 110, 115
U.S. Border Patrol, 33
U.S./Mexico border, 21–23, 31, 33, 34, 36–39, 45
U.S. Supreme Court, 36
Us vs. Them, 213, 243

V
Vasopressin, 308, 310
Ventral tegmental, 308, 310
Ventura, Deisy (Deisy de Freitas Lima Ventura), 117, 121, 122
Vietnam, 286, 304
Violence, 3–9, 13, 95, 96, 98, 102, 103, 112, 128, 140, 149, 150, 156, 162, 173, 174, 180, 183, 255, 259, 262, 275, 278, 295, 297, 304, 307, 325–327, 332
Virus, 220, 232–234, 245

## W

Waimiri-Atroari people (Brazil), 104
Wallace, B. Allan, 300
Waorani people (Ecuador), 317
Warfare, 311, 313, 317
Warfield Rawls, Anne, 183
Warren, Jonathan, 180
Washington, Booker T., 168
Washington, DC, 279, 280, 285, 287, 296
Washington, George (President of United States), 63
Welsh, 7, 325
West, Cornel, 152, 166, 182, 234
Western China, 96, 99–101, 127
White Buffalo, 179
Whitehouse, Harvey, 8, 150, 299, 309
White man's burden, 101
White nationalism, 2
Whites, 102–104, 111, 113, 118, 128
Wiesel, Elie, 309
Wilson, E. O., 221
Wimmer, Andreas, 27, 82
Wirangu and Kokatha people (Australia), 103
Witchcraft, 237, 246
Witch hunt/s, 212, 246, 329
World Health Organization (WHO), 229–231, 234
World Resources Institute (WRI), 228
World War I, 233, 303
World War II, 213, 234, 239, 240, 246, 303, 304
Wounded Knee Massacre (1890), 98, 102, 175, 177, 179
Wright, Robert, 298
Writing, 255, 306, 308, 311, 314
Wu, Katherine, 308

## X

Xenophobia, 6, 38, 45, 234, 243
Xingu National Park Reserve (Brazil), 117
Xinjiang Province, 100

## Y

Yang, Andrew (former U.S. presidential candidate), 234
Yanomami people (Brazil and Venezuela), 105, 107, 108, 110, 111, 116, 119, 124–127, 159, 160
Yellowstone National Park, 221
Young, Antonia, 209

## Z

Zaidel, Dahlia, 308
Zero tolerance border policy, 21

Printed in the United States
by Baker & Taylor Publisher Services